Analysis and Interpretation

of

Financial Statements

Third Edition

Analysis and Interpretation

of

Financial Statements

Third Edition

Boris Popoff
M Com, PhD (Otago), ACA,
Associate Professor of Accounting,
University of Otago

T K Cowan
M Com (NZ), FCA, CMA, MNZCS
Emeritus Professor of Accountancy
University of Otago

Butterworths

Sydney   Wellington

1989

AUSTRALIA

BUTTERWORTHS PTY LIMITED
271-273 Lane Cove Road, North Ryde 2113
Vanguard Insurance Building, 195 Victoria Square, Adelaide 5000
Commonwealth Bank Building, King George Square, Brisbane 4000
Canberra House, Marcus Clarke Street, Canberra 2600
161 Macquarie Street, Hobart 7000
160 William Street, Melbourne 3000
45 St Georges Terrace, Perth 6000

CANADA

BUTTERWORTHS CANADA LTD, Toronto and Vancouver

IRELAND

BUTTERWORTH (IRELAND) LTD, Dublin

MALAYSIA

MALAYAN LAW JOURNAL SDN BHD, Kuala Lumpur

NEW ZEALAND

BUTTERWORTHS OF NEW ZEALAND LTD, Wellington and Auckland

PUERTO RICO

EQUITY DE PUERTO RICO, INC, Hato Rey

SINGAPORE

MALAYAN LAW JOURNAL PTY LTD, Singapore

UNITED KINGDOM

BUTTERWORTH & CO (PUBLISHERS) LTD, London and Edinburgh

USA

BUTTERWORTH LEGAL PUBLISHERS, Austin, Texas; Boston, Massachusetts;
Clearwater, Florida (D & S Publishers); Orford, New Hampshire (Equity Publishing);
St Paul, Minnesota; and Seattle, Washington

National Library of Australia
Cataloguing-in-Publication entry

Popoff, B. (Boris).
Analysis and interpretation of financial statements.

3rd ed.
Includes index.
ISBN 0 409 49588 3.

1. Financial statements. I. Cowan, T. K. (Thomas Keith). II. Title.

657'. 3

Inquiries should be addressed to the publishers.
Typeset in Times and Optima by Excel Imaging Pty Ltd.
Printed in Australia by Hogbin Poole Printers Pty Ltd.

Contents

The effect of the human element on the preparation, presentation and interpretation of financial statements — Review questions.

Contents

Preface

The interpretation of financial statements is at the user end of the financial accounting and reporting process. According to the Trueblood Report, the basic objective in preparing financial statements should be the provision of information useful for the making of economic decisions. While the principal need for this information is that of those concerned with investment and financing, there are other important interests in business information including labour, social and government interests.

Before financial statements can be used effectively for the making of economic decisions, the analyst and interpreter should have adequate appreciation of the complexity of the economic phenomena which are the subject of accounting measurement and reporting, of the principles, methods and procedures employed, their effect on the nature of financial information and inherent limitations. Similarly, there should be adequate appreciation of both the uses and limitations of available analytical techniques.

In preparing the third edition, the authors have aimed at producing a text which meets dual needs. A test in analysis and interpretation would be superficial were it not backed by an extensive coverage of relevant aspects of financial accounting. Similarly, a text in financial accounting becomes more useful if it has an emphasis on how the end-products may be analyzed and used in a way which recognizes how those products have been derived. The book has been designed so as to be suitable for a basic course in financial accounting (above first year) and at MBA level, as well as for use as a specialized text in analysis and interpretation.

With these objectives in mind, the third edition has been substantially revised and expanded. The number of chapters has been increased from 20 to 23. New material has been added on the setting of financial reporting standards, on the informational content of financial statements in view of the efficient market hypothesis and the stockmarket crash of October 1987, on the allocation problem in financial accounting and reporting, on segment reporting, on foreign currency translation. Most of the existing chapters have been extensively revised and expanded to provide further background to financial analysis, in particular the chapters on some basic considerations in the financing of business enterprises, on aspects of statistical analysis, on the prediction of insolvency, and on analysis and interpretation for investors. Considerable additional real life cases and examples have been incorporated to illustrate the issues being discussed and to provide material for class assignments.

As was the case with the second edition, the third edition contains background coverage of legal requirements regarding contents of and disclosure in financial statements and financial reporting standards. In discussing financial reporting standards, the emphasis is again on issues as these both elucidate and transcend accounting practice. The study of these issues and the manner in which attempts are being made to deal with them is a necessary precondition for a more detailed study of particular aspects of current accounting practice and its impact on specific financial statements.

Throughout the book there is a strong emphasis on the human input (behavioural underpinnings) in financial accounting and reporting from the formulation of financial accounting principles to the preparation and presentation of financial statements and their analysis and interpretation.

In conclusion, we would like to express our appreciation to Dr R W Gibson for supplying some potential Australian case material and to Mrs Bev Brenssell and Ms Marie Kelly of the Department of Accounting and Finance of the University of Otago for readily typing the substantial revision and additional material for this third edition.

Dunedin   *B Popoff*
May 1989   *T K Cowan*

Chapter 1

The Nature and Function of Financial Statements

[101] We should like to point out at the outset that the objectives of this book are considerably broader than may be inferred from a narrow interpretation of its title.

[102] The analysis and interpretation of financial statements is a complex matter which extends well beyond the routine application of standard analytical techniques. Effective analysis and interpretation requires an understanding of the economic phenomena which are the subject matter of financial accounting and reporting, of the fundamental issues which underlie the financial accounting methods and procedures utilized in dealing with these issues, and the nature, significance and limitations of the end product of the financial accounting process — the published company report.

The book we present, therefore, is one on financial accounting and reporting, on underlying theoretical and practical issues and on accounting methods and procedures designed to deal with them. Throughout the book there is a natural emphasis on the analysis and interpretation of financial statements for decision-making through gaining insight into the operating results and state of affairs of companies in the context of a dynamic environment and accounting measurement, reporting and evaluative practices which are subject to serious limitations.

[103] It is generally recognized that accounting deals with economic events, in particular those which affect the operating results and state of affairs of business enterprises. Throughout the book reference is made to the human factor (behavioural underpinnings) in accounting for, interpretation of, and reaction to reported results and state of affairs of business enterprises, since economic phenomena are entirely the product of human activity and human experience.

[104] It is recognized that financial statements are produced also by government departments and not-for-profit organizations. It is hoped that our discussion will bring out some principles and tools of analysis and interpretation which may be applied with equal validity to the non-business field.

Some characteristics of financial statements

[105] Let us begin by noting some of the characteristics of financial statements. An appreciation of these characteristics is necessary if one is to get a fair view of the significance and limitations of these statements and of any data developed from them. This clear understanding is essential if the information so provided is to lead to sound decisions by those who have interests in the results of the operations and financial condition of business enterprises.

1

The characteristics of financial statements include:
• the use of money as a basis for the recording of transactions;
• the classification of transactions into account categories such as expenses and revenues and assets and equities;
• the periodic interrelating of the resulting account balances to produce income statements and balance sheets;
• the development of additional information such as statements of changes in financial position, trend statements, and statements of highlights.

[106] As the name indicates, financial accounting is monetary in that it records, classifies, interrelates and analyzes data expressed in monetary terms. Its real emphasis, however, is economic. Recorded transactions arise from activities which are economic in nature and the entities which carry out these activities are economic entities. For example, financial institutions like banks which are concerned primarily with monetary assets, liabilities, revenues and expenses are economic in nature in that they deal with a commodity which is scarce and has value only by reason of what it can buy.

The development of financial accounting and the uses of financial statements and reports

[107] The system of double entry bookkeeping which forms the basis of modern financial accounting appeared in medieval and Renaissance Italy as the product of the economic, social and political environment of the times: A C Littleton, *Accounting Evolution to 1900*, American Institute Publishing Co, New York, 1933, pp12–21. According to Littleton the following are some of the major factors leading to this development:
• the widespread private ownership of property and its active employment in commerce;
• the development of a sophisticated money economy with money being used in the generation of wealth through credit and lending;
• Large-scale commerce carried on internationally through partnerships and agencies;
• the use of capital in the form of money or money equivalent for the purpose of generating profit measured in monetary terms.

[108] The system of double entry bookkeeping described by Pacioli in his historic treatise *Particularis Computis et Scripturis* of 1494 (translation by J B Geijsbeeck, *Ancient Double-Entry Bookkeeping*, Denver, 1914), was proprietary oriented and was intended to assist merchants to better understand and manage their business affairs (Ch 23):

... if he (the merchant) follows this system... he will know all about his business and will know exactly whether his business goes well or not.

And regarding branch operations:

Thus at any time you desire, you may see how the store is running — that is at a profit or loss — so you will know what you will have to do and how you will have to manage it.

The key characteristics of the double entry system developed in Italy were:
• accounting records based on monetary measurement;

- distinction between capital and income in the analysis and classification of accounting transactions;
- the integrating role of the capital account which was the recipient of all gains and losses.

[109] That the above essential characteristics of the system have remained unchanged to this day is explained by the fact that in the context of the largely monetary economy of Renaissance Italy, as is true today, money was accepted and used as a basic means of exchange and a measure of income and wealth; it became a basic commodity, as is the case today, in the conduct of business and the evaluation of business results and state of affairs — through the investment of money capital in business operations for the purpose of generating income measured in monetary terms.

[110] While the basic structure of financial accounting has not changed for 500 years, the development of financial accounting and reporting as we know it today was the result of economic developments which were unknown in the days of Pacioli. Particularly notable were:

- the growth of the corporate form of business organization;
- the separation of company ownership from company management; and
- the growth in number, diversity and strength of other interests — social, economic, and political — in the operations of business enterprises.

In today's environment, the typical financial statements are primarily reports by management to shareholders on the results of operations and the state of affairs of the companies for which they are responsible; but it is recognized that they are also a major source of information to other persons including investors, creditors, organized labour and consumer groups, and the government as a taxing authority and a regulator of the economy.

[111] It has been generally recognized that the function of accounting statements is to provide information for the purpose of making economic decisions. For example, Statement No 4 of the Accounting Principles Board of the AICPA, *Basic Concepts and Accounting Principles Underlying Financial Statements of Business Enterprises*, October 1970, defined accounting as a service activity:

> Its function is to provide quantitative information, primarily financial in nature, about economic entities that is intended to be useful in making economic decisions — in making reasoned choices among alternative courses of action.

The report of the AICPA study group on the objectives of financial statements (the Trueblood Report) published in 1973 stated (p 13) that the provision of information useful for the making of economic decisions is the basic objective of financial statements. The report also emphasized the external uses of financial statements when it stated (p 17) that:

> An objective of financial statements is to serve primarily those users who have limited authority, ability, or resources to obtain information and who rely on financial statements as their principal source of information about an enterprise's economic activities.

This view was supported in Statement of Accounting Concepts No 1, *Objectives of Financial Reporting by Business Enterprises*, published in the United States in 1978 by the Financial Accounting Standards Board (FASB).

3

[112] The importance of financial statements as reports on the part of company management to external interests (primarily shareholders and investors) has long been recognized by British company law and professional recommendations on accounting reporting standards. For example, British company legislation requires audited financial statements to be sent to all shareholders, sets out certain minimum requirements regarding disclosure and requires financial statements to give a "true and fair view" of the profit or loss of a company and its state of affairs. For their part professional accounting bodies have shown their concern for the establishment and maintenance of financial reporting standards by the issuing of statements on standard accounting practice to serve as guidelines in dealing with specific problem areas in financial reporting.

Some fundamental problems in financial reporting

[113] The basic financial statements are the income, statement and the balance sheet. The income statement purports to show the "profit" or "loss" of a business enterprise for an accounting period, and the balance sheet the "state of affairs" or "financial position" of the enterprise at the end of the period.

At the heart of the problems associated with the determination and reporting of the profit or loss and state of affairs of business enterprises is the fact that, as yet, there is no explicit agreement among accountants regarding what the terms "profit", "loss", and "state of affairs" mean or ought to mean. Their meaning may be defined only by implication — in terms of the accounting practices applied in the preparation of financial statements.

[114] Similar problems arise in the interpretation of the requirement of British company legislation that financial statements should give a "true and fair view" of profit and loss and state of affairs. Since company legislation does not define what truth and fairness mean in the context of financial reporting, and there is little case law on the subject, the true and fair view requirement tends to be interpreted in terms of current accounting practice. This means that financial statements are assumed to give a true and fair view if they are prepared on the basis of current accounting methods and procedures. As we shall see later, this approach to the question of truth and fairness in financial reporting gives rise to some serious problems, because there is as yet no explicit frame of reference for the evaluation of existing accounting methods and procedures. As a result, alternative methods may be available for dealing with given problems in financial accounting each of which give an "acceptable" though different figure for profit or loss and an "acceptable" though different picture of the state of affairs. For example, fixed assets may be shown in a balance sheet (in New Zealand and Australia at least) at historical cost (depreciated when appropriate) or may be revalued and shown at valuation less depreciation since revaluation. As both methods are currently used in practice, both are generally accepted accounting principles. Further, since the legal requirement that financial statements should give a "true and fair view" is usually interpreted in terms of current accounting practice, the reporting of fixed assets at either cost or valuation will be assumed to give a true and fair view even though the reported asset values under the two methods may be significantly different. Alternatives have also been available in determining depreciation policies and charges, in the valuation of inventories, in the accounting treatment of the cost of major maintenance and renewals, in accounting for goodwill and leases, research and develop-

ment costs, gains and losses due to foreign exchange rate fluctuations, income tax concessions such as investment allowances, and government grants.

In the face of these problems, there has been a greatly increased emphasis on disclosure, in order to increase the total potential information content of financial statements and to offset to some extent the shortcomings and limitations of accepted practice in financial reporting.

Summary

[115] The purpose of this chapter has been to create a general awareness of:
- the evolutionary process at work in financial reporting;
- the perceived objectives of financial statements;
- the difficulties in the way of achieving these objectives, which include: the lack of definition of basic concepts such as capital and income, and of qualitative concepts such as "true and fair"; the lack of an explicit frame of reference on which to base detailed decisions in the problem areas of accounting practice; the limitations of "generally accepted accounting principles" (GAAP) as a standard;
- the roles of the law and the profession in the definition of accounting standards.

Much can be written on all these related topics. That, however, is beyond the objectives and scope of this book. Notwithstanding that, it is important that the analyst and interpreter of financial statements be aware of the nature and limitations of the material available. The nature of the financial information produced by current accounting practice and its uses and limitations in decision making will be discussed in the chapters that follow.

Chapter 2

Financial Statements — Statutory Requirements and Professional Standards

[201] Accounting statements are technical in nature. They are developed by systematically processing a great many transactions in ways which have become generally accepted within the business, professional and legal environments. Because they are technical statements, the analyst and interpreter has to be fully aware of their nature and limitations.

A further reason for understanding, if not caution, is that financial statements constitute a report on stewardship of resources by the stewards themselves (eg the directors of a company). Further, they are prepared by managers whose livelihood and reputation are affected by the information provided in the statements.

[202] Self interest is an important motivation when it comes to the content and presentation of accounting statements, in the choice of accounting methods from available alternatives, and in the exercise of judgment and expression of opinion in the context of current generally accepted accounting practice. Not everyone is honest. In this chapter we discuss the nature and effect of regulation on financial reporting practice.

[203] Traditionally, British financial reporting has been influenced strongly by legislation. Some of the reasons for the existence of company legislation in Britain can be traced back to the English experiences with joint stock companies in the early eighteenth century during a period which culminated in the financial disaster known as the South Sea Bubble (1711-20). Central to the events of that period was the formation of the South Sea Company with the idea that the State should sell trading monopolies in the South Seas in return for a sum of money to pay the national debt. The scheme caught the imagination of the public, fabulous profits were dreamed of with the result that the price of the stock rose out of all proportion to the earnings of the company. Imitative ventures also sprung up with the result that ruinous losses were suffered by many sections of the public. An investigation by a House of Commons committee revealed widespread fraud and corruption and an Act of Parliament known as the "Bubble Act" prohibited, in the public interest, the formation of joint stock companies. This prohibition lasted for a hundred years.

The "Bubble Act' was repealed in the nineteenth century and was replaced by a succession of Companies Acts which permitted the formation of joint stock companies, extended limited liability to registered companies, made mandatory the keeping of adequate accounts and enforced publicity of the operations of companies by requiring audited balance sheets to be sent to shareholders and to the Registrar of Companies.

These developments were significant for the future of British financial reporting in that they recognized:

- the importance of the company form of business organization as a means of utilizing the funds in the hands of the public for the economic development of the nation;
- the need to protect investors by making available to them relevant information about the operations and state of affairs of companies;
- the importance of financial statements as a means of communication from company management to shareholders and the need for such statements to meet certain standards.

[204] It has been said that the major advances in financial reporting have been caused by crises. One such crisis was the celebrated *Royal Mail Steam Packet* case in Britain which showed how the manipulation of reserves can be used to produce misleading statements. The case did much to change the attitude of the accounting profession and legislators in favour of the greater disclosure requirements embodied in current company legislation.

Financial reporting in Australia and New Zealand follows the British pattern in that it has been strongly influenced by legislation which, in the past at least, has followed many of the provisions of company legislation in Britain.

[205] In the United States of America the influence of the law has tended to be indirect. The position at this time turns around two bodies. The Securities and Exchange Commission (SEC) sets Rules to be followed in the submission of financial statements and related information by companies coming within its jurisdiction. An ostensibly independent body, the Financial Accounting Standards Board (FASB), sets down Statements of Financial Accounting Standards as guides to the profession but these have no direct legal standing.

General Statutory Requirements Regarding Annual Accounts

[206] Statutory requirements regarding annual company accounts in Australia and New Zealand are contained respectively in the Australian Companies Act of 1981 and corresponding laws of participating States and the Northern Territory, and the New Zealand Companies Act of 1955.

Balance sheet and profit and loss account

[207] Under the provisions of Australian and New Zealand companies legislation, the directors of every company are required to ensure that a balance sheet and profit and loss account are prepared and laid before the company at each annual general meeting.

A true and fair view

[208] The general overriding provision of company legislation is that every balance sheet must give a true and fair view of the state of affairs of the company as at the

end of the financial year, and every profit and loss account must give a true and fair view of the profit and loss of the company for the financial year (ss 269 and 285 of the Australian Act and s 153 of the New Zealand Act).

Under current company legislation the true and fair requirement is of paramount importance and as such overrides requirements for specific disclosure where compliance with these may cause the accounts not to give a true and fair view.

Directors' report

[209] A directors' report dealing with specific aspects of the operations and state of affairs of the company must be attached to every balance sheet.

The New Zealand Companies Act requires the directors' report to deal with:
  (i) the state of the company's affairs and, to the extent that in the opinion of the directors it will not be harmful to the business of the company, with any change during the financial year in the nature of the company's business;
  (ii) the amount of any recommended dividend;
  (iii) the amount of any recommended transfers to reserves.

Considerably wider requirements regarding the contents of the directors' report are contained in the Australian Companies Act.

Auditors' report

[210] The auditors' report must be attached to the balance sheet. In it the auditors must state whether in their opinion the accounts of the company or company group are properly drawn up in accordance with company legislation so as to give a true and fair view of the company's (company group's) affairs at balance date and the company's (group's) profit for the year ended at balance date.

[211] In addition to the above reports, Australian company legislation requires the directors to state in a statement attached to the accounts that, in their opinion, the accounts give a true and fair view of the profit and loss and state of affairs of the company or company group. There is no such requirement in the New Zealand Companies Act.

Some of the detailed requirements of company legislation and professional standards regarding disclosure in financial statements are discussed in Chapter 4.

Notes to the accounts

[212] These are used to disclose information not otherwise disclosed in the body of the accounts, including information required to be disclosed by company legislation. Notes to the accounts should be read in conjunction with the financial statements.

A Discussion on the True and Fair View Requirement

[213] Although company legislation sets out the giving of à true and fair view as the overriding consideration in financial reporting, it does not define what truth and fairness mean in the reporting context or the means by which truth and fairness should be attained.

"Truth" and "fairness" are general concepts and their interpretation in the financial reporting context depends heavily on subjective judgment. Let us consider this problem further.

The true and fair view may be interpreted in terms of the general principles applied in the interpretation of statutes. Two of these principles are that words of a statute must be given their ordinary or popular meaning unless there is something to the contrary in the context or scheme of the statute, and that "technical words or words of known legal import" must be given their technical meaning: T R Johnston, G C Edgar and P L Hays, *The Law and Practice of Company Accounting in New Zealand*, 6th ed, Butterworths, Wellington, 1986; T R Johnston, M O Jager and R B Taylor, *The Law and Practice of Company Accounting in Australia*, 6th ed, Butterworths, Sydney, 1987. Since "true" and "fair" are not technical words and have no "known legal import" in relation to financial reporting, it reasonably follows that they should be given their ordinary, popular meaning. In other words, "true" and "fair" should mean what people expect them to mean.

Dictionary definitions of "true" include "in accordance with fact and reality" and being "not false or erroneous", and of "fair" as being "just", "unbiased", "equitable". The unquestionable desirability of truth and fairness in financial reporting in the dictionary sense leads us to conclude that this interpretation is in accord with the popular interpretation of the words.

[214] As related to accounting, however, the concept of truth as being "in accordance with fact and reality" or being "not false or erroneous" is difficult to apply. While there may be little disagreement about the need for truth in accounting, people who speak about truth in accounting may have different "facts" in mind. For example, some people have argued that the facts in accounting are objectively determined historical costs while others have argued that the relevant facts for attaining truth in accounting are current market values represented by current market prices. Further, the "facts" in accounting are determined by generally accepted accounting principles such as those relating to the recognition of revenues and losses, the measurement and allocation of costs, valuation of assets, tax allocation, the treatment of research and development costs, etc. The availability of alternatives in dealing with specific accounting problems requires a choice of accounting methods and procedures which in turn requires the use of judgment; the choice may be influenced by expediency and bias.

[215] The lack of agreement among accountants on the meaning of profit and state of affairs further complicates the determination and reporting of facts in accounting. This is not to say that there are no facts about the subject matter of accounting. Had that been so, any arbitrary selection from among arbitrarily determined accounting principles would have sufficed and there would have been no grounds for dissatisfaction with current or any accounting procedures. The problems in financial reporting arise from the lack of a clear agreement on the objectives of financial statements in the face of diversity of user interests, from the absence of a frame of reference for the evaluation of existing or proposed accounting procedures, from the complexity of accounting phenomena in the context of a changing environment and from the uncertainty relating to accounting measurement.

[216] The uncertainty which attaches to business operations necessitates the expression of opinion and the exercise of judgment in the evaluation of operating

9

results and the state of affairs of business enterprises. Many students are taken aback when first confronted with the claim that profit, as measured by traditional accounting methods, is a statement of opinion based on expectations about the future. Yet the claim is very much correct. The use of a cost basis in accounting measurement is justified on the continuity assumption; depreciation charges, even when based on historical cost, are determined on the basis of the expected useful life of assets, any expected salvage value, and an assumed pattern of depreciation cost incurrence; the valuation of inventories at historical cost is based on the expectation that they will realise an amount greater than historical cost in the next accounting period, etc. Uncertainty is inherent in business operations: it cannot be avoided in accounting measurement and should be given adequate recognition in the interpretation of accounting reports. Since accounting measurement is based on expectations, judgment is an integral part of accounting measurement. Truth in financial reporting, therefore, must ultimately relate to the soundness of judgment.

[217] Similar problems arise when we attempt to relate the concept of fairness to accounting. Fairness as "impartiality", "justice', "freedom from bias" must inevitably relate to accounting truth. While truth in accounting has been usually associated with the contents of financial statements, fairness has been largely associated with the mode of presentation. Again the mode of presentation requires the exercise of judgment in the choice of format and manner of disclosure, in the presentation of summarized data and extent of disclosure beyond the legal minimum requirements, in the highlighting of significant items, in the provision of graphs, summaries and trend statements. As was the case in determining accounting truth, the presentation of financial statements may reflect the bias of those responsible for the preparation of the statements.

The accounting interpretation of the true and fair view

[218] The accounting interpretation of the true and fair view requirement is essentially a technical one — financial statements are deemed to give a true and fair view if they are prepared on the basis of generally accepted accounting principles (which is really just another name for current accounting practice). Since, as yet, there is no frame of reference for the evaluation of current accounting practice, the reasoning behind the current interpretation of the true and fair view is rather circular — financial statements are true and fair if they are prepared in terms of current accounting practice, therefore, financial statements which are prepared in terms of current accounting practice are true and fair. In this respect Australian and New Zealand accountants are not very different from their American counterparts who explicity qualify the "fairness" of financial statements in terms of "generally accepted accounting principles". A similar qualification is implicit in the Australian and New Zealand audit reports. Recently some New Zealand and Australian audit reports have explicitly qualified the truth and fairness of financial statements as being in terms of the historical cost convention. For a more extensive discussion of the true and fair view requirement see B Popoff "Some Conceptualising on the True and Fair View", *The International Journal of Accounting*, 19/1, Fall 1983.

[219] The foregoing does not mean that accounting methods and procedures are necessarily arbitrary or that the accounting profession is not concerned with the truth and fairness of financial statements. Accounting methods are generally logically conceived. A major problem is that they are not conceived and evaluated in terms of a fundamental frame of reference for the solution of accounting problems. As a result, accounting problems have been tackled in isolation and alternatives have become available for dealing with specific accounting issues.

Financial Reporting Standards

[220] The practical application of any standard requires its expression in terms of specific methods and procedures. In the field of financial reporting the objective of giving a true and fair view is translated into practical guidelines by way of official pronouncements by the accounting profession in the form of statements of standard accounting practice. The objective of such official accounting standards has been stated to be " ... to improve the quality and uniformity of reporting and introduce a definitive approach to the concept of what is a true and fair view". By way of general guideline a true and fair view is stated to imply: " ... disclosure and appropriate classification and grouping of all material items, and consistent application of acceptable accounting principles": Council of New Zealand Society of Accountants, *Explanatory Foreword to Statements of Standard Accounting Practice*, para 1.2.

By way of specific guidelines, pronouncements on standard accounting practice deal with problem areas in accounting such as disclosure of accounting policies, inventory valuation, depreciation, income tax allocation, consolidations, accounting for associated companies, and others.

Professional statements of standard accounting practice increase the informational value of financial statements and aid in their interpretation in a number of ways:

• they promote the standardization of reporting practices and, therefore, increase the comparability of financial statements;
• they require a higher level of specific disclosure than company legislation;
• they are more flexible than legislation in meeting the needs of a changing environment;
• departures from statements of standard accounting practice require certain disclosure if the effects of the departure are material.

Disclosure of Accounting Policies

[221] It should be clear by now that the understanding of financial reports will be enhanced if disclosure is made of the accounting principles used in their preparation. Accounting standards in Australia and New Zealand require the disclosure of the accounting policies used in the preparation of financial statements in a summary which is presented as an integral part of the financial statements. Such summaries are usually shown immediately preceding the financial statements or as the first item under the heading "Notes to the Accounts".

Authority Behind Generally Accepted Accounting Principles

[222] In most countries there is no direct legal backing for generally accepted accounting principles except to the extent that company legislation contains specific provisions regarding disclosure in financial statements. As such legal requirements regarding disclosure must be complied with, it follows that they are part of current accounting practice.

[223] In the United States the Securities and Exchange Commission (SEC) has vast powers to prescribe accounting methods for the preparation of the financial statements of companies listed on the national stock exchanges. While the Commission has generally left the matter of formulation and promulgation of accounting standards to the accounting profession or more precisely the ostensibly independent Financial Accounting Standards Board (FASB), it is in a position to mandate compliance with particular standards or procedures, should it so resolve.

[224] In Australia, the Accounting Standards Review Board (ASRB) has power to issue Approved Accounting Standards which then have legislative backing in that company law requires directors to ensure that accounts are drawn up in accordance with applicable approved accounting standards and auditors are required to inform the ASRB of any qualified reports they have issued on the grounds of non-compliance with approved accounting standards. There are provisions for penalties for non-compliance.

[225] Apart from the above the accounting profession has no direct legal power to enforce compliance with the reporting standards it defines and promulgates. Its major leverage is the requirement for auditors to issue qualified reports where financial statements fail to comply with professional reporting requirements.

[226] To a very large extent the application of accounting reporting standards in the preparation and presentation of financial statements depends on the acceptability of the standards to company management. This state of affairs gives company management considerable leverage to influence what are ultimately promulgated as financial reporting standards.

Implications for the Analysis and Interpretation of Financial Statements

[227] The analysis and interpretation of financial statements is not an easy task. Informed analysis and interpretation require good knowledge and understanding of current accounting practice and reporting standards. In the analysis of particular financial statements study should be made of the accounting policies applied in their preparation in order to determine their effect on what is held out to represent a true and fair view of company profit and state of affairs. In the chapters that follow we will discuss more specifically some of the major problems which underlie current financial accounting practice, the approaches used and methods developed to deal with them and their effect on financial statements. Methods of analysis and interpretation will be introduced in a graded manner.

It is hoped that discussion, side by side, of the methods of analysis and interpretation and the nature of the problems with which the interpreter of financial statements is faced will help to explain both the uses and limitations of financial statements and the uses and limitations of available analytical techniques.

Review questions

2.1 Discuss briefly and contrast the British and American backgrounds of financial reporting.

2.2 "In order to give a 'true and fair view' of a company's operating results and financial position, published company reports must be prepared in accordance with 'generally accepted accounting principles'."
Do you agree? Give reasons for your answer.

2.3 Discuss the responsibility of professional accountancy bodies regarding the external reports of companies, and the authority of their recommendations and published statements.

2.4 " 'Truth' and 'fairness' are subjective concepts and when related to financial reporting their interpretation depends heavily on subjective judgment."
Discuss.

2.5 "Related to accounting . . . the concept of truth as being 'in accordance with fact and reality' . . . is difficulty to apply . . . people who speak about truth in accounting may have different 'facts' in mind."
Discuss.

2.6 Discuss the use of notes in published financial statements. What are the advantages and disadvantages of this practice?

2.7 Discuss the objectives of the statements of standard accounting practice issued by the accounting profession.

2.8 Why the need to disclose the accounting policies followed in the preparation of published financial statements?

2.9 Comment on the following quotations:
- "Within certain flexible extremities 'true' and 'fair' can mean very much what the directors and auditors want them to mean."
- "The reform needed here is not the law which is clear enough. 'True and fair' are unambiguous words. Practice needs to conform to the legal obligation."

Chapter 3

Financial Information and the Politics of Standard Setting. The Efficient Market Hypothesis

[301] Business activities are economic in nature. They involve the investment of economic resources (capital) for the purpose of producing an output of economic benefits (income). In a society motivated to a very large extent by economic considerations, the operations and state of affairs of business enterprises and the financial statements which report on them are the focal point at which converge powerful, diverse and often conflicting economic interests.

[302] The diversity and conflict of sectional interests in financial reporting and the need for the accounting profession to rely on general acceptance for reporting standards have a profound impact on financial reporting practice and its evolution over time. For example, parties on whom the general acceptance of accounting promulgations depends are in a strong position to influence the contents and direction of what is promulgated. Further, sectional interests may introduce bias in the contents, presentation and interpretation of financial statements. The most favourable alternative accounting method or procedure may be followed rather than the most relevant. Advantage may be taken of the lack of clarity and precision in and any popular misunderstandings about the nature of the income and state of affairs of business enterprises to present a view that may pass as "true and fair" but which in fact is biased and liable to mislead the reader.

[303] It is generally accepted that, in the field of business activity, people are primarily motivated by economic self interest. It is in the context of economic self interest, therefore, that we will discuss the sectional interests in the operations and financial results of business firms.

Sectional Interests in Financial Statements

[304] The following are the major groups with special interests in the operations of business firms and their financial statements as reports on their operating results and state of affairs.

Directors

[305] Directors and the management team control the operations of the business enterprise with the ostensible aim of ensuring its continuing profitability and solvency. The securing of growth and the maintenance of risk at an acceptable level

14

may be subsidiary objectives. The results of a year are seen within the context of longer term objectives and plans.

In an environment which has long been characterized by the separation of business management and business ownership, the directors are required to provide periodic results to shareholders on the manner in which they have exercised their stewardship over the firm's resources. These reports provide a basis for the assessing by sharehodlers and investors of the effectiveness of managerial decision-making in the planning and control of business operations.

Company legislation and customary practice have placed upon the directors the primary responsibility for the provision of financial statements and (within the limits of certain legal requirements and accounting standards) for the contents of the statements.

It should be evident that directors have a strong vested interest in the financial statements of their firms and the manner in which they reflect their performance as directors. There are therefore, a number of motivating influences which affect the decision of directors regarding choices for income and asset measurement.

There is a natural desire on the part of directors to create a favourable impression in the minds of shareholders and investors about the performance and state of affairs of the enterprise under their control. The financial statements not only reflect the personal performance of the directors but also affect the attitude of investors and providers of credit to the firm and, therefore, the ability of the firm to raise additional finance as the need arises and the servicing cost of such finance. There may be a desire on the part of directors to create a favourable climate for the firm's operations through good public and industrial relations by recognizing in the preparation of financial statements the interests of employees and consumers. The directors may also want to limit disclosure for the purpose of restricting the information available to competitors or reducing the risk of takeover.

On the other hand, directors may decide to make additional disclosures regarding matters such as the current value of assets and perceived prospects of the firm in order to thwart an unwelcome takeover bid.

Shareholders and investors

[306] The main decisions faced by shareholders and investors relate to buying, selling or holding shares in companies. Normally, shareholders and investors will have alternative investments open to them. Since the economic value of an investment is dependent on the expected flow of material benefits arising from it, the information which is likely to prove most helpful to the shareholder/investor is that which provides a guide to the future.

The question of the uses made by shareholders and investors of financial statement information and the usefulness of the information for the making of investment decisions has been the subject of controversy. Available evidence appears to bear out the view that shareholders and investors do use financial statement information in the making of investment decisions (see section on the Efficient Market Hypothesis later in this chapter). On the other hand, not enough is positively known about shareholders' and investors' decision-making processes or the level of sophistication which they bring into the analysis and use of financial statement information. In a different way, it could be argued that to the extent that shareholders and investors use the advice of stockbrokers and other investment advisers, their decisions reflect a higher level of financial analysis than that of which they are personally capable.

[307] The following are some matters which may be considered in the analysis and interpretation of financial statements from the viewpoint of shareholders and investors:
- the nature and relative importance of the company's business activities including subsidiaries and associated companies;
- the amount and composition of share capital including any special rights attaching to particular classes of shares;
- details of capital changes and bonus issues;
- analysis of operating performance including sales and trends in sales, profit before and after tax, provisions for taxation and depreciation, trends in profits, abnormal and extraordinary items, earnings per share, etc;
- dividend policies and profit retention;
- composition and amount of reserves, in particular reserves available for distribution free of tax;
- liquidity position and overall financial structure including any trends;
- asset backing per share;
- the market value of the company's shares;
- dividends and earnings yield on market value; etc.

Organized labour

[308] Organized labour may use the techniques of financial statements analysis to determine the ability of firms to pay higher wages while, presumably, maintaining or expanding employment opportunities. Of particular interest to organized labour is the profitability of business and published financial statements may be used as a basis for assessing this profitability.

Recognizing the importance of employees as users, some companies produce simplified and abbreviated reports for staff members, and prepare statements such as the one (provided by a departmental store enterprise) shown as Figure 3.1.

Creditors

[309] Providers of credit and loan finance fall under a number of categories from trade creditors, to banks providing overdraft facilities, to long-term lenders.

Trade creditors have two major objectives in marketing: to achieve a planned volume of sales, and to avoid loss through bad debts and minimize the cost of delayed payments by debtors.

Financial statements of client companies may provide useful information for decisions regarding the granting and control of credit. The following are of interest to trade creditors:
- amount of trade creditors in relation to current assets (cash, debtors and stock) and changes in the composition of current assets in order to assess possible future cash flows from which creditors may be paid;
- details of secured creditors and their securities, and the position of unsecured creditors;
- rate of stock return;
- trends in sales, expenses and profits;

Figure 3.1

How the sales income was applied

	This year		Last year	
	$	%	$	%
Total Sales	22,058,200	100.0	20,211,300	100.0
Paid to suppliers for goods	13,686,600	62.1	12,670,500	62.7
Paid for expenses	2,059,300	9.3	1,849,200	9.1
Provided for depreciation	178,200	.8	134,500	.7
	15,924,100	72.2	14,654,200	72.5
Leaving	6,134,100	27.8	5,557,100	27.5
Which was used as follows				
Return to shareholders for capital invested	269,300	1.2	242,300	1.2
Return to employees for work performed	4,072,300	18.5	3,739,000	18.5
Return to employees superannuation fund	138,200	.6	118,300	.6
Return to employees profit participation	78,000	.4	70,300	.4
Return to government in income tax	850,200	3.8	731,200	3.6
Retention in company for the future development for the benefit of employees, shareholders and government	726,100	3.3	656,000	3.2
	6,134,100	27.8	5,557,100	27.5

- own firm's proportion in the total purchases of the client firm;
- the relationship between trade creditors and the average monthly cost of sales as an indication of the credit being taken, etc.

[310] Banks usually have more ready access to the accounting statements of client firms than trade creditors and may require additional statements including cash budgets. Two items of major concern to banks are the security for the advance and the liquidity of the client firm — the ability of the firm to repay the amount owing quickly. Items of interest to banks are the liquid position of the firm, its working capital and profits and trends in these.

[311] Long-term loans are usually secured by way of mortgages. Debentures may be issued with or without security and with or without the right to conversion into shares at a set date. The long-term lender will be concerned for the security of his advance and the regular payment of interest. The relevant value of assets pledged as a security is the current realizable value. The current realizable value of assets will depend on whether the assets are specialized and on the profitability of the enterprise overall, as in the case of a fertilizer works — or whether the assets are non-specialized, as in the case of an office building in a desirable city location. A mortgagee will generally be concerned with the capacity of the business to pay its way.

Where long-term loans are raised by the issue of debentures and trustees for the debenture holders are appointed under a trust deed, the trustees will be concerned with the adherence to the terms of the debenture trust deed and the safeguarding of the property pledged as security. They will be concerned with balance sheet relationships such as those between shareholders' funds and liabilities, and current assets and current liabilities; they will also be concerned with the relationship between interest charges and profit before tax and interest, and with the prospects for the continuing profitability of the enterprise.

Competitors

[312] Financial statements may be used by the management of competing firms in order to assess their own relative performance. The policy regarding disclosure in financial statements adopted by the directors of a firm may be motivated by a desire to restrict the information made available to competitors.

Consumer groups

[313] Rising prices and continuing inflation have led organized consumer groups to take a close interest in the reported profits of companies. Consumer organizations are partiuclarly concerned with prices set at a level which will produce what they consider to be excessive profits.

The government

[314] The interest of government in the operations of business enterprises stems from its role as a taxing authority and regulator of the economy. Analyses of published financial statements of companies provide a basis for government decisions regarding the economy in relation to the level of economic activity, the encouraging or discouraging of certain kinds of economic activity, price and profit controls, etc.

To the extent that it is perceived that the financial statements of companies reflect the degree of success of particular government economic policies, it could be said that the government which promotes such policies would have an interest in the manner in which financial statements reflect their outcome.

Conflict of interest

[315] It should be reasonably apparent that the wide diversity of interests in the operations of business enterprises often leads to conflict when it comes to the reporting and interpretation of the operating results and state of affairs of business firms. For example, the natural desire of management to present in financial statements the operations of their firm in a favourable light, may conflict with the interests of shareholders, investors and creditors to know the facts. The interests of organized labour and consumer groups may clash with the objectives of management. For example, in wage negotiations, trade unions and management are likely to draw different inferences from the firm's financial statements regarding the ability of the firm to pay higher wages. Sometimes, there are attempts by sectional interests, such as management, to achieve the "best of both worlds" in the face of a difficult dilemma. The following example has been taken from the 1973 annual accounts of a New Zealand meat processing company.

[316] In moving for the adoption of the 1973 accounts at the annual general

meeting of this company, the chairman noted an increase in net profit of some 65%. He noted also, however, that while operating costs had been quite satisfactory (based on the historic cost of buildings and plant), had these assets been related to 1973 prices, an entirely different picture would have emerged. The replacement value of the firm's assets at that time had been estimated as something like $25 million compared to a written down book value of $7 million. Had the assets been written up to their replacement cost, the earning rate on the resulting shareholders' funds even in that record year, would have been slightly in excess of 3%.

The seconder of the motion to adopt the annual accounts made the following interpretation of the operating results for the year:

> The profit achieved is an excellent one . . . The earnings rate for the year is a significant 55 cents per share compared with 33 cents per share last year. At first glance, this year's earnings rate and increase in profit appears high and comparable increases shown by other companies have led to adverse comments from government ministers. However, as illustrated in the chairman's address, the profit represents a return of about 3½% on the current cost of replacing the assets of the company. A return of 3½% is less than is paid on government loans and would not encourage an investor to sink funds in a freezing works — all this in a year in which favourable factors have produced good profits.

> The facts quoted above also illustrate the limitations of accounting reports in times of rapid inflation such as we have experienced in recent years. A balance sheet does not purport to show the current value of the enterprise. However, if those in employment are entitled (as they should be) to current wage rates surely investors are entitled to a return on the current value of their investment.

[317] One has some justification in saying that the above example implies an attempt by the management of the company, when faced with the difficulties of operating under conditions of high inflation, to impress shareholders and investors with the successful operations of the company, to counter criticisms of excessive profits by the government of the time and to lay the ground for resisting union demands for higher wages fuelled by the vast improvement in reported profit. Readers are referred to Chapter 19 where this example is discussed at greater length under the subheading "Price Changes, Behavioural Effects and Social, Economic and Political Implications: A Case Study of Two New Zealand Meat Processing Companies".

[318] So far the discussion of sectional interests in financial reporting has been concerned with the preparation, presentation and interpretation of financial statements. There is general recognition that sectional interests and conflict extend also to the formulation of the very principles and standards to be applied in the preparation of financial statements. This matter is considered below.

Financial Reporting and the Politics of Standard Setting

[319] There are strong incentives for the accounting profession to be concerned with the quality and reliability of financial statements. The standing of the profession in society depends on the quality of the services it provides. Failures in financial reporting reflect badly on the profession and particularly so if given media

publicity. Further, such failures may be taken to indicate an inability of the profession to require adequate standards of its members, and so may lead to demands for the regulation of financial reporting in detail by government agencies. Then, there is the ever present threat of litigation against auditors for giving credence to financial statements which may be found to have misrepresented the income and state of affairs of enterprises.

[320] Until the 1970s it was generally regarded that the formulation of financial accounting and reporting standards was primarily the concern and province of the accounting profession.

For example, in the United States, the deficiencies of financial reporting practices brought to light by the stock market crash of 1929 led to severe criticism of the profession and to the establishment of the Securities and Exchange Commission (SEC) with vast powers to regulate the reporting practices of companies listed on the national stock exchanges. The events stimulated the accounting profession into action to improve financial reporting practice. The steps taken ranged from ad hoc measures to deal with reporting matters of immediate urgency to attempts, in the early 1960s, to develop a basic frame of reference for the development of accounting principles following the Report to Council of the Special Committee on Research Program (*Journal of Accountancy*, December 1958, pp 62-8). Efforts to develop a frame of reference have also been made by the Financial Accounting Standards Board in its Statements of Financial Accounting Concepts, the first of which, "Objectives of Financial Reporting by Business Enterprises", was issued in 1978. For its part, the SEC, in spite of its vast regulatory powers, has generally chosen to leave the formulation of accounting principles primarily to the accounting profession and to reputedly independent bodies such as the FASB.

[321] Lacking direct legal power to ensure compliance with financial accounting standards, the profession has to rely on consultations with sectional interests in order to ensure the general acceptability of the standards it intends to promulgate. This opens the door for inputs into the processes of the formulation of accounting principles and the setting of specific accounting standards from the sectional interests outside the profession and the application of pressure, persuasion and lobbying tactics by those interests. Strongly influential inputs may be made by the company management section, the sector primarily responsible for the preparation and presentation of financial reports on their stewardship of enterprise resources and, therefore, for the application in practice of accounting principles and standards. This state of affairs has important implications for the accounting profession as it seeks to establish, perform and protect its role in the regulation of financial reporting practice.

[322] Stephen Zeff discussed the phenomenon of intervention by external parties in the standard setting process in terms of economic consequences ("The Rise of 'Economic Consequences' ", *Journal of Accountancy*, December 1978, pp 56-63). Financial reports impact on the behaviour of business, government, unions, investors and creditors; the resulting behaviour may have adverse effects on the interests of other persons and groups; in dealing with accounting matters, therefore, standard setters must take into consideration such possible adverse consequences. Zeff noted that the inability of the Accounting Principles Board to deal effectively with third-party intervention in the 1960s led to its demise and to the establishment in 1973

of the Financial Accounting Standard Board (FASB). He then expressed the opinion that the FASB would preside over its own demise if it were to make decisions primarily on other than accounting grounds. The FASB was, therefore, faced with a dilemma which required a delicate balancing of accounting and non-accounting considerations.

[323] In an article " 'Muddling through' with the APB" (*Journal of Accountancy*, May 1972, pp 42-9), Dale K Gerboth, manager in the accounting research division of the AICPA, argued for the largely policital approach adopted by the APB in the setting of financial reporting standards. He examined critically what he called the "comprehensive approach" of the critics of the APB (an approach which, in his view, required the definition of accounting objectives, the construction of comprehensive, internally consistent accounting theory suitable for analyzing problems, and an understanding of the interrelatedness and repercussions of the decisions associated with standard setting) and found it utopian. He then contrasted this "comprehensive approach" with the "incremental" approach adopted by the APB which, instead of aiming at total solutions to accounting problems concentrated on relatively small changes from the present state — incremental changes along the margin. The incremental approach was essentially remedial in coping with problems which could not be mastered in their totality, a series of incremental steps which, in impossible circumstances, diminish the need for any single action to be optimal. Gerboth argued that since, in most times, radical changes are not politically feasible, practical individuals should not waste time considering courses of action which do not have a reasonable chance of acceptance; in policy making they should be concerned with what they can get.

[324] In his article "The Politicization of Accounting" (*Journal of Accountancy*, November 1978, pp 65-72) David Solomons expressed deep concern about the implications for accounting if the standard setting process was to be dominated by political considerations and influences. He considered the arguments of some of the spokesmen for recognising the political nature of the standard setting process such as Dale Gerboth ("Research, Intuition, and Politics in Accounting Inquiry", *The Accounting Review*, July 1973, p 481) that, in a society committed to democratic legitimization of authority, only politically responsive institutions have the right to command others to obey the rules they set, and Charles Honngren ("The Marketing of Accounting Standards", *Journal of Accountancy*, October 1973, p 61) that, as standards place restrictions on behaviour, they must be accepted by the affected parties, a process which, in a democratic society, requires skillful marketing in a political arena. According to Solomons, the view that political considerations should enter into the formulation of accounting standards found its extreme expression in the position taken by David Hawkins that, as the FASB had the power to influence economic behaviour, it had the obligation to support government economic plans (David M Hawkins, "Financial Accounting, the Standards Board and Economic Development", 1973-74 Emanuel Saxe Distinguished Lectures in Accounting, Bernard M Baruch College, City University of New York, April 1975, pp 7-8).

According to Solomons, the future of the FASB and the integrity of accounting may depend on the better understanding of the role which politics should or should not play in standard setting. If accounting measurement is tampered with in order to achieve political aims, it would only destroy whatever credibility financial reports may have. Solomons argued instead for neutrality in the sense of representational accuracy. Comparing accounting with cartography he argued that a map is judged according to how well it represents the facts; how people reacted to it was another matter.

The Information Content and Objectives of Financial Statements

[325] FASB Statement of Financial Accounting Concepts No 1, "Objectives of Financial Reporting by Business Enterprises" (November 1978) which reflected many of the views expressed earlier in the report of the AICPA Study Group on the Objectives of Financial Statements (The Trueblood Report) made the following points about the function of financial reporting:
• The function of financial reporting is to provide information which is useful for making economic decisions about business enterprises and about investment in or loans to business enterprises (para 15).
• Financial reporting is concerned primarily with the needs of users who, because of limited authority to obtain the information they want from an enterprise, must use the financial statement information provided by management (para 28).
• The objectives recognize the diversity of interests in financial statements. The focal point of such interests, however, is the ability of the enterprise to generate cash flows. Financial statements, therefore, should provide users with information which will assist them in assessing the amounts, timing and uncertainty of future cash flows (para 37).
• Although the primary concern is with the ability of business enterprises to generate positive cash flows, earnings determined on an accrual basis are considered to be a better indication of performance than information about current cash receipts and payments during short periods such as a year (paras 43 and 44).
• Financial information is a tool for decision-making. If it is to be an effective tool, it must be comprehensible to users who have a reasonable understanding of business and economic activity and are prepared to study the information and its uses with reasonable diligence (paras 34 and 36).
• To the extent that financial reporting assists in identifying efficient and inefficient users of resources, it assists in promoting efficient capital and other markets. The function of financial reporting, however, is to provide evenhanded, neutral information for decision-making and not to determine or influence the outcome of such decisions (para 33).

The Efficient Market Hypothesis

[326] Since the late 1960s, alongside attempts to develop financial reporting standards in an environment characterized by external intervention into and politicization of the standard setting process, proponents and supporters of the Efficient Market Hypothesis (EMH) have seriously questioned the usefulness of financial statements for decision-making and, directly or by implication, the setting of reporting standards for the purpose of enhancing the information content and value of financial reports.

According to the EMH, the market impounds in share prices, promptly and without bias, all available information including financial statement data. That being so, share prices are the best available estimates of value and analysis based on financial statement data will not lead to abnormal returns being earned on security investments.

[327] Three levels of market efficiency have been defined in the literature:

(1) Weak level efficiency

At the weak level of market efficiency, share prices move independently of previous movements. Since share prices would respond only to new information or to new economic events, future price movements cannot be predicted from a study of past price movements.

(2) Semi-strong level efficiency

At the semi-strong level of efficiency, the market will respond promptly (instantaneously) and in an unbiased manner to all publicly available information. Although participants in the market may differ in their interpretation of the available information, their interaction will result in share prices which will represent the best available interpretation of the information. Therefore, it will be futile for investors to attempt to earn abnormal returns on the market from an analysis of available published data, including financial statements.

(3) Strong level efficiency

At the strong level of market efficiency share prices will reflect fully not only published information but also all relevant information including data not yet publicly available. If the market is efficient in the strong sense, then even insider information will not result in abnormal returns.

Statistical evidence has largely supported the assumption of market efficiency at the semi-strong level.

[328] One of the biggest barriers for the acceptance of the EMH by sceptics is the absence of a convincing rational explanation regarding how the interaction of a large number of market participants who possess different expectations and different analytical skills and use information of variable quality would consistently result in market prices which reflect the best estimates of share values.

One possible explanation which has been advanced is that market efficiency is the product of the averaging of the diverse expectations of different participants. Further, the market is likely to reflect the influence of sophisticated (expert) investors such as sharebrokers and investment advisers and institutional investors. If the actions of naive investors largely cancel out, the share prices which result will reflect sophisticated analysis, and hence the best estimate of market value.

Market efficiency and the investor

[329] The assumption of market efficiency, for example at the semi-strong level, implies that even the sophisticated, well-informed investor will not be able to earn abnormal returns at any risk/return combination since the market will value all

shares at that risk/return combination equally. There will be no advantage to the investor to hire an expert for the purpose of earning an abnormal return as the expert will not be able to do better.

Decisions regarding what shares to hold should relate to regulating the level of risk the investor is prepared to accept on his or her portfolio and in particular to maintain diversifiable risk at a minimum. In an efficient market, market return will compensate investors only for risk which cannot be diversified away. The services of an expert may be utilized for the purpose of planning an investment portfolio given the risk preferences of the investor, and where an expert may be expected to obtain information prior to its being made public.

Once an investor has established a portfolio at a given level of largely undiversifiable risk, he or she should pursue a buy-and-hold policy, since switching from one group of securities to another at the same level of risk would not hold advantages but will result in transactions costs.

Market efficiency and financial reporting

[330] An assumption of market efficiency would require a reconsideration of the role financial reporting plays or should play in the market for securities. This matter was considered by William H Beaver ("What Should Be the FASB's Objectives?", *Journal of Accountancy*, August 1973, pp 49-56).

[331] Statistical evidence lends support to the proposition of market efficiency at the semi-strong level; evidence also indicates that abnormal returns can be achieved through access to relevant inside information not available to the market.

Given the above, financial statements should be concerned with the expansion of disclosure in a manner designed to prevent abnormal returns being earned by investors who act on inside information not available to the market. In other words, financial statements should provide information which will increase market efficiency.

[332] It has been claimed by supporters of the EMH that the market "sees through" many accounting figures such as those produced by the application of different depreciation methods. That being so, standard setting should be concerned with "substantive" issues, those which are likely to affect the market's perception of the performance of firms and the value of their shares. The accounting methods and procedures used should be disclosed, however, to assist evaluation by the market.

[333] While financial statements cannot be used to achieve abnormal returns, they can be used to determine the relative risk of securities.

Complex accounting data should not be simplified in order to make it comprehensible to the "naive" user. Market interaction and efficiency impound the data in security prices and so will protect the naive investor.

[334] In an efficient market, financial statements are only one source of information used in the pricing of securities. By using a broad information base, eg interim reports, preliminary profit announcements, various types of information relating to the prospects of industries and firms, the effects of changes in government economic policies, analyses and comments in the business press, etc, the market reduces the impact on security prices of the release of financial statements. Even if the market does react to new information in the financial statements, the

adjustment is prompt and the usefulness of the information for the making of investment decisions is short-lived.

[335] An assumed efficiency of the market does not necessarily diminish the role financial statements play in the operations of the securities market. In fact it may be that it is the information disclosed in financial statements and impounded in share prices through analysis by sophisticated investors which keeps the market efficient. This leads to what has been referred to by some writers as a paradox — the market is kept efficient through analysis of information by sophisticated investors which in turn prevents sophisticated investors from earning the extra returns which were the objective of the analysis of information in the first place.

The Efficient Market Paradox

[336] R D Hines ("The Usefulness of Annual Reports: The Anomaly between the Efficient Markets Hypothesis and Shareholder Surveys", *Accounting and Business Research*, Autumn 1982, pp 296-309), examines the implications resulting from the EMH conclusion that shareholders cannot use publicly available information to earn returns in excess of expected equilibrium returns, and the evidence provided by shareholder surveys that shareholders do in fact use published financial statements as an important primary source of information.

A possible explanation of the anomaly is that shareholders may believe that publicly available information can be used to earn abnormal results while in fact it cannot. Such explanation is contradicted by evidence that sophisticated investors use annual reports to a greater extent than naive investors.

[337] If investors are heterogeneous, ie financial information has different implications for different investors, then investors' expectations would produce a dispersion around the resulting average market response. In this context, some individual expectation could be superior due to the superior analytical and predictive ability of some investors which will allow them to earn abnormal returns. According to Ray Ball, Philip Brown and Frank J Finn ("Published Investment Recommendations and Share Prices: Are There Free Lunches in Security Analysis?", *Journal of Australian Society of Security Analysts*, June 1978, p 9), in a well-functioning, competitive market "returns should be consistent with efforts (there should be no free lunches)".

Is there an efficient market paradox?

[338] The answer should be no. As we have seen in our discussion earlier in this chapter on the information content and objectives of financial statements as reflected in the FASB Statement of Financial Accounting Concepts No 1, the objectives of financial statements and the underlying financial reporting standards are to provide information on the basis of which rational and informed economic decision can be made — a major part of such decisions will be market-related investment decisions. If financial statements provided all the information which at the time is considered to be relevant for market decisions, then abnormal returns can only be earned by superior analytical and interpretative abilities on the part of investors. A subsequent study of the factors which have led to such abnormal

returns may point to a need to make further disclosures in financial statements and to further increase the analytical and interpretative skills of investors and those who advise them, factors which in turn will increase the efficiency of the market itself.

Some criticisms of the EMH

[339] It would be dangerous for investors to accept market efficiency at any of the three levels discussed earlier in this chapter.

[340] In an article entitled "Why Relative Cost is a Better Basis for Investment Decisions Than the 'Efficient Market' Fallacy" (*The Chartered Accountant in Australia*, May 1980, pp 10-17), Austin S Donnelly attacked the implication of the EMH, arising from the assumed random behaviour of share price, that shares could be bought with the same confidence at the peak of a share boom as when they are at a low point in a market cycle. He pointed out that there is a very low probability of shares producing sustained capital gains if investment is made when the price of shares is high relative to other investments. While the EMH suggests that there is nothing to be gained by attempts to time moves in and out of the market, the facts were that investment in shares should be limited when share prices are high in relation to other investments.

[341] In examining the conceptual weaknesses of the EMH, Donnelly argued that the EMH assumes only one kind of market speculation which moves prices towards an equilibrium. He pointed out that a good deal of speculation in the capital market is destabilising — eg when prices rise above a reasonable level, there is a tendency for the rise to attract interest which leads to further rises, a process which may be self-sustaining for a year or two. Further, market decisions are made by investors on their *perception* of information and that perception may be affected by the market mood of the moment. Donnelly cited the mining boom in the late 1960s and the boom in mineral exploration and mining shares in 1970-80 in which information played little part.

[342] The stock market crash of October 1987 has provided ample support for the above views expressed by Donnelly in 1980. The following are some observations from the New Zealand scene, many of which would be applicable to experiences during the period in Australia and elsewhere.

In the two years or so which preceded the stock market crash there was a growing feeling in New Zealand that shares were over-valued in relation to company earnings. Interest rates were high, at times exceeding 20%. Caught in a frenzy of speculation, many people borrowed at high interest rates to invest in company shares, whereas events were to show that, in fact, it was time to get out of the share market. Yet, to the knowledge of the authors, there was little evidence that sharebrokers advised their clients to do so (although there is evidence that such advice was given by some sharebrokers to their clients *after* the crash). The effects of the stock market crash fell differently on different companies. In some cases the fall in the market value of shares was catastrophic with corresponding losses to investors. Reference to the market value of the shares of such companies before the crash indicates that the market had failed to recognize the high risk nature of such companies in a grossly overvalued market — it should have done so as the information was publicly available.

Even the experts got caught! This is evident from the failure of a number of sharebroking firms in New Zealand, the substantial losses suffered by some banks and insurance companies and by the millions of dollars of losses suffered by pension funds.

Review questions

3.1 Discuss the nature of the decisions which may be made on the basis of the information disclosed in published financial statements.

3.2 Discuss the extent to which sectional interests and conflict of interests may affect the preparation, presentation and interpretation of financial statements.

3.3 "In the final count, groups with special interests in the financial statements of companies will see in the statements what they want to see." Do you agree?

3.4 (a) What do you see as the special interests in published financial statements, of the following groups:
- directors;
- shareholders and investors;
- organized labour;
- consumers;
- the government?

(b) To what extent is it necessary and practicable for the directors to ensure that the needs of these diverse interests are met? Is there any conflict of interests involved?

3.5 Examine critically the following statement:
"The profit achieved is an excellent one ... The earnings rate for the year is a significant 55 cents per share compared with 33 cents per share At first glance, this year's earnings rate and increase in profit appears high, and comparable increases shown by other companies have led to adverse comments from government ministers. However, ... the profit represents a return of about 3½% on the current cost of replacing the assets of the company. A return of 3½% is less than is paid on government loans and would not encourage an investor to sink funds in a freezing works — all this in a year in which favourable factors have produced good profits."

3.6 Compare and contrast the external and internal uses of financial information. State what you see as the main problems to be faced by the interpreter of financial data:
(a) operating within the business to produce information for use by management;
(b) operating outside the business to produce information for some outside interest.

3.7 "There are strong incentives for the accounting profession to be concerned with the quality and reliability of financial statements."
Discuss.

3.8 Consider the view that the FASB would preside over its own demise if it were to make decisions primarily on other than accounting grounds.

3.9 " . . . Share prices are the best available estimates of value and analysis based on financial statement data will not lead to abnormal returns." Discuss.

3.10 Is there an efficient market paradox?

3.11 How efficient is the share market?

Chapter 4
Components and Presentation of Financial Statements

[401] The contents and presentation of company reports will vary from firm to firm depending on the nature of the business, the size of the firm, and the policy of management regarding presentation and disclosure. Company reports may be modest in size, comprising little more than the basic financial statements and information required by company law and accounting standards, or they may assume the appearance of glossy magazines covering many pages and containing information in written, statistical, graphic and pictorial form.

Although the contents and form of presentation of company reports will show variations from one firm to another, company legislation and financial reporting standards ensure that certain common statements are presented, that some specific disclosures are made in the statements and that some general principles and guidelines are followed in their preparation and presentation.

Examples of components of financial statements and their presentation based on a relatively simple published financial report of what we will call The Mount Cargill Trading Co Ltd are shown as Figures 4.1 to 4.9 in this chapter.

Disclosure

[402] Disclosure is a fundamental issue in financial reporting. Financial statements should disclose information which is useful for decision-making. This requires not only that the contents are relevant, but also that they are effectively communicated to the decision-maker.

Classification

[403] Items should be classified and grouped in a manner which is appropriate to the business of the firm. The aggregates produced should be meaningful; they should facilitate the analysis of the operating results and state of affairs of the firm. Appropriate classification should lead to clarity of presentation with emphasis on important items.

Materiality

[404] Materiality is concerned with the relative importance of items to be disclosed — amounts, methods of accounting and changes, and the effects of changes in methods of accounting. If the amount or nature of an item is such as to affect the decisions of users of financial statements, the item should be disclosed separately.

Significant unusual and non-recuring items would fall under this category. On the other hand, the statements should not be concerned with the detailed disclosure of trivia. The items to be disclosed are those which have a significant bearing on the understanding by readers of the operating results and state of affairs of the firm.

Consistency and comparability

[405] The standard of consistency requires that once accounting principles for the preparation of financial statements have been selected, they should be consistently applied from one period to another. Any material effects on reported results and the state of affairs of changes in accounting principles should be adequately disclosed. The objective of the standard of consistency is to attain comparability in financial reports.

Accounting standards and legal requirements regarding disclosure in financial statements

[406] Company law requires financial statements to give a true and fair view of operatintg results and the state of affairs. As discussed in Chapter 2, the truth and fairness of financial statements is interpreted in terms of current accounting practice. Current accounting practice is governed by professional standards regarding the measurement of operating results and the determination of the state of affairs, and the disclosure requirements of professional standards and company law.

As company legislation sets out the true and fair view requirement as being of paramount importance, the specific disclosure requirements of company law and professional standards should be regarded as the minimum. The circumstances of a particular case may require disclosures beyond those prescribed.

In Australia the legal requirements regarding disclosure are contained in Schedule 7 of the Companies Regulations. In New Zealand the requirements are contained in the Eighth Schedule of the Companies Act of 1955.

The objectives of the legal and professional requirements regarding disclosure are to enhance the informational value and interpretability of financial statements, and to prevent manipulation and abuses in financial reporting of the kind revealed in the Royal Mail Steam Packet case. Discussed below are some of the main disclosure requirements of company law and professional standards.

The discussion is intended to illustrate the general nature and direction of legal and accounting standards disclosure requirements. For more detailed disclosure requirements in Australia and New Zealand for example, readers are refered to Schedule 7 of the Company Regulations in Australia and the Eighth Schedule of the New Zealand Companies Act (the disclosure requirements of the Australian Schedule are considerably wider than those of the New Zealand Schedule), and to financial reporting standards in the two countries, as significant differences may also exist, as for example in relation to the preparation of statements of sources and application of funds (AAS12) and statements of cash flows (SSAP10), equity accounting (accounting for associated companies), etc.

Disclosures in the profit and loss statement

[407] There are two main views regarding the contents of the profit and loss statement:

(a) the "exclusive" (current operating performance) view; and

(b) the "all inclusive" view.

The "exclusive" view holds that the profit and loss statement should report only current operating revenues and expenses and that unusual, non-recuring items should be adjusted to retained earnings and other reserves.

The "all inclusive" view holds that all items of profit and loss recognized in the current period should be dealt with in the profit and loss statement.

Current reporting practice tends to favour the "all inclusive" approach for reporting on profit or loss. The Australian Statement of Accounting Standards (AAS1) "Profit and Loss Statements" recommends (para 18) that, except for the revaluation of non-current assets:

... the profit (loss) for a period reported in the Profit and Loss Statement should take into account all items of revenue and expenses, and other gains and loses (whether of a capital or revenue nature), arising in that period —

(a) irrespective of whether they are attributable to the ordinary operations of the business entity during the period, or to events or transactions outside those operations; and

(b) even though they may relate to prior periods.

The adoption of this broad approach to the reporting of profits (losses) requires the clear disclosure of operating profit (loss) and the extent to which such profit (loss) has been affected by abnormal and extraordinary items.

[408] AAS1 defines abnormal items (para 4(c)) as items of revenue and expense and other gains and losses brought into account in the period which, although attributable to ordinary business operations, are considered abnormal by reason of their size and effect on the results for the period. Extraordinary items are defined (para 4(d)) as items of revenue and expense, gains and losses brought into account which are attributed to events, or transactions outside the ordinary operations of the business entity.

It should be readily apparent that, in order to assist in the effective analysis of trends, it would be necessary for the financial statements to disclose information about abnormal and extraordinary items in reported figures relating to past periods as well as information about abnormal and extraordinary items relating to the current period. A similar position is adopted in New Zealand by SSAP7: "Extraordinary Items and Prior Period Adjustments".

[409] Disclosure requirements in the profit and loss statement include:
- corresponding figures for the preceding period;
- sales;
- expenses, appropriately grouped and classified, showing separately: depreciation, interest expense, directors' remuneration, auditors' remuneration, and expenses associated with commitments under leases;
- income from investments showing separately dividends and interest from related companies, other companies and other sources;
- abnormal items;
- taxation;
- extraordinary items;
- dividends paid and provided for;
- transfers to and from reserves.

Taxation

[410] Taxation represents a complex reporting problem. Timing and permanent differences between accounting and taxable income; tax implications of losses brought forward or carried forward; taxation incentives to business; and tax implications of abnormal and extraordinary items all combine to make accounting for and reporting of taxation an important item in financial statements. Current accounting standards require a reconciliation to be provided of the tax applicable to reported profit at the normal tax rate and the actual tax provided for in the profit and loss statement.

Taxation may not only affect the analysis and interpretation of the reported profit for the period but also the analysis and interpretation of the retained earnings and reserves of companies. For example, until 1984 there were a number of provisions which enabled New Zealand companies to pay dividends which were tax-free in the hands of shareholders. This necessitated the classification and the disclosure of retained earnings and reserves in a manner which would enable users of financial statements to determine the ability of a company to pay tax-free dividends (see Figure 4.4, Note 3). These provisions for tax-free dividends were removed after the change of government following the 1984 general election. As tax regulations vary over time, however, the analyst and interpreter of financial statements should be aware of any tax implications regarding the distributability of a company's retained earnings and reserves which may apply at a particular time, especially if such tax implications have a bearing on the decisions to be made.

Disclosures in the balance sheet

[411] Disclosure requirements regarding the balance sheet include:
- Corresponding figures for the preceding period.
- Details of authorized and issues share capital including details of different classes of shares. Where redeemable preference shares have been issued, the earliest date the company has power to redeem the shares must be disclosed.
- Amount and description of reserves, showing separately the amount of the share premium account and any capital redemption reserves. Movements in reserves should be disclosed by way of a note if not otherwise shown.
- Long-term liabilities should be appropriately described and summarised. Where a liability is secured, the fact should be stated. Intercompany loans (that is, within a company group) should be disclosed separately, as should loans from associated companies and from directors. A summary of interest rates, repayment terms and conversion provisions (where applicable) should be provided.
- Short-term liabilities should be appropriately described and summarised. Where a liability is secured, the fact should be disclosed. The following should be disclosed separately:
  - bank loans and overdrafts;
  - trade creditors;
  - dividends payable;
  - intercompany indebtedness;
  - payables to associated companies.
- Fixed assets should be summarized in a manner appropriate to the company's business. The following fixed assets should be shown separately, divided further if material:

- freehold land;
- freehold buildings;
- leaseholds;
- plant and equipment.

• The normal method of disclosing fixed assets is to show for each item the gross amount at cost or valuation, as the case may be, less the aggregate amount of depreciation since acquisition or revaluation. Aggregates for assets which have been revalued should be shown separately from aggregates of assets carried at cost. The date and manner of any revaluation of fixed assets should be disclosed.

• Details of investments should be disclosed showing separately:
- investments in subsidiaries;
- investments in associated companies;
- investments in other companies;
- investments in public body stocks and bonds;
- other investments.

• The market value of stock exchange listed investments should be disclosed.

• Intangibles such as goodwill, patents and trademarks must be disclosed separately to the extent that they have not been written off.

• Current assets should be appropriately summarised showing separately:
- bank balances and cash;
- marketable securities not held as long-term investments — the market value should be disclosed if different from the carrying amount in the balance sheet;
- trade receivables;
- intercompany receivables;
- receivables from associated companies;
- other receivables;
- inventories further divided, where appropriate, into raw materials, work in process and finished goods.

Disclosure by way of notes

[412] Information required to be disclosed by way of notes to the financial statements if not otherwise disclosed includes:
• contingent liabilites including estimated amount if possible;
• commitments for future capital expenditure;
• guarantees to secure the liabilities of others and the amount of the guarantees.

Notes may be used to streamline the presentation of the main financial statements. A popular mode of presentation is to show only main totals in the profit and loss statement and balance sheet and to disclose details, for example, of expenses, capital and reserves, term and current liabilities, fixed and current assets, in notes to the accounts.

Other information disclosed by way of notes includes statements of acounting policies, analysis of income tax provided for, details of loan repayments, etc.

[413] An example of a profit and loss statement is given in Figure 4.1.

The balance sheet

[414] Extending our example, the balance sheet of the Mount Cargill Trading Co Ltd is shown in Figure 4.2.

Figure 4.1

The Mount Cargill Trading Co Ltd
Profit and loss statement for year ended 31 July 19A9

	19A9 $	19A9 $	19A8 $	19A8 $
Sales	29,309,792		24,729,084	
Less cost of goods sold	19,145,324		16,245,643	
Gross profit from trading		10,164,468		8,483,441
Less expenses —				
Advertising, salaries, rents etc	7,611,669		6,220,490	
Interest on term loans	287,790		76,848	
Depreciation	499,895		316,649	
Directors' fees	18,000		17,700	
Audit fees	24,242	8,441,596	19,125	6,650,812
Trading profit		1,722,872		1,832,629
Add income from investments —				
Dividends from companies	2,976		628	
Interest on government stock	299		—	
Interest on other investments	109,017	112,292	50,010	50,638
Net profit before tax		1,835,164		1,883,267
Less provision for tax (see note 5)		831,496		856,675
Net profit after tax		1,003,668		1,026,592
Add unappropriated profit from Previous year		2,378,225		2,368,412
Balance available for appropriation		3,381,893		3,395,004
Less transfer to general reserve	600,000		800,000	
Provision for dividend as recommended	459,950		423,703	
Less transfer from capital reserve	47,581	412,369	206,924	216,779
		1,012,369		1,016,779
Unappropriated profit carried forward		2,369,524		2,378,225

Figure 4.2

The Mount Cargill Trading Co Ltd
Balance sheet as at 31 July 19A9

	19A9 $	19A9 $	19A8 $	19A8 $
Shareholders' funds				
Authorized capital — 5,000,000 ordinary shares of $1 each	5,000,000		5,000,000	
Issued capital — 3,172,070 ordinary shares of $1 each fully paid		3,172,070		2,956,070
Capital reserves (note 3)				
General reserves	2,303,286		1,306,307	
Premium on shares	458,600	2,761,886	275,000	1,581,307
Revenue reserves				
General reserve (note 3)	2,740,045		2,138,716	
Unappropriated profit	2,369,524	5,109,569	2,378,225	4,516,941
Total shareholders' funds		11,043,525		9,054,318
Term liabilities				
Mortgages (secured) (note 4)		2,268,963		816,300
Bank term loan (secured)		2,009,635		421,435
Total term liabilities		4,278,598		1,237,735
Deferred taxation		—		33,070
Current liabilities				
Trade creditors		2,636,708		2,008,768
Unclaimed dividends		13,010		10,533
Money held on deposit		430,525		403,027
Provision for tax (note 5)		282,542		421,583
Bank overdraft and loans (secured)		2,279,342		489,078
Provision for dividend as recommended		459,950		423,703
Total current liabilities		6,102,077		3,756,692
		21,424,200		14,081,815

	19A9 $	19A9 $	19A8 $	19A8 $
Fixed assets				
Land (valuation 19A9)		3,411,470		1,239,250
Buildings (valuation 19A9)	3,371,939		2,181,950	
Less accumulated depreciation	52,497	3,319,442	144,490	2,037,460
Fixtures, fittings and plant (at cost)	4,583,302		3,936,376	
Less accumulated depreciation	2,988,427	1,594,875	2,611,806	1,324,570
Total fixed assets		8,325,787		4,601,280
Investments (at cost)				
Shares in other companies	15,134		5,368	
Advances to staff	92,391		49,712	
Sinking fund	26,160		21,800	
Government stock	39,000		10,494	
Total investments		172,685		87,374
Current assets				
Trading stock	7,731,123		6,119,157	
Trade debtors	3,985,702		2,845,077	
Cash in hand	28,311		24,427	
Money on deposit	1,180,592		404,500	
Total current assets		12,925,728		9,393,161
		21,424,200		14,081,815

Statement of accounting policies

[415] The overriding requirement in financial reporting is that financial reports should give a true and fair view of operating results and state of affairs. In Chapter 2 we discussed some of the difficulties in applying general standards such as truth and fairness to the preparation and presentation of financial reports. We also saw that the accounting interpretation of the true and fair view requirement was essentially a technical one — that financial statements are deemed to be true and fair if they are prepared on the basis of currently acceptable accounting methods and procedures. In the analysis and interpretation of financial statements, therefore, it is essential that the methods and procedures used are properly understood since these methods and procedures define, by implication, what is reported as operating results and state of affairs.

[416] The need for readers of financial statements to be informed about the methods and procedures used in the preparation of the statements is recognized by accounting standards in Australia and New Zealand. Current accounting reporting practice requires the inclusion in financial reports of summaries of accounting principles used, usually as the first item under the heading "Notes to the Accounts" or immediately preceding the financial statements.

The statement of accounting policies of the Mount Cargill Trading Co Ltd is reproduced as Figure 4.3.

Notes to the accounts

[417] Sometimes it is not feasible to incorporate in the profit and loss statement and balance sheet information which is an integral part of these statements or is

Figure 4.3
Statement of accounting policies

The general accounting principles recognized as appropriate for the measurement and reporting of results and financial position under the historical cost method have been observed in the preparation of these accounts except for the revaluation of land and buildings.

The following particular accounting principles which significantly affect the measurement of profit and financial position have been applied.
(a) Land and buildings have been adjusted in 19A9 to the latest government valuations after making an allowance for the value of lifts, escalators, heating and sprinkler plant. The revaluation adjustment has been transferred to capital reserves.
(b) Depreciation of fixed assets (other than land) has been calculated on the straight line basis at rates which are estimated to write off the cost less residual value of those assets over their economic lives. The principal rates in use are:
— Buildings 1% – 2½%
— Fixtures, fittings and plant and motor vehicles, etc 10% – 20%.
(c) Trade debtors are valued at expected realizable value.
(d) Valuation of stock has been made at the lower of cost or net realizable value on a basis consistent with last year. Cost means the actual cost of the relevant item. Allowance has been made to reduce the cost of ageing stock to net realizable value.
(e) Taxation charged against profits includes both current and deferred taxation. The latter arises from depreciation claimed for tax purposes but not charged in the accounts.

pertinent to them. Where this is the case disclosure may be made in "notes" which accompany and form part of the accounts.

Notes may also be used to simplify the presentation of the main financial statements. For example, details of fixed assets, of liabilities and investments, of changes in reserves and provisions, of tax calculation, etc may be disclosed in notes leaving the main financial statements free of excessive detail.

Notes to the accounts should be appropriately cross-referenced and should be read in conjunction with the financial statements to which they refer.

The notes to the accounts of the Mount Cargill Trading Co Ltd (with the exception of the statement of accounting policies) are shown as Figure 4.4.

The directors' report

[418] The directors' report of the Mount Cargill Trading Co Ltd is shown as Figure 4.5. The report follows New Zealand practice and is brief, the more detailed discussion of the operations of the company being left for the chairman's address to shareholders. Directors' reports attached to Australian financial statements are more extensive as a result of more comprehensive requirements of Australian company legislation.

The Auditors' Report

[419] Auditors' reports follow a fairly standard form, the contents being largely concerned with the discharge by the auditors of the duties imposed on them by statute. Of particular interest to readers of financial statements are any qualifications in the audit report.

The auditors' report to the shareholders of the Mount Cargill Trading Co Ltd is shown as Figure 4.6.

Statements of Changes in Financial Position (Funds Statements)

[420] A profit and loss statement reports the results of business activity during a period and a balance sheet the state of affairs of a business enterprise at the end of a period. A statement of changes in financial position (a statement of sources and application of funds, or funds statement) is used to highlight and explain changes which have taken place in the state of affairs of an enterprise between two consecutive balance dates.

[421] Company legislation does not mandate the inclusion of statements of changes in financial position in published company reports. Such statements have been included in company reports as voluntary additions or in order to comply with financial reporting standards.

[422] The aim of a statement of changes in financial position is to summarize the financing and investing activities of a business enterprise. It would show the funds provided during the period from operations and from other sources, such as borrowing and contributions to capital and how these funds were applied, for example,

in financing the acquisition of assets, repayment of liabilities, dividend distributions to shareholders, etc.

[423] The statement of changes in financial position may provide reasonably satisfying answers to questions such as:
  (a) where has the profit shown in the profit and loss statement gone to?
  (b) why cannot the firm pay a higher dividend?
  (c) why has working capital gone up (or down)?
  (d) what has happened to the extra capital or loan money put into the business during the year?
  (e) how was the year's capital expenditure financed?

[424] The form and content of the statement of changes in financial position would depend mainly on two factors:
  (a) the concept of funds used in the preparation of the statement; and
  (b) the particular aspects of the changes in the financial structure of the enterprise that the preparer of the statement wishes to highlight and explain.

For example, the statement may be so designed as to highlight changes in the cash position of the firm, or its net liquid resources (eg current assets and current liabilities but excluding inventories), or its working capital, or to provide an explanatory link between the balance sheets at the beginning and end of an accounting period by concentrating on changes in total resources.

[425] The practice and financial reporting standards regarding the contents, presentation and emphasis in statements of changes in financial position have varied. For example, SSAP10: "Statement of Changes in Financial Position" issued by the New Zealand Society of Accountants in July 1979 recognized a need for flexibility in form and content of the statement but stated that the statement should show:
  (a) funds derived from or used in operations, based on the reported results;
  (b) all other financing and investing operations;
  (c) changes in working capital.

[426] SSAP10: "Statement of Cash Flows" issued by the New Zealand Society of Accountants in October 1987 to replace the statement of July 1979 (discussed above) abandoned what had been the more traditional approach to the preparation of financial statements (based essentially on the notion of funds as total resources but also highlighting changes in working capital) in favour of a statement of cash flows.

[427] SSAP10 (1987) defines cash as cash on hand, demand deposits and other highly liquid investments in which a firm invests as part of its day-to-day cash management; it excludes from the definition of cash accounts receivable, accounts payable, equity securities or any borrowing subject to a term facility. The objective of the statement (para 4.1) is stated to be to provide information which, if used with information in the other statements, should help users to estimate the ability of the firm to generate positive net cash flows, to assess its financial needs and ability to pay dividends, and to note the difference between income and associated receipts and payments. The cash flow statement should show separately cash flows from operating activities, investing activities and financing activities (para 5.3). The statement should be presented in a manner that will reconcile the cash at the start of the period with the cash at the end (para 5.6).

Figure 4.4

Notes to the accounts

(1) *Statement of accounting policies*
   [Shown as Figure 4.3.]

(2) *Changes in the basis of accounting*
   A change to straight line depreciation for all assets has resulted in an additional $85,756 in this year's charge for depreciation as compared with tax rates.

(3) *Capital reserves*

	Share premium reserve $	Available for tax free dividend $	Available for tax free bonus distribution $	Other $	Total $
Balance as at 31/7/A8	275,000	53,321	542,866	710,120	1,581,307
Less transfer to P&L a/c for dividend as recommended		(47,581)			(47,581)
Adjustment for asset disposal		1,943			1,943
Premium on issue of 216,000 shares being part of the purchase price of Beath's assets	183,600				183,600
Revaluation of assets			903,230	139,387	1,042,617
	458,600	7,683	1,446,096	849,507	2,761,886

Revenue reserves	$
Balance as at 31/7/A8	2,138,716
Add unclaimed dividends forfeited in accordance with Articles of Association	1,329
Transfer from profit and loss account	600,000
Balance as at 31/7/A9	2,740,045

(4) *Mortgages*
   Repayable as under

	$
19B1	63,000
19B3	500,000
19B5	166,250
19B7	425,800
19C1	425,813
19C4	465,000
19C8	223,100
	2,268,963

(5) *Provision for tax*

	$
This year's provision for tax	831,496
Add last year's provision for deferred tax now due	33,070
	864,566
Less provisional tax paid	582,024
Balance as per accounts	282,542

(6) Estimated amount of the company's commitments for capital expenditure not provided for in the accounts amounts to $790,000.

Figure 4.5

Directors' report

The directors present to shareholders the ninety-third annual report and statement of accounts of the company for the year ended 31 July 19A9.

Turnover

Turnover for the year was $29,309,792, an increase of $4,580,708 or 18.5% as compared with $24,729,084 last year.

Profit and appropriation	$	$
Net profit before tax is		1,835,164
Provision for tax amounts to		831,496
Leaving a net profit after tax of		1,003,668
Plus unappropriated profit from previous year		2,378,225
Leaving a balance for appropriation of		$3,381,893
Your directors recommend		
A dividend of 14½ cents per share	459,950	
Less transfer from capital reserve	47,581	412,369
A transfer to general reserve		600,000
A carry forward balance to next year		2,369,524
		3,381,893

Directorate

In accordance with the Articles of Association Messrs JP Wells and GD Mowbray retire from the Directorate, and being eligible, offer themselves for re-election.

Audit

In accordance with s 163(3) of the Companies Act 1955, Murchison, Ball, & Co continue in office.

By order of the board.

7 October 19A9

JP WELLS
GD MOWBRAY   Directors

Figure 4.6

Auditors' report

To the members of the Mount Cargill Trading Co Ltd.

We have obtained all the information and explanations that we have required. In our opinion proper books of account have been kept by the company so far as appears from our examination of those books.

In our opinion, according to the best of our information and the explanations given to us and as shown by the books, the balance sheet and the profit and loss account together with the notes thereto, are properly drawn up so as to give a true and fair view of the state of the company's affairs as at 31 July 19A9 and the results of its business for the year ended on that date.

According to such information and explanations the balance sheet and the profit and loss account give the information required by the Companies Act 1955 in the manner required.

MURCHISON, BALL & CO, Chartered Accountants.

Dunedin, 9 October 19A9.

[428] In contrast to SSAP10, the Australian standard AAS12: "Statement of Sources and Application of Funds" is based on a broad concept of funds which includes cash and cash equivalents. The concept has been adopted so that statements of sources and application of funds can disclose information about all the investing and financial activities of the reporting enterprise. Each of the transactions of the enterprise with external parties would involve funds flows in the form of cash or cash equivalents, such as credit or the issuing of shares. The funds statement will summarize such flows showing sources of funds and how the funds were applied (paras 6 and 7). In the case of equity accounting and provisions for dividend and taxation, however, the funds statement should be limited to the disclosure of cash flows — eg dividends received from associated companies and dividends and taxation paid. The requirements of AAS12 are reflected in Approved Accounting Standard ASRB1007: "Financial Reporting of Sources and Applications of Funds".

[429] It is evident from the preceding discussion that statements of changes in financial position can be prepared in different ways, using a variety of concepts of funds and can be designed to analyse, explain and highlight changes in different aspects of the financial structure of an enterprise. Notwithstanding the particular financial reporting standard regarding the preparing of statements of changes in financial position applicable at a particular point of time, the analyst and interpreter of financial statements should be able to use funds flows analysis as a flexible tool for a wide range of purposes — from the study of overall changes in the financial position of an enterprise to an analysis and study of working capital, or more narrowly still, of liquid or cash resources.

[430] In the immediate aftermath of the stock market crash of October 1987 there were calls for increased concern with cash flows and cash flow analysis in the interpretation of the results and state of affairs of business firms. This should not be surprising considering the substantial losses which many investors suffered from investments in companies which had reported high profits arising to a large extent from holding or exchanging shares in various intercompany arrangements or takeovers in a rising but overpriced market which had little by way of cash flow implications. On the other hand, one should not ignore the informational potential of funds flows analysis based on concepts of funds broader than cash.

A funds statement (statement of changes in financial position) for the Mount Cargill Co Ltd is shown in Figure 4.7. The statement is prepared in a manner which highlights movements in liquid funds. Statements of changes in financial position based on alternative concepts of funds are illustrated in Chapter 6.

Optional Statements and Reports

[431] The profit and loss statement, balance sheet, directors' report, and auditors' report are statements and reports required to be incorproated in the overall report of a company by statute. The inclusion of a statement of changes in financial position is required by financial accounting standards. In addition to these, the financial report of a company may include optional statements and reports such as:
• statement of highlights;
• trend statement;

• chairman's address;
• graphs and charts, etc.

Figure 4.7
Funds statement for year ended 31 July 19A9

		19A9 $000		19A8 $000
Source of funds				
Net profit after tax		1,004		1,027
Adjustments of items not involving				
the movement of funds				
Depreciation	500		317	
Increase in deferred tax	—	500	33	350
Total generated from operations		1,504		1,377
Funds from other sources				
Increase in creditors (including				
tax)	422		166	
Bank term loan	1,704		75	
Mortgages	1,453		(57)	
Share issue	400	3,979	—	184
		5,483		1,561
Application of funds				
Dividends proposed	460		424	
Purchase of fixed assets	3,223		262	
Increase in stocks	1,612		730	
Increase in debtors	1,140	6,435	421	1,837
		(952)		(276)
Movement in net liquid funds				
Decrease in cash balances	1,037		288	
Increase in short term investments	85		12	
		Dec (952)		Dec (276)

Statement of highlights

[432] The purpose of providing a statement of highlights in published financial reports is to communicate to readers statistical information about what are considered significant aspects of the operations and state of affairs of the business firm such as turnover, profit before and after taxation, shareholders' funds and rate of return on these, earnings per share and dividend distributions, working capital and working capital ratios, debt equity ratios, etc.

A three-year statement of highlights of the Mount Cargill Trading Co Ltd is shown in Figure 4.8.

Trend statement

[433] Analysis of trends is important in the interpretation of financial statements — it allows the analysis of results and state of affairs to be made in an historical perspective and provides a basis for projections. The statement of highlights shown

in Figure 4.8 is a form of a trend statement covering a period of three years. Trend statements covering longer periods such as five or 10 years are also included in financial reports. Graphs and charts may also be used as means of illustrating significant trends.

A five-year trend statement included in the published financial report of the Mount Cargill Trading Co Ltd is shown in Figure 4.9.

Figure 4.8

Trading highlights

	19A9 $	19A8 $	19A7 $
Turnover	29,309,792	24,729,084	21,469,150
Net profit after tax	1,003,668	1,026,590	671,043
Net profit after tax per $ of sales (cents)	3.42	4.15	3.13
Taxes paid	831,496	856,675	520,644
Dividends — ordinary	14½% 459,950	14⅓% 423,703	14% 413,850
Revenue profit retained	543,718	602,887	257,193
Shareholders' funds	11,043,525	9,054,318	8,460,268
Earning rate on shareholders' funds	9.09%	11.34%	7.93%
Total remuneration paid to employees	5,461,649	4,396,596	3,953,098

Chairman's address

[434] While the directors' report, in New Zealand at least, tends to be brief and limited largely to meeting the requirements of company legislation regarding disclosures in the directors' report, published financial reports usually contain more comprehensive reviews of operating results and state of affairs in a chairman's address to shareholders.

In the case of the Mount Cargill Trading Co Ltd the following were among the matters discussed in the chairman's addres:
- the acquisition of additional stores during the year;
- review of profit performance including a decline in profit in the second half of the year;
- a proposal to obtain the aproval of the court for the payment of tax-free dividend from the share premium account;
- a proposed issue of specified preference shares and making some of the shares available for subscription by employees of the company;
- a proposal to increase the capital of the company;
- announcement of the retirement of the managing director with a review of his work for the company and tribute;
- other changes in the executive.

The address ends with a statement affirming the confidence of the board of directors in the future of the company.

Projects
1.   Referring to Figure 4.1 and the Chairman's address, prepare a statement showing the factors contributing to the reduction of net profit after tax in the

Figure 4.9
Comparisons 19A5-19A9

	19A9 $	19A9 $	19A8 $	19A8 $	19A7 $	19A7 $	19A6 $	19A6 $	19A5 $	19A5 $
Shareholders' funds										
Capital issued and fully paid — preference	—		—		—		500,000		500,000	
ordinary		3,172,070		2,956,070		2,956,070	*2,731,070	3,231,070	2,275,892	2,775,892
Reserves — capital	2,303,286		1,306,307		1,523,344		1,523,344		1,756,990	
premium on shares	458,600		275,000		275,000		—		78,108	
revenue	5,109,569	7,871,455	4,516,941	6,098,248	3,705,854	5,504,198	3,447,499	4,970,843	2,776,841	4,611,939
Total shareholders' funds		11,043,525		9,054,318		8,460,268		8,201,913		7,387,831
Represented by following assets										
Fixed assets, land, buildings, plant, etc	8,325,787		4,601,280		4,665,782		4,511,960		4,944,871	
Less mortgages	2,268,963	6,056,824	816,300	3,784,980	873,500	3,792,282	930,700	3,581,260	987,900	3,956,971
Investments		172,685		87,374		75,033		65,785		51,293
Current assets	12,925,728		9,393,161		8,240,991		8,400,836		6,434,792	
Less liabilities	8,111,712		4,211,197		3,648,038		3,845,968		3,055,225	
Working capital		4,814,016		5,181,964		4,592,953		4,554,868		3,379,567
Total net assets		11,043,525		9,054,318		8,460,268		8,201,913		7,387,831
Profit before tax	1,835,164		1,883,265		1,191,687		1,962,621		1,857,316	
Provision for tax	831,496		856,675		520,644		880,800		868,695	
Net tax-paid profit	1,003,668		1,026,590		671,043		1,081,821		988,621	
Less dividends	459,950		423,703		413,850		412,350		371,384	
Profits retained	543,718		602,887		257,193		669,471		617,237	
Ratio current assets to current liabilities	2.12		2.50		2.59		2.40		2.11	
Dividend per share, ordinary	14½ cents		14⅓ cents		14 cents		14 cents		†15 cents	
Percent net profit to shareholders' funds	9.09		11.34		7.93		13.18		13.38	

*Bonus issue, 1 for 5

†Inc 1% bonus

19A8/9 year of $22,924 from the operations of The Mount Cargill Trading Co Ltd.

2. Referring to Figure 4.2 and drawing on the other information provided, prepare statements showing for (a) the assets, (b) the liabilities, and (c) the shareholders' funds:
    (1) the differences of 19A9 over 19A8; and
    (2) the possible contributing factors to these differences.

Review questions

4.1 In your view, what order should be followed in the presentation of financial and statistical data in the annual report of a company with diverse shareholding? Give your reasons.

4.2 Explain the function in financial reporting of each of the following presentations:
(a) the profit and loss statement;
(b) the balance sheet;
(c) the statement of changes in financial position;
(d) the trend statements;
(e) the statement of highlights.

4.3 What in your opinion should be the contents of a statement of highlights?

4.4 What do you understand by the "inclusive" and "exclusive" viewpoints regarding the contents of the profit and loss statements? Which do you consider to be the better of the two? Give reasons.

4.5 How much understanding of financial statements should be attributed to shareholders in determining the form and content of the statements and amount of detail disclosed?

4.6 Discuss the importance of classification, materiality and consistency in the preparation and presentation of financial statements.

4.7 Discuss the considerations which determine the size, contents and layout of a company report and the degree of disclosure.

4.8 Which do you consider is the more important — the profit and loss statement or the balance sheet?

4.9 Shown below are the operating statement of the XYZ Co Ltd for the year ended 30 September 19A1 (Figure 4.11) and its balance sheet as at 30 September 19A1 (Figure 4.10).

You are provided with the following additional information:

1 The figure for administration expenses includes the amounts of directors' and audit fees. The company regards these as part of the overall expenses of administration.

2 The amount of the current provision for taxation was arrived at after allowing for an overprovision for taxation of $8000 in the year ended 30 September 19A0.

3 The authorized capital of the company consists of 500,000 ordinary shares of $1 each and 250,000 10% preference shares of $1 each.

4 The dividend equalisation account was created for the purpose of ensuring stability in dividend payments in view of possible profit fluctuations. The

current balance of the account represents two transfers of $20,000 each from general reserve made in the years ended 30 September 19A0 and 30 September 19A1.

5   A contract of $86,000 for expansion of buildings has been let with a contracting firm.

6   Provisions for doubtful debts and discounts amounting to $18,500 have been deducted from sundry debtors and only net debtors are shown in the balance sheet.

7   Included in the figure for creditors is bank overdraft of $18,350.

8   There is uncalled capital on shares in companies of $1950.

9   The XYZ Co Ltd has guaranteed the bank overdraft of a client company up to a limit of $20,000.

Required:

Examine critically the presentation of the operating statement and balance sheet of the XYZ Co Ltd, listing what you consider to be errors of presentation. In making your critical review, you should take into account what you consider to be good accounting reporting practice.

Figure 4.10

The XYZ Co Ltd

Balance sheet for year ended 30 September 19A1

	$	$	$
Capital and reserves			
400,000 ordinary shares of $1 each fully paid	400,000		
250,000 10% preference shares of $1 each fully paid	250,000		
Issued and paid up capital	650,000		
50,000 10% debentures of $1 each	50,000		
Reserves			
Share premium reserve	18,500		
General reserve	154,550		
Profit and loss appropriation account	24,578		
Total shareholders' funds	897,628		
Term liabilities			
Dividend equalisation account	40,000		
Current liabilities	$		
Creditors	227,750		
Provision for taxation and dividend	98,300		
	326,050		
	1,263,678		

	$	$
Fixed assets		
Freehold land		22,500
Buildings — at book value		198,800
Furniture and fittings —		
Book value 30/9/A0	20,038	
Less depreciation year ended 30/9/A1	4,000	16,038
Plant and machinery at cost less depreciation to date		271,555
Investments		
Shares in companies and government stock		508,893
Current assets		
Stock in trade		92,000
Debtors	431,220	
	231,565	
		662,785
		1,263,678

47

Figure 4.11

XYZ Co Ltd
Operating statement for year ended 30 September 19A1

	$	$
Sales		1,650,000
Income from investments		
Interest on government stock and dividends from		
companies		7,250
Total revenue		1,657,250
Less cost of sales		
Opening stock	463,200	
Purchases	1,040,000	
Selling and distribution expenses	238,900	
	1,742,100	
Less closing stock	431,220	1,310,880
Gross profits from trading		346,370
Less		
Administration expenses	135,290	
Occupancy costs and depreciation	70,290	
Interest paid on debentures and bank overdraft	6,660	
Interim dividend paid		
Ordinary 3%	12,000	
Preference 4%	10,000	234,240
Net profit before tax		112,130
Less provision for taxation		59,300
Net profit after tax		52,830
Profit and loss appropriation account — balance		
brought foward		10,748
Total available for appropriation		63,578
Provision for final dividend		
Ordinary 6%	24,000	
Preference 6%	15,000	39,000
Balance carried forward		24,578

Chapter 5
Some Basic Considerations in the Financing of Business Enterprises

[501] In Chapter 1 we traced the origins of the double entry system of bookkeeping to the monetary economy which had evolved in medieval and Renaissance Italy and in particular the key role money had come to play in trade and commerce.

[502] In the context of a monetary economy, business activities are carried on through the investment of money for the purpose of generating income measured in monetary terms. This basic characteristic of business activity is best seen in the lending of money at interest. In the majority of cases however, business operations involve investment in non-monetary assets such as goods for resale, or in raw materials and plant and machinery for the purpose of production, as an intermediate step in the income earning process. The basic objective of such operations, however, is not in essence different from lending money at interest, since the ultimate destination of non-monetary assets employed in business is their conversion into cash. In this context, profit is ultimately measured by the matching of two monetary amounts — cash outlays and cash inflows. In a monetary economy, therefore, the business cycle may be defined as:

$$\text{cash} \rightarrow \text{non-cash assets} \rightarrow \text{cash}.$$

This cycle is most easily seen in the venture trading and accounting for trading ventures in medieval and Renaissance Italy. It is also the cycle which underlies contemporary business operations. In the modern context, however, the cycle is more difficult to discern because of the continuity of business operations which requires continuing reinvestment in non-monetary assets. In continuing operations there is a need to account for the status of non-monetary assets at balance date in the preparation of periodic financial reports on the results and state of affairs of business enterprises.

[503] In this chapter we will consider the financing of business operations. Extended discussions on this subject will be found in a variety of texts on business finance and financial management. Our objective is to consider some issues which underlie the financing of business enterprises from a financial accounting and reporting point of view, and their implications for the analysis and interpretation of financial statements.

Sources of finance

[504] Money for use in business operations comes from two major sources:

49

(a) *proprietorship* (shareholders' equity — paid in capital and retained earnings), and

(b) *debt*, which may range from long-term debt, such as loans on mortgage, to medium debt like most debentures, to short-term debt such as trade creditors and loans on call.

Risk and Its Implications

[505] Investment in business operations is based on expectations about an uncertain future — it involves an element of risk. In the business context, risk may be defined as the perceived probability that actual returns on investment may turn out to be different from what is expected. A measure of the risk associated with a given investment is given by the standard deviation of expected future returns — the greater the dispersion of expected returns around the expected average, the greater the perceived risk.

[506] It is generally accepted that investors (providers of finance) are risk averse and that, other things being equal, they will prefer an investment of lower risk to one of a higher risk, or, to put it differently, an investment which carries a higher perceived level of risk should offer investors a higher rate of return as a compensating incentive.

[507] There are two main sources of risk associated with business operations: business risk and financial risk.

Business risk

[508] Business risk arises from the nature of the activities carried on by a business enterprise. For example, prospecting for oil in an unproven area (wild cat drilling) involves a high degree of business risk, whereas an established and profitable food manufacturing business has a low level of business risk.

The notion of business risk may be extended to include what has been referred to as "operating risk". Operating risk relates to the cost structure of an enterprise, in particular to the relative level of fixed costs incurred by the enterprise and the resulting sensitivity of profit to changes in the level of sales, as studied for example in break-even analysis. Operating risk may be imposed by the economic environment within which business operations take place, such as having to employ capital intensive methods of production and operations which require a major investment in fixed assets and the incurrence of a high level of fixed costs. The level of operating risk may also be the result of managerial decisions regarding the methods to be employed in production and operations.

Financial risk

[509] Financial risk is associated with the use of debt finance.

A business enterprise financed entirely from proprietary (shareholders') funds would carry only business risk. The incentive to introduce debt finance in the financial structure of such an enterprise is the opportunity to earn a higher rate of return on proprietary (shareholders') investment. There are two reasons why this may be achieved:

(a) interest paid on debt would normally be lower than the overall return generated by operations;

(b) interest paid is tax-deductible which reduces the net cost of servicing debt to the borrower.

Further, in times of inflation, there is both added need and incentive for firms to borrow, a matter which will be discussed later in this chapter.

[510] Where the expected rate of return on investment is higher than the interest rate, the introduction of debt into the financial structure of a hitherto debt-free enterprise will increase the return on shareholders' funds but will also introduce financial risk. In this context, financial risk is represented by the commitment to pay interest regardless of profit, hence increasing the volatility of profit available to shareholders, and to repay principal at a stated future date, regardless of the state of affairs of the enterprise. This increase in return with an increase in risk is consistent with the assumption of a risk-averse investor. Similar considerations apply to providers of debt finance. As the debt finance employed by an enterprise increases relative to the total investment, the risk to the lender of default by the borrowing enterprise will also increase. One would, therefore, expect that with the increase in risk the lender would expect a higher rate of interest. There is no evidence that there is a linear relationship between the relative level of debt employed by firms and the rate of interest they are required to pay. As debt increases relative to total investment, however, a point wil be reached where additional debt can be raised only at a higher rate of interest. This trade off between risk and rate of return on both proprietary investment and debt raises the question of an optimal financial structure for a firm and the criteria to be used in attaining such a structure.

[511] In an accounting context, the above categories of risk may be reflected in a sectionalized income statement as follows:

(a) *Net operating income before interest and tax* would represent the amount available first to providers of debt finance and then, after allowing for taxation, to providers of equity finance. Its volatility reflects primarily business risk. An analysis of disclosed fixed costs will provide a measure of the operating risk involved in the firm's activities.

(b) *Net operating income after interest and tax* will reflect the amount of income accruing to the shareholders' equity and ostensibly available for distribution by way of dividends or for retention and reinvestment in the operations of the enterprise. The size of financial costs incurred by the enterprise in relation to its income before interest and tax will provide a measure of its financial risk.

[512] It should be noted that using income statements for risk assessment will be done in an "accounting context" in that the figures do not reflect strictly cash flows which are the basis of analysis in finance texts. For example, the income figure may be affected by non-cash flow items such as depreciation, various deferrals and some effect of inventory valuation, etc. Depending on the extent of disclosure, adjustments may be made to reported income figures to make them reflect more closely cash flows for the period.

The Cost of Finance — The Required Rate of Return

[513] In the case of an unincorporated enterprise, such as a sole proprietorship, the employment of debt and the level at which it is employed will reflect the entrepreneur's personal risk preferences and his or her intuitive or explicit perception of an optimum relative use of proprietary and debt finance. Similar situations may exist in closely held private companies.

[514] In the case of incorporated enterprises, especially listed public companies the shares of which are widely traded, the notions of cost of finance and of an optimal financial structure are more complex. In listed companies financial decisions are made by company management using funds provided by investors with indidivudal risk preferences and perceptions of the company's operating results, state of affairs and prospects. The interests of such investors would range over the array of alternative investment opportunities offered by the market and their perceptions of such alternative investment opportunities would vary over time. Investors' evaluations of investment alternatives offered by the market and changes in these evaluations affect the ability of companies to raise equity and debt finance and the cost to service such finance.

[515] In the case of an unincorporated proprietary enterprise, an optimal use of proprietary and debt finance may be perceived as that which maximizes the return on the proprietor's/entrepreneur's investment, given the proprietor's/entrepreneur's attitude to risk. Such optimal use then may be deduced by attempting to rationalize the observed decisions regarding the financing of the enterprise. Even if a particular pattern or model cannot be discerned, it would hardly matter. In the case of companies, however, the concern with an optimal financial structure becomes important as a basis for financial decisions by management and for the evaluation of such decisions. An approach to deal with the problem is to assume that the objective of management in making financial decisions is to maximize the market value of the firm.

[516] The notion of maximizing the market value of the firm as a managerial objective creates a complex problem. For example, the maximization of market value must be perceived in the context of management's own attitude to risk. This makes difficult the evaluation of managerial decisions since any financing decision may be explained in terms of managerial risk preferences. An alternative approach for dealing with the problem of evaluating financial decisions by management could be as follows:

(a) The objective of managerial decisions regarding the financing of business operations should be to achieve a rate of return which would at least maintain the present market value of the company's ordinary shares.

(b) Since the current market value of company ordinary shares reflects expectations of growth, the rate of return should be such that would lead to attaining the expected growth.

(c) In order to maintain a competitive position on the market, the objective of managerial financial decisions should be to achieve a rate of return on existing ordinary shareholders' equity in excess of that achieved by other firms of similar perceived levels of risk.

[517] If the cost of finance or required rate of return is viewed as the rate of return an enterprise needs to achieve in order to maintain the market value of its share-holders' equity (ie the market value of the firm), rate of return may be calculated as the weighted average rate of return reflected in the curent market value of the company's equity and debt securities. Such a rate of return could then be taken to reflect the current market perceptions of the relative risk associated with the company's operations and existing financial structure. This required rate of return would provide a guide to management for the evaluation of investment projects. For example, the undertaking of major projects which will not attain the required rate of return would be expected to lead to a fall in the market value of the company, while projects which will attain a higher rate of return would be expected to lead to an increase in its market value.

The cost of debt finance

[518] The cost to service debt finance is the interest the borrowing firm has to pay. In addition to interest payments, expenses associated with raising debt finance and any continuing expense in monitoring adherence to the terms of debenture trust deeds should be taken into account. As interest paid by the borrowing firm is a tax-deductible expense, the net cost of debt is interest after tax.

[519] In times of inflation business enterprises have tended to rely more heavily on debt finance than under what may be termed normal conditions. There are two main reasons for this:
 • debt has to be repaid at face value regardless of loss of purchasing power;
 • under conditions of continuing inflation firms are likely to be forced into heavier borrowing because of liquidity problems arising from the taxation of over-stated profits, from the need to replace inventories at an ever-increasing cost, and the need to finance an increasing amount of debtors. Further, in the long run, it will be necessary to replace fixed assets at prices which may be very much higher than the historical cost of the assets used up.

[520] In times of inflation interest rates are likely to be high because of a high demand for debt finance, the concern of lenders to protect the real value of their investment, and tight monetary policy adopted by governments as an anti-inflation measure. The real interest cost, however, will be lower than implied by the nominal interest rate, and may even be negative. For example, we may calculate the "real" rate of interest on a debt at 20% interest and tax rate of, say, 40% during a year when 18% inflation took place as follows:

	%
Interest	20
Less tax	8
	12
Less inflation rate	18
Net real interest cost	(−6)

In the above example, the "real" interest cost turns out to be negative. There is another side to this, however. Debt imposes upon a firm the obligation to pay interest at regular intervals and to repay principal as it falls due. Inflation brings serious cash flow problems so that the possibility of financial embarrassment and even failure is very real where business enterprises become excessively dependent on debt finance.

[521] *Trade creditors.* We may consider at this point trade creditors as a special source of debt finance. It is normal for about a month's credit to be given on trade accounts. As a result, the inventory of a retail business may be financed by trade creditors to the extent of one month's purchases. For example, if inventory turnover is four times a year, then about a third of inventory may be financed by trade creditors (eg given a reasonably stable stock level and purchases, average inventory will represent approximately three months' purchases, and average monthly purchases approximately one third of average inventory.

Trade creditors are not necessarily a costless source of debt finance. A firm will incur costs in using this source of finance where there is a difference in the price of purchases for cash and on credit or where the firm loses discounts allowed for the timely payment of accounts or for payment within a period shorter than the normal trade period. In such cases management should be aware of the cost of using trade creditors as a source of finance. On the other hand, trade creditors would be left out of the calculation of the weighted average cost of capital (which we will discuss later in this chapter) on the grounds that the higher cost of purchases would be reflected in the calculation of income (and cash flows) and, therefore, in the cost of capital and the required rate of return.

The cost of equity finance

[522] Equity finance consists of ordinary share capital and retained earnings. It is usually the most important and most difficult component of the cost of capital to calculate. Earlier we stated that the cost of ordinary capital may be regarded as the rate of return a company needs to achieve in order to maintain the market value of its ordinary shares. In this context, the market value of ordinary shares may be regarded as the present value of expected dividend flows associated with the shares, produced by a discount rate which reflects the market assessment of the company's business and financial risks. This discount rate is the minimum required rate of return to be attained by the company in respect of its ordinary capital — it is the cost of ordinary capital. Let us assume for example that a company's income is measured entirely in terms of net cash flows and that, each period, the total of this income after providing for taxation is distributed by way of cash dividend. In this case we may determine the company's cost of capital by finding the rate of discount which will reduce the expected stream of ordinary dividends to a present value equal to the market value of the ordinary shares.

We can express the above relationship between cost of ordinary capital, expected dividend flows and the current market value of ordinary shares as follows:

$$P_O = \sum_{t=1}^{\infty} \frac{D_1}{(1 + ke)^t}$$

where

P_O = the current market price per ordinary share;

D_1 = the dividend expected next period;

K_e = the cost of ordinary share capital.

[523] From an investor's point-of-view, one of the most important features of investing in ordinary shares is the expectation of growth and, therefore, of expanding future dividend flows. The stream of expected dividend flows reflected in the current market value of shares therefore will include the investors' expectations of growth. If we can assume a constant rate of expected growth then the cost of ordinary capital will be

$$K_e = \frac{D_1}{P_O} + g$$

where

P_O = the current price per ordinary share;

D_1 = the dividend expected in the next period;

g = the expected constant rate of growth in dividend.

[524] The calculation of the cost of ordinary capital on the basis of the above discussion is illustrated in Example 5.1.

Example 5.1

An ordinary share of $1 nominal value has a market price of $2.50. Next dividend per share is expected to be 30c. The company is taxed at the rate of 40%. If the expected annual rate of dividend growth is 10%, the cost of ordinary capital will be calculated as follows:

$$K_e = \frac{D_1}{P_O} + g = \frac{0.30}{2.50} + 0.10 = 22\% \text{ after tax}$$

or

$$K_e = \frac{0.22}{1-0.4} = 0.3367 = 36.67\% \text{ before tax.}$$

We may note the following regarding the use of the above method for the measurement of the cost of capital:
• the current market prices of shares are observable;
• the next expected ordinary dividend may be estimated;
• the estimated rate of growth may be based on an analysis of past dividend flows and an assumption that the view of the market is that this rate will continue into the future.

[525] The major difficulty in applying the above method in the calculation of the cost of ordinary capital is the estimation of expected rate of constant growth. Both the assumption of a constant rate of growth and the estimation of the rate from, say, past dividend data will be essentially conjectural.

[526] Marked differences in the dividend yields of companies may be explained by the existence of markedly different allowances for growth by the market. It seems reasonable to assume that, where business risk and financial risk would appear to be comparable, the market cost of equity capital would be comparable. In such circumstances, the differences in dividend yield between two companies can be taken to be due to differences in the allowances for growth. This still does not give us the cost of equity capital of one of these companies — for this one requires a comparable company with no growth expectations but with an equivalent level of risk. Alternatively, one has to take a no-risk investment and make assumptions about what the market would allow for risk in the particular case. In the last approach to measuring the cost of capital, use can be made of the Capital Assets Pricing Model (CAPM).

[527] CAPM is a model for the valuation of assets under which the required rate of return of a security is represented by the return on risk-free securities plus a premium which reflects the risk of the security being valued. The risk of the security being valued is calculated by taking the differences between the expected return on the market portfolio (the average market return) and the expected return on risk-free securities and multiplying it by the beta of the security being valued.

[528] The beta of a security measures the extent to which the return on the security varies in relation to the return on the market portfolio. The higher the beta of a security, the more volatile its return is expected to be in relation to the average market return. The beta of the market portfolio is assumed to be 1. The return on a share with a beta of 2 is likely to be twice as volatile as the average market return. Similarly, the return on a share with a beta of 0.5 is likely to be half as volatile as the average market return.

[529] In light of the above discussion, the CAPM approach to the calculation of the cost of ordinary share capital may be expressed as follows:

$$K_e = K_f + (K_m - K_f)\beta_e$$

where

K_e	=	cost of ordinary share capital;
K_f	=	expected return on risk-free shares;
K_m	=	return on the market portfolio (average market return);
β_e	=	the beta of the ordinary shares.

For example, using the CAPM method, we can calculate the cost of ordinary shares with a beta of 2, and given a risk-free return of 10% and average market return of 14% as follows:

$$K_e = 0.10 + (0.14 - 0.10)\,2 = 0.18 = 18\%$$

[530] The main problems associated with using the CAPM for the calculations of the cost of ordinary share capital is the availability of betas for particular shares and the degree of stability/volatility of such betas over time as investors revise their relative expectations regarding such securities. In our discussion on the efficient market hypothesis in Chapter 3 we noted that the market cannot be relied on to always act on a rational evaluation of the relative risks of investment alternatives and to adjust prices to reflect corresponding expected rates of return. Sometimes investors act according to the mood and general trends of the market to produce prices which cannot be justified by the performance of companies or reflect rationally based expectations of prospects. Such investor attitudes may relate to individiual enterprises, to industries, or to the market as a whole. In extreme cases the result may be cataclysmic adjustments to market prices.

[531] Before we leave the question of the cost of equity capital, we will return briefly to the matter of taxation. A major factor in the attractiveness of debt as a source of finance is the deductibility for tax of the amount of interest paid — ie the cost of debt finance is met from income before tax. On the other hand, dividends on equity capital are paid from income after tax and after providing for sufficient profit retention to meet the growth expectations on investors in ordinary shares.

Tax considerations may affect the market demand for securities and, therefore, the cost of finance in another way. From the viewpoint of investors the relevant return on investment is that after tax. Therefore, differences in the liability for taxation of income from different investment sources will affect the expectations of after-tax income by investors and, therefore, the cost to a company to raise finance from such sources. Consider for example a situation where the dividend income of companies is not assessable for tax purposes but is assessable income to individual investors, and where interest income of both companies and individuals is assessable subject to a lump sum exemption in the case of individuals. Such differential tax treatment of investment income in the hands of corporate and individual investors may have important impact on share markets, where corporate investors play an important role in setting market prices.

The cost of retained earnings

[532] Profit retention is a universal practice the purpose of which is, ostensibly, to finance growth. As we stated earlier, ordinary shares are attractive to investors because of the expectations of growth in dividend income in future years. In order to achieve growth, retained earnings must be profitably invested in the operations of the company. In this context retained earnings may be regarded as additions to the company's ordinary capital with the same required rate of return.

In two respects, however, retained earnings may be regarded as a cheaper source of finance than an issue of ordinary capital. First, there is the saving of flotation costs which would be incurred if the same amount were to be raised by an issue of shares. Second, if all earnings where distributed to shareholders, the shareholders would be liable to any tax that might be levied on dividends. On the other hand, retention of earnings would, presumably, lead to growth and a consequent increase in the market value of ordinary shares. To the extent that gains from increases in the market value of shares are not taxable or are taxable at a lower rate than the marginal tax rate of individual shareholders, retention of earnings represents an advantage to shareholders in comparison to distribution by way of cash dividends. It could be argued, therefore, that the cost to the company to service retained earnings is lower than that of ordinary share capital.

The cost of preference capital

[533] In addition to equity capital represented by ordinary shares, a company may issue preference shares. These normally carry a right to dividend at a fixed rate and a right to return of capital up to the nominal value of the shares. The cost to service existing preference shares is higher than that of borrowing because dividend is paid out of tax-paid profit. Further, preference shareholders rank after lenders in the payment of dividend or return of capital so that the rate of dividend payable on preference shares must provide an inducement to investors to invest in this form of security rather than in company debentures. On the other hand, the servicing cost attached to preference share capital is lower than that attached to ordinary share capital because it (typically) ranks before ordinary capital for dividend payments and on winding up and, therefore, involves a lower level of risk to the investor. The higher servicing cost of ordinary share capital is evidenced by the aggregate of dividend paid and profit retained per share.

The weighted average cost of finance

[534] In its operations, a company would normally employ finance from a variety of sources which will make up its financial structure. The cost to the company of the particular sources of funds it utilizes, ie its individual securities, is said to be the discount rate which equates the present value of the cash flows associated with a security with the current market value of the security. The overall cost of the finance used by a company may then be calculated as the weighted average cost of all the sources of finance which comprise the financial structure of the company after making an adjustment for the tax deductibility of interest. The use of current market rates in determining the cost of capital tends to reflect investors' assessment of the current business and financial risks of the company. The overall cost of finance so calculated gives a measure of the overall rate of return the company would need to earn to maintain the market value of its shares.

[535] Instead of calculating the weighted average cost of capital on the basis of the existing financial structure of the company, the calculation may be made on the basis of a "target" financial structure if there is a perceived imbalance in the company's existing structure.

[536] The calculation of a weighted average cost of finance is illustrated in Example 5.2 below. The cost of equity capital (K_e) is calculated on the basis of an expected constant rate of growth.

Example 5.2

Shown below are details of the capital employed by the XYZ Co:

	Nominal value ($000)	Market value $	Dividend per share $
Ordinary shares of $1 each	2,600	2.50	0.20
Retained earnings	2,400		
	5,000		
10% Preference shares of $1 each	500	0.69	0.10
12% Debentures	2,000	0.89	

- The expected average dividend growth on ordinary shares is taken to be 10%.
- The expected next ordinary dividend is 20c per share.
- The company is taxed at the rate of 50%.

The calculation of the weighted average cost of capital of the XYZ Co is shown below.

Market value and current servicing cost

Source	(1) Total nominal value ($000)	(2) Market price $	(3) Total market value ($000)	(4) Payout $	(5) Yield per $ of market value $	(6) Tax effect $	(7) Net cost per $ $
Ordinary shares	2,600	2.50	6,500	0.20	0.180*		0.180
Retained earnings	2,400						
	5,000		6,500				
10% Preference Shares	500	0.69	345	0.10	0.145		0.145
12% Debentures	2,000	0.89	1,780	0.12	0.135	-0.067	0.067
	7,500		8,625				

$$*K_e = \frac{D_1}{P_o} + g = \frac{0.20}{2.50} + 0.10 = 0.18 = 18\%$$

Weighted average cost of capital after tax

Source	(1) Total market value ($000)	(2) Weight	(3) Cost per $ of market value $	(4) (2)x(3)
Shareholders' equity	6,500	0.7536	0.180	0.1356
Preference shares	345	0.0400	0.145	0.0058
Debentures	1,780	0.2064	0.067	0.0138
	8,625	1.0000		0.1552

The weighted average cost of capital after tax = 15.52%

Weighted average cost of capital before tax

Source	(1) Cost per $ of market value $	(2) Tax effect $	(3) Cost per $ of market value before tax $	(4) Weight	(5) (3)x(4)
Shareholders' equity	0.180	0.180	0.360	0.7536	0.2713
Preference shares	0.145	0.145	0.290	0.0400	0.0116
Debentures	0.135	—	0.135	0.2064	0.0279
				1.0000	0.3108

The weighted average cost of capital before tax and interest = 31.08%

59

Financial Gearing or Leverage

[537] In the broadest sense financial gearing, or leverage, refers to the relative amounts of shareholders' equity and borrowing employed by a business enterprise. The proprietary (equity/debt) ratio is a measure of this kind of gearing.

In a narrower sense, gearing may be thought of as the relationship between the shareholders' equity and debt requiring the payment of interest. Trade creditors will be left out of the calculation of a ratio designed to measure gearing of this kind.

A third way of looking at gearing is to relate the shareholders' equity to term borrowing — the borrowing which involves the company in a fixed commitment for the payment of interest. In this case, bank overdraft as well as trade creditors will be omitted from the calculation of the gearing ratio. However, where a portion of the overdraft appears as a permanent feature of the financial structure of the firm, that permanent portion may be included with long-term debt in determining the gearing position of the firm.

In considering financial gearing from the viewpoint of ordinary shareholders, preference capital should be included with borrowing since the fixed commitment by the company to the payment of preference dividend, especially where dividend is cumulative, gives preference capital the characteristics of a debt, at least from the viewpoint of ordinary shareholders.

In the narrowest sense, gearing can be conceived of as the relationship between the equity of the ordinary shareholders and preference capital.

[538] All these approaches to the measurement of financial gearing are based on the balance sheet, and are dependent for their validity on the relevance of the measures placed on assets and liabilities. For example, writing up land and buildings adds equal sums to both assets and the equity of ordinary shareholders, and so affects the calculation of gearing.

Long-term leases which are used as means of financing the purchase of property (financing leases) may limit the validity of the gearing based on balance sheet data alone. Let us take for example two companies which are identical in all respects except in their decisions on financing the acquisition of a property valued at $500,000. Company A decides on a 20-year non-cancelable lease with right of purchase at a very favourable figure, whereas company B decides to buy the property, financing the purchase in part by mortgage and in part by increased short-term finance. The two balance sheets might then show:

	Co A $000	Co B $000
Share capital and reserves	1,000	1,000
Long term debt	600	950
Current liabilities	400	550
Total to finance assets	2,000	2,500
Equity/debt ratio	1:1	0.67:1

The gearing of company A appears to be much lower than that of company B, whereas the fact is that the gearing levels are virtually identical.

[539] An alternative to the balance sheet approach to gearing as the expression of the relative dependence of an enterprise on debt finance is to measure gearing by relating the expense associated with debt finance of a year to profit before charging debt finance expense. Some ways of measuring gearing in this matter are as follows:

Interest	:	Net profit before interest and tax
Interest adjusted for tax effect	:	Net profit after tax, plus interest adjusted for tax effect
Interest plus non-cancellable lease rentals	:	Net profit before interest, non-cancellable lease rentals, and taxation

This last overcomes the financing lease problem. Obviously these ratios will be less stable than balance sheet based measures of gearing, as profits will tend to vary more than interest expense and rentals.

Risk and income considerations in financial gearing

[540] We have already seen that in the majority of cases borrowed funds are less costly to service than finance provided by shareholders. If profitability were the only consideration then it would pay a firm to obtain all its funds from loan finance.

Risk, however, is an equally important consideration in financing. Lenders recognize this too. It is far from likely that they will be prepared to provide all the funds required by an enterprise. Further, the servicing cost of loan finance will increase as an enterprise goes beyond what is considered as prudent in the use of loan finance.

[541] The effect of loan finance on the return on shareholders' funds may be determined by comparing the rate of return on the shareholders' equity and the rate of return on total assets. Successful employment of loan finance should result in the return on shareholders' funds being higher than that on total assets. A test of this success may be provided by a financial gearing profitability ratio calculated by the formula:

$$\frac{\text{Return on shareholders' equity}}{\text{Return on total assets}}$$

For example:

$$\frac{\dfrac{\text{Net profit after tax}}{\text{Shareholders' equity}}}{\dfrac{\text{Net profit after tax} + \text{Interest } (I\text{-}T^*)}{\text{Total assets}}}$$

*T = rate of tax.

Where the tax relating to a particular year has been significantly affected by extraordinary factors (such as a flow through of tax benefits from investment allowances), the rates of return on shareholders' funds and total assets may be calculated on the basis of profit before tax or by using a profit after tax figure which has been adjusted for extraordinary tax items.

[542] Where a company has issued preference share capital, the assessment of the profitability of financial gearing should be made in relation to the ordinary shareholders, since advantages or disadvantages of using borrowed funds and preference capital will ultimately affect the amount of profit available to ordinary shareholders and the rate of return on the investment attributable to them.

Example 5.3

The Mount Cargill Trading Co Ltd
Financial gearing and rate of return

Net profit before tax	$1,835,164
Less provision for tax	831,496
Net profit after tax	$1,003,668
Interest paid	$287,790
Shareholders' equity	$11,043,525
Total funds employed (= total assets)	$21,424,200
Rate of tax 45%	

Rate of return on shareholders' equity and total assets
(net profit after tax)

Rate of return on shareholders' equity

$$\frac{\text{Net profit after tax}}{\text{Shareholders' equity}} \times 100 = \frac{\$1,003,668}{\$11,043,525} \times 100 = 9.1\%$$

Rate of return on total assets

$$\frac{\text{Net profit after tax} + \text{interest } (1-0.45)}{\text{Total assets}} \times 100 =$$

$$= \frac{\$1,003,668 + \$287,790.(1-0.45)}{\$21,424,200} \times 100 =$$

$$= \frac{\$1,161,952}{\$21,424,200} \times 100 = 5.4\%$$

Financial gearing profitability ratio $\frac{9.1}{5.4} = 1.69:1$

The effect of financial gearing on the rate of return on shareholders' funds is illustrated in Example 5.3. The figures are taken from the financial statements of the Mount Cargill Trading Co Ltd used as illustration in Chapter 4.

A gearing profitability ratio higher than 1:1 indicates a favourable effect of borrowing on the rate of return on the shareholders' equity; a ratio of less than 1:1 will indicate an unfavourable effect.

[543] An examination of the balance sheet of the Mount Cargill Trading Co Ltd reveals a large increase in borrowing and total assets during the year. A better measure of the effect of gearing on the rate of return on shareholders' funds, therefore, may be given by comparing the rates of return on average shareholders' funds and average total assets. This is done in Example 5.4.

The financial gearing profitability ratio again shows that borrowing has had a favourable effect on the rate of return on shareholders' funds.

Example 5.4
The Mount Cargill Trading Co Ltd
Rate of return on average shareholders'
funds and average total assets

Average shareholders' funds $= \dfrac{\$11,043,525 + \$9,054,318}{2} = \$10,048,921$

Average total assets $= \dfrac{\$21,424,200 + \$14,081,815}{2} = \$17,753,007$

Rate of return on average shareholders' funds $= \dfrac{\$1,003,668}{\$10,048,921} \times 100 = 9.99\%$

Rate of return on average total assets $= \dfrac{\$1,161,952}{\$17,753,007} \times 100 = 6.54$

Financial gearing profitability ratio $\dfrac{9.99}{6.54} = 1.53:1$

Financial gearing and the vulnerability of profit

[544] The use of borrowed funds commits an enterprise to the payment of interest regardless of the profitability of operations. The higher the level of borrowing (ie the more highly geared the enterprise), the greater will be the amount of this commitment. High gearing results in greater fluctuations in profits attributable to ordinary shareholders. At high levels of income the ordinary shareholders have much to gain from high gearing. At low levels of income the profit attributable to their equity may be greatly reduced or eliminated altogether.

An analysis of the financial structure of a company may be extended to include a study of the cost structure of the company. The profits of a company incurring a high level of fixed costs are vulnerable to fluctuations in trading conditions in a similar manner as in the case of a company with a highly geared financial structure. There will be a significant relationship, therefore, among the cost structure of a company, the level of business risk associated with its operations and what may be considered to be appropriate financial gearing for the company.

The effects of high and low financial gearing on profits attributable to ordinary shareholders are illustrated in Examples 5.5 and 5.6. Example 5.5 considers gearing where only ordinary share capital has been issued and Example 5.6 extends the illustration to include the effect of preference capital.

The effect of high and low gearing will be evaluated by assuming that profit before interest and tax is alternatively 20%, 15%, 10% and 5% of the total funds employed.

Example 5.5 shows that with high gearing (eg borrowing at 60% of total funds) and high level of profit (eg profit before tax and interest at 20% of total funds) a much higher rate of return is earned on the equity of ordinary shareholders (17½% compared with 11¼% with low gearing). The profit, however is highly susceptible to adverse trading conditions. With profit before tax and interest at 5% of total funds, the ordinary shareholders' equity incurs a loss of $10,000 compared with a profit of $15,000 under low gearing.

Example 5.5

Financial gearing and profit attributable to ordinary shareholders

		$
(a)	High gearing	
	Ordinary capital and reserves	400,000
	Borrowing	600,000
	Total funds employed	1,000,000
(b)	Low gearing	
	Ordinary capital and reserves	800,000
	Borrowing	200,000
	Total funds employed	1,000,000
	Interest on borrowing	10%
	Rate of taxation	50%

Alternative profit results (percentage of total funds)

		20% $	15% $	10% $	5% $
(a)	Effect of high gearing				
	Profit before interest and tax	200,000	150,000	100,000	50,000
	Less interest	60,000	60,000	60,000	60,000
	Profit before tax	140,000	90,000	40,000	(−10,000)
	Less tax	70,000	45,000	20,000	NIL
	Profit after tax (attributable to ordinary shareholders)	70,000	45,000	20,000	(−10,000)
	Rate of return on ordinary shareholders' funds	17½%	11¼%	5%	—
(b)	Effect of low gearing				
	Profit before interest and tax	200,000	150,000	100,000	50,000
	Less interest	20,000	20,000	20,000	20,000
	Profit before tax	180,000	130,000	80,000	30,000
	Less tax	90,000	65,000	40,000	15,000
	Net profit after tax	90,000	65,000	40,000	15,000
	Rate of return on ordinary shareholders' funds	11¼%	8⅛%	5%	1.88%

[545] Example 5.6 extends the analysis to include the effect of preference capital on profit attributable to ordinary shareholders. The data is the same as in Example 5.5 except that it is assumed that the shareholders' equity includes $100,000 of 11% cumulative preference share capital.

[546] From the viewpoint of the ordinary shareholders, the effect of the preference capital in Example 5.6 is to further increase the gearing of the company and the volatility of the profit attributable to ordinary shareholders. With borrowing at 60% of total funds the rate of return on ordinary shareholders' funds is 19.7% when

Example 5.6

Preference capital and profit attributable to ordinary shareholders

			$
(a)	**High gearing**		
	Ordinary share capital and reserves		300,000
	11% preference share capital		100,000
			400,000
	Borrowing		600,000
	Total funds employed		1,000,000
(b)	**Low gearing**		
	Ordinary share capital and reserves		700,000
	11% preference share capital		100,000
			800,000
	Borrowing		200,000
	Total funds employed		1,000,000

Alternative profit results
(percentage of total funds)

		20% $	15% $	10% $	5% $
(a)	*Effect of high gearing*				
	Profit after interest and tax (from				
	Example 8.5)	70,000	45,000	20,000	(−10,000)
	Less preference dividend	11,000	11,000	11,000	11,000
	Profit attributable to ordinary				
	shareholders	59,000	34,000	9,000	(−21,000)
	Rate of return on ordinary				
	shareholders' funds	19.7%	11.33%	3%	—
(b)	*Effect of low gearing*				
	Profit after interest and tax (from				
	Example 8.5)	90,000	65,000	40,000	15,000
	Less preference dividend	11,000	11,000	11,000	11,000
	Profit attributable to ordinary				
	shareholders	79,000	54,000	29,000	4,000
	Rate of return on ordinary				
	shareholders' funds	11.29%	7.7%	4.14%	0.57%

profit before tax and interest is at 20% of total funds. However, when profit before tax and interest is at 5% of total funds, $21,000 deficiency accrues to the ordinary shareholders for loss and arrears of cumulative preference dividend. With low gearing there is greater stability of profit attributable to the ordinary shareholders.

The Analysis of Financial Structure

[547] We may view the balance sheet of a firm as a form of funds statement which shows a summary of the assets held by the firm at balance date and the manner in which the assets were being financed at that date.

In the analysis of the balance sheet, financial ratios and percentages are used to test the financial structure of the firm for strengths and weaknesses at a point of time and for changes over time.

Let us consider the abbreviated balance sheet of the assumed company Manufacturers Co Ltd shown in Figure 5.1. In the exhibit the components of the balance sheet are shown as amounts and as percentages; in the latter case the different classes of assets are shown as percentages of total assets, and the shareholders' equity and liabilities as percentages of total funds employed. The two percentage columns in Figure 5.1 represent a "common size" balance sheet which may be used for comparison of the financial structure with that of other firms or for a study of the changes in the financial structure of the firm over time by the comparison of common size balance sheets in succeeding periods. In the present example, however, our concern will be primarily with the financial relationships disclosed in the balance sheet itself. Some of the financial relationships disclosed in the balance sheet of Manufacturers Co Ltd are illustrated diagrammatically in Figure 5.2.

The following relationships shown in the balance sheet of Manufacturers Co Ltd may be considered:

(1) *Equity finance to borrowing (proprietary or equity/debt ratio)*. In the example the ratio is 1:1 or, to put it differently, the shareholders' equity represents 50% of the total funds used.

(2) *Current assets to current liabilities (curent ratio)*. The ratio in the example is 2:1.

(3) *Term liabilities to fixed assets*. In the example the ratio is 0.5:1. Put another way, term liabilities are 50% of the book value of fixed assets.

(4) *Fixed assets to total assets*. The fixed asset requirements of a firm will depend on the nature of its business. The ratio or percentage of fixed assets to total assests (in this case 30%) will indicate the relative distribution of funds over fixed and current assets and will have evaluative significance if compared to some standard.

(5) *Fixed assets to shareholders' equity*. Like the previous ratio, this ratio is concerned with the relative distribution of funds between fixed and current assets.

Figure 5.1

Manufacturers Co Ltd
Balance sheet as at 31 December 19A1

	$	%		$	%
Share capital	500,000		*Fixed assets*		
Retained earnings	500,000		(at cost less depreciation)		
Shareholders' equity	1,000,000	50	Land and buildings	200,000	
			Plant	400,000	
				600,000	30
Term liabilities	300,000	15	*Current assets*		
Current liabilities	700,000	35	Inventories	800,000	
			Debtors	600,000	
				1,400,000	70
	2,000,000	100		2,000,000	100

Figure 5.2
Manufacturers Co Ltd
Financial relationships as at 31 December 19A1

50%	Equity	Fixed assets	30%
15%	Long term borrowing	Current assets	70%
35%	Short term borrowing		

(50% left total)

The difference is that this ratio is concerned also with prudent financing. In our example the ratio is 0.6:1 which means that fixed assets are 60% of shareholders' funds. If the percentage is too high, the firm will either have a low working capital or will have to finance its working capital from long-term borrowing.

Shareholders' Equity as a Safety Margin for Creditors

[548] From a creditor's point of view the shareholders' equity provides a safety cushion, a net asset margin against loss in times of economic adversity. In our example the shareholders' equity represents 50% of the total investment in the firm (an equity/debt ratio of 1:1) which means that for every $1 of debt in the firm there is $2 backing of assets at book value.

The relationship between the shareholders' equity and borrowing provides only a general indication regarding the security of creditors. Conclusions regarding creditors' safety would require detailed examination of the following:

(a) the composition of the shareholders' equity with particular attention to any redeemable preference shares, options regarding redemption and earliest date of redemption;

(b) the composition of creditors with particular attention to priority of payment (in particular any security given and the assets to which it relates), and the timing of repayment of major loans;

(c) the composition of assets and their curent value, in particular their net realizable value.

Finally, it should be kept in mind that the realization of a firm's assets for the repayment of loans is regarded as a last resort action by lenders. The lending of money to business firms usually envisages repayment "in the normal course of operations" and this does not include the forced realization of assets with a possible liquidation of the firm as a consequence. Whether a firm represents a good risk for lenders would depend on its ability to meet interest payments and repayment of principal in the course of its continuing operations. Its ability to repay principal is likely to depend on its ability to either refinance the debt or to replace the debt with additional equity capital. Both are dependent finally on the confidence of investors in the continuity and profitability of the business. From a lender's viewpoint, it is not only a concern for the difference between recorded asset values and asset values in liquidation (which can be really material where the assets are specialized); no lender wishes to be faced with the risk that action will be necessary to protect the loan.

Analysis of the Shareholders' Equity

[549] In the preceding section we considered the shareholders' equity as a safety margin for creditors. A detailed analysis of the composition of the shareholders' equity is also important particularly from the viewpoint of shareholders and investors. The following are some purposes of such analysis:

(a) to determine the rights and priorities attaching to different classes of shares;

(b) to determine the existence of any liability on the part of shareholders for uncalled capital on shares;

(c) to establish whether special conditions apply in regards to the retained earnings and reserves of the company such as restrictions on distribution, and tax implciations of distribution in the form of cash dividends or bonus shares;

(d) to analyse the implications of a pending conversion into ordinary shares of convertible preference shares, notes, etc.

Share Capital

[550] The common classes of shares issued by companies are ordinary shares and preference shares. Shares with varying rights may be issued within these two major classifications.

(a) Ordinary shares

The equity of ordinary shareholders represents the residual (or proprietary) interest in a company. Ordinary shareholders bear the maximum risk in the operations of the firm and are entitled to the residual profits after the payment of interest on loans and dividends to preference shareholders. Changes in the value of assets which are recognized in the books of the firm (such as the revaluation of fixed assets) are adjusted to the equity of the ordinary shareholders. Usually only ordinary shareholders have the right to vote at general meetings of the company, and to appoint and dismiss directors.

(b) Preference shares

[551] Preference shares may be issued with a variety of rights and conditions. These rights and conditions will be specified in the company's memorandum or (more usually) articles of association.

Usually, preference shares entitle the holders to a fixed rate of dividend before dividend is paid to the holders of other shares. The rights attaching to preference shares may also provide for the repayment of capital on winding up before capital is returned to other shareholders; the conditions of issue may specify that such a return of capital will be limited to the nominal value of the shares or may stipulate that preference shares will participate in the sharing of any surplus on winding up and the manner of such participation.

Unless otherwise stated, dividends on preference shares are deemed to be cumulative — non-payment of dividend in one year must be made good in subsequent years.

[552] A company may issue redeemable preference shares. Where that is the case, company law requires the disclosure of the earliest date at which the company has power to redeem the shares. In the analysis of the shareholders' equity it is important to be aware of the conditions attaching to redeemable shares, in particular whether redemption is mandatory at the end of a specified period or whether it is at the option of the company or the shareholders. Taking the example where redemption at the end of a specified period is a condition of issue, redeemable preference shares can be regarded as little more than a debt though one ranking for repayment after creditors. Redeemable preference shares also must be treated as a debt where a decision has been made to redeem the shares even though redemption is not a compulsory condition of issue.

(c) Specified preference shares

[553] In New Zealand companies have issued "specified" preference shares. These shares have been issued with a variety of rights, options and conditions attached to them, ranging from the shares being convertible to ordinary shares on a set basis to their being redeemable in cash at a future date. The salient characteristic of specified preference shares is that dividend paid on them is tax-deductible by the company. This will normally make them less costly to service than non-specified preference shares. The issue of specified preference shares improves the security of creditors as specified preference shares rank after creditors for the payment of dividends or return of capital.

The Analysis of Reserves

[554] The breakdown of reserves into significant components is necessary where conditions have been set out restricting their use for dividend or other purposes, and also to inform the reader regarding the tax implications of their distribution. For example, the ability of companies to pay dividends from reserves free of tax is significant information for investors.

The capitalization of reserves for the issue of bonus shares is a common practice by companies. When accompanied by an increase in the amount of dividend paid, it usually leads to an increase in the market value of shareholdings and provides a tax-free return to shareholders. A study of the past policy of the company regarding bonus issues and cash dividends is important from the viewpoint of intending investors. Such a study should be combined with an analysis of the company's reserves — their composition and size in relation to paid up capital. Related to the analysis of reserves should be a study of operating results to determine the ability of the company to pay higher dividends.

[555] Tax laws regarding bonus issues and cash dividends would vary over time. Such existing tax laws should be considered as their effect could impact on investors decisions.

The Analysis of Debt

[556] A study of the financial structure of a business enterprise requires a careful analysis of its long- and short-term debt.

Long-term debt

Examples of long-term debt are mortgages and debenture stock. A special kind of long-term debt is convertible debentures. The following considerations are important in the analysis of long-term debt:

[557] (a) *Maturity dates*. These should be studied in order to determine the future financial demands on the firm. So far as debt is concerned, solvency is dependent not only on the ability to meet interest payments as they fall due but also to meet repayment on due date. The latter may well require the refinancing of the debt. In view of the uncertainties of the future market for finance and of the fortunes of the business, it is usual to spread the maturity dates for debt over a series of years. Debt due for repayment in the near future may well be a critical factor in the assessment of the financial position of a business.

[558] (b) *Interest rates*. It is important to compare the interest rates applicable to the loan finance used by the firm with current and projected interest rates in order to determine the likely servicing cost the company will have to face if loans are refinanced by further long-term debt.

[559] (c) *Secured loans*. A study should be made of secured loans and the assets over which security is given in order to determine the priorities of different types of lenders and the capacity of the firm to raise additional loans on the security of its assets. In this regard, the realizable value of the assets is the relevant measure, and not the book value.

[560] (d) *Restrictions imposed by lenders*. Debenture trust deeds impose restrictions on the firm such as requiring the maintenance of a minimum equity/debt ratio. Knowledge of these constraints is necessary for an adequate interpretation of the financial statements of the firm. If a company is constantly close to the trigger levels of lender imposed constraints, then the likelihood is that it is suffering financial stress and could be at risk.

[561] (e) *Convertible debentures*. Convertible debentures are a convenient source of funds especially when used to finance assets which will take some time to become fully productive. In such cases the servicing cost of the debentures will be relatively low in the years of establishment (because of the tax-deductibility of the interest); the conversion of the debentures into shares at a later date when, hopefully, the assets have become fully productive will find the company better able to meet increased dividend payments from tax-paid profits. In the analysis of debt it is important to consider the date of conversion and any options. Regarding the latter it is important to determine whether conversion is mandatory under the terms of the issue or whether redemption in cash is possible at the option of the company or the debenture holders.

Short-term debt

[562] Examples of short-term debt include bank overdraft, deposits on call and trade creditors. Short-term debt affects the liquidity of the firm.

[563] (a) *Bank overdraft.* When properly used, bank overdraft is a relatively cheap and convenient source of finance. Subject to an overdraft limit, the arrangement with the bank is flexible and interest is tax-deductible and is calculated on the actual amount of the overdraft on a day-to-day basis. On the other hand, in theory at least, bank overdraft is on call.

Bank overdraft is best used to finance the fluctuating day-to-day needs of the firm. Over-reliance on overdraft as a source of finance should be avoided as it may lead the firm into financial difficulties. For example, overdraft lending may be restricted as a result of government policy to reduce the availaiblity of credit in the economy. Further the bank may call up the overdraft in times of a downturn in trading which is a time the firm may need the finance most.

In the analysis of short-term debt it is important to consider the amount of overdraft in relation to any limit imposed by the bank and the nature of the security given. Consideration of operating results is also important. For example, within the limit imposed by the bank, well secured overdraft extended to a profit-able company may carry little risk of being called up. On the other hand, the overdraft of a firm which is experiencing serious trading difficulties may be in the nature of a highly liquid liability. From a banker's viewpoint, the fact that an overdraft is steadily around the limit is evidence of overtrading — of a level of need in excess of the financial resources available.

A study of variations in the amount of overdraft over time is also necessary in order to determine whether overdraft is being used to meet what may in fact be a long-term need for finance. If, for example, the overdraft of a firm never falls below, say, $200,000, the indication is that the firm needs additional long term finance in the vicinity of $200,000. In such cases it may be advisable for a firm to replace the more or less permanent portion of its overdraft by a long-term loan.

[564] (b) *Trade creditors.* It is normal for about a month's credit to be given on trade accounts. As a result, the inventory of a retail business may be financed by trade creditors to the extent of one month's purchases.

Trade creditors are little worry when their accounts are paid regularly or where the debtor is of such financial standing that creditors are willing to wait. On the other hand, if accounts are not paid regularly, and if the debtor is an uncertain financial risk, trade creditors can be a source of financial embarrassment for a firm and may even bring about its downfall.

In the analysis of financial statements a measure of the average period taken to pay creditors may be given by the ratio:

$$\frac{\text{Trade creditors}}{\text{Average monthly purchases}}$$

The ratio will give a measure of the number of average monthly purchases reflected in the figure for trade creditors. A ratio of say 2:1 would indicate that trade creditors represent two months of average purchases which in turn would imply that the firm takes about two months to pay its accounts.

Where the figure for purchases is not available, the average monthly cost of sales may be used instead, as an approximation.

The ratio, however, should be used with caution:

(i) Trade creditors may contain significant amounts which are unrelated to purchases and, therefore, may produce a misleading ratio.

(ii) An average rather than end-of-period figure for creditors may have to be used where end-of-period purchases are not representative of normal monthly purchases and the figure for trade creditors they have produced, therefore, is not representative of normal trade creditors.

Some further debt-related ratios

[565] (a) *Profit before tax and interest to interest expense.* The number of times interest is covered by an operating surplus such as profit before tax and interest is a measure of the ability of the company to service its debt. For example, the 1983 financial statements of a New Zealand company reported the following operating figures:

Profit before tax and extraordinary items	22,513
Interest expense	36,817
Profit before tax and interest	59,330

In the above example interest represents 62% of profit before tax and interest indicating a heavy commitment by the company for the payment of interest and vulnerability of the company's profits to fluctuations in operating results.

[566] (b) *Total assets less secured debt to unsecured debt.* The purpose of this ratio is to provide a measure of the assets available to meet claims of unsecured creditors. The most useful ratio is one calculated on the basis of the current realizable value of assets.

Asset Turnover and Efficiency in the Use of Finance

[567] The extent to which funds invested in assets generate income depends on the use made of the assets in operations. This point is best illustrated with inventories.

Inventories earn profit only as they are sold. The gross return earned on inventories depends on the gross profit mark up on cost, and at the rate at which the investment in inventories turns over in terms of sales.

Let us assume there are two inventory lines in relation to which the following information applies:

Line A: mark up on cost 50%, annual rate of turnover 2;

Line B: mark up on cost 30%, annual rate of turnover 4.

The percentage contribution to profit per $100 invested in each inventory line may be calculated as follows:

Line A: investment $100, mark up $50, annual turnover 2;
        contribution per $100 = 2x$50 = $100 = 100%

Line B: investment $100, mark up $30, annual turnover 4;
        contribution per $100 = 4 x $30 = $120 = 120%.

Disregarding variable costs, and other things being equal, funds invested in Line B will be more productive than funds invested in Line A.

The relationship among the rate of return on investment, the rate of profit to sales, and the rate of asset turnover in terms of sales may be expressed in what is referred to as the Du Pont formula:

$$\text{Rate of return} = \frac{\text{Profit}}{\text{Sales}} \times \frac{\text{Sales}}{\text{Investment}}$$

Following the example above:

$$\text{Return on Line A} = \frac{100}{300} \times \frac{300^*}{100} = 100\%$$

$$\text{Return on Line B} = \frac{120}{520} \times \frac{520^*}{100} = 120\%$$

Line A: sales per $100 investment = ($100 + $50) x 2 = $300.
Line B: sales per $100 investment = ($100 + $30) x 4 = $520.

[568] Similar considerations, though not as easy to see, apply to the use made of fixed assets. Other things being equal, funds invested in plant which is used 24 hours per day will be more productive than funds invested in plant which is used only eight hours per day. Further, the firm which uses its plant 24 hours per day will be in a stronger competitive position and will be better placed to maintain the efficiency of its plant by updating it for technological improvements than a firm which uses its plant only eight hours per day. For example, a rate of return of 20% on investment in assets which turn over once per year would require a rate of profit to sales of 20%:

$$\text{Rate of return} = \frac{20}{100} \times \frac{100}{100} = 20\%$$

If the investment were made to turn over three times per year, the rate of profit to sales would need to be 6.7%:

$$\text{Rate of return} = \frac{20}{300} \times \frac{300}{100} = 20\%$$

[569] It is possible to develop complete sets of ratios aimed at expressing detailed relationships within the broad context of the Du Pont formula. Movements in these detailed relationships may be significant for management, and particularly so if they are interpreted as part of a whole and as integrated into an overall plan.

Review questions

5.1 Prepare schedules of sources of finance ranked in order of:
(a) cost to service;
(b) risk.

5.2 "In a soundly financed business enterprise there should be a proper balance between funds obtained from shareholders' equity and from debt, and between short-term debt and long-term debt."
Discuss.

5.3 Discuss the effect of financial gearing on security and profitability.

5.4 Explain the meaning of "financial gearing" or "leverage". What is the relevance of financial gearing to the analysis and interpretation of financial statements?

5.5 "The gearing of a firm's financial structure depends on the risks its management chooses to take and the risks creditors are prepared to allow it to undertake."
Discuss.

5.6 Obtain copies of the annual reports of a finance company and a manufacturer and:
(a) calculate the cost of capital;
(b) determine the gearing of the companies;
(c) consider the reasons for the differences in the financial policies of these companies.

5.7 Why the need to analyse the composition of the shareholders' equity?

5.8 List and discuss five balance sheet ratios which may be used in the analysis of the financial structure of a firm.

5.9 Consider the wisdom of using bank overdraft in business operations in view of a recent major company failure brought about by the bank appointing a receiver to ensure the repayment of the overdraft.

5.10 "In a specialized business enterprise like a woollen mill or cement works the extent of gearing is related more closely to earnings and cash flows than to the equity/debt relationship."
Explain why this may be so.

5.11 Consider the "real" cost of using debt finance in times of inflation.

5.12 The share capital and reserves of A Ltd and B Ltd at 31 March 19A1 are as follows:

	A Ltd $	B Ltd $
Issued and paid up capital		
Ordinary	1,000,000	600,000
11% preference	200,000	400,000
Reserves		
Share premium reserve	100,000	
Asset revaluation reserve	80,000	
General reserve	240,000	200,000
P & L appropriation account	220,000	200,000
	1,840,000	1,400,000
The companies have long term liabilities as follows		
13% debentures	160,000	200,000
Mortgage on property at 12%		400,000
	160,000	600,000

Both companies have similar assets and earn a similar rate of return on total funds employed.

Required:
(a) Calculate and compare the gearing ratios of both companies.

      (b) Calculate the average cost of capital of each company, making any necessary assumptions.

      (c) Contrast the financial structures of the two companies from the viewpoints of profitability and risk.

5.13 Discuss the notion of cost of capital of a business enterprise, its intended use, and problems with its determination.

Chapter 6
Analytical Techniques and Tools: An Introduction

Analysis as a Breaking-down Process

[601] "Analysis" is normally understood as the resolution of a complex substance or statement into basic elements and "interpretation" as the "expounding" of meaning. In this context, the analysis of financial statements involves normally the separating out of the components of an aggregate in order to increase the interpreter's and decision-maker's understanding of the factors which have contributed to the aggregate, for example the breaking down of sales into sales by segments, the breaking down of expense into categories such as administration, marketing and financial expenses (and the further breaking down of such expenses into subcategories), the separation from reported profit of the effect of extraordinary items, the breaking down of the amount of taxation charged against a years' reported profit into, say, timing and permanent differences between reported and taxable income and the implications of such differences for projections by decision makers.

Financial Statements are Technical Documents

[602] Financial statements are technical documents prepared by the aplication of certain accounting principles, methods and procedures. The message of financial statements, therefore, is a specialized one and its interpretation requires certain specialist skills.

It is necessary also that the analyst and interpreter have an adequate knowledge and understanding of the ongoing activity and of the economic environment of the business whose data are under study. For useful interpretation one must be able to see behind the figures to the decisions and activity that led to their generation. For example, it is inadequate to think of sales merely as so many dollars. Retail sales consist of customers buying a range of goods and services. Behind these sales are a set of marketing decisions and the efforts of all those employees involved in purchasing and marketing. In order to appreciate the significance of data, one must appreciate the business context from which the data have flowed.

A person analyzing financial statements should have adequate knowledge of the principles and procedures used in their preparation. This person should know how amounts have been arrived at and their significance to the objectives of the analysis and interpretation, and, if necessary, should be able to make appropriate adjustments to reported amounts to ensure, for example, their comparability where there have been changes in accounting methods and procedures. Sufficient understanding of accounting processes to be able to use data presented for one purpose, such as the calculation of income and the determination of financial position, for another, such as the study of cash flows, are also necessary attributes.

Analysis and interpretation should be carried out with adequate appreciation of the limitations of financial statements and particularly those limitations which arise from the nature of the subject matter and the principles and procedures used in the preparation of the financial statements.

The Importance of Comparisons and Analysis of Relationships

[603] Accounting numbers have limited information value if taken by themselves. Their significance becomes evident in making comparisons (for example, of this year's sale with last year's sales) and as we consider relationships (for example, between earnings and the funds used to generate them). The development of comparative data and the calculation of absolute and percentage differences are elementary exercises. So too is the measurement of relationships in terms of ratios and percentages. The fair and helpful assessment of the significance for particular purposes of differences and relationships and changes in relationships from period to period and from enterprise to enterprise may be fraught with complexity.

[604] Let us take sales as an illustration of this. The information from the income statement that sales for the last financial year totalled $11 million is useful in its own right. It is from this gross revenue that the expenses of the year have to be met. But this information is of a limited value only if we wish to evaluate the company's performance over the period. A comparison of this year's sales with last year's sales will provide useful information of the change in dollar value of sales; but if prices are, say, 20% higher on average than last year, then a 10% increase in money sales would signify a significant fall in the physical quantity of sales. Then some products sold may produce higher percentage margins of profit than others, so that the significance of the comparison cannot be determined fairly without a comparison of the sales mix for the two periods. A fuller appreciation of the significance of the results for an assessment of performance would be obtained if we were able to compare actual sales to budgeted sales, and if we could assess our market share in total and by product line and compare these with previous periods and budgets. And even if all these comparisons were made and changes determined, the relating of these changes to causes would be at best difficult and at worst impossible. Yet, notwithstanding such difficulties, analysis has to be carried out in order to add to the information and understanding of the interpreter and decision-maker and to improve the basis for making judgments.

[605] The fair interpretation of relationships between aggregates and changes in those relationships from period to period and enterprise to enterprise is doubly complex because aggregates and changes in aggregates are complex in themselves. For example the measurement of the earnings of a period involves the offsetting

against revenue of a whole set of expense items each with its own problems of calculation. There may be significant differences in the components from period to period. The calculation of the investment which was used to generate this income may be far from a straightforward exercise involving as it does the measurement of both assets and liabilities.

[606] Both the measurement of earnings and the measurement of investment are complicated by changing money and asset values. The relating of income to the investment used to generate it produces the key figure of the rate of return, and this is used in making comparisons between periods and among business enterprises. The superficial measurement of such relationships is an elementary exercise, but the fair interpretation of the results requires an appreciation of the complexity which lies behind the calculations, an understanding of the business and its environment, and considerable judgment. The objective of analysis and interpretation is to provide a more informed basis for judgment.

The Use of External Information

[607] Business firms do not operate in a vacuum; their operations are affected by the interaction of complex economic conditions. The effective analysis and interpretation of financial statements often requires the use of information outside that contained in the statements. Comparisons with competing firms and trade and industry performance are necessary in the evaluation of operating performance and the state of affairs. Analysis of prevailing economic conditions is equally important. For example, the fortunes of the fertilizer industry are closely related to the fortunes of farming. It will be difficult, therefore, to make an effective evaluation of the performance of a fertilizer firm without an analysis of the economic conditions affecting farming and the demand for fertilizer in particular.

Analysis, Interpretation and Prediction

[608] Financial statements deal with past events. On the other hand analysis and interpretation are oriented towards the future. Implicit in the processes of analysis and interpretation is the belief that understanding the past is an important factor in forecasting the future. The past, however, is not an infallible guide to the future. In making projections based on past events, it is important to decide what conditions which have affected the past are likely to continue into the future and what changes the future is likely to bring. In the absence of a reliable crystal ball, predictions are likely to be permeated by uncertainty and their validity will depend very largely on the soundness of the judgment of the decision-maker.

Analytical Techniques and Tools

[609] The common techniques and tools for the analysis of financial statements include:
  (a) comparative financial statements;
  (b) common size financial statements;

78

(c) percentages and ratios;

(d) statements of changes in financial position (funds statements).

Where analysis involves the development of time series, it may be considered useful to analyze trends, and to illustrate changes through graphs and charts.

Comparative financial statements

[610] Under this method the financial statements of a firm (balance sheets, income statements, statements of changes in financial position etc) are set side by side and are examined for changes from year to year over the years. Most important in this process is the discernment and study of trends.

Comparative statements may be prepared to include only selected items such as sales, certain types of expenses, profit before and after tax, rate of return, dividends paid, working capital, and shareholders' equity, which are considered to have particular importance to the reader.

Comparisons may be made in absolute amounts or percentages. For example, trend analysis and comparisons may be facilitated by converting absolute amounts into index number series. This is done by selecting a base year (usually the first year in the series) and expressing the amounts in subsequent years as a percentage of the corresponding amounts in the base year. The procedure is illustrated in Example 6.1.

Example 6.1

A five year comparison of the sales and net profit of the ABC Co Ltd is given below:

	19A1 $	19A2 $	19A3 $	19A4 $	19A5 $
Sales	1,000,000	1,120,000	1,570,000	1,730,000	2,150,000
Net profit	100,000	109,000	117,000	128,000	142,000

An index number series prepared from the above figures and using 19A1 as a base year will be as follows:

	19A1	19A2	19A3	19A4	19A5
Sales	100*	112**	157	173	215
Net profit	100*	109***	117	128	142

*19A1 = 100   **$\dfrac{1,120,000}{1,000,000} \times 100 = 112$ ***$\dfrac{109,000}{100,000} \times 100 = 109$ etc

From the figures in the example we can see that over the five-year period there have been increases in both sales and net profit. Referring to the index number comparison, it is more readily aparent that net profit for the period has increased at a considerably lower rate than sales.

[611] Comparative financial statements should be analyzed and trends interpreted with caution. There may be good reasons why the data and data relationships shown in the series are not fairly comparable period by period and do not provide a fair impression of the firm's performance. For example, there may be no allowance for the effects of material extraordinary items and changes in accounting policies.

[612] Basing predictions on past performance assumes, at least implicitly, that the operating conditions prevailing in the past will continue in the future. In an environment characterized by change, this is likely to be the exception rather than the rule. In making projections, therefore, it is necessary to consider the business environment expected in the future in terms of general economic conditions, and any special conditions likely to effect the particular trade or industry and the firm under consideration.

Common size financial statements

[613] The analysis of comparative statements and trends is sometimes referred to as *horizontal analysis*.

[614] Common size financial statements involve what is referred to as *vertical analysis*. Under this method the components of a financial statement are expressed as a percentage of a base amount in that statement — for example, the components of the income statement may be expressed as percentages of total net sales, and the components of the balance sheet as percentages of total assets. Similarly, the components of a subgroup within a financial statement may be expressed as percentages of the total of the subgroup — for example, cash, debtors, inventories and any other current assets as percentages of total current assets.

Common size statements may be used to study the operational structure of a firm in terms of the relationship between costs and revenues, the relative proportions of finance obtained from different sources (such as shareholders' funds and long- and short-term borrowing) and relative investment in different classes of asset (such as land and buildings, plant and machinery, inventories, debtors, etc).

Common size statements may be used in trend (horizontal) analysis. By comparing common size statements of a firm over time, changes, for example, in the composition of the firm's assets and its financial structure can be highlighted and studied.

Common size financial statements may be used to compare the financial statements of firms of different sizes. In such comparisons use may be made of trade or industry averages to evaluate the performance of the firm and that of other firms in the trade or industry and their relative financial structures.

Percentages and ratios

[615] Some uses of percentages in financial analysis have already been discussed. Percentages and ratios are used to study the relative importance of absolute amounts. Let us take an example.

Example 6.2

Companies A and B are competitors in the same trade and for the last financial year they report net profit as follows:

Company A	$270,000
Company B	$420,000

How well did the two firms perform in relation to each other?

A superficial conclusion would be that, since Company B achieved a greater amount of net profit, it performed better than Company A.

Let us assume, however, that the following additional information is provided regarding the sales and the shareholders' investment in the two companies:

	Company A $	Company B $
Sales for period	3,000,000	6,000,000
Shareholders' funds	2,700,000	5,400,000

We can now evaluate the relative performance of the two companies by relating their profit to the amount of sales which produced them and the amount of the shareholders' investment used in the operations of the two firms:

	Company A	Company B
Net profit as a percentage of sales	9%	7%
Net profit as a percentage of shareholders' funds	10%	7.8%

The percentage analysis above shows that on the average, Company A earned 9 cents of profit per dollar of sales while Company B earned only 7 cents and that Company A earned 10% profit on its shareholders' investment while Company B earned 7.8%. This relative evaluation of the operating results of the two companies gives reasons to believe that Company A had operated more effectively during the period than Company B.

[616] Percentages and ratios should be used to analyze significant relationships between components of financial statements. For example, the significance of an increase in an item of operating expense in a transport business cannot be determined by reviewing the change in isolation. It is reasonable to expect that there will be some correlation betwen the level of operating expenses and the level of cartage charges. Therefore one relates the particular operating expense of each year to the cartage charges of that year, and compares the percentages. One may then look for explanations, such as increases in fuel prices, or wages from period to period, or changes in the nature of work done. In the operations of a department store there will be a very close relationship between sales and the cost of goods sold in each department. Management wil also be concerned with the relationship between departmental sales wages and departmental sales because sales wages are the main controllable expense. The relationship between sales and cost of sales, and between sales wages and sales will be the main factors leading to profit or loss on departmental operations.

Some expenses can be expected to vary more or less in proportion to sales. Examples are delivery expenses and cash discounts to customers. Other expenses are less susceptible to changes in sales volume, and study of cost behaviour at different sales levels is necessary if one is to interpret changes fairly. Within certain levels of activity, some expenses such as depreciation and occupancy costs are likely to be fixed. One can expect there to be a relationship between the level of sales and the level of inventory carried, and between the level of sales and the level of accounts receivable (trade debtors); but these relationships are not clearcut. Inventory of finished stock is held to service *future* sales, and not past sales. Accounts receiveable arise from *recent* sales on *credit*, and not the sum of cash and credit sales for the previous year. Changes in the relationship between past sales and expected future sales and between credit sales just made and total sales could explain the differences in inventory/sales and debtor/sales relationships from those which applied last year. Where fundamental relationships are unclear, interpretation requires considerable care if it is to be useful.

[617] A large number of percentages and ratios may be developed for use in financial analysis, some having general application, others having more specialized uses in specific circumstances or industries. The choice of percentages to use in particular circumstances would depend on the objectives of the analysis and on the significance of the relationships of financial statement items which the analysis aims to highlight. For example, a set of ratios covering the production side of a business could relate the various cost inputs like materials and wages to total production. Marketing and administrative cost inputs would be related to sales. Ratios would show asset turnover in terms of the relationships between productive assets and the total cost of production, the rate of stock turn of finished goods, and the relationship between sales and debtors. Ratios would be developed to reflect investment in the financing of assets, and basic balance sheet relationships. Measures of the rate of return on sales, on total assets, and on proprietorship would complete the picture. Top management seeking to exercise broad control may find sets of ratios of this kind of some value, as suggesting areas for more detailed enquiry.

[618] In the interpretation of financial statements reference should be made to both percentages and absolute amounts. This is so because a large percentage change can be produced by changes in amounts which themselves may not be significant. For example, an increase in advertising expense from, say, $1000 to $2000 will be an increase of 100%. Yet $1000 or $2000 may be a relatively insignificant amount when compared to the amount of sales and other items of expense.

[619] If properly used, percentages and ratios may bring to notice conditions which may need further enquiry and in some cases corrective action. Percentages and ratios, however, should be interpreted with caution. The interrelationships which underlie business operations are complex. The manner in which ratios and percentages drawn from financial statements reflect these interrelationships is subject to limitations. In the study of financial statements adequate recognition should be given to both the complexity of the subject matter and to the limitations of financial statements and of the tools available for the analysis of the data they contain.

Statements of changes in financial position (funds statements)

[620] Statements of changes in financial position are useful analytical tools in that they can help explain changes in the financial structure of a firm during a period as a result of the firm's trading and financing activities. A statement of changes in financial position may be so prepared as to highlight changes in particular aspects of the financial position of the firm such as working capital or net liquid assets.

The Application of Analytical Techniques

[621] This section will introduce, discuss and illustrate some of the comparisons, percentages and ratios commonly used in the analysis and interpretation of financial statements. The analytical use of statements of changes in financial position

will also be discussed and illustrated. In subsequent chapters these and other analytical techniques will be examined in greater depth having regard to the complexity of the subject matter and to the inherent limitations of both the techniques themselves and the financial statements the interpretation of which they are designed to facilitate.

The discussion and illustrations will be based on the assumed income statement and balance sheet of the XYZ Co Ltd which are reproduced as Example 6.3. The purpose of the analysis will be to comment on the operations and state of affairs of XYZ Co Ltd to the extent that this is possible with the information provided.

Example 6.3
XYZ Co Ltd
Income Statement for year ended 31 March 19A2

	19A2 $	19A2 $	19A1 $	19A1 $
Sales		1,725,000		1,380,000
Cost of sales				
Opening stock	299,200		227,000	
Purchases	1,323,700		966,500	
	1,622,900		1,193,500	
Closing stock	458,900		299,200	
Cost of sales		1,164,000		894,300
Gross profit		561,000		485,700
Expenses				
Administration	138,100		125,500	
Selling salaries and wages	141,200		116,000	
Advertising	10,300		5,800	
Sundry selling expenses	6,200		5,400	
Depreciation	19,500		12,800	
Interest	14,400		2,500	
Directors' fees	2,300		2,300	
Audit fees	3,900	335,900	3,400	273,700
Net profit before tax		225,100		212,000
Less provision for tax		105,200		111,000
Net profit after tax		119,900		101,000
Add unappropriated profit from previous year		118,400		92,400
		238,300		193,400
Less provision for dividend		95,000		75,000
Unappropriated profit carried forward		143,300		118,400

Analysis of the Income Statement

Sales and cost of sales

[622] A comparison of the sales figures of XYZ Co Ltd for the two years shows that sales have increased in 19A2 by $345,000 or 25%. During the same period the cost of goods sold has increased by $269,700 or 30.2%.

XYZ Co Ltd
Balance Sheet as at 31 March 19A2

	19A2 $	19A2 $	19A1 $	19A1 $
Capital and reserves				
Issued and paid up in $1 ordinary shares		760,000		600,000
General reserve	180,000		180,000	
P & L appropriation a/c	143,300	323,300	118,400	298,400
Total shareholders' funds		1,083,300		898,400
Term liabilities				
Mortgage		200,000		20,000
Current liabilities				
Bank overdraft	90,800		4,200	
Trade creditors	145,200		92,000	
Provision for tax	105,200		111,000	
Provision for dividend	95,000		75,000	
Total current liabilities		436,200		282,200
		1,719,500		1,200,600

	19A2 $	19A2 $	19A1 $	19A1 $
Fixed Assets				
Land (at cost)		340,000		230,000
Buildings (at cost)	591,000		450,000	
Less depreciation to date	50,900	540,100	45,000	405,000
Furniture and fittings (at cost)	216,800		174,800	
Less depreciation to date	94,800	122,000	81,200	93,600
Total fixed assets		1,002,100		728,600
Current assets				
Debtors	258,500		173,000	
Stocks	458,900		299,000	
Total current assets		717,400		472,000
		1,719,500		1,200,600

On the basis of the information provided there is little one can say about the sales performance of the company apart from noting the amount and percentage of increase. The evaluation of the company's sales performance will be greatly facilitated if comparisons were made with budgeted sales, with the sales achieved by competitors and the sales and trend in sales in the trade to which the company belongs.

[623] The cost of goods sold and its relationship to sales is most important in the analysis of operating results. Sales less cost of sales gives gross profit — the amount from which the expenses are recovered and net profit is made. The relationship between sales and cost of sales determines the rate at which gross profit is generated by sales and is an important indicator of the profit potential of a business enterprise. In the example the fact that the cost of sales has increased relatively to sales (eg by 30.2% compared with an increase in sales of 25%) indicates that in 19A2 less gross profit was earned per sales dollar than in 19A1. This may be illustrated by expressing cost of sales as a percentage of sales — 67.5% in 19A2 and 64.8% in 19A1.

A more common way of analyzing the relationship between sales and cost of sales is to consider the amount of gross profit and the gross profit rate.

Gross profit and the gross profit rate

[624] The gross profit of XYZ Co Ltd in 19A2 in $561,000 compared with $485,700 in 19A1, an increase of $76,000 or 15.4%. On the other hand the gross profit rate (gross profit as a percentage of sales) has fallen from 35.2% in 19A1 to 32.5% in 19A2.

The gross profit rate is important and changes in it should be investigated since what may appear to be a small variation in the gross profit rate may have a significant effect on net profit. In the example, the drop in the gross profit rate of 2.7% (35.2% − 32.5%) amounts to a reduction in the gross profit rate of 7.7% ($\frac{2.7}{35.2} \times 100$). Had the gross profit rate of 35.2% been maintained in 19A2, the amount of gross profit on sales of $1,725,000 would have been $607,200 (eg 35.2% of $1,725,000) or $46,200 more than achieved. This would have resulted in that much higher net profit before tax.

Some common reasons for variations in the gross profit rate are inability on the part of the firm to reflect higher cost of sales in higher selling prices, deliberate mark down of selling prices, increases in selling prices in excess of increases in the cost of sales, changes in sales mix where different lines are sold at different mark ups, and the effect of inventory valuation on cost of sales.

Inventory levels and stock turn

[625] Where business operations involve the acquisition of goods (through purchase or manufacture) for the purpose of earning profit by selling the goods at a price above cost, the examination of inventory levels will be an important part of the analysis of financial statements. In a well-managed business enterprise the level of stocks carried should be adequate to meet the needs of sales and production without the problems and losses associated with stockouts such as lost sales, emergency purchases from uneconomic sources and higher production costs which may arise with emergency attempts to make up stock deficiencies. On the other hand, inventory levels should not be higher than necessary to meet the needs of the firm. Over-stocking may involve the firm in excessive cost of storage and of servicing the excessive amount of investment tied up in stocks, as well as the risk of loss through obsolescence and deterioration of stocks. In a well-managed firm there should be, under normal circumstances, a reasonable correspondence between the level of sales and the level of stocks carried by the firm.

[626] A study of stock levels can be made by relating changes in stocks to changes in sales and the calculation and comparison of rates of stock turn.

In the example, the stock of XYZ Co Ltd has increased in 19A1 by 24.1% from $227,000 to $299,200 and in 19A2 there has been a further increase of 53.4% from $299,200 to $458,000. The increase in stock of 53.4% in 19A2 compares with an increase in sales in the same period of 25%. The implication is that, since stock has increased at twice the rate of the increase in sales, the company is carrying excessive stocks. At least two matters should be considered, however, before a conclusion is reached on the appropriateness of the amount of stock carried by the company.

(a) what is considered to be the normal level of stock to carry in relation to sales in this type of business; and

(b) the level of sales of the company towards the end of 19A2 as compared with the sales for the same period in 19A1 and the expected sales for 19A3. The reasonableness of the current stock level should be determined by reference to current and expected sales and not necessarily by reference to the sales, for, say, the preceding 12 months.

[627] The rate of stock turn aims to measure the number of times the investment in stocks turns over in terms of sales during a given period. Since investment in stocks earns income when the stocks are sold, the rate of stock turn is a measure of the efficiency with which investment in stocks is used.

The rate of stock turn is calculated by the formula

$$\frac{\text{Cost of sales}}{\text{Average stock}}$$

with average stock usually calculated as follows:

$$\frac{\text{Opening stock + closing stock}}{2}$$

[628] A more accurate rate of annual stock turn may be arrived at by averaging the stock held at the end of each month of the year.

The rate of stock turn of XYZ Co Ltd for 19A2 and 19A1 is calculated as follows:

$$19A2 \ \frac{\$1,164,000}{\frac{1}{2}(\$299,200 + \$458,900)} = 3.1 \text{ times per annum}$$

$$19A1 \ \frac{\$894,300}{\frac{1}{2}(\$227,000 + \$299,200)} = 3.4 \text{ times per annum}$$

What is an "appropriate" rate of stock turn will vary from one type of business to another. In our example the rate of stock turn of XYZ Co Ltd is 3.4 in 19A1 and 3.1 in 19A2. From the figures provided we can say that in 19A2 the rate of stock turn was lower than in 19A1 because of the build-up of stocks. However, in order to say whether a stock turn of, say, 3.1 is good or bad we must compare this figure with some standard for the particular type of business or with budget. For example, a rate of stock turn of 3.1 may be considered to be very satisfactory in the case of a business selling furniture; on the other hand the same rate of stock turn would be inadequate in the case of a butcher shop purporting to sell fresh meat (to take a rather extreme case).

Expenses

[629] Table 6.1 shows the expenses of XYZ Co Ltd for 19A2 and 19A1 — the amount and percentage differences in the two years and the expenses in the two years expressed as a percentage of sales.

[630] Expenses may be compared individually or by significant categories with corresponding amounts for the previous year or, where possible, with budget. It is common practice to relate many items of expense to sales. In the process of analysis care should be taken to ensure that comparisons are valid and that percentages reflects significant relationships between the expense items and the base (such as sales) to which they are related. Let us look at the expense items disclosed in the income statement of XYZ Co Ltd.

Table 6.1
XYZ Co Ltd
Comparison of expenses

	19A2 $	19A1 $	Increase 19A2 $	Percen- tage of increase %	Expenses as a percentage of sales 19A2 %	Expenses as a percentage of sales 19A1 %
Administration	138,100	125,500	12,600	10.0	8.00	9.09
Selling salaries and wages	141,200	116,000	25,200	21.7	8.19	8.41
Advertising	10,300	5,800	4,500	77.6	0.60	0.42
Sundry selling expenses	6,200	5,400	800	14.8	0.36	0.39
Depreciation	19,500	12,800	6,700	52.3	1.13	0.93
Interest	14,400	2,500	11,900	476.0	0.83	0.18
Directors' fees	2,300	2,300	—	—	0.13	0.16
Audit fees	3,900	3,400	500	14.7	0.23	0.25
	335,700	273,700	62,200	22.7	19.47	19.83

[631] Table 6.1 shows that administration expenses have increased by 10% from $125,500 in 19A1 to $138,100 in 19A2. In relation to sales, however, administration expenses have fallen from 9.09% in 19A1 to 8% in 19A2. To gain a better understanding of these figures and comparisons, a study would be necessary of the items comprising administration expenses and the extent to which these items can be expected to vary with sales. In most cases administration expenses will be largely fixed within a certain level of operations. To the extent that this is the case with the XYZ Co Ltd, this would explain the reduction of administration expenses as a percentage of sales in 19A2. To the extent that administration expenses are fixed in relation to sales, the increase in the amount of administration expenses may be explained by cost increases in 19A2 such as increase in salaries and wages and

administration staff or increases in the cost of some expense items such as power and postal charges, etc. To the extent that some expense items vary with sales the increase in the amount of administration expenses can be explained by the increase in sales in 19A2.

[632] Continuing with the example, the selling salaries and wages have increased by 21.7% from $116,000 in 19A1 to $141,200 in 19A2. In relation to sales selling salaries and wages have fallen from 8.41% in 19A1 to 8.19% in 19A2. Again a study would need to be made of selling salaries and wages to determine the extent to which they vary with the level of sales. For example the increase may be explained by increase in sales staff to handle increased sales, or salary and wage incentives related to sales. In relation to sales selling salaries and wages are likely to be semi-variable rather than fully variable. This may partly explain the fall in the percentage of selling salaries and wages to sales. As in the case of administration expenses, part of the explanation for the increase in the expense item may be found in cost increases such as an increase in salaries and wage rates.

[633] Going on to advertising we see that this expense has increased by 77.6% from $5800 in 19A1 to $10,300 in 19A2. In relation to sales, advertising has increased from 0.42% to 0.60%. Advertising expense is difficult to interpret both in terms of absolute amounts and in relation to sales. While it is reasonable to assume that there is some positive relationship between the amount spent on advertising and the level of sales, it is usually very difficult to quantify this relationship in terms of advertising input and sales output. Advertising may be specific, aimed at promoting specific products of the firm, or it may be of a general nature, promoting the activities of the firm as a whole. Specific advertising may result in general sales benefits and the benefit of current advertising may extend into the future. Advertising costs may be incurred at different rates in different sales areas to achieve different results. Comparing advertising cost with trade averages may not be conclusive since each firm may have unique features. A shop on a side street may have to spend a higher proportion of turnover on advertising than a shop in the main street. To a large extent the amount spent by a firm on advertising would be discretionary and it would be difficult to say whether the same level of sales would not have been achieved with a lower level of advertising or that a higher level of advertising would have resulted in higher sales. In our example, the amount spent on advertising has increased at a much greater rate (77.6%) than the amount of sales (25%). In absolute terms, however, the amount spent on advertising is relatively small compared with sales (0.60% of sales in 19A2) and other expenses. We may compare the increase in advertising expense of $4,500 with the increase in sales of $345,000. To the extent that one can attribute the increase in sales to the increase in advertising expenditure, the additional amount spent on advertising could well be regarded as having been worth while.

[634] The analysis of sundry selling expenses would require a study of the components of this item in order to determine the extent to which the amounts should vary with sales and thus the extent to which the level of expenditure in 19A2 and 19A1 may be regarded as reasonable.

[635] Depreciation is a cost item which should be interpreted with considerable caution. Its amount depends on the amount of depreciable assets carried by the firm, the basis on which these assets are valued, and on the depreciation policy

adopted by the firm's management regarding method and rate of depreciation. In our example the charge for depreciation has increased by 52.3% from $12,800 in 19A1 to $19,500 in 19A2. In relation to sales, depreciation has increased from 0.93% to 1.13%. With a given operating set up in terms of, say, floor space, plant and machinery, furniture and fittings, delivery vehicles, etc, depreciation is likely to be fixed in relation to sales. If, however, the level of operations increases to an extent which requires expansion of operating facilities by the acquisition of additional depreciable assets, then depreciation charges will increase. It is very unlikely, however, that there will be a linear relationship between the level of operations and the amount of depreciation charges. Expressing depreciation charges as percentages of sales, therefore, will be of limited analytical value. It would be more informative to relate depreciation charges to the amount of depreciable assets carried by the firm and to examine how depreciation charges have been arrived at — the basis of valuation of depreciable assets, the method and rate of depreciation used and the consistency with which depreciation charges have been calculated from one period to another. The relative importance of depreciation charged against revenue will vary from firm to firm. Where depreciation represents a significant proportion of the costs incurred by a firm, relating depreciation to profit may throw light on the "quality" of the reported profit figure. For example, a firm reports profit of $3 million after a charge for depreciation of $2 million. Since depreciation is to a significant extent a matter of opinion, the reported profit is vulnerable to opinion, judgment and even to manipulation. In our example an explanation for the increase in the depreciation charge in 19A2 may be found in the fixed assets held by the XYZ Co Ltd at the end of 19A2. The increases in fixed assets and sales may indicate an expansion of the operations of this firm.

Interest

[636] The use of loan money is a common practice in the financing of business operations and the interest paid by a business firm is the cost of using loan money. The amount of interest paid is a function of the amount and time span of borrowing, and the rate of interest applying to different loans. As discussed in Chapter 5, a major attraction of using borrowed money is the comparatively low servicing cost in terms of tax-deductible interest payments. Further, the manner in which business operations are financed is to a large degree determined by managerial policy. Therefore, interest expense should be related to the level of borrowing used rather than to sales, and the impact of interest payments on profit before tax should be examined. In the example, interest charges have increased by 476% from $2500 in 19A1 to $14,400 in 19A2. An explanation of this increase will be found in the much greater use of borrowed funds in 19A2 — at the end of 19A2 there is an increase in bank overdraft of $86,600 and mortgage of $180,000. Since borrowing commits a firm to a payment of interest irrespective of profits, it may be useful in many cases to examine the relationship between interest paid and profit before interest in order to determine the demand the servicing of borrowing makes on the earnings of the firm. Since interest is deductible for tax purposes and, therefore, affects the amount of tax paid profit, the comparison should be made with net profit before interest and tax. In our example the profit before interest and tax comes to $239,500 and the interest paid of $14,400 is 6% of that figure. A high percentage of interest paid

to profit could indicate that the firm's profits and the firm itself are vulnerable to changes in trading conditions.

The remaining two expense items in our example are directors' fees of $2300 and audit fees of $3900. Relating these to sales is unlikely to have significant informational value. What may be considered is the materiality of the amounts and their reasonableness for a firm of this kind and size.

[637] It should be apparent from the preceding discussion that the analysis and interpretation of expenses is not an easy task. Expenses vary in nature; not all expenses are directly related to sales. While sales may be a useful basis to which to relate expenses, the interpretation of expenses in relation to sales should be made with caution. What we should be concerned with is the reasonableness of the expenses given the nature of the firm and the level of its operations. Comparisons with previous years, trade and industry averages and other firms in the trade or industry could be helpful and so would comparisons with budgets. The effective analysis and interpretation of expenses would require considerably more information than is available in published financial statements. In the absence of such information the interpretation of expenses cannot but involve a considerable amount of guesswork.

Net profit and taxation

[638] In the analysis and interpretation of the income statement a study should be made of both profit before and after tax.

In the process of analysis, distinction should be made between profit from the normal operations of the firm and non-operating income such as income from investments. The figures may have to be adjusted for abnormal and extraordinary items relating both to revenue and expense. Operating profit represents the surplus of revenue over expense earned by the firm and measured by the application of a set of currently accepted accounting principles.

Taxation is an expense which is determined in accordance with current tax legislation and rules, as applicable to the firm. As there may be significant variation between the accounting methods applied in the measurement of reported profit before tax and the tax rules applied to determine taxable profit, the amount of taxation deducted from pre-tax income should be the subject of close scrutiny. This is necessary in order to determine whether special tax provisions and allowances have significantly affected the amount of tax provided and, therefore, the amount of net profit after tax. A relevant percentage in this regard is to relate taxation to net profit before tax. Current accounting practice requires the notes to the financial statements to include an explanation and reconciliation of any difference between the income tax expense shown in the profit and loss account and the tax calculated at the current rate on the reported accounting profit before tax: see Example 14.5 in Chapter 14.

[639] The net profit after tax is the amount generated by the activities of the firm and ostensibly available for distribution to shareholders or retention in the business.

Net profit before and after tax may be expressed as a percentage of sales. This percentage, however, is more difficult to interpret than, say, the gross profit rate since the relationship between expenses and sales is not as direct as that between sales and cost of sales. A comparison of the percentages of net profit to sales of different firms in the same industry or trade may give some insight into the relative efficiency of the firms provided the statements are reasonably comparable.

Let us return to our example. The following figures and comparisons are shown below: the change in the amount of net profit before and after tax in 19A2, net profit before and after tax for 19A2 and 19A1 as a percentage of sales, and taxation for 19A2 and 19A1 as a percentage of net profit before tax.

Increase in amount of profit

	19A2 $	19A1 $	Increase $	Percentage of increase
Net profit before tax	225,100	212,000	13,100	6.18
Net profit after tax	119,900	101,000	18,900	18.42

Net profit as a percentage of sales

	19A2	19A1
Net profit before tax	13.05	15.36
Net profit after tax	6.95	7.32

Taxation as a percentage of net profit before tax

$$19A2 \quad \frac{\$105,200}{\$225,100} \times 100 = 46.7\% \qquad 19A1 \quad \frac{\$111,000}{\$212,000} \times 100 = 52.4\%$$

[640] From the comparisons shown above it can be seen that net profit before tax has increased in 19A2 by $13,100 or 6.18%. As a percentage of sales, however, net profit before tax has fallen from 15.36% in 19A1 to 13.05% in 19A2. Since total expenses to sales have remained relatively stable (19.83% in 19A1 and 19.47% in 19A2 — see Table 6.1), the reason for the drop in the percentage of net profit before tax to sales is the reduction in 19A2 in the gross profit rate.

The net profit after tax has increased by $18,900 or 18.42%; as a percentage of sales it has dropped from 7.32% in 19A1 to 6.95% in 19A2. The reason for the higher increase in the amount of net profit after tax than net profit before tax and the relatively smaller fall in the percentage of net profit after tax to sales is taxation.

In 19A1 taxation represented 52.4% of profit before tax and in 19A2 the percentage was 46.7%. Given a rate of taxation of, say, 50%, the figures show some divergence between accounting profit and taxable profit in the two years and in particular in 19A2. Some possible reasons are tax benefits received by the company in the form of investment allowances, special depreciation allowances, export incentives, etc. The question of taxation in the analysis and interpretation of financial statements will be discussed in detail later in this book.

Profit and Profitability — The Rate of Return

[641] The terms "profit" and "profitability" are not synonymous. "Profit" refers to an absolute amount such as $235,189. "Profitability" on the other hand is a relative concept. To determine the "profitability" of a firm, for example, we need to relate the "profit" of the firm to the investment used to generate it. It is reasonable to expect that a higher level of investment in business operations would need to generate a higher level of profit. Since it is inconvenient and difficult to compare

and evaluate absolute amounts of profit and investment, a measure of profitability is provided by the rate of return.

The rate of return is one of the most important measures of profitability. The ability of a firm to earn an "adequate" return on investment determines its ability to attract investment and to survive financially in the long run.

The rate of return is usually calculated by expressing net profit after tax as a percentage of shareholders' funds. The following rates of return were earned by the XYZ Co Ltd in 19A2 and 19A1:

$$19A2 \ \frac{\$119,900}{\$1,083,300} \times 100 = 11.07\% \qquad 19A1 \ \frac{\$101,000}{\$898,400} \times 100 = 11.24\%$$

[642] A refinement in the calculation of the rate of return would be to use the average shareholders' funds especially where there has been a significant increase in the shareholders' funds during the period. For example using the average of the shareholders' funds at the beginning and end of the period, the rate of return of the XYZ Co Ltd for 19A2 would be as follows:

$$\frac{\$119,900}{\frac{1}{2}(\$1,083,300 + \$898,400)} = 12.10\%$$

The above figures show that the XYZ Co Ltd has achieved a comparable rate of return in two years and, if anything, has earned a somewhat higher rate of return in 19A2 if the calculation is based on the average shareholders' equity. Whether the rate of return earned by the company is a reasonable one would depend on the rate of return achieved by other firms in the trade or industry and in business in general.

[643] A measure of operating effectiveness may also be obtained by calculating the rate of return on total assets:

$$\frac{\text{Net profit before tax + Interest}}{\text{Total assets}}$$

If there has been a significant change in total assets during the period, the average total assets may be used:

$$\frac{\text{Net profit before tax + Interest}}{\frac{1}{2}(\text{Beginning total assets + Ending total assets})}$$

This rate of return concentrates on the efficiency in the use of assets. By adding back interest paid we remove from profit the effect of financing the firm's operations through borrowing. By using the amount of profit before tax we add back the tax benefit relating to interest payments and remove the tax effects of any special tax allowances and provisions which will be reflected in the net profit after tax figure.

[644] Alternatively the rate of return on total assets may be calculated by removing from the profit figure the tax relating to interest payments only:

$$\frac{\text{Net profit after tax + Interest} \times (1 - \text{tax rate})}{\text{Total assets}}$$

or

$$\frac{\text{Net profit after tax + Interest} \times (1 - \text{tax rate})}{\frac{1}{2}(\text{Beginning total assets + Ending total assets})}$$

[645] These latter calculations may be used where it is considered that special tax provisions are such as to significantly affect the manner in which the assets of the firm are used, as would be the case where an enterprise has adjusted its operations in order to take advantage of a tax concession designed to encourage exports.

Regarding our example, the following rates of return on total assets may be calculated for the XYZ Co Ltd:

Net profit before tax and interest to total assets:

$$19A2 \quad \frac{\$225,100 + \$14,400}{\$1,719,500} = 13.93\%$$

$$19A1 \quad \frac{\$212,000 + \$2,500}{\$1,200,600} = 17.87\%$$

Net profit before tax and interest to average assets:

$$19A2 \quad \frac{\$225,100 + \$14,400}{\frac{1}{2}(\$1,719,500 + \$1,200,600)} = 16.40\%$$

Net profit after tax plus interest less tax benefit on interest paid (assuming "normal" tax rate of 50%) to total assets:

$$19A2 \quad \frac{\$119,900 + \$14,400.(1 - 0.5)}{\$1,719,500} = 7.39\%$$

$$19A1 \quad \frac{\$101,000 + \$2,500.\ (1 - 0.5)}{\$1,200,600} = 9.35\%$$

Net profit after tax plus interest less tax benefit on interest paid (assuming "normal" tax rate of 50%) to average total assets:

$$19A2 \quad \frac{\$119,900 + \$14.400.(1 - 0.5)}{\frac{1}{2}(\$1,719,500 + \$1,200,600)} = 8.71\%$$

[646] From the information provided in the example we cannot calculate the rate of return on average total assets for 19A1. We will consider, therefore, possible comments on the rate of return on total end of year assets for 19A2 and 19A1.

[647] The rate of return on total end of year assets before taxation and interest has fallen from 17.87% in 19A1 to 13.93% in 19A2 or 22% (ie $\frac{3.94}{17.87}$). At the same time the rate of return on end of year shareholders' funds has remained relatively stable (11.07% in 19A2 and 11.24% in 19A1). The implication is that in 19A2 total assets were used less efficiently than in 19A1. The rate of return on shareholders' funds, however, has not been unduly affected because the interest paid to service the increased borrowing used to finance the higher level of assets in 19A2 is deductible for tax purposes and because in 19A2 the rate of tax to profit before tax is lower than in 19A1. If we incorporate 19A2 tax advantage, the rate of return has dropped from 9.35% in 19A1 to 7.39% in 19A2, a drop of 21% (eg $\frac{1.96}{9.35}$). The implication is again one of reduced efficiency in the use of asets in 19A2. Another possible explanation is that the expansion of the company's operations which has taken place in 19A2 has not taken full effect by the end of 19A2. If that is the case, one could expect a better return on assets and shareholders' funds when the expansion becomes fully effective, say in 19A3 and, presumably, afterwards.

[648] The rate of return on total assets may be used to compare the relative performance of different firms, especially where different policies are being fol-

lowed by the management of the firms regarding the financing of operations.

Dividends and profit retention

[649] Net profit after tax represents a source from which dividends are paid and funds are retained for use in operations. An analysis of the dividend/profit retention policy of a firm is important. Dividend payments are income in the hands of shareholders and are a significant determinant of the market value of shares. Profit retention provides for growth and in times of rising prices helps counter the effects of inflation.

The provisions for dividend, the rate of dividend and the amounts and rate of profit retention of the XYZ Co Ltd for 19A2 and 19A1 are shown in Table 6.2.

As shown in Table 6.2, the XYZ Co Ltd has retained $24,900 or 20.77% of its reported profit in 19A2 compared to $26,000 or 25.74% in 19A1. The rate of dividend has remained stable in the two years at 12½%.

Table 6.2
XYZ Co Ltd
Dividend and profit retention policy

	19A2	19A1
Net profit after tax	$119,900	$101,000
Provision for dividend	95,000	75,000
Retained profit	$ 24,900	$ 26,000
Rate of profit retention*	20.77%	25.74%
Rate of dividend**	12.5 %	12.5 %

*Retained profit as a percentage of net profit after tax
**Provision for dividend as a percentage of paid up capital.

Analysis of Balance Sheet Relationships

[650] The purpose of the balance sheet is to present the "financial position" or "state of affairs" of the firm at a given point in time. The analysis of balance sheet relationships aims to test the financial structure of the firm for strengths and weaknesses. A firm is in a sound financial position if it can pay its way in the short and long run. The fundamental test of a sound financial position is solvency. In the long run solvency is closely related to profitability since only profitable business enterprises can be expected to pay their way. Solvency is the first priority since it is a precondition for the very survival of the firm. But satisfactory financing implies more than solvency. It requires an appropriate spread of financing among alternative sources designed also to keep down the average cost of capital. These concerns were discussed in some detail in Chapter 5.

Working capital, current ratio and short-term solvency

[651] Short-term solvency relates to the ability of the firm to meet its current obligations. The ability of a firm to meet its current obligations is very important since failure to do so will place the firm's long-term prospects in serious jeopardy.

Working capital and the current ratio are two measures of the short-term solvency of the firm.

Working capital is the excess of current assets over current liabilities. Current assets are defined as those expected to be realised within 12 months of balance date or within the normal trading cycle of the firm, if longer, and current liabilities as those which fall due within 12 months of balance date or within the trading cycle of the firm if longer. Working capital, therefore, represents a kind of safety margin of current assets over current liabilities in meeting short-term debts and contingencies in the face of the uncertainty which, to some degree, inevitably accompanies business operations.

[652] It should be noted, however, that solvency is an ongoing condition and that current obligations, including wages and expenses, are met from available cash and cash inflows in the normal course of business operations, or from cash made available through arrangements with lenders such as banks. Solvency is not a question of liquidating the current assets (eg stocks and debtors) shown in the balance sheet for the purpose of paying the current liabilities shown in the balance sheet.

[653] Referring to our example, the details of the current assets and liabilities and the calculation of the working capital of XYZ Co Ltd are shown in Table 6.3.

The figures in Table 6.3 show that the working capital of XYZ Co Ltd has increased during 19A2 by $91,400 or 48.2%. To evaluate the significance of the amount of working capital in the two years and the change in working capital in 19A2 we must refer to a variable which is related to working capital in a meaningful way. Such a variable is sales on the assumption that a higher level of working capital would be required to service a higher level of sales.

Table 6.3

	19A2 $	19A1 $
Current assets		
Debtors	258,500	173,000
Stocks	458,900	299,000
	717,400	472,000
Less current liabilities		
Bank overdraft	90,800	4,200
Trade creditors	145,200	92,000
Provision for tax	105,200	111,000
Provision for dividend	95,000	75,000
	436,200	282,200
Working capital	281,200	189,800

[654] Relating working capital to sales we see that while sales increased in 19A2 by 25%, working capital increased by almost twice that rate or 48.2%. As a percentage of sales working capital was 16.3% in 19A2 and 13.8% in 19A1. Whether these relationships are satisfactory or not would depend on the particular type of business in which the firm is involved and on the particular circumstances surrounding its operations. We might say, for example, that in view of the increase in sales an increase in working capital was to be expected. Whether this increase should have been as large as has occurred, however, would depend, among other things, on the

adequacy of working capital in 19A1, on the level of sales of the firm towards the end of its financial year and on the expected level of sales in 19A3.

If one is to make a useful assessment of the level of working capital, one needs to consider all its components. While working capital has increased by $91,400, one notes that there has been an increase of $159,900 in inventories, $86,600 in bank overdraft and $53,200 in creditors. These are significant changes. Without study at some depth, including an examination of company policy, it would be superficial to describe the change in working capital as "satisfactory". In a high interest cost situation, for example, the position may be far from optimal.

[655] The current ratio is a measure of solvency which concentrates on the relative total amounts of current assets and current liabilities. The implication is that a high ratio of current assets to current liabilites represents a high degree of assurance that current liabilities will be paid out of current assets. Let us consider for example the following combination of current assets and current liabilities:

	A $	B $	C $
Current assets	320,000	400,000	480,000
Current liabilities	120,000	200,000	280,000
Working capital	200,000	200,000	200,000
Current ratio (Current assets to current liabilities)	2.67:1	2:1	1.7:1

In the above comparison the relative amounts of current assets and current liabilities under A with a current ratio of 2.67:1 indicate a better solvency position than under C with a current ratio of 1.7:1. For example, under A there are $2.67 of current assets for every $1 of current liabilities, while under C there are only $1.70 of current assets for every $1 of current liabilities.

[656] In using the current ratio as a measure of solvency, however, it should be remembered that solvency depends on the timing of receipts and payments over time and not on the ratio of current assets to current liabilities at a point of time. If the timing of receipts and payments is such that cash is always available to pay debts as they fall due, the firm wil be solvent regardless of what the current ratio looks like at a given point of time. The current ratio is a measure of solvency to the extent that it indicates potential future cash flows.

The current ratio is a relative rather than an absolute measure of solvency. What is a good current ratio would depend on the nature of the business enterprise and the circumstances surrounding its operations. For example, a retailer selling for cash can operate on a lower current ratio than a retailer selling on credit because of the time lag in the latter case between making the sale and the collection of cash from debtors. Similarly, in the case of a manufacturing enterprise the current ratio would need to be still higher because of the greater time lag between the acquisition of, say, raw materials, their conversion into finished goods and sales, and the collection of cash from debtors.

A cursory examination of the financial statements of business firms would show that, in the normal course of business operations, firms find it necessary to maintain a margin of current assets over current liabilities. What this margin should be, however, would depend on the nature of the enterprise and on the particular circumstances under which it operates.

[657] The question of business solvency should be considered in a dynamic context. Since the crux of the matter is cash flows, the interpretation of the current ratio should involve the analysis of the composition of current assets and current liabilities. Important in this regard are the rate of stock turn and debtors turnover and the timing at which current liabilities fall due.

The liquid (acid test) ratio

The liquid ratio is:

$$\frac{\text{Liquid assets}}{\text{Quick liabilities}}$$

and is used to provide a supplementary basis for the assessment of short-term solvency. The broad aim is to isolate assets which may be expected to contribute to cash becoming available in the next month or two to help meet the liabilities due for payment during that period.

Liquid assets consist roughly of current assets less stock on hand, that is:
• cash;
• current debtors;
• marketable investments not set aside for a special purpose.

Stock is excluded from liquid assets because of the time lag associated with converting stock into cash through sale and collection of debts.

[658] Some liabilities such as trade creditors fall clearly under the heading of quick liabilities. Whether other liabilites should be classified as quick would depend on the circumstances surrounding the case. For example, if bank overdraft is adequately secured and within the limit set by the bank, it may be omitted from the calculation of the liquid ratio. If the overdraft is above the limit, then at least the excess over the limit should be treated as a quick liability. If the circumstances surounding the operations of the firm and its state of affairs are such as to be a cause for concern at the bank, then the total overdraft should be regarded as a quick liability. Provision for taxation may be another problem item. If the payment of tax is not due for several months, the provision for taxation may be excluded from the calculation of the liquid ratio.

It has been suggested that the liquid ratio should not be less than 1:1. There are no hard and fast rules, however, and generalisations are dangerous. To take a rather extreme case, a restaurarant doing a cash trade at the rate of $20,000 per month may show in its accounts a stock of $4000, no debtors, no money in the bank and creditors of $10,000. If it pays creditors on monthly terms it may be able to pay all accounts as they fall due.

The calculation of the liquid ratio of XYZ Co Ltd is shown below. The provision for taxation is excluded from the calculation and the ratio is calculated alternatively excluding and including bank overdraft:

Exluding overdraft, the liquid ratio has remained stable in 19A2 and 19A1. Including overdraft, the liquid ratio shows that in 19A2 liquid assets do not cover quick liabilites. We do not know the overdraft limit of the company or details of its arrangements with the bank. Assuming that the overdraft limit is in excess of $90,000 (the amount of overdraft at the end of 19A2), the liquid position of the

	19A2 $	19A1 $
Liquid assets		
Debtors	258,500	173,000
Liquid liabilities		
Trade creditors	145,200	92,000
Provision for dividend	95,000	75,000
Total (excluding overdraft)	240,200	167,000
Overdraft	90,800	4,200
Total (including overdraft)	331,000	171,200
Liquid ratio		
Excluding overdraft	1.08:1	1.04:1
Including overdraft	0.78:1	1.01:1

company as revealed by the liquid ratio does not suggest any reason for anxiety.

Long-term borrowing and short-term solvency

[659] A firm which finds itself in short-term liquidity difficulties may correct its liquid position by long-term borrowing. The ability of a firm to borrow long term may be regarded as a second line of defence in meeting its short-term obligations. Where long-term loans are secured over the fixed assets of the firm, property in particular, relating long-term loans to fixed assets, in particular property, may give an indication of the extent to which fixed assets have been mortgaged and a measure, therefore, of the remaining capacity of the firm to raise additional long-term loans should the need arise.

Returning to the example, in 19A1 XYZ Co Ltd had a mortgage of $20,000 or 4.9% of the book value of its property (eg $\frac{\$20,000}{\$405,000}$) and in 19A2 the mortgage was $200,000 or 37% of the book value of property (eg $\frac{\$200,000}{\$540,100}$).

Assuming that the property can be mortgaged to 50% of its value, the XYZ Co Ltd still has some capacity left to raise additional long-term finance on the security of its property. It should be noted also that long-term loans are made on the basis of the current realizable value of assets. If the current value of the property is significantly higher than its book value, the borrowing capacity of the company wil be greater than shown by the above figures.

Proprietary (equity/debt) ratio

[660] The proprietary (equity/debt) ratio is the ratio of the shareholders' equity (paid up capital and reserves) to total liabilites. The ratio indicates how much of the total assets of the business is financed by the shareholders' funds and how much by outside interests. For example, a proprietary ratio of 1:1 indicates that half of the total assets of the business are financed by shareholders' funds and half by creditors. The percentage stake of the shareholders in the assets of the business is an indication of the security of creditors, since this stands between the creditors and a loss on realization of assets in a winding up. For example, a ratio of 1:1 indicates

that there is $2 of asset backing (at book value) for every $1 of creditors. The proprietary ratio may be calculated, alternatively, by expressing the shareholders' funds as a percentage of total assets. This latter method has the advantage that it gives us directly the percentage of assets financed by the shareholders' interest.

There are no hard and fast rules regarding what the proprietary ratio should be. In most business undertakings it is not regarded as sound for creditors to have a larger financial stake in the business than shareholders. What is an appropriate proprietary ratio in a particular case would depend on the nature of the business and its history. For example, a finance company would usually have a high dependence on borrowed funds and would, therefore, operate on a lower proprietary ratio than, say, a manufacturer or a trading firm.

[661] A high proprietary ratio is not necessarily good as it may indicate a failure on the part of management to utilize relatively cheap to service borrowed funds and thereby increase the rate of return on the shareholders' equity. The objective of management policy regarding the financing of the firm's operations should be to avoid imbalance developing between the shareholders' equity and liabilities to an extent that the firm will find itself in financial difficulties, say, in a time of recession.

In our example, the proprietary ratio of XYZ Co Ltd can be calculated as follows:
   (a) Shareholders' equity to total liabilities:

19A2	19A1
$\dfrac{\$1{,}083{,}300}{\$636{,}200^*} = 1.7{:}1$	$\dfrac{\$898{,}400}{\$302{,}200^*} = 2.97{:}1$

	19A2 $	19A1 $
Mortgage	200,000	20,000
Current liabilities	436,200	282,200
*Total liabilities	636,200	302,200

Or
   (b) Shareholders' equity as a percentage of total assets:

19A2	19A1
$\dfrac{\$1{,}083{,}300}{\$1{,}719{,}500} = 63\%$	$\dfrac{\$898{,}400}{\$1{,}200{,}600} = 74.8\%$

[662] The above figures show that the proprietary ratio of XYZ Co Ltd has dropped from 74.8% at the end of 19A1 to 63% at the end of 19A2. The drop has been caused by the relative increase in the use by the company of loan finance in 19A2. This is not necessarily a bad development because a proprietary ratio of 74.8% was probably too high. It is quite possible that a ratio of 63% still leaves some room for a further increase in the use of borrowed funds.

It should be noted that where the book value of assets is significantly different from current value, a notional revaluation of assets with an apropriate adjustment of the shareholders' equity may give a better picture of the firm's equity/debt position and its capacity for greater use of borrowing.

Debtors' turnover — Average collection period for debtors

[663] The average collection period for debtors may be calculated by dividing the amount of debtors by the average daily or monthly credit sales. The formula is

$$\text{Debtors} \div \frac{\text{Credit sales for year}}{365}$$

for calculation of the average collection period in days, or

$$\text{Debtors} \div \frac{\text{Credit sales for year}}{12}$$

for calculation of the period in months.

Alternatively we can obtain a figure for turnover of debtors by dividing the credit sales for the year by the amount of debtors. A figure for the average collection period in months may then be obtained by dividing 12 by the debtors' turnover.

Assuming that all the sales of XYZ Co Ltd are on credit, we may calculate an average collection period for debtors for the company as follows:

19A2	19A1
$258,500 \div \dfrac{\$1,725,000}{365} = 54.7$ days	$173,000 \div \dfrac{\$1,380,000}{365} = 47.8$ days

Or

19A2	19A1
$258,500 \div \dfrac{\$1,725,000}{12} = 1.8$ months	$173,000 \div \dfrac{\$1,380,000}{12} = 1.57$ months

Or

$$\textit{19A2}$$
$$\text{Debtors' turnover} = \frac{\$1,725,000}{\$258,500} = 6.67 \text{ times}$$

$$\text{Average collection period} = 12 \div 6.67 = 1.8 \text{ months.}$$

[664] The above calculations are based on the end of year debtors. Since there has been a significant increase in debtors and sales during 19A2, it may be more appropriate to base the calculation on average debtors. For example, the calculation for 19A2 will be

$$\tfrac{1}{2}(\$173,000 + \$258,500) \div \frac{\$1,725,000}{365} = 45.7 \text{ days}$$

Or if average monthly sales are used

$$\tfrac{1}{2}(\$173,000 + \$258,500) \div \frac{\$1,725,000}{12} = 1.5 \text{ months}$$

A calculation of the average collection period for debtors aims to throw light on the rate at which debts are collected, ie the rate at which debtors generate cash flows for use in operations. The collection period for debtors may also give an indication of the credit policies followed by the firm, the average age of debtors, and their value.

[665] The average collection period for debtors, however, should be interpreted with caution. The calculations above show that, based on end of year debtors, the

average collection period for 19A2 was 54.7 days (1.8 months) compared to 47.8 days (1.57 months) in 19A1. The figures indicate a slowing down of the rate of debt collection in 19A2 and, perhaps, a need for review by management of its credit policy. Given the significant increases in sales and debtors in 19A2, however, a better indication of the rate of debt collection may be given by the calculation based on average debtors — eg 45.7 days (1.5 months) in 19A2 (we cannot calculate the corresponding figures for 19A1). The point is that what we are interested in is the rate at which current debts are collected. A detailed analysis of debts may require an individual examination of large debts and an "ageing" of all debts showing details of amounts overdue. Such an analysis, however, even if considered desirable, cannot be undertaken by a person relying primarily on the information disclosed in published financial statements.

[666] Two further cautionary notes. Where the level of debtors varies significantly during the year (for example, as a result of seasonal variations in sales) and end of year debtors are not representative of the average debtors carried by the firm, an average of monthly debtors' balances may be necessary in order to arrive at a representative rate of debt collection. Also, where there are different categories of debtors (eg hire purchase and budget accounts) separate calculations of collection rates may be desirable.

Statement of Changes in Financial Position

[667] The aim of the statement of changes in financial position is to summarize the financing and investing activities of a business enterprise, including the use of funds generated from operations, and to highlight changes in the financial position of the enterprise during the period.

[668] Shown below are statements of changes in financial position of XYZ Co Ltd:
   (a) based on changes in total resources (Figure 6.1) (p 102), and
   (b) highlighting changes in working capital (Figure 6.2) (p 103).

[669] It is not the objective of this chapter to deal with the techniques and problems associated with the preparation and rationalization of statements of changes in financial position. The following points will be made, however, in connection with the statements shown as Figures 6.1 and 6.2:

   (a) The first item in both statements is net profit after tax. This is a common starting item. Net profit after tax is ostensibly the amount generated by operations which is available for distribution or retention and use in the operations of the firm. In this regard the statement provides, among other things, an explanation regarding how reported profit has been utilized.

   (b) The statement highlighting changes in working capital (Figure 6.2) can be derived directly from the general statement shown as Figure 6.1. This is done by taking those items in the latter statement which do not represent changes in current assets and current liabilities. Changes in current assets and liabilities may be summarized separately in a statement of working capital changes as has been done in Figure 6.2

   (c) Although the statement highlighting changes in working capital (Figure 6.2) contains the same items as that in Figure 6.1, the former statement is more informative than the latter. For example, it shows that during 19A2 the funds obtained by the company from profit retention and long-term sources (share capital and mortgage) exceeded expenditure on long-term assets by $91,400 which is why working capital was increased by that amount. For further discussion of statements of changes in financial position see Chapter 4, paras [420]–[430].

Figure 6.1
XYZ Co Ltd
Statement of changes in financial position for year ended 31 March 19A2
(Total resources)

	$	$
SOURCES OF FUNDS		
From operations		
Net profit after tax		119,900
Plus depreciation written off		19,500
Total funds from operations		139,400
Funds from other sources		
Share capital	160,000	
Mortgage	180,000	
Increase in current liabilities —		
Bank overdraft	86,600	
Trade Creditors	53,200	
Provision for dividend	20,000	499,800
Total sources of funds		639,200
APPLICATION OF FUNDS		
Purchase of fixed assets		
Land		110,000
Buildings		141,000
Furniture and fittings		42,000
Increase in debtors		85,500
Increase in stock		159,900
Reduction in provision for tax		5,800
Provision for dividend		95,000
		639,200

Review questions

6.1 "The message of financial statements is a specialized one and its interpretation requires certain specialist skills."
Discuss.

6.2 "The informational value of accounting numbers is relative and is brought out in meaningful comparisons and in the analysis of the interrelated processes which they reflect."

Discuss. Give examples.

Figure 6.2

XYZ Co Ltd
Statement of changes in financial position for year ended 31 March 19A2
(Working capital)

	$	$
SOURCES OF FUNDS		
From operations		
Net profit after tax		119,900
Plus depreciation written off		19,500
Total funds from operations		139,400
Funds from other sources		
Share capital	160,000	
Mortgage	180,000	340,000
Total sources of funds		479,400
Application of funds		
Purchase of fixed assets		
Land	110,000	
Buildings	141,000	
Furniture and fittings	42,000	293,000
Provision for dividend		95,000
Increase in working capital		91,400
		479,400

Change in working capital

	Increase $	Decrease $
Debtors	85,500	
Stock	159,900	
Provision for tax	5,800	
Bank overdraft		86,600
Trade creditors		53,200
Provision for dividend		20,000
	251,200	159,800
Net increase in working capital		91,400
	251,200	251,200

6.3 To what extent can financial statements derived from the past be regarded as guides to the future?

6.4 Why are comparisons important in the analysis and interpretation of financial statements?

6.5 Define and examine the problems associated with the analysis of comparative financial statements and with the interpretation of changes and trends.

6.6 What are common size financial statements? How are they used in analysis and interpretation?

6.7 How are percentages and ratios used in analysis and interpretation of financial statements?

6.8 Explain the calculation and uses of the following ratios:
(a) gross profit rate;
(b) rate of return;
(c) current ratio;
(d) liquid ratio;
(e) proprietary (equity/debt) ratio;
(f) rate of stock turnover.

6.9 Examine the usefulness of ratios and percentages in the interpretation of financial statements.

6.10 (a) Why is the gross profit rate important?
(b) What are some reasons for variations in the gross profit rate?

6.11 How do you calculate the rate of stock turn? What is its significance for the analysis and interpretation of financial statements?

6.12 How would you go about determining an "appropriate" rate of stock turn for a firm?

6.13 "Percentages and ratios should be used to analyse significant relationships between components of financial statements."
How useful would it be in the analysis of the income statement to express the following expense items as a percentage of sales?

- administration salaries;
- salaries of sales office;
- travellers' salaries and expenses;
- bad debts;
- depreciation;
- interest paid;
- directors' fees;
- audit expenses;
- advertising;
- rent paid;
- marketing research;
- executive travel;
- taxation.

6.14 "The analysis and interpretation of expenses is not an easy task."
Discuss.

6.15 Discuss some of the problems likely to be encountered by an external analyst of financial statements.

6.16 "The terms 'profit' and 'profitability' do not mean the same thing."
Discuss.

6.17 How is the rate of return calculated? What is its significance in the analysis and interpretation of financial statements?

6.18 Discuss the analytical uses of the rate of return on shareholders' equity and the rate of return on total assets.

6.19 During the year ended 31 March 19A2 the working capital of ABC Co Ltd increased from $562,381 to $621,493. Is that good or bad?

6.20 "The higher the current ratio, the better!" Do you agree?

6.21 "In order to be solvent, a firm must have a current ratio of not less than 2:1."
Discuss

6.22 Discuss the treatment of the following items in the calculation of the liquid ratio:
- taxation;
- debtors;
- trading stocks;
- bank overdraft.

6.23 "Solvency is an ongoing condition."
Discuss.

6.24 Is a proprietary (equity/debt) ratio of 75% better than one of 65%?

6.25 Discuss the usefulness of statements of changes in financial position in the analysis and interpretation of financial statements.

6.26 The revenue accounts of Service Wholesalers Ltd for the years ended 31 March 19A1 and 19A2 showed the following results:

	19A1 $	19A2 $
Sales	390,000	480,000
Gross profit	99,000	114,000
Net profit (before tax)	42,000	48,000

What are the significant features of the 19A2 results as compared with the 19A1 results? Has 19A2 been more profitable than 19A1?

6.27 The following are comparative statements of operating results and state of affairs of AB Traders Ltd for the years ended 31 December 19A1, 19A2 and 19A3:

	Operating results					
	19A1		19A2		19A3	
	$	$	$	$	$	$
Sales		600,000		720,000		900,000
Cost of goods sold		400,000		540,000		720,000
Gross profit		200,000		180,000		180,000
Selling expenses	80,000		80,000		90,000	
Administrative expenses	60,000		60,000		70,000	
		140,000		140,000		160,000
Net profit		60,000		40,000		20,000

State of affairs as at 31 December

	19A1 $	19A1 $	19A2 $	19A2 $	19A3 $	19A3 $
Current assets						
Debtors	80,000		120,000		160,000	
Stock	100,000	180,000	160,000	280,000	200,000	360,000
Fixed assets						
Buildings and plant	140,000		200,000		200,000	
Less provision for depreciation	50,000	90,000	66,000	134,000	86,000	114,000
		270,000		414,000		474,000
Current liabilities						
Creditors		60,000		60,000		100,000
Bank		10,000		134,000		74,000
Capital and reserves		200,000		220,000		300,000
		270,000		414,000		474,000

Stock on 1 January 19A1 was $100,000.

Required:

Comment on the operating results and state of affairs of AB Traders Ltd for the three years covered by the above figures under the following headings: (a) sales; (b) gross profit; (c) net profit; (d) rate of return; (e) rate of stock turn; (f) working capital and current ratio; (g) liquid ratio; (h) proprietary (equity/debt) ratio; (i) collection period for debtors; (assume all sales are on monthly credit).

6.28 The following information has been extracted from the final accounts of Anchor Ltd:

	Years ended 30 June 19A1 $	Years ended 30 June 19A2 $
Sales	360,000	480,000
Cost of sales	252,000	300,000
Net profit before tax	36,000	48,000
Tax payable	18,000	24,000
The expenses charged in arriving at net profit included:		
Depreciation — buildings	3,000	3,000
plant and machinery	4,800	7,200

	As at 30 June 19A1 $	As at 30 June 19A2 $
Assets		
Land and buildings (at cost less depreciation)	60,000	57,000
Plant and machinery (at cost less depreciation)	44,700	69,300
Preliminary expenses	5,400	—

Continued p 107

Stock	49,800	55,200
Debtors	44,400	41,700
Cash at bank	18,900	1,800
	223,200	225,000

Shareholders' funds and liabilities

Paid up capital	106,800	106,800
Appropriation account	20,100	25,200
Mortgage	24,000	12,000
Proposed dividend	6,000	13,500
Provision for tax	18,000	24,000
Creditors	48,300	43,500
	223,200	225,000

Note:

The mortgage was reduced by $12,000 on 15 July 19A1. The remaining
balance of $12,000 is due for payment on 15 July 19A2.

Required:

Comment on the operating results and financial position of Anchor Ltd
under the following headings:
(a) sales;
(b) gross profit;
(c) net profit;
(d) rate of return on shareholders' funds;
(e) stock carying policy;
(f) dividend policy;
(g) working capital and current ratio;
(h) liquid ratio;
(i) proprietary (equity/debt) ratio.

6.29 Good Foods Ltd and Best Foods Ltd are competitors in the food processing
industry. The following information has been extracted from their latest
published accounts:

	Best Foods Ltd $	Good Foods Ltd $
Shareholders' funds	1,300,000	850,000
Fixed assets (at book value)	1,600,000	840,000
Bank overdraft	60,000	150,000
Trade creditors	380,000	390,000
Stocks	580,000	500,000
Debtors and other current assets	540,000	350,000
Mortgages	980,000	300,000
Sales	3,400,000	3,000,000
Net profit after tax	160,000	285,000

Required:
(a) Set out your calculations of the working capital of the two companies.
(b) Calculate, compare and comment *briefly* on:
    (i) the current (working capital) ratios; and

(ii) the proprietary ratios of the two companies.

(c) Comment, as far as it is possible from the figures provided, on the trading results and relative profitability of the two companies. Support your answer with such data or calculations as you consider appropriate.

6.30 The following figures have been extracted from the accounts of ABC Ltd for the year ended 31 March 19A3:

    (i) The profit of the company before tax was $490,000. This profit figure was arrived at after deducting normal depreciation of $236,000 and $3400 being the book value of plant scrapped.

    (ii) Provision for taxation amounted to 50% of the profit before tax shown above.

    (iii) A short-term investment with a book value of $20,000 was sold for $25,000. In last year's balance sheet this investment was shown as a current asset.

    (iv) Fixed assets were purchased at the cost of $400,000. A mortgage of $200,000 was raised to help pay for the purchase. The balance was paid in cash.

    (v) A new share issue was made during the year: 200,000 $1 ordinary shares were issued at a premium of 20%. This issue was fully subscribed and at the end of the year all the capital had been called up. All the money due on the shares had been received except for $10,000 final call in arrears.

    (vi) Provisions for dividends were made as follows: 12% on ordinary capital of $600,000 and 10% on preference capital of $300,000.

Required:

Calculate the change in total working capital of ABC Ltd at the end of the year as compared to its working capital at the beginning of the year. You should present your answer in the form of a funds statement prepared for the purpose of explaining changes in working capital. (*Note:* statement of changes in current assets and current liabilities is not required.)

6.31 The following are the summarized balance sheets of XYZ Co Ltd for the years ended 31 July 19A2 and 19A3:

	19A2 $000	19A3 $000
Issued and paid up capital	3,000	3,000
Revenue reserves	3,000	3,300
	6,000	6,300
Mortgages	500	500
Current liabilities		
Bank overdraft	60	—
Sundry creditors	640	700
Provision for dividend	400	400
Provision for taxation	580	680
	8,180	8,580

Continued p 109

Fixed assets (at cost less depreciation)

Land and buildings	5,000	4,900
Furniture and fittings	240	220

Current assets

Stocks	2,140	2,440
Debtors	800	1,000
Bank	—	20
	8,180	8,580

The sales and net profit of the company for the two years were as follows:

	19A2 $000	19A3 $000
Sales	8,000	8,900
Net profit after tax	600	700

Required:

(a) Comment on the operating results of XYZ Co Ltd for the year ended 31 July 19A3 using such ratios, percentages and comparisons as you consider appropriate.

(b) Comment on the financial structure of XYZ Co Ltd as at 31 July 19A3 and changes in it during the year ended 31 July 19A3 using such comparisons, ratios and percentages as you consider appropriate.

6.32 The operating statements and balance sheets of Progresive Traders Ltd for the years ended 30 September 19A1 and 19A2 are shown on the following pages.

Required:

(a) Comment on the operating results of Progressive Trades Ltd in 19A2 using appropriate ratios and percentages.

(b) Examine the changes in the financial structure of the firm during 19A2 using appropriate ratios of percentages and giving, if possible, probable reasons for the trends shown.

Operating statements				
	19A1		**19A2**	
	$	$	$	$
Sales		260,000		286,000
Cost of sales				
Opening stock	25,000		37,000	
Purchases	194,000		235,500	
	219,000		272,500	
Closing stock	37,000		58,000	
Cost of sales		182,000		214,500
Gross profit		78,000		71,500

Continued p 110

109

Continued

Expenses

Occupancy	2,500		3,200	
Administration	15,000		15,500	
Selling	18,000		20,000	
Advertising	4,000		7,000	
Other	14,000	53,500	14,200	59,900
Net profit		24,500		11,600
Provision for tax		13,200		5,300
Net profit after tax		11,300		6,300
Profit and loss appropriation account —				
Balance brought forward		22,300		25,600
		33,600		31,900
Provision for dividend		8,000		8,000
Balance carried forward		$25,600		$23,900

Balance Sheets

	19A1 $	19A2 $
Left hand side		
Authorised and issued capital		
60,000 ordinary shares of $1 each fully paid	60,000	60,000
Profit and loss appropriation account	25,600	23,900
	85,600	83,900
Current liabilities		
Bank	—	21,800
Sundry creditors	16,000	44,000
Provision for tax	13,200	5,300
Provision for dividends	8,000	8,000
	37,200	79,100
Total	$122,800	$163,000
Right hand side		
Fixed assets (net book value)		
Freehold property	35,000	52,000
Motor vehicles	5,000	7,000
Furniture and fixtures	6,000	10,000
	46,000	69,000
Current assets		
Bank	11,800	—
Debtors	28,000	36,000
Stock	37,000	58,000
	76,800	94,000
Total	$122,800	$163,000

Chapter 7
Some Limitations of Financial Statements

[701] The road of the interpreter of financial statements is studded with man-sized potholes, the signposts are often quite unreliable, and the journey may have to be made in the half-dark. Some of the difficulties have been mentioned in the preceding chapters. In this chapter we shall discuss in greater detail difficulties and problems in analysis and interpretation arising from the accounting and reporting processes themselves:
- the principles and practices used in accounting measurement;
- the uncertainty factor;
- the form and content of financial statements; and
- the effect of the human element on the preparation, presentation and interpretation of financial statements.

The Principles and Practices Used in Accounting Measurement

[702] The nature of generally accepted accounting principles has already been discussed; the term refers to the principles, methods and procedures which comprise current accounting practice. It is essential that the analyst and interpreter of financial statements has understanding of the principles, methods and procedures used in their preparation in order to appreciate the basis of accounting measurement and, therefore, the significance of what is reported as profit and state of affairs, and to assess the relevance of the reported figures for the particular purpose for which the analysis and interpretation is required.

The following are some of the principles currently applied in the preparation of financial statements and some of the limitations of financial statements which result from their application.

(1) The monetary principle

[703] Accounting transactions are recorded, analyzed and interpreted in terms of money. According to Moonitz:

> The use by accountancy of money as a common denominator is merely a specific example of the logical requirement that two or more objects must be expressed in identical units before we can perform operations on them such as adding them together, or subtracting one from the other. [Maurice Moonitz, *The Basic Postulates of Accounting*, Accounting Research Study No 1, AICPA, New York, 1961, p 18]

111

The term "common denominator", however, assumes a stable measurement unit, which money is not. Current accounting practice uses monetary measurement without regard for changes in the purchasing power of the monetary unit (the dollar). Since business operations are economic in nature, accounting for them should be in economic terms. The economic significance of money is its purchasing power. The failure of current accounting practice to account for changes in the purchasing power of the monetary unit imposes severe limitations on the informational value of financial statements and may lead to error in the evaluation of the operating performance of business firms.

[704] The use of money as the basis for accounting measurement, however, has deeper significance than that associated with a basic measuring unit. Accounting in terms of money reflects the manner in which business operations are launched and maintained — through the input of money for the purpose of generating a monetary output over and above the amount of monetary input. To quote Moonitz again on the cyclical circulation of invested capital in the course of business operations (Maurice Moonitz, *Changing Prices and Financing Reporting*, Stipes Publishing Co, Champaign, Illinois, 1974):

> Each cycle starts with capital in the form of money ("free capital") invested in "real" capital goods and services other than money and ends up with disinvestment and reconversion into money or "free capital". [p 31]

> . . . Ultimately the gain or loss on the entire cycle is measured by comparison of two money amounts, the amount invested at the outset and the amount recovered at the end of the cycle. To make the comparison properly, the two amounts should be expressed in terms of a uniform scale of measurement, the exchange value of the monetary unit at a single point of time. [ibid]

In traditional accounting, the monetary principle coupled with the historical cost and realization conventions results in the measurement of monetary assets at face value and of non-monetary assets in terms of the number of dollars involved in the original outlay, reduced where appropriate by provisions for depreciation.

[705] Current accounting practice ignores changes in the purchasing power of the monetary unit. As a result, transactions are recorded, classified, aggregated and interpreted in dollars of different purchasing power, dollars which are not really comparable. It may be argued, therefore, that in times of significant price level changes, accounting numbers are not additive and that the aggregates of such numbers cannot be meaningfully interpreted. For example, in the process of income measurement, original investment outlays are matched against revenue in terms of the number of dollars involved and not in terms of what is economically significant: purchasing power. Further, investment outlay is one dimension of business reality. Current value is another. The latter reflects the current state of the firm's investment in business operations given current costs and prices, and the firm's expectations about the future.

[706] In the evaluation of results and state of affairs, it is necessary to take into account the effects of both general and specific price changes if significant price changes have taken place.

For example, A acquires a property at the start of the year for $200,000, and obtains a loan secured by mortgage of $100,000, with interest at 10%, from lender B. Inflation for the year was 8%, so that B would require $108,000 at the end of the year to be as well off in terms of purchasing power. A and B paid taxation at 40%.

In accounting terms, B made a profit in the form of interest $10,000 less taxation $4000 = $6000. His capital of $100,000 was represented by the $100,000 advance, and so remained intact.

In economic terms, B needed $108,000 to be as well off as he was at the start of the year, whereas he had only $6000 income after tax and the $100,000 advance = $106,000. In fact, he had incurred a loss in purchasing power of $2000.

In accounting terms, A borrowed $100,000 and still owed $100,000 at the end of the year. In economic terms, A borrowed $100,000 in purchasing power at the start of the year. This is equivalent to $108,000 of purchasing power at the end of the year. But he owes only $100,000 of end-of-year purchasing power. He has made a purchasing power gain of $8000. His interest expense was $10,000 less tax benefit $4000 = $6000 (we have assumed that the property is used for income earning purposes so that the interest is tax deductible). The interest cost for A was negative by $2 000!

For A this is only one side of the story. The other is the worth of the property at the end of the year. There may have been a specific price change — the worth of the property may have increased at a higher rate than the rate of general inflation, as often happens, say by 10% in the face of general inflation of 8%. His investment of $200,000 in purchasing power will be represented by $220,000 in end-of-year purchasing power. His equity at the start of the year was $100,000 but is now $220,000 less $100,000 = $120,000. He needed an equity of $108,000 to maintain the purchasing power of his original investment. He is $12,000 better off, $8000 at the cost of B and $4000 because the value of the property rose more than the rate of inflation — increase in the money value of the property $20,000 less effect of inflation $16,000 (ie 8% of $200,000) = "real" increase in value $4000 the total of which accrues to A.

This leads on to another principle of accounting, historical cost, which warrants further consideration.

(2) Historical cost

[707] The historical cost convention emphasizes that accounting provides a historical record of transactions expressed in monetary terms. Accordingly, a balance sheet does not purport to show the current value of assets but only that residue of historical cost which has yet to be charged to operations in the process of matching cost with revenue.

Although current accounting practice includes some departures from historical cost (such as the revaluation of some fixed assets, in particular land and buildings, and the lower of cost or market basis of valuation of inventories), historical cost has been and continues to be the most common concept applied in accounting measurement and valuation.

What are the reasons for this continuing survival of historical cost as a fundamental factor in accounting measurement?

Transactions are at the heart of business operations. Accounting involves the maintenance of a detailed historical record and analysis of transactions of business enterprises as a starting point in the process of accountability and performance evaluation. Further, the historical cost of non-monetary assets represents the initial investment in income generating activities against which income performance will be measured.

[708] The criticisms of historical cost arise from a recognition of a need to reflect in accounting measurement the effects of price and price level changes. The failure of current accounting practice to reflect the effects of price level changes means that the original investment in assets is measured and recovered from revenue in terms of the number of dollars involved and not in terms of the purchasing power of the original monetary outlay. Further, in times of significant price changes, the effective evaluation of performance requires knowledge of the current value of assets and not the residuals of the historical costs of those assets.

For example, take the case of a depreciating asset with an estimated useful life of 10 years which cost $100,000 five years ago. Depreciation is charged against the revenue of year five of $10,000. Due to inflation over the five years, the equivalent purchasing power invested originally in the asset is now $140,000. Depreciation expense in purchasing power terms would be $14,000. Further, if the cost of replacing the asset now is $160,000, then one would argue that the fair depreciation expense was $16,000, and that an appropriate balance sheet value of the asset net of depreciation would be $80,000 and not $50,000 (ie $160,000 less five years depreciation at $16,000). The question of accounting for the effects of general and specific price changes is discussed in greater length in Chapter 19.

[709] The objectivity of historical cost, which is often claimed as a justification for its continued use in accounting, merits close scrutiny. The usefulness of financial statements for decision-making depends much more on the relevance of the data they contain than on the objectivity of the data as such. Further, the valuation of depreciable assets at historical cost loses, over time, not only its relevance to decision-making but also its objectivity. This is because the determination of periodic depreciation charges is a highly subjective exercise. The depreciation expense of a year may be taken to result from judgments regarding the estimated useful life of assets, the estimated residual value (if any), and the pattern of depreciation cost incurrence considered appropriate to the asset.

[710] Further, it may be unwise to consider depreciation and asset value apart from repairs and maintenance. Programs of maintenance, claimed as an expense for tax purposes, may provide for the constant updating and improvement of production facilities out of revenue. How else can one explain the following case, which illustrates how historical cost data can lose relevance over an extended period of years?

Some years ago the annual accounts of a New Zealand company engaged in the manufacture of fertilizers showed, among other things, the data shown on p 115.

In his address to the shareholders at the annual meeting the chairman of directors made the following statement: "It is of interest to note that the plant, machinery and fittings appear in the balance sheet at $260,000 against an indemnity value for insurance purposes of $1,782,000 and a replacement value of $2,260,000".

Given the above figures and the wide discrepancy they indicate between book and current value, the question arises regarding the relevance of both the profit figure based on the historical cost depreciation and the asset values at the written down cost figures reported in the accounts. Both of these suspect items would enter into an evaluation of the profitability of this firm in particular and of the fertilizer

	$	$
Profit before tax		356,916
Provision for tax		176,000
Net profit for year		180,916
After providing for		
depreciation		
Buildings	32,846	
Plant	57,184	
Fixtures and fittings	4,222	
Total	94,252	

	Cost $	Depreciation to date $	Book value $
Plant and machinery	822,054	597,230	224,824
Fixtures and fittings	82,776	47,704	35,072
	904,830	644,934	259,896
Share capital, fully paid			1,100,000
Shareholders' funds			2,160,524
Proposed dividend 10%			110,000

industry in general. At the time pressure was being exerted by some farmers to secure government support for the establishment of a cooperative fertilizer works in the South Island of New Zealand: see for example, T K Cowan, "Figures, Facts and Fertilizers', *The Accountants' Journal*, October 1965, pp 101–3. In this connection, the reported results of this company could scarcely be regarded as relevant information. For a discussion of the effects of rejuvenating maintenance over an extended period of time on the value of the plant of this company see B Popoff, "The Price-Level Adjustment and Accounting Realism: A Case Study of a New Zealand Company", *The International Journal of Accounting*, Spring 1971, pp 15–35.

[711] It should be noted that the historical cost convention is not strictly adhered to in current accounting practice. The writing down of items included in inventories to net realizable value when this falls below historical cost is an example of a departure from a strict application of historical cost. Another departure from historical cost is the writing up of fixed assets (land and buildings in particular) which has gained acceptance, in New Zealand and Australia at least. So too is the non-provision of depreciation on buildings by some enterprises, on the grounds that the buildings are considered to have at least maintained their value over the period.

(3) Realization

[712] The realization convention prohibits the recognition of gains until these have been realized, normally by way of sale. The realization convention is related to historical cost in that it implies that assets should not be valued at a figure above cost: like the historical cost convention, it affects both the measurement of profit

and the balance sheet valuation of assets.

One effect of the realization constraint on profit reporting is that what may be the "holding gains" of one period will be reported as the operating gains in the period in which sale takes place. (A holding gain is the excess of the current replacement cost of an item over its historical cost.) For example, gains from speculative buying of, say, raw materials will be reported as the operating gains of the period of sale of the finished goods produced from the cheap raw materials.

Current accounting practice accepts certain departures from the principle of realization such as the writing up of fixed assets and where profit is taken on long-term contracts prior to completion. Investment companies investing mainly in real estate may revalue their holdings at the end of each accounting period and recognise the gain (or loss) in their revenue statements separately from operating income (from rents, less expenses and taxation). These unrealized gains are of a lower quality than realised income from operations. They lack certainty until actually realized.

(4) Continuity

[713] Under the continuity convention it is assumed that the business will continue in existence "indefinitely". The continuity assumption reflects the fact that most business enterprises are established for indefinite periods of time, and the observable phenomenon that many business enterprises have continued in operation over lengthy time periods.

The continuity convention has important implications for the valuation of assets and the measurement of profit. It has been used to justify the use of historical cost in accounting as a basis of valuation and profit measurement. Other cost-based methods of accounting, such as proposals for accounting based on current replacement cost, also require an assumption of continuity for logical justification. In a cost-based system of accounting there is an implicit assumption that operations will continue into the future for a period sufficient to cover the expected useful lives of the existing assets of the firm. As the firm replaces assets used up, this period will be extended further into the future.

The continuity principle underlies the processes of accrual accounting and, indeed, of all carrying forward of expenditure to future periods. Its application has been regarded as acceptable and useful practice provided that there is an acceptable level of assurance that the business entity will indeed continue during the expected economic life of the assets concerned and will produce future benefits at least equal to the book value carried forward. The principle becomes critical where the level of assurance is reduced to the point where continuity becomes uncertain. A possible outcome is liquidation and the results of liquidation could be realization of assets at figures below their book value and also the incurrence of related costs such as liquidation expenses and redundancy pay. It is well to realize the dilemma of the auditor in such circumstances. If he yields to the persuasion of the directors that liquidation values are inappropriate as the enterprise has plans to trade its way out of difficulty, and the enterprise fails soon after the accounts are produced, then he may well be charged with negligence. If he stands his ground, he may well ensure that the outcome is indeed liquidation, with losses which might have been avoided. It may be worth noting that the former course of action is the easier and the more likely to be followed.

(5) Accounting period convention

[714] The continuing nature of business operations has created the need for regular reports on the results of operations and state of affairs of business firms. This need has given rise to the presentation of annual financial reports and, more recently, of interim financial reports.

The practice of periodic reporting has given rise to the problems of accrual accounting — the necessity to accrue and defer items of income and expenditure and to separate capital expenditure from revenue expenditure. This apportionment of amounts between past and future periods requires the use of judgment and brings a considerable degree of subjectivity into accounting measurement.

(6) Consistency and comparability

[715] The need for consistency in the application of accounting principles has arisen because of the alternatives available for dealing with some important problems in financial accounting and reporting.

The accounting notions of consistency and comparability are related; for example, it is generally regarded that the consistent application of accounting principles is a necessary precondition for ensuring comparability in financial statements over time and across firms.

From the viewpoint of the analysis and interpretation of financial statements, it should be noted that the selection and consistent application of a set of accounting principles will not automaticaly produce financial statements which are comparable. For example, in times of price changes and inflation the consistent application of historical cost in the preparation of the financial statements of a firm will not result in comparable statements in terms of sales, expenses and rates of return. Similarly, the consistent application of historical cost in the preparation of the financial statements of different firms, say, in the same industry, will not necessarily result in an intercompany comparability of financial statements. The investment of funds in assets at different points of time will not be reported in comparable terms, nor will asset values and depreciation expense. As a result, the reported rates of return of different firms in the industry will not necessarily be comparable. In order to ensure the comparability of financial statement data, we may have to depart from the consistent application of historical cost and make restatements of some revenue and balance sheet items for general and specific price changes so that costs and asset values are expressed in comparable terms.

This is not to say that there is anything wrong with a principle of consistency in itself. Comparability is a highly desirable quality in financial reporting. Rather, accountants appear to have adopted a somewhat simplistic view of the twin issues of consistency and comparability. It seems that there has been an implicit assumption that any selection of a set of accounting principles from available alternatives will result in the comparability of financial statements provided that the selected set of principles is consistently applied from one period to another and from one firm to another.

(7) Conservatism

[716] Conservatism is a doctrine which, it has been claimed, permeates the principles of valuation in accounting: see for example R Sterling, "Conservatism: The

Fundamental Principle of Valuation", *Abacus*, December 1967, pp 107–32. The uncertainty which pervades business life and the need to exercise judgment in the measurement of profit and the assessment of asset values have bred an attitude of caution and the belief that, in the reporting of the profit and state of affairs of a business firm, it is better to be on the side of caution. For example, the principle of realization prohibits the recognition of gains until these have been realized by way of sale; on the other hand it is a generally accepted accounting principle to provide for anticipated losses, as is done by the writing down of inventories to market value when this falls below cost, and by creating provision for doubtful debts.

In the past, the doctrine of conservatism has been used to justify the deliberate understatement of assets and overstatement of liabilities with the resulting creation of secret reserves. For example, at the beginning of the century the undervaluation of assets and the creation of secret reserves was generally approved by the courts and the accounting profession. The practice was discredited, however, following the celebrated Lord Kylsant case and the consequent moves towards fuller disclosure in financial statements: for a discussion on secret reserves see T R Johnston, M O Jager and R B Taylor, *The Law and Practice of Company Accounting in Australia*, 6th Ed, Butterworths, 1987, pp 89–92; or T R Johnston, G C Edgar and P L Hays, *The Law and Practice of Company Accounting in New Zealand*, 6th Ed, Butterworths, Wellington, 1986, pp 98–102.

In the modern setting, conservatism can be conceived of as that degree of prudence in accounting measurement and reporting which is required by the uncertainty and risk attaching to business operations. At the same time it should be kept in mind that undue conservatism can produce misleading financial statements and be as harmful to the interests of users of financial statements, such as shareholders and investors, as excessive optimism. Further, the undue conservatism of one period may well be reflected in a higher profit figure in the next.

(8) Matching expense with revenue

[717] Profit is traditionally measured by matching expense with revenue. Implicit in this process is the concept that expense measures the resources given up in the process of earning revenue and revenue represents the inflow of resources as a result of operations. Profit then is the net increment to the total resources of the enterprise.

The process of matching expense with revenue in detail may make it possible to determine the sources from which profit was derived, such as particular operating and investment activities.

An alternative method for the measurement of profit, which would produce similar reuslts, would be to value, on the basis of generally accepted accounting principles, the net assets of the enterprise at the beginning and end of an accounting period and then to take as profit the increase in net assets after making appropriate adjustments for any contributions to capital, or profit distributions. Such a profit figure, however, would be of limited informational value because of the lack of detail.

[718] A narrow view of the matching concept would require matching on the basis of a cause and effect relationship between expense and revenue — it would require some positive correlation between expense and revenue. Such a positive correlation, however, does not always exist, as not all cost inputs result in revenue. For

example, the expense of calls by salesmen, in the short run at least, may be incurred regardless of revenue. Further, the revenue effect of some kinds of expenditure, such as advertizing, is difficult to determine. The fact that depreciation is largely regarded as a fixed cost indicates that at least a significant portion of depreciation is unrelated to the level of operations. Also, since only expenditures which embody benefits to future business operations may be properly carried forward, many costs would have to be written off in a given period simply because they are not regarded as containing such future benefits.

In the measurement of profit, therefore, the matching concept is conceived within a broader context than one requiring a narrow cause and effect relationship between expense and revenue. Rather than matching in a narrow sense, we may speak broadly of allocating expenses to different accounting periods. The major problems in this process of allocation are the difficulties and subjectivity involved in determining the future benefits embodied in unexpired expenditures such as, for example, research and development costs, and in assets generally. Further, the quality of the profit figure determined by means of the matching process will be affected by the accounting principles applied in the recognition and measurement of assets and asset-related expenses, in the recognition of revenue, in the recognition and measurement of liabilities, and in dealing with uncertainty.

The Uncertainty Factor

[719] The analysis and interpretation of financial statements is usually carried out with the future in mind. The common objective is to use data drawn from the past as a guide to the future. Projections based on the study of the past events depicted in financial statements require the exercise of judgment and will be permeated with uncertainty. What may not be so readily apparent to the lay reader of financial statements, however, is the extent to which opinion and judgment affect the accounting evaluation of the past events that is reported in published financial statements and therefore, the potentially high degree of uncertainty which may attach to the figures contained in these statements which the reader is using as a basis for projection.

The uncertainty attaching to accounting measurement arises from the allocation of costs and revenues among accounting periods (in particular joint costs and revenues) and the determination of period income by matching the costs and revenues so allocated. As the allocation of joint costs and revenues to different accounting periods is, unavoidably, a subjective exercise reflecting expectations about the future (for example, regarding the collectibility of debtors, the market value of inventories, expected economic lives of fixed assets, etc) accounting income measurement is "conditional' in nature in the sense that the fairness (or otherwise) of the expectations embodied in the income figure can be judged only in the light of future events.

Since continuing operations require continuing reinvestment in assets, income measurement will be "conditional" to the extent of the values assigned to assets carried forward into successive accounting periods. This "conditionality" of accounting income measurement is "in the nature of things" as far as the subject matter of accounting is concerned and cannot be avoided. In the accounting context, therefore, the "truth" and "fairness" of what is reported as "income" and "state of affairs" must, to a very large extent, relate to the exercise of informed and responsible judgment regarding expectations about the future.

Since uncertainty is inherent in business operations and cannot be avoided in accounting measurement, it must be given adequate recognition in any analysis and interpretation of financial statements. For example, the level of uncertainty regarding income and asset measurement is affected by changes in the nature and spread of investment in assets and by changes in the prospects for the particular enterprise. To illustrate, a higher investment in finished stock by a manufacturer, offset by a lower investment in raw materials may indicate a rise in the level of uncertainty regarding the measurement of period income and of inventory.

The Form and Content of Financial Statements

[720] In an enterprise of even average size and complexity the need for accountability and for effective planning and control of each segment of the undertaking makes it essential to incorporate a large number of accounts in the data processing system. Financial statements prepared for senior management will consolidate the detail to some extent, in order to make communication easier and to provide a broader picture. Further consolidation and condensation is necessary in preparing the published financial statements. There are space constraints — reports are costly to produce and to circulate. There are also communication constraints. Most of the readers will be concerned with the broad picture of the undertaking as a whole, and excessive detail may hamper the communication of that broad view. There are also constraints of privacy. Management may consider it desirable for competitive and other reasons to restrict the information that is given in a public report.

For these reasons, financial statements prepared under current reporting practice are likely to lack important details which, if disclosed, will greatly facilitate the decisions of users of financial statements. As currently prepared, financial statements lack detail both laterally and vertically. By this is meant that separate transactions coming within a certain classification are grouped together, and similar transactions occurring at different times during an accounting period are grouped also. The result is not only a lack of detailed information on the nature of each item, but also a lack of knowledge of trends during the accounting period. For example, information about the trend in sales towards the end of the accounting period may be necessary in order to determine the reasonableness or otherwise of the reported amounts of trade debtors and inventories. Further, it is quite possible to have a situation where the total sales this year are higher than those for last year, but where the trend in sales is actually falling because sales towards the end of the year are lower than those for the same months of the preceding year.

[721] The lack of detail is particularly evident in the statements of diversified companies and company groups. The problem here relates to the interpretation of the financial statements of companies or the consolidated financial statements of company groups involved in diverse business activities which carry different degrees of risk, rates of profitability, and opportunities for growth. Where these variations are significant, the analysis and interpretation of the aggregated data contained in the financial statements will be difficult and may yield information of limited value for the projection of future trends. Consider for example the case of a

brewery which owns and operates a chain of hotels and taverns. While an analysis of the aggregate results of the company will yield some useful information, it will be considerably more informative, from the viewpoint of evaluating the performance of the company, to analyse the separate results and profitability of brewing and hotel and tavern ownership.

[722] Financial statements deal with past events. To most of the people who examine financial statements the future is more important than the past. Financial statements reveal only partially and indirectly the basic factors affecting the future of the business. Vital matters are prospective changes in management, development plans, forward orders in hand, improvements in productive efficiency, plans for bonus share issues and the like. Information on these matters must be sought largely outside the financial statements.

[723] The interpreter of financial statements may also encounter difficulties in relating results to managerial decisions. The profits attributed in financial statements to particular periods reflect the decisions and performance of management not just in the current year but also to some extent in earlier years: for example, current performance may be to a considerable extent the result of capital investment decisions in the past. Similarly, the wisdom of current long-term decisions may not become evident until several years have passed.

[724] Finally, the preparation of financial statements involves choice and judgment. Bias may affect the choice and judgment of those responsible for the preparation of financial statements and, therefore, the contents of the statements and the manner in which they are presented.

The Effect of the Human Element on the Preparation, Presentation and Interpretation of Financial Statements

[725] Financial statements are prepared by people and are analysed, interpreted and acted upon by people. The human element in the process is reflected in the judgment, subjectivity and bias which may, and do, enter into the preparation and presentation, and the analysis and interpretation of financial statements. The quality of financial statements depends on the skill, honesty and fairness of those who prepare them and those who give formal opinion on them. Equally, the quality of the analysis and interpretation of financial statements for the benefits of decision-makers is dependent on the skill, honesty and fairness of the analysts and interpreters.

[726] As far as the preparation and presentation of financial statements is concerned, the effect of the human element relates to the choice of accounting principles from available alternatives and the manner and extent of disclosure. Areas where options regarding accounting methods and procedures are available include depreciation, inventory valuation, taxation, accounting for research and development costs, foreign exchange transactions, leases, and the cost of major maintenance and renewals. The decison made by management regarding the choice of accounting methods may be motivated by other than purely "accounting" consid-

erations with their overriding aim of producing financial statements which give a "true and fair view" of profit and state of affairs.

For example, selecting the "flow through" method of accounting for the tax benefit arising from investment allowances will increase the reported profit for the period; decisions regarding the timing of major maintenance and renewals may be affected by available finance and reportable profit, while the accounting treatment of the cost of major maintenance and renewals (for example, the extent to which such cost is treated as a current expense or is capitalized) may be influenced by tax considerations such as the amount the company is allowed to claim as a tax deduction. During periods of inflation, there is evidence to suggest that company management has attempted to get the "best of both worlds" by reporting what appear to be record profits to shareholders and investors and, at the same time, stressing the illusory nature of such profits when seeking tax concessions or relaxation of price and profit controls from the government, or resisting union demands for higher wages.

[727] Regarding the interpretation of financial statements, bias may be reflected in an attitude of interested parties to see in reported figures what they want to see. For example, management, consumers, and organized labour could well come to different conclusions regarding the ability of a company to, say, hold prices or pay higher wages by looking at the same reported profit figures.

[728] Regarding the effect of the human element on the presentation of financial reports, let us look at three examples from published company reports (the examples are not intended to be exhaustive).

Example 7.1

In 19A1 company A reported net profit after tax of $1,139,000. During the year the company had incurred overseas exchange losses of $1,094,000. In its published profit and loss statement the company deducted the overseas exchange losses after the amount of unappropriated profit brought forward from the preceding year had been added to the current year's profit so leaving the reported profit for 19A1 at $1,139,000. Had the overseas exchange losses been charged against the profits for the year, the reported profit would have been $45,000. The following year (19A2) the reported profit of the company after tax but exclusive of overseas exchange losses was $3,351,000. Exchange losses for the year amounted to $807,000. That year the company charged its exchange losses directly against current profits and reported profit after tax of $2,544,000.

Example 7.2

Company B deals in insurance. In 19A1 the company had incurred a deficit of $264,000 on compulsory third party motor insurance which, when set of against the surpluses the company had generated from underwriting and life insurance, left a reported net loss for the year of $35,000. The following year (19A2) the deficit from third party insurance incurred by the company was $614,000. That year, this deficit was shown in the income statement of the company opposite the corresponding figure for 19A1 but rather than being deducted from the surpluses from underwriting and life insurance, as had been done in the previous year, it was explained in the notes to the accounts that the deficit had been transferred to general reserve. As a result, the company reported a net profit of $203,000. Had the deficit been treated in a manner consistent with the previous year, the company would have reported a loss of $411,000. No attention was drawn in the accounts to the effect of this inconsistency in the treatment of the third party motor insurance deficit in the two years.

Example 7.3

It is necessary for the interpreter of financial reports to treat graphical and similar illustrations of numerical data with considerable caution. This is made evident from the example which follows.

In its annual report company C included graphs to illustrate the growth of shareholders' funds, profits and dividends, over a period of 10 years. The graphs were shown side by side and are reproduced in Figure 7.1 (p 124). In studying the graphs it is important to note the differences in the scale in which they are drawn. For example, the horizontal scale of the graph showing growth in profits and dividends for the 10-year period is smaller than that of the graph showing growth of shareholders' funds. On the vertical scale of the profit graph the distance used to show $100,000 of profit is equivalent to the distance used to show $3 million on the graph illustrating the growth in shareholders' funds. The combined result is a profit line which rises much more steeply than the line showing growth in shareholders' funds, indicating, presumably, a rising rate of return. An examination of the report revealed that the company had been expanding by a series of takeovers. No mention was made of rates of return in the 19-year trend statement shown in the report. The rates of return for each of the 10 years, however, could be calculated from the figures in the trend statement and are shown graphically in Figure 7.2 (p 125). The trend in the rate of return is quite different from that which may be suggested by a cursory examination of the graphs in Figure 7.1.

Review questions

7.1 "The objective of brevity in financial reporting is to highlight material items."
"Financial statements as currently prepared are likely to lack important details which, if disclosed, will facilitate the decisions of the users of the statements."
Discuss. Can you reconcile these apparently conflicting viewpoints regarding the contents and degree of disclosure in financial statements?

7.2 What special problems may arise in the analysis and interpretation of the financial statements of diversified companies and company groups?

7.3 "Financial statements reveal only partially and indirectly the basic factors affecting the future of the business."
Discuss.

7.4 Why is it important that the analyst and interpreter of financial statements understands the principles on which the statements are prepared?

7.5 Discuss the use of the monetary unit as a basis for accounting measurement and reporting.

7.6 How does the continuity assumption affect the reporting of profit and state of affairs of business enterprises?

7.7 Explain the accounting principles of consistency and comparability. To what extent does the consistent application of a set of accounting principles ensure comparability in the financial statements of a firm over time and the financial statements of different firms at a point of time?

FIGURE 7.1

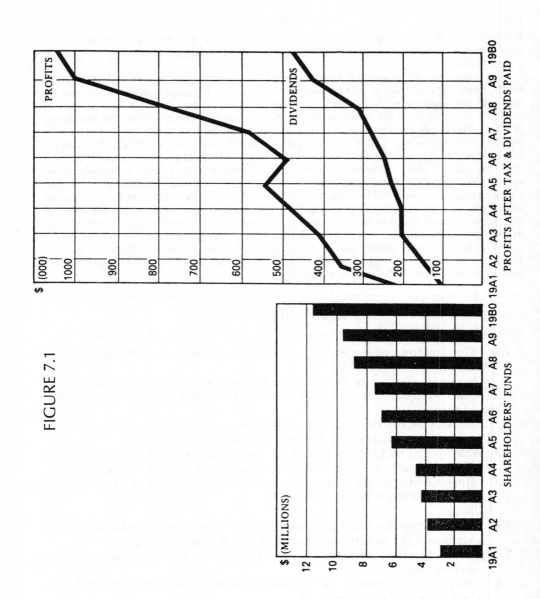

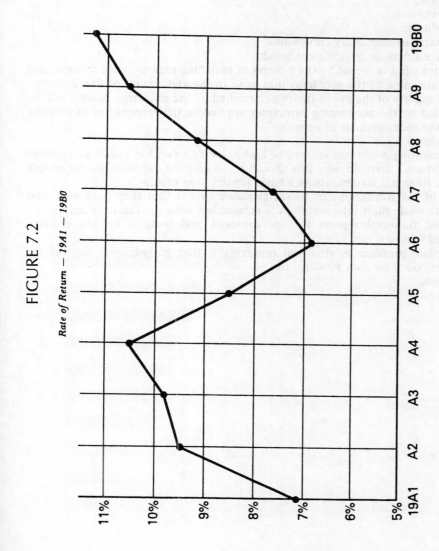

FIGURE 7.2

Rate of Return — 19A1 — 19B0

7.8 Consider the effect of the historical cost convention and the doctrine of conservatism on each of the following types of assets shown in the balance sheet of a manufacturer who has been in business for 25 years:
- land;
- buildings;
- plant;
- inventories;
- debtors;
- shares in subsidiary companies;
- investment in government bonds.

7.9 Explain what is meant by the process of matching expense with revenue and indicate some of the problems that arise in the application of this process.

7.10 "The quality of the profit figure determined by the matching process will be affected by the accounting principles applied in the recognition of revenue and the measurement of expense."
Discuss.

7.11 "Accounting profit can seldom be looked on as a fact but rather as a matter of opinion." Explain why this should be so and the implications for people using financial statements as a basis for decision-making.

7.12 One of the limitations of financial statements is that they deal with past events while their interpretation is carried out with the future in mind.
Should financial reports include forecasts and budgets for the ensuing period?

7.13 "A basic problem in financial reporting is that management control the reports on their own stewardship."
Discuss.

Chapter 8
Problems of Interpretation and Limitations of Ratio Analysis

[801] It was pointed out in Chapter 6 that accounting numbers have little informational value if taken by themselves — their informational value is obtained by relating them to other numbers through the processes of comparison and analysis. An adequate appreciation of their significance may be dependent on knowledge of the data from which they have been derived, and, further back still, of the sets of circumstances and actions which produced the primary data. Percentages and ratios are used to study the relative importance of absolute amounts, in particular where a significant relationship exists between components of financial statements such as, equity and debt, current assets and current liabilities, revenue and expense, and profit and investment.

The analysis of financial statements by means of ratios and percentages, however, is subject to a number of limitations. Some of these limitations relate to the nature of financial statements and the data disclosed in them; others are inherent in the financial ratios themselves. An understanding of the limitations of financial ratios as analytical tools is essential if ratio analysis is to be employed usefully in the interpretation of financial statements.

Let us consider some of these limitations.

Lack of Detail

[802] The data disclosed in financial statements lack details — they are summaries of many transactions and totals of often diverse items within a class. The lack of details relates both to trends within an accounting period and to the "mix" factor (composition) of totals.

For example, a reported sales figure will lack details of trends during the accounting period and in particular towards the end of the period. There may be little detail regarding sales mix such as sales by products, divisional sales in a company group, sales by territories and market segments, and local and export sales.

[803] The submerging of detail in totals will hinder the analysis of expenses. Such analysis involves the breaking down of expenses into significant classes, the comparison of the amounts with previous years and with budget, and the relating of expense items to some base, such as sales, which is assumed to have a significant bearing on the amount of the particular expense items. The lack of detail regarding expenses in published financial statements gives little scope for analysis of this kind. Where detail is provided expenses may be compared with the preceding year and percentages of expenses to sales may be calculated and compared. However,

where a total under a particular expense classification is an aggregate of diverse items (for example, selling expenses disclosed as one total), it may not be possible to determine the extent to which individual items and, therefore, the aggregate can be expected to vary with sales. Further, it may not be possible to determine if there have been any significant changes in the "mix" of expenses from the preceeding year which could affect the comparability of the data for the two years.

[804] Lack of detail in the published statements of diversified companies means that often averages have to be used in the analysis and interpretation of the results of operations — for example, average rate of return and average rates of inventory turnover. Averages are seldom useful for decision-making; rates of return by segments and rates of inventory turnover by product lines will be more informative. For example, it is more useful to know that the rate of return in one segment of a business is 5% and in another 15% than to know that the rate of return overall is, say, 10%. The issue of segment reporting is discussed in Chapter 15.

The Relevance of Financial Data

[805] Added to the problem of lack of detail is the problem of the relevance of reported financial data to the purposes for which the data are used. The latter problem arises largely from the principles used in accounting measurement and valuation (such as historical cost, realization and conservatism), and the methods and procedures applied in dealing with specific accounting problems (such as inventory valuation, depreciation, the valuation of fixed assets, the measurement of investments, accounting for the cost of major maintenance and renewals, for income taxes, for foreign exchange differences, etc).

[806] Some of the major limitations of accounting data arising from the principles used in accounting measurement and valuation were discussed in Chapter 7. Problems associated with and limitations of financial data arising from the application of accounting methods and procedures in specific areas of accounting measurement and valuation are discussed in subsequent chapters.

The Effects of Price and Price Level Changes

[807] The usefulness of financial data and ratios derived from them depends on how well they represent reality.

In Chapter 7 we pointed out two fundamental deficiencies of current accounting practice: its failure to apply a constant measuring unit in the determination and evaluation of the results and state of affairs of a business firm, and, generally, its failure to reflect the current value of assets to the firm given current costs and prices and the expectations of the firm regarding its future operations. As a result, in periods of significant price and price level changes, financial statement presentations may be far removed from the reality they are supposed to portray. In interpreting financial statements, the analyst should be aware of these deficiencies and the effects of any revaluations of assets.

Let us take some examples.

(a) Assessment of profitability

[808] The profit performance of a business firm is usually measured by the rate of return. The rate of return concentrates on the relationship between the amount of profit and the resources used in generating the profit — shareholders' funds or total investment in assets. The formula for the calculation of the rate of return (ROR) is

$$\text{ROR} = \frac{\text{Profit}}{\text{Investment}} \times 100$$

In times of rising prices and inflation, traditional accounting will report an overstated profit figure and an understated investment in assets. The resulting rate of return will compound the deficiencies of the component figures.

(b) Evaluation of proprietary (equity/debt) position

[809] Because the balance sheet does not reflect the current value of assets, it will be difficult to evaluate the proprietary (equity/debt) position of the firm at a point of time and changes over time.

(c) Evaluation of borrowing capacity

[810] A measure of the capacity of a firm to raise additional long-term loans may be obtained by expressing existing long-term loans as a percentage of fixed assets, in particular property. As security for loans is assessed on the basis of the current value of assets, in times of rising prices this percentage may understate the borrowing capacity of the firm if the book value of assets is significantly lower than their current value.

(d) Sales comparisons

[811] In times of inflation reported sales increases may be largely fictional, as, for example, the reporting of a 10% increase in sales during a period in which 15% inflation has taken place.

Window Dressing of Balance Sheets

[812] It is possible to "window dress" a balance sheet. This may take the form of pre-balance sales, of reduced buying prior to balance date, of delaying of payments until after balance date, of temporary realization of assets, and even of temporary loans. Window dressed balance sheets mean window dressed balance sheet ratios. For example, a delay of inventory purchases on credit in the last month of the financial year until after balance date will "improve" the current ratio reported at the end of the year; similarly, a liquid ratio of less than 1:1 can be brought closer to 1:1 by increasing "quick" borrowing. This is illustrated in Example 8.1.

The Balance Sheet is a Still Picture of an Ongoing Concern

[813] The balance sheet is a still picture at a point of time of an ongoing concern. Continuity of operations means that the position of the firm is in a state of

Example 8.1

Window dressing of balance sheet ratios

Current ratio

	Position if purchases not delayed $	Amount of purchases delayed $	Reported current position $
Current assets	450,000	50,000	400,000
Current liabilities	250,000	50,000	200,000
Current ratio	1.8:1		2:1

Liquid ratio

	Position at end of year $	Increase in "quick" borrowing $	Reported liquid position $
Liquid assets	240,000	100,000	340,000
Quick liabilities	380,000	100,000	480,000
Liquid ratio	0.63:1		0.71:1

continuous change over time — within the timespan of an accounting period and from one accounting period to another.

[814] In the study of the results of operations and position of a business firm over time we are likely to discern certain monthly and annual cycles. For example, there will be a monthly cycle of cash receipts from trade debtors and cash payments to trade creditors. For many companies the accounting period of one year will coincide broadly with what may be termed a trading cycle. At certain points in the annual cycle, the position disclosed is affected by the annual determination of profit, the assessment of liability for taxation, the declaration of dividends, and the payment of taxation and dividends.

It follows that the current position of the firm at the middle of the month may be quite different from that at the end of the month. Similarly, a balance sheet taken at, say, 31 July may produce a set of financial ratios which are significantly different from those derived from a balance sheet taken at 31 December, as in the case of a manufacturer building up inventories during the year for a seasonal peak of retail sales during the Christmas period.

[815] Ratios calculated at a point of time to test aspects of the economic condition of the firm need to be used with considerable care. Let us take for example the current ratio. It is calculated at a point of time and may be used as an indicator of the solvency of the firm — the ability of the firm to pay its debts as they fall due. Yet the solvency of a business firm depends primarily on the amounts and timing of future receipts and payments over time and not on the relationship, between current assets and current liabilities at a point of time.

Some Inherent Limitations of Financial Ratios as Tools of Analysis

[816] It should be evident from the discussion so far that, in the analysis of financial statements, ratios and percentages should be used with caution. For example, the ratio and percentages will reflect the limitations of the data on which they are based. Further limitations may be introduced into the analysis of financial data because of the nature of the percentages and ratios themselves.

Percentages and ratios are used to analyse significant economic relationships between components of financial statements. The calculation of a percentage or a ratio requires the compression of financial data into two totals which are then related. Problems, however, may arise from the following:

(a) the loss of detail and the submerging of some quality factors; and

(b) the complexity of the relationships being analysed and studied.

Let us consider these in turn.

(a) Loss of detail and the submerging of some quality factors

[817] The data disclosed in financial statements often lacks important detail because it has been compressed and summarized. The use of such data in the calculation of financial ratios may require its further compression into totals. The result may be a further loss of detail and the submerging of some important quality factors underlying the composition of the totals. Let us consider the current ratio as an example.

[818] The principal current assets included in the calculation of the current ratio are cash, inventories, debtors and marketable securities. The rate of flow through of current assets into cash will vary. For example, the work in progress of a major contractor may include work done on which there can be no recovery for several months; debtors may be on monthly or time payment terms; the rate of inventory turnover may be high or low. In other words, a quality factor enters into the current ratio calculation, and may be relevant to an assessment of the significance of the ratio.

Current liabilities include bank overdraft, trade creditors, bills payable, accrued charges, loans maturing within a year, provision for current income tax, and provision for dividend.

The composition of current assets and current liabilities is important. The relative proportions of cash, inventories and debtors affect solvency. Some substantial current liabilities may be semi-permanent in nature (bank overdraft may be at least partly in this category), or not payable until several months later, as with the provision for taxation.

[819] It should be evident, therefore, that an effective interpretation of the current ratio as an indicator of solvency would require an analysis of the components of current assets and liabilities and a study of the changes in the composition of current assets and liabilities over time. Let us look at Example 8.2 which compares the 19A1 and 19A2 end-of-year current assets and current liabilities of the A Co Ltd and the company's current ratio at the end of the two years.

The figures in Example 8.2 show similar *totals* for current assets and current

Example 8.2

A Co Ltd
Current assets and current liabilities

	19A1 $	19A2 $
Current assets		
Trade debtors	123,000	99,000
Inventories	200,000	240,000
	323,000	339,000
Current liabilities		
Trade creditors	50,000	51,000
Bank overdraft	35,000	104,000
Provision for dividend	40,000	30,000
Provision for tax	90,000	40,000
	215,000	225,000
Current ratio	1.5:1	1.5:1

liabilities at the end of the two years and a stable current ratio at 1.5:1. A conclusion may be reached from a superficial examination of the totals of current assets and current liabilities and the current ratios that there has been no significant change in the solvency position of the company during 19A2.

[820] A closer examination of the composition of the current assets and current liabilities at the end of the two years, however, reveals a different picture. Trade debtors have dropped by $24,000 or 18.6%, inventories have increased by $40,000 or 20%, trade creditors are up by $1000 or 2% and bank overdraft has trebled from $35,000 to $104,000. At the same time the provision for dividend has been reduced from $40,000 to $30,000 and the amount provided for taxation at the end of 19A2 is $40,000 compared with $90,000 at the end of 19A1. Let us examine the possible significance of these changes.

The drop in the amount of debtors and the significant increase in the level of inventories at the end of 19A2 may indicate a major downturn in sales in the last months of 19A2 with a resulting build up of unsold inventories. At least there is reason to conclude that at the end of 19A2 sales may well have been running at a considerably lower level than in 19A1. A result of such a downturn in trading could have been a drop in the profit of the company. The much reduced amount provided for taxation at the end of 19A2 and the reduction in the provision for dividend do suggest that there has been a large fall in profit in 19A2. While, on the face of it, there has been only a marginal increase of $1000 or 2% in trade creditors, this increase related to possible lower sales and (presumably) a reduced level of purchases may indicate a deterioration in the liquidity position of the company resulting in a slow payment of creditors. The much increased reliance on bank overdraft in 19A2 also indicates at least some liquidity difficulties. To conclude, the provision and study of the detail has indicated a need for further inquiry which would not have been evident from the totals and the ratios alone.

(b) Complexity of relationships

[821] Business events (and the data they produce) involve a mix of interacting processes operating in a changing environment. The data which they produce reflect this interaction. Financial data alone are often an inadequate expression of the processes which underlie business events. Similarly, financial ratios and percentages as tools of analysis are often inadequate to capture the complex relationships which exist within the business situation.

For example, a relationship exists between delivery expenses and sales which may be studied by expressing delivery expenses as a percentage of sales and comparing the percentage from one period to another. The relationship, however, may be too complex to be captured by the interrelating of two totals, since it may be affected by selling prices, product mix, market mix, order size, freight rates, means of transport, delivery times, etc.

[822]   A complicating factor in the analysis of expenses by relating them to a volume base such as sales is the fact that at least part of most expenses is fixed in relation to sales. For example, a reduction in the percentage of administration expenses to sales may suggest higher efficiency and better use of resources in the admininistrative area, whereas the facts may be that these expenses are largely fixed in nature and the reduction in the percentage is due to an increased sales figure (which in turn may be due to an increase in prices rather than an increase in volume).

The Need for Standards in Ratio Analysis

[823] It is a relatively simple matter to select and to calculate ratios which are regarded as significant — but considerable care is required in their interpretation. It is not just that the data are drawn from a complex environment, and that the nature of the relationships between the data is also complex. There are more elementary reasons for care in interpretation.

For example, it does not necessarily follow that if, in a given set of circumstances, an increase in a particular financial ratio indicates improvement in the position of the firm, then the higher the ratio the better. Too high a current ratio may mean an inefficienct use of working capital, and too high a proprietary ratio may indicate a failure on the part of the firm to utilize relatively cheap borrowed funds. What then is the optimal size for a particular financial ratio?

[824] Because business firms are different, there are no standard ratios which are applicable to all firms. Some general standards have been suggested such as that the current and liquid ratios should not be less than 2:1 and 1:1 respectively, and that the shareholders' equity should not be less than 50% of total assets. The use of such arbitrary standards in practice does not indicate that they are useful in all circumstances. Indeed the cynic would say that they are properly regarded as little better than financial folklore. What is an appropriate ratio would depend rather on the nature of the firm's business and on its particular circumstances. For example, a retailer selling for cash will normally be able to operate on a significantly lower current ratio than a manufacturer having a lengthy production period and carrying substantial stocks of raw materials. A new firm with good prospects and a high

credit rating may begin with a high level of borrowing (low proprietary ratio) and let its proprietary position build up through profit retention as the operations of the firm develop.

[825] Industry averages have been used as a way out of the problem of determining ratio standards. The approach is useful to the extent that it reflects common experience of firms in an industry. It is questionable, however, whether industry averages can be used to determine optimal ratio sizes. Alternatively, guides to ratio standards may be sought in the experience of trendsetting firms, keeping in mind the diversity of size, conditions and stages of development of firms within an industry, and differences in managerial attitudes regarding financing and risk.

Ratio analysis creates special problems when related to the financial statements of diversified firms. In such cases ratio analysis and standards may be meaningful only when applied to definable and reasonably independent segments of the firm.

Summary

[826] Ratios are not important in themselves; they are important as indicators of the economic conditions which underlie the operations and state of affairs of the firm, and then they may not always be reliable indicators.

Ratios should supplement, not supplant financial data. They do not necessarily provide the final answer. While ratios may point out areas which require further investigation, a careful analysis of the underlying data and the events and conditions from which the data arose may be necessary before a conclusion is reached. Above all, quick conclusions based on superficial examination of ratios should be avoided. Let us illustrate this last point with a rather extreme example.

Example 8.3

Shown below is a four year comparison of the current assets, current liabilities, working capital and current ratio of a New Zealand cement works of some years ago.

	19A1 $	19A2 $	19A3 $	19A4 $
Current assets	217,577	198,324	163,969	227,617
Current liabilities	155,973	248,201	488,200	448,507
Working capital	61,604	−49,877	−324,231	−220,890
Current ratio	1.4:1	0.8:1	0.34:1	0.51:1

[827] The above figures indicate what appears to be a very unsatisfactory current position for the firm with negative working capital for three of the four years and a current ratio of less than 1:1. An examination of other trend figures from the company's published reports showed that during the period the company had expanded its fixed assets from $278,900 at the end of 19A1 to $990,000 at the end of 19A4. The sharp deterioration in the working capital and current position of the firm was caused by the increase in fixed assets being partly financed from short-term borrowing, in particular, bank overdraft. The figures indicated a classical case of a firm finding itself in severe liquidity difficulties because it had disregarded the cardinal rule that the acquisition of long-term assets should not be financed from short-term sources. A closer study of the case, however, revealed a different picture. The expansion of the company's production capacity had been undertaken in order

to meet demand for cement because of pending construction of hydro-electric dams in the proximity of the works. The overdraft of the company had been guaranteed by the government and had been used to partly finance the expansion of fixed assets because of its convenience and relatively low interest cost.

Review questions

8.1 "Ratio analysis should be used with caution because of the limitations inherent in the ratios themselves."
Discuss

8.2 "Averages are seldom useful for decision-making."
Discuss in relation to the interpretation of an overall inventory turnover rate and an overall rate of return of a diversified enterprise.

8.3 "Financial data alone are often an inadequate expression of the processes which underlie business events."
Discuss.

8.4 "The balance sheet is a still picture of an ongoing concern."
Discuss in relation to the limitations of the balance sheet as a statement of financial position.

8.5 The following are the sales figures of XY Co Ltd for the last five years:

19A5	19A4	19A3	19A2	19A1
$1,180,000	$1,100,000	$1,050,000	$900,000	$1,000,000

Comment on the above sales figures and list any further details you would require to facilitate you in your analysis and interpretation of the trends shown.

8.6 How useful for the analysis and interpretation of operating results is the relating of expenses to sales?

8.7 How reliable a guide to solvency is the current ratio?

8.8 The following are the current ratios of three firms in the same line of business:
A Ltd 1.9:1   B Ltd 2.3:1   C Ltd 2.5:1
Which of the three firms is best able to pay its debts as they fall due?

8.9 Discuss the need to consider the composition of current assets and current liabilities in the use of the current ratio as a guide to solvency.

Chapter 9
Some Examples of Analysis and Interpretation

[901] In this chapter we shall consider three examples of analysis and interpretation. The purpose of the examples is to illustrate the application of some of the analytical techniques considered previously before extending our discussion into some major problem areas of financial reporting such as inventory valuation, depreciation, taxation, foreign currency transactions, and a more detailed discussion of the problems associated with accounting for the effects of price changes.

Example 9.1
Superficial Interpretation

Shown below, in abbreviated form, are the end-of-year accounts of Downtown Traders Co Ltd prepared by its recently appointed young accountant. The company owns premises in an important city shopping area.

Downtown Traders Co Ltd
Operating statement for year ended 31 March 19A5

	19A5 $	19A5 $	19A4 $	19A4 $
Sales		1,760,000		1,600,000
Less cost of sales				
Opening stock	312,000		304,000	
Purchases	1,435,200		1,227,200	
	1,747,200		1,531,200	
Less ending stock	374,400	1,372,800	312,000	1,219,200
Gross profit		387,200		380,800
Less expenses				
Wages and salaries	192,000		188,800	
Advertising	96,000		80,000	
Maintenance	12,800		10,360	
Rates and insurance	7,000		6,400	
Depreciation				
Buildings	3,840		3,840	
Other	4,800		5,280	
General expenses	6,670	323,200	6,120	300,800
Net profit before tax		64,000		80,000
Provision for tax		24,000		31,360
Net profit after tax		40,000		48,640

Appropriation statement

	19A5 $	19A4 $
Undistributed profit brought forward	40,000	23,360
Net profit for year	40,000	48,640
	80,000	72,000
Less provision for dividend 10%	32,000	32,000
	48,000	40,000

Balance sheet as at 31 March 19A5

	19A5 $	19A5 $	19A4 $	19A4 $
Equities side				
Authorized and issued capital				
320,000 ordinary shares of $1 fully paid		320,000		320,000
Revenue reserves				
General reserve	112,000		112,000	
Appropriation account	48,000	160,000	40,000	152,000
Shareholders' funds		480,000		472,000
Current liabilities				
Trade creditors	76,800		96,640	
Provision for taxation	24,000		31,360	
Provision for dividend	32,000	132,800	32,000	160,000
		612,800		632,000
Asset side				
Fixed assets				
Land and buildings, at cost	192,000		192,000	
Less depreciation to date	76,800	115,200	72,960	119,040
Plant, fittings and vehicles, at cost	73,600		72,000	
Less depreciation to date	32,000	41,600	27,200	44,800
Goodwill		8,000		8,000
		164,800		171,840
Current assets				
Bank	22,400		100,000	
Stocks	374,400		312,000	
Debtors	51,200	448,000	48,160	460,160
		612,800		632,000

The examples are relatively simple and are concerned with superficial interpretation (Example 9.1), routine analysis and comparability of data (Example 9.2), and intercompany comparison and the financing of expansion (Example 9.3).

The following are the main points in the report of the company accountant to the directors of the company on the results for the year:

(1) Sales

[902] Sales are up 10% on last year. This is a satisfactory increase. In view of the 19A3 sales of $1,520,000 a very favourable trend is apparent.

(2) Inventory turnover

[903] In spite of the higher inventory level at 31 March 19A5, stock turnover has been maintained at approximately four times per year. This indicates that the company's efficiency in the merchandizing of goods is being maintained.

(3) Gross profit

[904] There has been a slight fall in the rate of gross profit from 23.8% to 22%, a fall of 1.8%. The gross profit rate for 19A3 was 23.5%. However, in spite of the fall in the gross profit rate, the amount of gross profit in 19A5 has increased by $6400.

(4) Expenses

[905] Expenses have increased by $22,400, the major increases being in advertizing $16,000; salaries and wages $3200; maintenance $2540. In view of the fall in net profit which is discussed below, these expenses should be kept firmly under control.

(5) Net profit

[906] Net profit before tax is down $16,000 on last year in spite of the increase in the amount of gross profit. This is due mainly to the higher expenses incurred (see (4) above). The rate of net profit before tax to sales is 3.64% compared with 5% last year, a fall of 1.36%. This is partly compensated by the reduced taxation cost (down $7360).

(6) Current ratio

[907] The current ratio of the company is 3.4:1 compared with 2.9:1 last year. There is no hard and fast rule regarding what the current ratio should be but a ratio of 2:1 is generally considered to be adequate. The liquidity position of the firm, therefore, is particularly good.

(7) Balance sheet

[908] The balance sheet of the company is really better than it looks in view of the recent offers made to the company to either:
   (a) sell the property for $400,000, or
   (b) lease the property for 10 years at a rental of $40,000 per year (plus rates and insurance premiums).

Required:

Comment on the report given by the accountant to the directors of the company under the seven points given above.

Some possible comments

[909] The report on the financial statements of the Downtown Traders Co Ltd has been prepared by the accountant of the company. Unlike external users who must rely primarily on the data disclosed in the financial statements for their analysis and conclusions, he has access to details regarding the operating results and state of affairs of the firm which should facilitate his analysis and interpretation. What stands out about the report of the accountant is the superficiality of his comments, his failure to study the details underlying the summarized data in the statement and, therefore, his failure to produce a detailed, well-reasoned, and informative report for the use of the directors of the company.

Let us consider in turn the seven points raised in the report:

(1) Sales

[910] The report fails to consider a number of important considerations in an analysis of sales such as:
   (i) the extent to which the increase is the result of increases in selling prices or of the volume of goods and services sold;
  (ii) any changes in sales mix;
 (iii) a comparison of the sales performance with other firms in the same trade in order to determine relative performance;
  (iv) a comparison with budgeted sales in order to determine the extent to which management has attained its objectives;
   (v) trends in sales over the 19A5 year as an indication of possible sales trends in the coming period.

Answers to these questions may well indicate that the level of sales achieved was far from satisfactory and that the sales trend towards the end of the year was in fact unfavourable.

(2) Inventory turnover

[911] The calculation shows an overall inventory turnover based on opening and closing stock. Information about the rates of turnover by products or sections of the business would be more useful to management.

There is no indication that the comments regarding the inventory turnover are the result of a comparison with some standard or budget.

Is the company overstocked? Ending stock is up by $62,400 on the previous year (or 20%) while sales are up 10%. The increase may be justified if, for example, the level of sales at the end of 19A5 was something like 20% higher than at the same time last year or if inventory levels had been built up in expectation of higher sales in 19A6. No attempt is made in the report, however, to provide an explanation for the higher inventory level.

(3) Gross profit

[912] The drop in the gross profit rate is not 1.8% but 8% and, therefore, is not slight. When related to sales of $1,760,000, a reduction in the gross profit rate of 1.8% represents a fall in the amount of gross profit of $31,680 which will be reflected in the amount of net profit before tax; the significance of this amount becomes apparent when one considers that the net profit before tax in 19A5 was $64,000.

No attempt is made in the report to examine the reasons for the reduction in the gross profit rate. There is a dollar for dollar relationship between the gross profit shown and the valuation placed on inventory. In this example, the inventory at the end of the year of $374,400 was $62,400 higher than at the start of the year. How conservative was this valuation?

(4) Expenses

[913] No attempt has been made to examine the reasons for the increases in expenses in 19A5 in order to determine whether the amounts are reasonable. For example, advertizing is up $16,000 but with what results? What was the objective of the higher expenditure on advertizing in 19A5 and how successful was the company in attaining this objective?

(5) Net profit

[914] The fall in net profit before tax is $16,000 or 20%, not 1.36%. This is due in part to the higher expenses in 19A5 but a more important cause was the reduced gross profit rate. It is possible to distinguish the broad factors contributing to the profit fall in this way:

Extra sales:	
Had last year's gross profit rate been maintained, extra gross profit would have been 23.8% of $160,000 =	$38,080
Lower gross profit rate: ·	
The gross profit rate fell 1.8% on $1,760,000 sales	(31,680)
Rise in gross profit	6,400
Less increase in expenses	22,400
Fall in net profit before tax	(16,000)

The reference to the reduced amount of taxation is superfluous as, in the absence of extraordinary circumstances, one would expect a lower amount of tax with lower profit.

No attempt has been made to determine the reasonableness of the amount of profit by the calculation of, say, the rate of return.

(6) Current ratio

[915] The "improvement" in the ratio is reflected mainly in the increase of inventories of $62,400. On the other hand the bank balance is down by $77,600. Can one

really say that "the liquid position" has improved significantly? What are the overdraft arrangements with the bank?

A 2:1 "standard" may not be appropriate to this firm. Solvency is concerned with the continuing ability to pay debts as they fall due; it is not merely a matter of ratios.

(7) Balance sheet

[916] No attempt has been made to relate the current value of the property or its lease value to the operating results of the company. For example, the lease value of the property could have been used to determine the incremental income the company has earned from its trading operations and to calculate a rate of return on the company's investment in trading assets:

	$	$
Net profit before tax (as shown in the accounts)		64,000
Less notional rental (plus rates and insurance)	40,000	
Less depreciation	3,840*	36,160
Extra profit before tax attributable to trading operations		27,840
*The depreciation charge is probably too low in view of the current value of the property.		
Total assets		612,800
Less property		115,200
Investment in trading assets		497,600

This gives a pre-tax rate of return on investment in trading assets of 5.6% or 5.7% if goodwill is excluded from the trading assets ($\frac{\$27,840}{\$497,600} \times 100$).

Some other critical comments:
- a funds statement would have been useful in explaining changes in the financing of the company during the year;
- there is no evidence of budgeting in the accountant's report;
- if the annual accounts provide the only occasion for the survey of operating results, then this is certainly too infrequent.

Example 9.2
Routine Analysis: Comparability of Data

Shown on pp 142-3 are the financial statements of Retailers Co Ltd for the year ended 30 September 19A1.

Required:

(a) Comment on the operating results of Retailers Co Ltd for the year ended 30 September 19A1.

(b) Comment on the financial structure of the company as at 30 September 19A1 and any changes which have taken place during the year; give as far as possible, reasons for the changes.

Retailers Co Ltd

Operating statement for year ended 30 September 19A1

	19A1 $	19A1 $	19A0 $	19A0 $
Sales		3,564,000		2,690,000
Cost of sales				
Opening stock	821,600		673,000	
Purchases	2,270,120		1,917,100	
	3,091,720		2,590,100	
Closing stock	846,400		821,600	
Cost of sales		2,245,320		1,768,500
Gross profit		1,318,680		921,500
Less operating expenses				
Wages and salaries	590,000		448,000	
Administration expenses	50,400		33,800	
Repairs, maintenance and renewals	6,500		115,000	
Depreciation	94,400		99,600	
Advertising	158,400		93,000	
Sundry marketing expenses	52,000	951,700	16,700	806,100
Net profit before tax		366,980		115,400
Less provision for tax		164,800		50,400
Net profit after tax		202,180		65,000
Unappropriated profit brought forward		43,500		78,500
		245,680		143,500
Provision for dividend 10%		100,000		100,000
Unappropriated profit carried forward		145,680		43,500

Some possible comments

(a) Operating results

[917] A routine analysis of the operating statement will bring out the following matters:

(i) *Sales*

19A1	$3,564,000	
19A0	2,690,000	
Increase	$ 874,000	or 32.5%

Balance Sheet as at 30 September 19A1

	19A1 $	19A0 $
Issued and paid up capital in $1 ordinary shares	1,000,000	1,000,000
General reserve	400,000	400,000
P & L appropriation account	145,680	43,500
Capital and reserves	1,545,680	1,443,500
Term liabilities		
Debentures (secured)	300,000	—
Current liabilities		
Sundry creditors	288,000	338,800
Bank	36,920	443,900
Provision for dividend	100,000	100,000
Provision for taxation	164,800	50,400
	589,720	933,100
	2,435,400	2,376,600

	19A1 $	19A0 $
Fixed assets — at cost less depreciation	1,101,600	1,196,000
Current assets		
Inventories	846,400	821,600
Debtors	487,400	359,000
	1,333,800	1,180,600
	2,435,400	2,376,600

Note: Extensive renovations and extensions of premises were carried out in 19A0. These renovations and extensions were completed in May of the same year.

143

(ii) *Gross profit*

19A1	$1,318,680
19A0	921,500
Increase	$ 397,180 or 43.1%

Gross profit rate

19A1 $\dfrac{\$1,318,680}{\$3,564,000} \times 100 = 37.0\%$

19A0 $\dfrac{\$ 921,500}{\$2,690,000} \times 100 = 34.3\%$

Increase in the gross profit rate 2.7 or 7.9%.

The above figures show a substantial increase in sales accompanied by increases in both the amount and rate of gross profit. The increase of $397,180 in gross profit may be explained as due to:

(1)   increase in sales:
       $874,000 at the 19A0 gross profit rate (34.2565) = $299,402
(2)   increase in the gross profit rate:
       2.7435% of $3,564,000   97,778
                                                               $397,180

[918] In interpreting the sales figures it is necessary to consider the effect of the renovations and extension of premises in 19A0. Sales in 19A0 could have been affected by disruption of store traffic, but, perhaps more significantly, operations in the renovated and extended premises applied to four months in the year ended 30 September 19A0 and to all of the year ended 30 September 19A1.

(iii) *Expenses*

	19A1 $	% of sales	19A0 $	% of sales	Increase (decrease) $
Wages and salaries	590,000	16.55	448,000	16.65	142,000
Administration	50,400	1.41	33,800	1.26	16,600
Repairs, maintenance and renewals	6,500	0.18	115,000	4.28	(108,500)
Depreciation	94,400	2.65	99,600	3.70	(5,200)
Advertising	158,400	4.45	93,000	3.46	65,400
Marketing	52,000	1.46	16,700	0.62	35,300
	951,700	26.70	806,100	29.97	145,600

The analysis of expenses shows that, overall, expenses have increased in 19A1 by $145,600 but have fallen relative to sales from 29.97% in 19A0 to 26.70% in 19A1. An examination of the individual expense items shows increases in the amounts of wages and salaries and administration, advertizing and marketing expenses. The increase in wages and salaries is in line with sales, and administration, advertizing and marketing expenses have increased at a higher rate than sales.

[919] Regarding wages and salaries, and administration expenses, an explanation for the increases should be sought in a further breakdown of these expense items, in comparisons with budget and the study of relevant factors such as increases in staff employed and wages and salaries increases.

The increases in advertizing and marketing expense indicate increased marketing effort during the year. Relating marketing expense (including advertizing) to sales would generally be of limited value because it is unlikely that there will be a one-to-one correspondence between marketing expense input and sales revenue output. A better analysis would be to relate the level of marketing expense to budget and to overall sales and profit performance. For example, the increase in advertising and marketing expense is $100,700 and the increase in sales is $874,000. Further, as shown below, there has been a significant improvement in the profit performance of the company. In order to draw proper conclusions about the effectiveness of the marketing effort, however, one would need to relate the expenditure to budget and to the trading conditions prevailing during the period.

[920] A salient point in the comparison of expenses is the substantial drop in the repairs, maintenance and renewals expense from $115,000 in 19A0 to $6500 in 19A1. The reason for this drop may be found in the note to the balance sheet that extensive renovations and extension of premises were carried out in 19A0. This fact is important in drawing any conclusions about the performance of the company in 19A1 as it raises the question of the comparability of the 19A1 and 19A0 figures. We have to consider the extent to which the 19A0 figure for repairs, maintenance and renewals expense represents abnormal expense in view of the renovation of premises which took place in 19A0.

(iv) *Net profit*

	19A1 $	% of sales	19A0 $	% of sales
Net profit before tax	366,980	10.30	115,400	4.29
Less tax	164,800		50,400	
Net profit after tax	202,180	5.67	65,000	2.42
Tax as a percentage of net profit before tax	44.91%		43.67%	

Net profit both before and after tax has shown substantial improvement in 19A1.

Assuming that the normal tax rate is 50% of assessable income, the reported tax rates in the operating statement of 44.91% for 19A1 and 43.67% in 19A0 imply that the firm has taken some advantage of special tax concessions or that it has applied different methods in the calculation of its reported profit such as, for example, in the calculation of depreciation charges for reporting and tax purposes. The question of taxation in the analysis and interpretation of financial statements will be discussed at greater length in Chapter 14.

(v) *The rate of return*

The rate of return (net profit after tax to shareholders' funds) has increased from:

4.5% in 19A0 ($\frac{\$65,000}{\$1,443,500} \times 100$) to 13.1% in 19A1 ($\frac{\$202,180}{\$1,545,680} \times 100$).

Summary:

[921] The operating statement shows a marked improvement in operating results in 19A1 over those in 19A0. Sales, gross profit, net profit before and after tax, and the rate of return have increased to a marked extent. It should be noted, however, that 19A0 may not have been a "normal" year because of the major renovations and extension of premises carried out. It is important also to know the extent to which the 19A1 results were in line with the expectations of management.

(b) Financial structure

[922] (i) *Working capital and current ratio*

	19A1	19A0
	$	$
Current assets	1,333,800	1,180,600
Current liabilities	589,720	933,100
Working capital	744,080	247,500
Increase in working capital	$496,580	
Current ratio	2.26:1	1.27:1

The above figures show a large improvement in the current and working capital position of the firm in 19A1. The amount of working capital at the end of 19A1 is three times that at the end of 19A0, and the current ratio has increased from what was probably a low ratio of 1.27:1 to a more satisfactory 2.26:1. Relating working capital to sales, we see that while sales have increased by 32.5% in 19A1, the amount of working capital has trebled. The explanation of the much higher increase in working capital may be found in an attempt by the company to correct a strained working capital position in 19A0.

The increase in working capital can be explained as follows:

	$
Net profit after tax	202,180
Less provision for dividend	100,000
Retained profit	102,180
Add back depreciation written off	94,400
	196,580
Plus term loan raised — debentures	300,000
Increase in working capital	496,580

(ii) *Liquid ratio*

The provision for taxation has been exluded from the liquid ratio on the assumption that it is not payable until several months after balance date. The bank overdraft has also been excluded from the calculation in view of the vastly reduced amount of overdraft at the end of 19A1 and the marked improvement in the operating results and working capital position of the firm.

The indications again are of a strained liquid position in 19A0 (especially if one includes in the calculation the large bank overdraft) and a significant improvement in 19A1.

	19A1 $	19A0 $
Liquid assets		
Debtors	487,400	359,000
Quick liabilities		
Creditors	288,000	338,800
Provision for dividend	100,000	100,000
	388,000	438,800
Liquid ratio	1.26:1	0.82:1

(iii) *Term liabilities to fixed assets*

$$19A1 \quad \frac{\$300,000}{\$1,101,600} \times 100 = 27.2\%$$

The debentures represent 27.2% of the book value of fixed assets. This indicates that the firm may have some further capacity to raise term loans on the security of its fixed assets should the need arise.

(iv) *Proprietary (equity/debt) ratio*

Shareholders' funds as a percentage of total assets:

$$19A1 \quad \frac{\$1,545,680}{\$2,435,400} \times 100 = 63.5\%$$

$$19A0 \quad \frac{\$1,443,500}{\$2,376,600} \times 100 = 60.7\%$$

The proprietary (equity/debt) ratio of the company has increased. The reason for the increase is the profit retention in 19A1. Assuming that a ratio of 50% is appropriate for this firm, the firm can utilize further borrowing in its operations.

(v) *Inventory levels*

Inventories at the end of 19A1 are $24,800 or 3% higher than at the end of 19A0. On the other hand sales during 19A1 have increased by 32.5%. An explanation for the rather small increase in inventory as compared with the increase in sales may be that there was a build-up of inventories at the end of 19A0 to meet the expected expansion of sales in 19A1. But there may have been other reasons, such as overstocking due to sales below budget levels at the end of 19A0.

Rate of inventory turnover:

$$\frac{\text{Cost of sales}}{\text{Average inventory}}$$

$$19A1 \quad \frac{\$2,245,320}{\frac{1}{2}(\$821,600 + \$846,400)} = 2.7 \text{ times per annum.}$$

$$19A0 \quad \frac{\$1,768,500}{\frac{1}{2}(\$673,000 + \$821,600)} = 2.4 \text{ times per annum.}$$

The figures indicate some improvement in the rate of inventory turnover. The above rates of turnover should be compared with some standard for the trade before conclusions are drawn.

Summary:

[923] The financial structure of the firm has shown a marked improvement in 19A1. The working capital, current and liquid positions at the end of 19A0 appear to have been under considerable strain, probably because of the renovations and expansion of premises in 19A0 being at least partly financed from working capital. The position has been corrected in 19A1 through profit retention and the raising of a loan by the issue of debentures which has been used to reduce the large overdraft at the end of 19A0. The firm appears to be in a position to utilize further loan finance should the need arise.

Example 9.3

Intercompany Comparison and the Financing of Expansion

The managing director of X Ltd consults you about the comparative operating performance and financial position of his company in relation to its major competitor — Y Ltd. He provides you with the following information:

Operating results
Year ended 30 September 19A5

	X Ltd	Y Ltd
Sales	$2,450,000	$3,290,000
Net profit before tax	340,000	362,000
Provision for tax	153,000	181,000
Net profit after tax	187,000	181,000

Abbreviated balance sheets
as at 30 September 19A5

	X Ltd	Y Ltd
Capital and reserves	$1,360,000	$2,100,000
Mortgages	200,000	500,000
Current liabilities	600,000	550,000
	$2,160,000	$3,150,000
Fixed assets (net book value)	$1,200,000	$1,900,000
Current assets	960,000	1,250,000
	$2,160,000	$3,150,000

The following additional information is also provided.

(a)   *Details of current liabilities*

	X Ltd	Y Ltd
Bank overdraft	$184,000	$49,000
Provision for tax	153,000	181,000
Provision for dividends	103,000	110,000
Sundry creditors	160,000	210,000
	$600,000	$550,000

Continued p 149

(b)   *Details of current assets*

	X Ltd	Y Ltd
Debtors	$335,000	$493,000
Inventories	625,000	757,000
	$960,000	$1,250,000

(c)   *The amount of interest on borrowing paid by the two companies during the year was*
       X Ltd $54,000
       Y Ltd $76,000

X Ltd is considering an expansion of its operations which is estimated to require additional finance of $1 million. The additional investment required by the expansion is summarized as follows:

Fixed assets	$550,000
Inventories	300,000
Debtors	$150,000
	$1,000,000

Required:

(a) Comment on and compare the operating results of X Ltd and Y Ltd, using appropriate ratios, percentages and comparisons.

(b) Comment on and compare the financial position of X Ltd and Y Ltd, using appropriate ratios, percentages and comparisons.

(c) Suggest how the proposed expansion of X Ltd can be financed and discuss the effect of your proposals on the financial structure of the company.

(d) How, if at all, would you modify your answers to (a) and (b) if you were informed that the fixed assets of Y Ltd are shown at a recent valuation while the fixed assets of X Ltd are shown at their written down historical cost, their current value being considerably higher than their book value.

Comments

[924] (a) *Comparison of operating results*

The sales of the two companies are: X Ltd $2,450,000, Y Ltd $3,290,000. The sales of Y Ltd are $840,000 or 34.29% higher than those of X Ltd, indicating that Y Ltd has a higher share of the market for the trade.

Net profit

	X Ltd $	Y Ltd $
Net profit before tax	340,000	362,000
Provision for tax	153,000	181,000
Net profit after tax	187,000	181,000
Tax as a percentage of net profit before tax	45%	50%

149

The net profit before tax of Y Ltd is $22,000 higher than that of X Ltd; the net profit after tax of Y Ltd, however, is $6000 lower. Provision for taxation is 45% of net profit before tax in the case of X Ltd and 50% in the case of Y Ltd. These differences should be examined to determine the extent to which taxation has affected the comparability of the profit figures.

[925] The rates of net profit to sales for the two companies are as follows:

	X Ltd	Y Ltd
Net profit before tax	13.9%	11.0%
Net profit after tax	7.6%	5.5%

X Ltd has achieved a higher rate of net profit to sales both before and after tax. Since both companies are in the same trade and assuming that their selling prices are similar, the indication is that X Ltd has relatively lower costs and is, therefore, more efficient. Before such a conclusion can be drawn, however, it would be necessary to examine the accounting principles applied by the two companies in the measurement of their profit to see whether the profit figures are properly comparable. The difference in the rate of taxation to net profit before tax for the two companies indicates that the two profit figures may not have been determined on a fully comparable basis.

Rate of return

	X Ltd	Y Ltd
(i) Net profit before tax to shareholders' funds	25%	17.24%
(ii) Net profit after tax to shareholders' funds	13.75%	8.62%
(iii) On total assets — net profit before tax plus interest to total assets	18.24%	13.90%

The above figures show that X Ltd has achieved a better rate of return on shareholders' funds both before and after tax and has achieved also a better rate of return on total assets.

[926] We can calculate gearing profitability ratios for the two companies by relating their rates of return on shareholders' funds (before tax) to the rates of return on total assets:

$$\text{X Ltd } \frac{25\%}{18.24\%} = 1.37{:}1$$

$$\text{Y Ltd } \frac{17.24\%}{13.90\%} = 1.24{:}1$$

The above figures show that X Ltd has achieved a higher gearing profitability than Y Ltd.

Summary:

[927] Although the sales of Y Ltd are 34.29% higher than those of X Ltd, X Ltd has achieved better overall results in terms of net profit per sales dollar and rate of return on shareholders' funds and total assets. X Ltd, therefore, appears to be the more effiicent of the two companies. Before reaching such a conclusion, however, it would be necessary to examine the principles used to measure the profit (and value

the assets) of the two companies in order to determine whether the figures are properly comparable.

[928] (b) *Comparison of financial position*

Working capital and current ratio

	X Ltd	Y Ltd
Current assets	$960,000	$1,250,000
Current liabilities	600,000	550,000
Working capital	$360,000	$700,000
Current ratio	1.6:1	2.27:1

With its sales 34.29% higher, Y Ltd has almost twice the working capital of X Ltd. The current ratio of Y Ltd is considerably better than that of X Ltd.

Liquid ratio

	X Ltd	Y Ltd
Liquid assets		
Debtors	$335,000	$493,000
Quick liabilities		
Creditors	$160,000	$210,000
Provision for dividend	103,000	110,000
	$263,000	$320,000
Bank overdraft	184,000	49,000
	$447,000	$369,000
Liquid ratio (excluding overdraft)	1.27:1	1.54:1
Liquid ratio (including overdraft)	0.75:1	1.34:1

Y Ltd has a better liquid ratio than X Ltd, especially if bank overdraft is taken to be a quick liability. The overdraft limits of the two companies are not known but X Ltd appears to be relying on overdraft to a much greater extent than Y Ltd.

It could be that the working capital position of X Ltd is under some strain.

Inventory levels

[929] From the information provided one cannot calculate rates of inventory turn-over for the two companies. A rough comparison of inventory levels, however, can be made by comparing inventories as a percentage of sales:

$$X \text{ Ltd } \frac{\$625,000}{\$2,450,000} \times 100 = 25.5\%$$

$$Y \text{ Ltd } \frac{\$757,000}{\$3,290,000} \times 100 = 23.0\%$$

X Ltd is carrying a higher level of inventories in relation to its sales than Y Ltd.

Mortgages to fixed assets:

$$X \text{ Ltd } \frac{\$200,000}{\$1,200,000} \times 100 = 16.7\%$$

$$Y \text{ Ltd } \frac{\$500,000}{\$1,900,000} \times 100 = 26.3\%$$

Y Ltd has mortgaged its fixed assets to a greater extent than X Ltd. Both companies appear to have capacity to raise further long-term loans on the security of their fixed assets.

Y Ltd has much larger long-term borrowing ($500,000) than X Ltd ($200,000). This would explain the better working capital and liquid position of Y Ltd.

Proprietary (equity/debt) ratio:

Shareholders' funds as a percentage of total assets:

$$\text{X Ltd } \frac{\$1,360,000}{\$2,160,000} \times 100 = 63\%$$

$$\text{Y Ltd } \frac{\$2,100,000}{\$3,150,000} \times 100 = 66.7\%$$

The shareholders' equity in both companies is in excess of 50% of total assets, in fact about two-thirds of total assets. Before a further comment could be made, one would need to know what equity/debt ratio is considered normal for this kind of business.

Summary:

[930] X Ltd has a considerably lower working capital than Y Ltd even when the difference in sales is taken into account. X Ltd relies much more heavily on bank overdraft and its working capital and liquid position may be under some strain.

Y Ltd has made greater use of long-term finance than X Ltd which accounts for its better working capital and liquid position. For example, long-term finance (shareholders' equity and mortgages) represents 85.54% of the total funds employed by Y Ltd and 72.22% of the total funds employed by X Ltd. Both companies appear to have further capacity for long-term borrowing on the security of their fixed assets.

The equity/debt position appears to be strong in both companies. The shareholders' equity represents two-thirds of the total funds employed by Y Ltd and just under two-thirds of the total funds employed by X Ltd.

[931] (c) *The financing of the proposed expansion of X Ltd*

The objective in arranging the finance for the expansion program will be to end up with a post-expansion financial structure which is regarded by management as appropriate to the business. This appropriateness applies particularly to the level of debt finance and to the spread between short- and long-term debt. As this is related to the nature of the business and of its assets, it is a useful first step to determine the post-expansion investment in assets:

Assets	Pre-expansion $	Expansion $	Post-expansion $
Debtors	335,000	150,000	485,000
Inventories	625,000	300,000	925,000
= Current	960,000	450,000	1,410,000
Fixed	1,200,000	550,000	1,750,000
Total	2,160,000	1,000,000	3,160,000

[932] The balance sheet at 30 September 19A5 shows current liabilites of $600,000

and a current ratio of 1.6:1. The current ratio appears to be too low if Y Ltd is taken as a guide to what is desirable. If we assume that the directors are of the opinion that a current ratio of 2:1 is desirable, then a further $100,000 of short-term debt would be acceptable:

	$
Post-expansion current assets	1,410,000
Post-expansion current liabilities	
($600,000 + $100,000)	700,000
Current ratio	2:1

If the inventory turns over four times per year and is obtained on monthly terms, then trade creditors will be $100,000 higher. There would be no need to seek other sources of short-term finance. This leaves $900,000 to finance long term.

[933] Long-term finance may be obtained from debt and from equity sources. The main sources of long-term debt are mortgages and debentures. The extent of use of debt depends on the views of management and lenders on what is an appropriate equity/debt ratio. The present financing is 63% by way of equity (shareholders' funds). Let us assume that the acceptable ratio is 60%. Then 40% of assets may be financed by debt:

	$
40% of $3,160,000 =	1,264,000
Less current liabilities after expansion	700,000
Long term liabilities could be	564,000
Present level of long term debt	200,000
Balance which the company might endeavour to raise	364,000

[934] Without some knowledge of the fixed assets, including their market value, one cannot assess how much could be raised by way of mortgage of land and buildings and on the security of plant. The company is not a large one, and a debenture issue could be difficult. There are considerable current assets on which a floating charge could be given (subject to the security of the bank).

The balance would have to be raised by means of an issue of shares:

	$
60% of assets ($3,160,000)	1,896,000
Less present shareholders' funds	1,360,000
Additional share capital, approximately	536,000

On these calculations, the funds would be obtained, if possible:

	$
From extra trade creditors, approximately	100,000
From extra long term debt, approximately	400,000
From an issue of shares, approximately	500,000
	1,000,000

subject to the assumptions incorporated in the discussion set out above.

[935] The above calculations indicate that it may not be feasible for X Ltd to raise the finance needed entirely from borrowing. For example, lenders may not be prepared to make loans to the extent of 63% of the book value of fixed assets. In fact, the ability of the company to borrow on the security of its fixed assets would depend on the nature of the assets and their realizable value and not on their book value. Further, there is the risk factor to consider, both from the viewpoint of the lenders and the company, associated with a considerably worsened equity/debt position, ie in the shareholders' equity falling from 63% of total funds to 43%.

[936] It appears that the best way to finance the expansion would be by a combination of long-term borrowing and share capital. The actual proportions in which these two sources of finance will be used will depend on the availability of finance from the two sources and on the level of gearing management desires to achieve. The latter may depend on the expected level and stability of the company's profits.

[937] (d) *Revision of comments under (a) and (b) if the fixed assets of Y Ltd are shown at recent valuation and the fixed assets of X Ltd at a written down historical cost.* At least a notional adjustment should be made of the financial statements of X Ltd to make them more comparable with those of Y Ltd.

As currently reported, the profit of X Ltd is overstated to the extent that the charge for depreciation of fixed assets is based on their historical cost and not on the higher current value. The rate of return of X Ltd on the shareholders' equity and total assets is also overstated to the extent that profit is overstated and the shareholders' equity and total assets are understated.

The equity/debt position of X Ltd is stronger than reported and therefore the company has a better security base to borrow than currently indicated.

[938] We will end this chapter with a case study on analysis and interpretation based on the 1980 published financial statements of a New Zealand company, DIC Limited. Some matters which arise from the analysis and interpretation of these financial statements, such as the effects of taxation and price changes, are discussed in later chapters. The case study may, therefore, be tackled by users of this book at two levels. The study may be attempted on the basis of knowledge acquired to this stage and then it may be reviewed after a study of the chapters on taxation and price changes.

[939] It may be pointed out that many of the taxation rules which applied to DIC Limited in 1980 do not apply to companies at a time when the study is tackled by users of the book. Taxation rules change over time. In dealing with taxation in this book, the objective of the authors has been to consider the effects of taxation on the operations of business firms and its implications for the anlaysis and interpretation of financial statements over time. The exposure of analysts and interpreters to these effects should better prepare them to understand the impact of taxation on reported results and state of affairs of business enterprises, even when taxation rules are different from those which have applied in the past.

A Case Study — The DIC Limited

[940] The DIC Limited operated departmental stores in many of New Zealand's larger cities. Its trading covered the typical range for departmental stores including

clothing, cosmetics, home appliances, and television, furnishings, hardware, etc.
Shown below are extracts from the 1980 financial statements of the company.

Trading Highlights

	1980	1979	1978
	$	$	$
Turnover	43,428,280	33,857,202	31,239,750
Net profit after taxation	1,368,738	976,411	569,071
Net profit after taxation per $ of sales (cents)	3.15	2.88	1.82
Taxation	—	475,612	—
Net profit after extraordinary items	1,610,009	982,377	478,488
Dividends — ordinary	16%507,531	15%475,810	12½%396,509
Dividends — 12% specified preference	180,000	180, 000	90,000
Revenue and extraordinary profit retained	922,478	326,567	(8,021)
Shareholders' funds	14,814,153	13,852,144	12,596,592
Earning rate on shareholders' funds	10.86%	7.05%	3.80%
Total remuneration paid to employees	8,288,685	6,023,989	6,188,152
Number of employees at year end	1,135	1,032	932

Each dollar of income has been applied as follows:

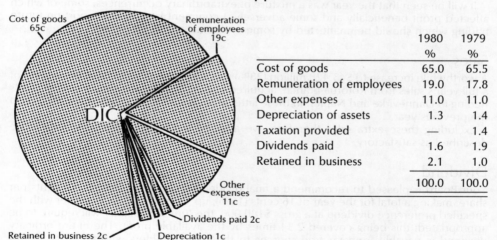

Cost of goods 65c

Remuneration of employees 19c

DIC

Other expenses 11c

Dividends paid 2c

Retained in business 2c

Depreciation 1c

	1980	1979
	%	%
Cost of goods	65.0	65.5
Remuneration of employees	19.0	17.8
Other expenses	11.0	11.0
Depreciation of assets	1.3	1.4
Taxation provided	—	1.4
Dividends paid	1.6	1.9
Retained in business	2.1	1.0
	100.0	100.0

Chairman's Review

The year in retrospect

In my review with the 1979 accounts, when the company was able to increase its ordinary
dividend from 12½% to 15%, I noted that should the dividend be approved, it would be

covered only 1.49 times: and consequently that the directors' recommendation was "a mark of their belief that the present trend of profits is not just a short term one". With a capital profit from the sale of our old Christchurch property of $734,000 about to be realized within days of the annual meeting, that prophecy was perhaps not as incautious as it might have seemed.

Nevertheless, it is a pleasure to report a profit of $1.6million — a record — for the year ended 31 July 1980. Shareholders should be aware, however, that there were several circumstances surrounding the attainment of that profit which are unlikely to be repeated in the immediate future.

1. It was contributed to by extraordinary items of *income* totalling $819,107, less of course, extraordinary items of *expenditure* which netted the increment down to $241,271.
2. As a consequence of the costs of strengthening and refurbishing our Wellington building, *no tax* was payable. Nor does it seem likely that the company will incur anything other than a minimal tax liability in its 1981 year.
3. Trading profit was severely affected by some of the expenses of continuing to trade at Lambton Quay while massive structural and strengthening operations were in progress. These included some $335,000 in written-down values of stock and $160,000 paid out for wages for shifting and cleaning stocks while work was in progress.
4. It should be appreciated that massive expenditures on our new premises at Lower Hutt were incurred, for which we received only a three-month return: similarly there were heavy progress payments at Lambton Quay where sales were much on a par with last year. In other words, there were heavy payments for no commensurate return and consequently our interest bill was inflated by 108% from these and other causes.

It will be seen that the year was a mixture of extraordinary occurrences, some of which affected profit beneficially and some adversely. I comment later in this report on future trading which should be unaffected by some of the factors occurring this year.

Sales

A worthwhile increase to $43.428 million (28%) was achieved. We did have the benefit of a full year's sales from Rotorua branch, acquired in August 1979 and similarly a full year's trading in Dannevirke and Napier: in these latter areas we traded for only three months in the previous year.

Excluding these extra sales therefore, we attained a 17% increase which could be described as satisfactory.

Dividend

Your Board is pleased to recommend a final dividend on ordinary shares of 9 cents per share, making a total for the year of 16 cents (16%), up 1 cent on 1979. Together with the specified preference dividend at a gross $180,000, the sum of $687,531 will require to be appropriated: this being covered 2.34 times by the available profit. The entire ordinary dividend is payable from tax-free sources to those shareholders who so elect. In this connection I shall hope to be in a position to make a further announcement at the annual general meeting.

Shops

In Dunedin the DIC–DCC–YMCA carpark was duly completed at the end of 1979 and patronage has been growing steadily, contributing an increased customer count to our premises.

Lambton Quay has already been mentioned briefly and work there is expected to be complete as regards our shop premises by the time our annual meeting is held. Some five months' further work is required in the areas occupied by tenants.

Lower Hutt new store was opened by Mrs Muldoon, assisted by Mr Kennedy-Good, the Mayor of Lower Hutt, in late April of this year. This magnificent new shop has earned favourable comments from the trade and customers alike, and its sales are up to budget expectations. The old premises have been disposed of for cash at a modest capital profit.

As already mentioned, leasehold premises at Rotorua were acquired at the beginning of the year and we have traded successfully in these. We believe there is considerable potential yet to be achieved in this prosperous city.

No major alterations have been undertaken at other branches. They have been maintained in first-class order.

The future

I make no apology for the fact that this review contains many references to our Lambton Quay store. The refurbished and strengthened shop is due to be opened in the presence of the prime minister and the mayor of Wellington on November 18. It is no secret that we shall be looking for a contribution before tax and head office charges in the seven-figure area on a yearly basis once trading can be resumed without interruption. That will represent a very significant improvement upon current returns.

At Lower Hutt we will receive a full year's return from our new store, which with its open plan and good access, can be operated most economically. That store too will return a significant extra contribution.

I have already remarked upon the interest bill we have had to meet in 1980. These charges are unlikely to decrease in 1981. Therefore, as a matter of prudence, we have deferred some improvements which we would have liked to carry out in various branches until the 1981-82 year: but we certainly do not anticipate that after July 1981, the very heavy expenditures on refurbishing incurred in the three years to that date, will continue.

In summary, therefore, in 1981, given no undue or unusual disruptions to business conditions, we are looking to produce an improved result upon that reported to you this year.

P W Fels
Chairman

The DIC Limited
Profit and Loss Account
for the year ended 31 July 1980

	Notes	1980 $	1980 $	1980 $	1979 $
Sales				43,428,280	33,857,202
Gross Profit from Trading				15,204,453	11,678,969
Less Expenses					
Advertising, salaries, rents, insurances, etc			12,328,966		9,395,289
Interest on mortgages and term loans			468,403		333,668
Interest on bank overdraft, loans and					
short term deposits			462,563		114,685
Depreciation			573,987		494,929

157

	Notes	1980 $	$	$	1979 $
Directors' fees			25,000		18,000
Audit fees			38,398		32,170
				13,897,317	10,388,741
Trading profit				1,307,136	1,290,228
Add dividends from companies			1,050		350
Interest on government stock			4,144		3,400
Interest on other investments			56,408		158,045
				61,602	161,795
Profit before taxation				1,368,738	1,452,023
Less taxation	6			—	475,612
Profit after taxation				1,368,738	976,411
Add extraordinary items	3			241,271	5,966
Profit after tax and extraordinary items				1,610,009	982,377
Add retained profits brought forward				5,379,151	1,757,222
				6,989,160	2,739,599
Add transfer from general reserve				—	3,301,328
				6,989,160	6,040,927
Dividends paid and recommended					
7% interim dividend paid			222,045		222,045
Provision for 9% final dividend as recommended			285,486		253,765
12% specified preference dividend paid			180,000		180,000
Total dividends			687,531		655,810
Transfer to capital replacement fund			21,727		246,549
			709,258		902,359
Less transfer from share premium reserve		21,727			
Transfer from capital reserve	4(d)	138,414	160,141		246,549
				549,117	655,810
				6,440,043	5,385,117
Transfer to capital profits reserve	4(d)			813,869	5,966
Retained profits at 31 July 1980				$5,626,174	$5,379,151

The DIC Limited
Notes to the Accounts
for the year ended 31 July 1980

1. Statement of accounting policies

The general accounting principles recognized as appropriate for the measurement and reporting of results and financial position under the historical cost method have been observed in the preparation of these accounts except for the valuation of land and buildings. The significant accounting policies adopted are:

(a) Land and buildings are shown at the latest government valuations after making allowances for the value of lifts, escalators, heating and sprinkler plant. This adjustment is shown in the property revaluation reserve. All other assets are valued at cost.

(b) Depreciation of Fixed Assets (other than land) has been calculated on the straight line basis at rates which are estimated to write off the cost, or in the case of buildings the revalued amount, less the residual value of those assets, over their economic lives. The principle rates in use are:

Buildings	1–2½%
Fixtures, fittings and plant	10%
Motor vehicles and computer equipment	20%

(c) Trade debtors are valued at expected realizable value. Profit on hire purchase transactions is included at the time the sale is made and interest charged on these transactions included evenly over the term of each agreement.

(d) Valuation of stock has been made at the lower of cost or net realizable value on a basis consistent with previous years. Cost means the actual cost of the relevant stock item. This year the allowance made to reduce the cost of ageing stock to net realizable value has been changed and the effect of this change is described in Note 2.

(e) Taxation charged against profits includes current taxation and deferred taxation based on the partial concept. This year, because of allowances relating to the strengthening of the Wellington building to comply with latest seismic regulations, no tax is payable. Details are shown in Note 6.

2. Changes in accounting policies

The basis of reducing the cost of ageing stocks to net realizable value was changed this year and an additional $63,591 written off. This amount has been included with the extraordinary items and shown in Note 3.

3. Extraordinary items

Extraordinary items consist of:

		1980	1979
Capital profits on the sale of the Christchurch and Lower Hutt buildings		819,107	5,966
Costs associated with the strengthening of the Wellington building			
• Stock write downs	335,000		
• Additional payroll and other costs	179,245		
Additional provision for aged stock (see Note 2)	63,591	577,836	—
		$241,271	$5,966

The DIC
Balance
as at

	Notes	1980 $	1979 $
Shareholders' Funds			
Authorised Capital —			
8,500,000 Ordinary Shares of $1 each		8,500,000	8,500,000
1,500,000 12% Specified Preference Shares of $1 each		1,500,000	1,500,000
		$10,000,000	$10,000,000
Issued Capital —			
3,172,070 Ordinary Shares of $1 each fully paid		3,172,070	3,172,070
1,500,000 12% Specified Preference Shares of $1 each fully paid		1,500,000	1,500,000
		4,672,070	4,672,070
Reserves —			
Share Premium Reserve	4(a)	—	21,727
Capital Replacement Fund	4(b)	458,600	436,873
Property Revaluation Reserve	4(c)	3,368,205	3,328,674
Capital Profits Reserve	4(d)	689,104	13,649
Retained Profits		5,626,174	5,379,151
		10,142,083	9,180,074
Total Shareholders' Funds		14,814,153	13,852,144
Deferred Taxation	6(b)	168,977	168,977
Term Liabilities			
Mortgages (secured)	5	2,605,476	2,511,179
Bank Term Loans (secured)		455,000	587,000
Other Term Loans (secured)		691,275	157,155
Long Term Commercial Bill Facility		1,500,000	—
Total Term Liabilities		5,251,751	3,255,334
Current Liabilities			
Trade Creditors		6,130,681	3,694,647
Unclaimed Dividends		16,507	14,983
Short Term Deposits and Loans (secured $236,989)		1,558,733	1,379,460
Bank Overdraft and Loans (secured)		3,043,982	1,007,426
Current Portion of Mortgages (secured)	5	100,251	91,524
Provision for Taxation	6	—	352,794
Provision for Dividend		285,486	253,765
Total Current Liabilities		11,135,640	6,794,599
		$31,370,521	$24,071,054

Limited
Sheet
31 July 1980

	Notes	1980 $	1980 $	1979 $
Fixed Assets	7			
Land		4,127,523		4,388,610
Buildings		7,092,581		4,869,364
Fixtures, Fittings and Plant		1,496,457		1,195,040
Motor Vehicles		241,298		120,683
Computer Equipment		337,650		302,484
Total Fixed Assets			13,295,509	10,876,181
Investments (at cost)				
Government Stock		39,409		22,000
Shares in Subsidiary Companies	8	5,100		5,100
Shares in Companies		19,644		16,792
Advances to Staff		103,124		33,720
Life Assurance Premiums Paid		39,240		34,880
Mortgages and Loans		343,033		479,521
Total Investments			549,550	592,013
Current Assets				
Trading Stock		12,164,909		8,580,485
Debtors	9	5,120,348		3,989,446
Taxation Refund Due		203,262		—
Cash in Hand		36,943		32,929
Total Current Assets			17,525,462	12,602,860
			$31,370,521	$24,071,054

On behalf of the Board
P W Fels
F R M Watson, Directors

4. Reserves

(a) *Share premium reserve*

In terms of a resolution dated 16 November 1977, sanctioned by the Supreme Court of New Zealand, the sum of $458,600 in the reserve was available for distribution in cash to ordinary shareholders.

	1980	1979
Balance at 1 August 1979	21,727	268,276
Plus adjustment to distribution in lieu of dividend in 1978 accounts	—	40,924
	21,727	309,200
Less interim distribution in lieu of dividend	21,727	167,695
	—	141,505
*Less provision for final distribution	—	119,778
Balance at 31 July 1980	$ —	$21,727

(b) *Capital replacement fund*

The Supreme Court approval to make distributions from share premium reserve is conditional upon an equivalent amount being transferred from retained profits to a capital replacement fund. This fund equates the amount provided for distributions to 31 July 1980.

(c) *Property revaluation reserve*

	1980	1979
Balance at 1 August 1979	3,328,674	2,384,444
Less Transfer on sale property	414,961	—
	2,913,713	2,384,444
Plus Adjustment on reclassification of reserves	—	17,102
Revaluation of land and buildings this year	454,492	927,128
	$3,368,205	$3,328,674

$2,500,371 is available for tax-free bonus distribution to shareholders being revaluations in excess of cost and the balance is depreciation previously provided.

(d) *Capital profits reserves*

	1980	1979
Balance at 1 August 1979	13,649	7,683
Transfer from profit & loss account being profits on disposal of assets	813,869	5,966
	827,518	13,649
Less Distribution to Shareholders	138,414	—
Balance at 31 July 1980	$689,104	$13,649

This balance represents realized capital profits available for tax-free distribution to shareholders. Shareholders are entitled to elect whether their payment of dividend is made from capital profits or from trading profits. This figure will be adjusted when final advice is received.

5. Term liabilities

The company's mortgages secured over various properties are due for repayment as follows:

	Interest Rates	1980	1979
Within 1 year	13%	100,251	91,524
From 1 to 5 years	13%	1,690,505	985,443
From 5 to 10 years	12%	828,271	1,013,917
Over 10 years	7%	86,700	511,819
		$2,605,476	$2,511,179

The bank term loans are repayable between 1 and 5 years at interest rates of 11% and 15½%. The other term loans are repayable within three years at interest rates of 12% to 12½%. In addition to these loans, the bankers hold a debenture securing the assets of the company for their remaining advances.

6. Taxation

(a) *Current taxation*

No taxation is payable this year. In determining the taxation liability the following allowances have been taken into account.

	1980	1979
Profit for the year	1,368,738	1,452,023
Less Extraordinary cost	577,836	—
Specified preference dividend	180,000	180,000
Decrease in unearned profit on hire purchase sales	(3,001)	58,472
Allowance for strengthening of Wellington building (see below)	696,445	—
Loss carried forward	—	270,484
	82,542	943,067
Add other adjustments, chiefly depreciation on revalued portion of buildings	82,542	113,850
Taxable income	$NIL	$1,056,917
At 45%	$NIL	$475,612

The Inland Revenue have approved the deduction for tax purposes, which may be spread over a period of up to five years, of the costs associated with the strengthening of the Wellington building to comply with local by-laws. For accounting purposes this expenditure has been capitalized and is shown as part of construction in progress in Note 7. At 31 July 1980, $1,494,081 had been expended on this project and a further $1,130,000 committed. (Of these amounts $696,445 has been claimed against this year's profit).

(b) *Deferred taxation*

	1980	1979
The provision in the balance sheet consists of		
Difference between accounting and taxation treatment of hire purchase profits	197,977	197,977
Difference between financial and tax rates of depreciation (except buildings)	(29,000)	(29,000)
	$168,977	$168,977

As described in Note 1 the partial concept of deferred taxation is used. The liability for deferred taxation on all hire purchase profits reported for financial purposes but not included for taxation is $347,860 (1979 $349,211) leaving a balance of $149,883 (1979 $151,234) not provided as deferred taxation.

7. Fixed assets

	Valuation	1980 Original cost	Accumulated depreciation	Book value	Book Value 1979
Freehold land	4,127,523	—		4,127,523	3,934,110
Freehold buildings	5,766,609	—	275,469	5,491,140	4,126,610
Construction in progress	—	1,601,441	—	1,601,441	1,197,254
Fixtures, fittings and plant	—	5,014,393	3,517,936	1,496,457	1,195,040
Motor vehicles	—	306,337	65,039	241,298	120,683
Computer equipment	—	594,896	257,246	337,650	302,484
Total 1980	$9,894,132	$7,517,067	$4,115,690	$13,295,509	$10,876,181
Total 1979	$8,260,411	$6,317,057	$3,701,287	$10,876,181	

Land and buildings have been revalued to latest government valuations dated 1975 to 1979 after making allowance for the value of building services such as lifts, escalators, heating and sprinkler plant.

8. Subsidiary companies

All subsidiary companies balance as at 31 July 1980. Group accounts have not been prepared as in the opinion of the directors it would be of no real value to members in view of the insignificiant amounts involved.

One subsidiary company traded during the year and the results have been included in the profit and loss account of the parent company by crediting an inter-company charge of $NIL.

No subsidiary or any nominee of the subsidiaries hold shares in the company. No directors' fees have been paid by subsidiary companies.

9. Debtors

	1980	1979
Debtors consist of		
Trade debtors	4,495,993	3,792,289
Less provision for unearned interest	236,522	173,966
	4,259,471	3,618,323
Sundry debtors	860,877	371,123
	$5,120,348	$3,989,446

10. Capital commitments and contingent liabilities

An estimate of the company's commitments for capital expenditure not provided for in the accounts amounted to $1,183,000 (1979 $2,600,000).
Deferred taxation not accounted for Note 6(b) $149,883 (1979 $151,234).

Auditors' Report
To the members of The DIC Limited

We have obtained all the information and explanations that we have required. In our opinion, proper books of account have been kept by the company so far as appears from our examination of those books.

In our opinion, according to the best of our information and the explanation given to us and as shown by the books, the financial statements on pages 7 to 13 are properly drawn up using the historical cost method modified by the revaluation of certain assets so as to give a true an fair view of the state of the company's affairs as at 31 July 1980, and the results of its business and the changes in financial position for the year ended on that date.

According to such information and explanations, the financial statements give the information required by the Companies Act 1955 in the manner so required.

Dunedin, 24 October 1980   *Hutchison, Hull & Co, Chartered Accountants*

Note: a five-year trend statement is reproduced on p 166

Required:

Comment on the results of DIC Limited and its state of affairs as disclosed in its financial statements for the year ended 31 July 1980.

Some comments and suggestions on how to approach the study

[941] The financial statements of DIC Limited which have been reproduced above with relatively minor abbrevations provide an interesting exercise in analysis and interpretation by the application of analytical techniques and the drawing of inferences from ratios, percentages and comparisons.

The authors suggest the following progressive approach to the case study which follows the order in which the data are presented in the financial statements:

(1) Study and comment on the data disclosed in the statement of trading highlights and the "pie chart" and the related percentages for 1980 and 1979. The pie chart and percentages illustrate how each dollar of "income" was applied (the term

COMPARISONS 1976–1980

	1980 $	1979 $	1978 $	1977 $	1976 $
Shareholder's Funds:					
Capital issued and fully paid — Preference	1,500,000	1,500,000	1,500,00		
Ordinary	3,172,070	3,172,070	3,172,070	3,172,070	2,956,070
	4,672,070	4,672,070	4,672,070	3,172,070	2,956,070
Reserves — Capital	—	21,727	268,276	458,600	275,000
Reserves — share premium					
Reserves — revenue	5,626,174	5,379,151	5,073,795	5,109,569	4,516,941
	10,142,083	9,180,074	7,924,522	7,871,455	6,098,248
Total shareholders' fund	14,814,153	13,852,144	12,596,592	11,043,525	9,054,318
Represented by the following assets:					
Fixed assets, land, buildings, plants, etc	13,295,509	10,876,181	8,648,122	8,325,787	4,601,280
Less term liabilities and deferred taxation	5,420,728	3,424,311	3,145,891	2,268,963	816,300
	7,874,781	7,451,870	5,502,231	6,056,824	3,784,980
Investments	549,550	592,013	604,357	172,685	87,374
Current assets	17,525,462	12,602,860	10,977,489	12,925,728	9,393,161
Less liabilities	11,135,640	6,794,599	4,487,485	8,111,712	4,211,197
Working capital	6,389,822	5,808,261	6,490,004	4,814,016	5,181,964
Total net assets	14,814,153	13,852,144	12,596,592	11,043,525	9,054,318
Profit before tax	1,368,738	1,452,023	569,071	1,835,164	1,883,265
Provision for taxation	—	475,612	—	831,496	856,675
Extraordinary items	241,271	5,966	(90,583)	—	—
Net profit after tax and extraordinary items	1,610,009	982,377	478,488	1,003,668	1,026,590
Less dividends	687,531	655,810	486,509	459,950	423,703
Profits retained	922,478	326,567	(8,021)	543,718	602,887
Ratio current assets to current liabilities	1.57	1.85	2.45	2.12	2.50
Dividend per share, ordinary	16 cents	15 cents	12½ cents	14½ cents	14½ cents
Percent net profit including extraordinary items to shareholders' funds	10.86	7.05	3.80	9.09	11.34

"income" was used in the published financial statements — a more common term would have been "revenue"). After studying this part of the financial statements, answer the following questions:

   (i) What are your initial impressions of the operations and results of the company in 1980?

   (ii) What additional information would you be looking for as you extend your study of the financial statements?

   (iii) What financial statement user group do you believe the pie chart is aimed at?

(2) Study the chairman's review. What matters discussed in the review do you consider to be of particular importance to you as an analyst and interpreter of the statements?

(3) Extend your analysis to the profit and loss account. Consider in particular:

   (i) The amount and treatment of extraordinary items.

   (ii) Taxation. Taxation is discussed in Chapter 14. Some information on taxation as it affected the company in 1980 is provided below.

   (iii) Consider the effects of rising prices on the operations of the company. For the purposes of this case you may assume that during the year general inflation was 15% and that the selling prices of the company and the cost to it to replace the inventories sold increased on the average, by a similar percentage. (The effects of price changes and inflation on the operations of business enterprises are discussed in Chapter 19.)

(4) Calculate and comment on what you consider to be the significant balance sheet ratios and what they imply about the state of affairs of the company.

(5) Note 6 to the accounts discloses that the costs associated with the strengthening of the Wellington building has been capitalized for accounting purposes but has been claimed as a tax deduction. Should the company have capitalized the total cost of strengthening the buildings in view of the fact that it has been claimed for taxation?

(6) What do you think the future held for the company at 31 July 1980?

[942] Some additional notes and comments on the accounts of DIC Limited:

(a) *Reserves (Note 4) — share premium reserve and capital replacement fund.* Until 1984 New Zealand companies could with the approval of the court, make tax-free cash distributions from their share premium reserves. In granting approval, a condition the court usually imposed was that an amount equivalent to the distribution be transferred from retained profits to a non-distributable capital replacement fund (reserve).

Until 1984 New Zealand companies could make tax-free cash distributions from various capital reserves, depending on the origins of the reserves. These provisions for tax-free cash distributions were largely removed following the change in government in 1984. The exent to which the reserves of DIC Limited were available for tax free aistributions at the end of its 1980 financial year is disclosed in Note 4 to the financial statements.

(b) *Specified preference shares.* Some New Zealand companies have issued specified preference shares. The dividends paid on specified preference shares are tax-deductible, unlike those on non-specified preference shares which must be paid from profit after tax.

Review questions

9.1 The following information has been extracted from the published accounts of Jones and Brown Trading Co Ltd for the years ended 30 September 19A1 and 19A2.

	19A1 $	19A2 $
Capital and reserves (see note 1)	764,000	867,200
Fixed assets at cost less depreciation (see note 2)	460,400	808,000
Government stock	120,000	—
Term liability — mortgage		40,000
Working capital (see note 3)	183,600	99,200
Sales	2,040,000	3,560,000

Notes

1 During the year ended 30 September 19A2 the company increased its capital by $80,000. Net profit after tax for the year amounted to $107,200. The net profit after tax for the year ended 30 September 19A1 was $84,200.
2 There were no sales or other disposals of fixed assets during the year ended 30 September 19A2. Depreciation written of amounted to $50,000.
3 The following are the details of current assets and liabilities as disclosed in the published accounts:

	19A1	19A2
Current assets		
Bank	50,000	—
Debtors	184,000	288,000
Trading stock	256,000	504,000
	490,000	792,000
Current liabilities		
Bank	—	158,400
Creditors	128,000	352,000
Provision for tax	106,400	98,400
Provision for dividend	72,000	84,000
	306,400	692,800

The firm's overdraft limit is $40,000.

Required:

(a) Prepare a statement of sources and disposition of funds for the year ended 30 September 19A2, with emphasis on changes in working capital.
(b) Comment *briefly* on the trading results and profitability of Jones and Brown Trading Co Ltd for the year ended 30 Septmeber 19A2. Support your comments as far as possible with figures and percentages.
(c) Comment *briefly* on the changes which have taken place in the financial

position of the company during the year ended 30 September 19A2. Support your answer with appropriate comparisons, ratios and percentages. State how the company may correct any unfavourable aspects of its financial position.

9.2 The following are the summarized balance sheets of ABC Ltd for the years ended 30 September 19A3 and 19A4.

The sales of the company for the two years were as follows:

19A3	$4,000,000
19A4	$4,450,000

The following net profit after tax was reported:

19A3	$300,000
19A4	$350,000

Required:

Comment on the operating results and financial structure of ABC Ltd for the year ended 30 September 19A4 using such ratios, percentages and comparisons as you consider appropriate.

	19A3 $000	19A4 $000
Paid up capital	1,500	1,500
Revenue reserves	1,500	1,650
	3,000	3,150
Mortgages	250	250
Current liabilities		
Bank overdraft	30	—
Sundry creditors	320	350
Provision for dividend	200	200
Provision for tax	290	340
	4,090	4,290
Fixed assets at cost less depreciation		
Land and buildings	2,500	2,450
Furniture and fittings	120	110
Current assets		
Stocks	1,070	1,220
Debtors	400	500
Bank	—	10
	4,090	4,290

9.3 The tabular information on p 170 has been extracted from the accounts of the XYZ Co Ltd for the three years ended 31 May 19A5, 19A6 and 19A7.

Required:
(a) Comment on the operating results of the XYZ Co Ltd for the three years ended 31 May 19A5, 19A6, and 19A7. You should support your comments with appropriate comparisons and percentages.
(b) Calculate and compare the rate of stock turn for the three years.
(c) Comment briefly on the significance of the following ratios and percentages given in the table:

	19A5	19A6	19A7
Sales	$600,000	$950,000	$1,000,000
Gross profit rate (as a percentage of sales)	42%	38%	37%
Net profit after tax	$ 59,000	$ 72,000	$ 74,000
Provision for dividend	$ 30,000	$ 40,000	$ 40,000
	$	$	$
Capital and reserves			
Ordinary capital	200,000	300,000	300,000
Reserves	150,000	182,000	216,000
Capital and reserves	350,000	482,000	516,000
	$	$	$
Average stocks	120,000	230,000	210,000
Debtors (31 May)	74,000	129,000	125,000
Fixed assets (cost less depreciation)	400,000	660,000	610,000
Term liabilities	100,000	160,000	200,000

In addition to the above information, the following ratios and percentages have been extracted from the Accounts.

	19A5	19A6	19A7
Current ratio	1.35:1	0.95:1	1.46:1
Proprietary ratio (capital and reserves as a percentage of total assets)	59%	47%	54.6%
Term liabilities as a percentage of net fixed assets	25%	24%	33%

- current ratio;
- proprietary ratio;
- term liabilities as a percentage of net fixed assets.

Give, where possible, likely reasons for the trends shown by these ratios and percentages.
(d) Assuming that all the sales are credit sales made on a monthly basis, calculate and compare the average colection period for debtors for 19A6 and 19A7.

9.4 The annual accounts of Hamilton Wholesalers Ltd (pp 171-2) as prepared by a member of their staff in respect of the years ended 31 March 19A1 and 19A2 are submitted to you.

You are asked to prepare a formal report for submission to the board of directors covering the progress of the company during the two years ended 31 March 19A1 and 19A2.

Your report should cover the following points:

1 trading results;
2 liquid position;
3 working capital;
4 stock carrying and credit policies;
5 dividend policy;

Trading account

	19A1 $	19A2 $		19A1 $	19A2 $
Stock (beginning)	700,000	500,000	Sales (net)	5,000,000	5,200,000
Purchases	4,150,000	4,760,000	Stock (end)	500,000	600,000
Gross profit	650,000	540,000			
	5,500,000	5,800,000		5,500,000	5,800,000

Profit and loss account

	19A1	19A2		19A1	19A2
Salaries and wages	240,000	250,000	Gross profit	650,000	540,000
Advertising	10,000	20,000			
Interest	25,000	45,000			
Vehicle running	18,000	20,000			
Printing and stationery	6,500	8,000			
Telephone and tolls	4,500	6,000			
Bad debts	45,000	50,000			
Depreciation					
Buildings	9,000	13,200			
Office furniture	2,470	2,620			
Motor vehicles	12,000	18,000			
Directors' fees	30,000	20,000			
General expenses	7,530	7,180			
Net Profit	240,000	80,000			
	650,000	540,000		650,000	540,000

Appropriation account

	19A1 $	19A2 $		19A1 $	19A2 $
Provision for dividends	100,000	30,000	Balance (beginning)	150,000	170,000
Provision for taxes	120,000	40,000	Net profit	240,000	80,000
Balance (end)	170,000	180,000			
	390,000	250,000		390,000	250,000

Balance sheets

	19A1 $	19A2 $		19A1 $	19A2 $
Provision for dividend	100,000	30,000	Office furniture	30,500	32,000
Mortgage on realty	400,000	800,000	Cash	5,500	3,000
Bad debts provision	60,000	80,000	Land	160,000	160,000
Authorized capital			Stocks	500,000	600,000
(fully paid)	1,200,000	1,200,000	Sundry		
General reserve	200,000	200,000	debtors	1,360,000	1,680,000
Appropriation a/c	170,000	180,000	Prepayments	16,000	8,000
Taxes provision	120,000	40,000	Buildings	500,000	780,000
Bank overdraft			Motor		
	110,000	405,000	vehicles	48,000	72,000
Trade creditors	260,000	400,000			
	2,620,000	3,335,000		2,620,000	3,335,000

6 statement of source and application of funds (year ended 31 March 19A2);

7 general conclusions.

Where possible, percentages and ratios, and the basis of their calculation, should be given to illustrate the points made.

You may make any reasonable assumptions you consider necessary.

9.5 The following data have been extracted from the financial statements of the XYZ Co Ltd for the three years ended 31 March 19A3, 19A4, and 19A5.

	19A3	19A4	19A5
Current ratio	2.3:1	1.6:1	1.1:1
Liquid ratio	1.6:1	1.1:1	0.5:1
Inventory turnover pa	12	11	9
Average collection period for debtors (months)	1.3	1.5	1.9
Proprietary ratio	30%	34%	41%
Gross profit ratio	39%	32%	34%
Net profit to total funds	4.1%	5.1%	7%
Net profit to sales	8.3%	10%	13%
Reserves to paid up ordinary capital	48%	33%	22%
Net profit to ordinary paid up capital	20%	21.3%	20.9%

	19A3 $	19A4 $	19A5 $
Sales	1,200,000	1,600,000	1,920,000
Paid up ordinary capital	500,000	750,000	1,200,000
Total shareholders' funds	740,000	1,000,000	1,460,000

Required:

Comment on the trends of the business.

9.6 The information below has been extracted from the annual report of Donaghys Industries Limited for the year ended 31 March 1986:

Consolidated Profit Statement

	1986 $000	1985 $000
Sales	57,255	59,968
Trading profit		
Non-trading income (interest and dividends received and other income)	27	504
Net profit before tax	3,328	6,964
Provision for tax	(387)	2,088
Net profit after tax	3,715	4,876
Extraordinary items after tax	—	2,533
Net profit after extraordinary items	3,715	7,409

The following details were disclosed in the notes to the accounts:

(a) Net profit before tax was arrived at after charging the following interest and rental costs:

	1986 $000	1985 $000
Interest paid	3,325	2,581
Leasing and rental costs	699	257
	4,024	2,838

(b) At the nominal rate of tax of 45% taxation would have been $1,497,000. However, export tax incentives, investment allowances and other sundry allowances had reduced taxation to a credit of $387,000.

The balance sheet included the following figures:

	1986 $000	1985 $000
Shareholders funds (capital and reserves)	34,474	31,918
Current Assets		
Short-term deposits	895	3,000
Debtors	8,201	8,914
Stocks and work in progress	19,329	20,022
Prepayments	1,633	319
	30,058	32,255

Continued

173

Current liabilities

Bank overdraft	1,211	4,035
Bills payable	6,409	2,158
Term liabilities payable within 12 months	1,630	1,978
Trade creditors and accrued charges	3,923	4,987
Provision for tax	—	385
Provision for dividend	1,210	1,008
	14,383	14,551

In his review of the year's operations the managing director stated that the year had been one of the most difficult the company had experienced in recent years because of the effect structural changes to the New Zealand economy had had on the company's principal market—the pastoral and horticultural sectors. As a result, profit after tax for the year had fallen by 23.7% from the 1985 record profit of $4,876,000. The profit for 1985 was further increased by an extraordinary gain of $2,533,000 as a result of the sale of group property, while in the 1986 financial year extraordinary items were nil.

Required:

(a) Comment on the operating results of Donaghys Industries Limited for its financial year ended 31 March 1986, including the interest and leasing and rental costs incurred by the company. Support your comments with such comparisons, ratios and percentages as you consider appropriate.

Note: Export incentives were to be phased out by the end of the 1987 calendar year.

(b) Calculate and comment briefly on the working capital and current ratio of the company at 31 March 1986 and 1985.

(c) Comment briefly, as far as possible from the information provided, on the changes which have taken place in the current assets and current liabilities of Donaghys Industries during the year ended 31 March 1986.

Chapter 10
Ratio Analysis Extended

[1001] In the preceding chapters we considered a number of financial ratios and percentages and illustrated some of their uses in the analysis and interpretation of financial statements. The purpose of this chapter is to consider some further ratios and percentages, in particular some which are frequently used by investors and financial analysts. Some of these ratios and percentages, like earnings yield and dividend yield, make use of share market prices in addition to information contained in the financial statements themselves.

Earnings Per Share (EPS)

[1002] The earnings per share ratio measures the amount of net profit attributable to one ordinary share and is calculated by dividing net profit after tax and preference dividend by the number of issued ordinary shares. The calculation of the earnings per share of an assumed company X Ltd is illustrated in Example 10.1.

Earnings per share data have been used as a measure of business performance and a basis for predicting dividends and growth and, therefore, future market prices of ordinary shares.

[1003] Earnings per share is a simple concept which has some serious limitations as an indicator of business performance. For example, the ratio concentrates on the *number* of issued ordinary shares rather than on the amount of the investment attributable to ordinary shareholders. This limits the value of earnings per share as a means of comparing the performance of different firms or the evalutaion of the performance of the same firm over time. These limitations will be illustrated in Examples 10.2 and 10.3.

[1004] Example 10.2 shows that even though the shareholders' funds, profit after tax and rate of return of the two companies are the same (and we may assume that the companies are identical in every other respect), A Ltd shows a higher earnings per share figure than B Ltd. This difference is caused solely by the different *number* of shares isued by the two companies.

[1005] The figures in Example 10.3 illustrate that earnings per share may show a rising trend over time while, in fact, the rate of return on the shareholders' equity is falling. This phenomenon is caused by the fact that the calculation of earnings per share ignores retained earnings. As one may expect that, over time, the profits of a firm will increase with the growth of investment through profit retention, earnings per share is not a substitute for other measures of performance such as the rate of return.

Example 10.1
X Ltd
Capital and reserves as at 31 March 19A1

400,000 ordinary shares of $1 each	$400,000
100,000 10% preference shares of $1 each	100,000
Issued and paid up capital	$500,000
Reserves	300,000
Shareholders' equity	$800,000

Net profit after tax	$90,000
Preference dividend to be provided for	10,000
Earnings per share	
Net profit after tax	$90,000
Less preference dividend	10,000
Profit attributable to ordinary shares	$80,000

$$EPS = \frac{\$80,000}{400,000} = 20¢.$$

Example 10.2

Shown below are details of the capital and reserves of A Ltd and B Ltd, the net profit after tax of the two companies and their earnings per share and rate of return calculated on the basis of these figures.

	A Ltd	B Ltd
Paid up capital in $1 ordinary shares	$400,000	$600,000
Retained earnings	400,000	200,000
Shareholders' funds	$800,000	$800,000
Net profit after tax	$120,000	$120,000
Earnings per share	30¢	20¢
Rate of return	15%	15%

Example 10.3

Shown below is a four years comparison of the capital and retained earnings, net profit after tax, earnings per share and rate of return of C Ltd.

	19A1 $	19A2 $	19A3 $	19A4 $
Ordinary capital in $1 shares	500,000	500,000	500,000	500,000
Retained earnings	300,000	360,000	430,000	520,000
Shareholders' funds	800,000	860,000	930,000	1,020,000
Earnings per share	32¢	34¢	36¢	38¢
Rate of return	20%	19.8%	19.4%	18.6%

The earnings per share ratio is based on a simple concept. There are, however, a number of problems associated with its calculation. Some of these are discussed below.

176

Net profit after tax

[1006] The problem here is to determine the extent to which the reported net profit after-tax figure reflects the "normal" operations of the firm. The concern should be with extraordinary items, the effects of changes in accounting policies, tax distortions arising from investment allowances, special tax concessions, losses brought forward, etc. It may be necessary to make appropriate adjustments in order to arrive at a more representative profit figure to use in the calculation of the earnings per share ratio. A treatment of extraordinary items is illustrated in Example 10.4.

Example 10.4

	19A1	19A2
Net profit before extraordinary items	$140,000	$124,000
Profit attributable to extraordinary items	50,000	2,000
Total profit	$190,000	$126,000
Issued ordinary shares	1,000,000	1,000,000
Earnings per share		
Excluding income from extraordinary items	14¢	12.4¢
Income from extraordinary items	5¢	0.2¢
Including income from extraordinary items	19¢	12.6¢

Issues of ordinary shares during the period

[1007] An issue of ordinary shares may involve a cash issue, a bonus issue, or an issue on the acquisition of an interest in another company. Where bonus shares are issued, retrospective adjustments of previously reported earnings per share are necessary to ensure the comparability of the figures over time. The calculation of earnings per share when there have been issues of ordinary shares during the period and necessary retrospective adjustments, are illustrated in the examples which follow.

[1008] *Issue of ordinary shares for cash.* Where there is an issue of shares for cash during a period, additional funds are made available for use in operations. It is considered, therefore, that, in such cases, earnings per share should be calculated on the basis of the weighted average number of shares for the period.

Example 10.5

	19A2	19A1
Issued ordinary capital in $1 shares (200,000 $1 shares issued for cash in 19A2 3 months before balance date)	$1,200,000	$1,000,000
Net profit after tax	$90,000	$75,000
Average number of shares:		
19A1		1,000,000
19A2 (1,000,000 + 25% of 200,000)	1,050,000	
Earnings per share	8.57¢	7.5¢

[1009] *Issue of bonus shares.* A bonus issue of shares by the capitalization of reserves will affect the comparability of earnings per share with previous years. The adjustment necessary to earnings per share for previous years is illustrated in Example 10.6.

It should be noted that without an adjustment of the 19A1 calculations the comparison shows a drop in earnings per share from 11.80 cents to 11.64 cents while in fact there has been an increase from 10.72 cents to 11.64 cents.

Example 10.6

	19A2	19A1
Issued ordinary shares after 1 for 10 bonus issue in 19A2	1,100,000	1,000,000
Profit after tax	$128,000	$118,000
EPS without adjustment for bonus issue	11.64¢	11.80¢
To make the figures comparable, EPS for 19A1 is recalculated on the basis of 1,100,000 shares	11.64¢	10.72¢

[1010] *Issue of ordinary shares on the acquisition of an interest in another company.* Where ordinary shares are issued on the acquisition of a subsidiary, earnings per share for the period during which the acquisition took place should be calculated on the basis of the consolidated profit figure and the weighted average number of ordinary shares of the holding company. For example, the consolidated financial statements of the holding company and its subsidiary will show a consolidated profit figure consisting of the holding company's profit plus the holding company's share of the subsidiary profit since the time of acquisition; and the issued ordinary capital will be that of the holding company, including the shares issued on the acquisition of the subsidiary. As the acquisition took place during the period, the earnings per share should be calculated on the basis of the weighted average number of shares of the holding company.

Example 10.7

In 19A2, six months before balance date, A Ltd, acquired a controlling interest in B Ltd, by the issue to shareholders of B Ltd, of 500,000 ordinary shares. The figures shown below have been extracted from the financial statements of A Ltd for 19A2 and 19A1. The 19A2 figures are after the consolidation of the financial statements of A Ltd and its subsidiary B Ltd.

	19A2	19A1
Ordinary shares	1,500,000	1,000,000
Profit after tax	$226,250	$172,500
Earnings per share	18.10¢*	17.25¢
*Calculated on the basis of $226,250 profit and the weighted average number of shares of 1,250,000 (1,000,000 plus ½ of 500,000).		

Share splits

[1011] Share splits involve the conversion ("splitting") of shares into smaller denominations. For example $1 shares may be split into 50c shares.

A split of ordinary shares requires retrospective adjustment of earnings per share in order to effect comparability over time.

Basic and diluted earnings per share

[1012] The preceding examples dealt with what is known as basic earnings per share — the ratio of net profit attributable to ordinary shares.

Example 10.8

In 19A2 X Ltd split its 1 million $1 shares into 2 million 50¢ shares. The following figures relate to the operations of the company for 19A2 and 19A1:

	19A2
Profit after tax	$259,600
Ordinary shares (50¢ each)	2,000,000
Earnings per share	12.98¢

	19A1
Profit after tax	$225,000
Ordinary shares ($1 each)	1,000,000
Earnings per share	22.5¢

Because of the share split in 19A2, to make the earnings per share figures for the two years comparable, the 19A1 earnings per share should be recalculated on the basis of 2 million 50¢ shares. The comparison will then be:

	19A2	19A1
Earnings per share	12.98¢	11.25¢

[1013] Where a company has issued convertible securities such as convertible preference shares or debentures, or has given options to take up shares to employees, creditors or business associates, it is considered useful to calculate "diluted" earnings per share. "Diluted" earnings per share are calculated on the assumption that convertible securities are converted into shares and that share options are taken up. The purpose of the calculation is to determine the dilution of earnings per share which may be caused by existing convertible securities and options. The calculation may require an adjustment of the profit figure as well as of the number of ordinary shares. The basis of these adjustments is the notional conversion of the convertible preference shares or debentures into ordinary shares in accordance with the specified terms of conversion, and the notional taking up of share options by those entitled to do so. The profit figure applicable to ordinary shareholders will be affected by any changes in interest expense, income tax expense, and preference dividends. The result of the notional conversion or issue of options is the "dilution" of the earnings per share applicable to ordinary shareholders. The calculation of diluted earnings per share is illustrated in Example 10.9.

[1014] Example 10.9 deals with convertible debentures. Where a company has issued convertible preference shares, earnings are adjusted by adding back preference dividend. In recent years New Zealand companies have issued "specified" preference shares the salient characteristic of which is that the dividend paid on them is tax-deductible. Where a company has issued convertible specified preference shares, it will be necessary to allow for notional tax on the preference dividend. The earnings after tax now applicable to the increased ordinary shares will be:

- *net profit after tax*, before notional conversion of specified preference shares;
- *plus* dividends on specified preference shares;
- *less* tax benefit no longer applicable as these dividends were deductible for tax purposes.

Example 10.9
Diluted earnings per share

	19A2	19A1
Issued $1 ordinary shares	1,000,000	1,000,000
$1 convertible notes (interest 10%, convertible at the rate of 10 notes for 6 shares)	200,000	200,000
Rate of tax 50%		
Net profit after tax	$180,000	$150,000
Earnings per share		
(a) *Basic*	18¢	15¢
(b) *Diluted*		
Issued ordinary shares	1,000,000	1,000,000
Plus notional conversion of notes		
$(\frac{6}{10} \times 200,000)$	120,000	120,000
Adjusted number of shares	1,120,000	1,120,000
Net profit after tax	$180,000	$150,000
Plus interest on convertible notes $20,000		
Less tax saving on this 10,000	10,000	10,000
Adjusted net profit after tax	$190,000	160,000
Diluted earnings per share	16.96¢	14.29¢

Cash Flow and Cash Flow per Share

[1015] As pointed out earlier in this book, profit measurement, even when based on the traditional accounting concepts of historical cost and realization, is largely the product of judgment and opinion in the face of an uncertain future. Profit measurement, therefore, is subject to bias because of difficulties associated with the proper matching of revenue and expenses and the arbitrary nature of some procedures for the allocation of both revenues and expenses to different accounting periods.

[1016] Let us take depreciation as an example. The allocation of depreciation expense to different accounting periods is a highly subjective exercise which requires the estimation of the expected useful life and residual value of depreciable assets. In addition, it requires a choice of an "appropriate" method of depreciation such as straight line or reducing balance. The allocation of total estimated depreciation cost to different accounting periods, therefore, is, at best, the result of responsible and informed opinion; at worst it could be the product of deliberate bias. For example, let us assume that two capital intensive companies have identical assets and identical operating results in every respect except for depreciation policies. If depreciation expense is a material item in the measurement of the profit of the two companies, the reported profit figures may be significantly different because of the differences in the depreciation policies.

[1017] The subjectivity which attaches to the measurement of profit, in particular the allocation of depreciation expense, has led analysis of financial statements to sometimes ignore charges for depreciation and to concentrate instead on what has been termed "cash flow" — net profit after adding back depreciation (and, strictly speaking, other non-cash charges against revenue). Published financial reports frequently include *cash flow per share* figures calculated by dividing the amount of cash flow by the number of shares.

[1018] The concept of cash flow is most useful in considering the short- to medium-term results of capital intensive enterprises with substantial investments in specialized assets. Much of the investment, once made, is "sunk", as the realizable value of the plant and buildings may be negligible. In the short run, depreciation of what is a sunk cost is less significant than current operating expense. A useful measure of performance is the net profit before allowing for this depreciation expense. For example, it could be regarded as more useful to continue to operate the enterprise in difficult economic conditions than to shut it down provided that there was some surplus "cash flow" to indicate a recovery of part of the sunk investment in specialized plant and buildings.

[1019] It has been held that cash flow information assists investors in the prediction of future dividends, and creditors in the prediction of the availability of cash for the payment of interest and the repayment of principal. Cash flow projections may be used to determine the degree of risk associated with an investment. For example, where the risk associated with an investment project is higher than normal, the "payback period" may be used to determine how soon the original investment may be recovered in terms of the positive "cash flows" the project is expected to generate.

Some limitations of cash flow analysis

[1020] Cash flow anlaysis is subject to a number of serious limitations which arise to a large extent from misconceptions about the meaning of the term. "Cash flow" is not really what the term suggests.

Cash flow (profit before non-cash expenses, including depreciation) does not represent the "flow" of cash through the enterprise, as it is, in fact, a net amount, nor does it represent a residual of cash received less cash disbursed. At best, cash flow can be used to approximate the amount of "funds" (resources) generated from operations, with "funds" being conceived in a broader context than strictly cash.

[1021] Another possible misconception is that the cash flow calculation removes the subjectivity from profit measurement. The fact is that adding back depreciation removes only one of the subjective elements included in the measurement of profit. Other subjective cost allocations include inventory valuation, the allocation of research and development costs to different accounting periods, and the treatment in the accounts of the cost of major maintenance including maintenance which extends the economic life of the asset.

[1022] Cash flow does not necessarily represent a surplus available for discretionary use by management. The continuation of business operations requires reinvestment in inventories, the continued financing of debtors and, in the long run, the replacement of fixed assets. The conception of cash flow as surplus funds is particularly misleading in times of rising prices when inventories cost more to maintain and higher selling prices require higher investment in debtors.

Overemphasis on cash flows as a measure of performance may lead to the dangerous misconception that depreciation is not an expense in the "proper" sense of the word. It may be regarded as different from materials used and labour costs incurred, and from other expenses requiring more or less immediate cash outlays. If this difference is accepted, then one might form the opinion that cash flow is a better measure of operating results and "real" profitability than profit as normally measured. Further, the fact that cash flow will show a higher amount than profit may lead management to emphasise cash flow rather than profit in times when profits are low.

[1023] Depreciation involves the allocation of the cost of an asset over the estimated useful life of the asset; it provides for the recovery from revenue of the investment in depreciable assets over the assets' useful lives. The problems associated with accounting for depreciation expense arise mainly from the subjectivity associated with both the estimation of useful lives and the selection of an "appropriate" method of depreciation. The fact of depreciation is generally accepted and with it the need to allow for depreciation expense against period revenue. The recovery of investment in depreciable assets through depreciation charges is similar to the recovery of investment in inventories through charges against revenue for cost of sales. The difference is in the time length of the cycle between investment and recovery and this is a difference of degree, not of substance.

[1024] The foregoing is not to say that cash flow is without merit in the interpretation of financial statements. Used in conjunction with an analysis of reported profit, it may lead to better informed decisions. The danger in the use of cash flow in decision-making lies in possible misconceptions regarding the meaning of the term and of its significance in the interpretation of financial statements.

Cash flow and rising prices

[1025] In times of rising prices firms are faced with rising monetary outlays for the replacement of inventories sold, in financing an increasing level of debtors (even if physical sales remain unchanged), and, in the long run, with the need to replace the productive capacity of depreciable assets at prices which may be many times higher than historical cost. Under conditions of rising prices, therefore, cash flow when measured by adding depreciation to reported profit can be particularly misleading. This point will be illustrated in Example 10.10.

Example 10.10

This example deals with an operating cycle of X Ltd. Shown below is the balance sheet of the company at the beginning of the cycle

X Ltd
Balance Sheet

	$		$
Capital (in $ shares)	200,000	Inventories at cost	150,000
		Depreciable assets at cost	50,000
	200,000		200,000

The following simplifying assumptions are made:
1 The total inventory of X Ltd is sold for $210,000.
2 The only expense incurred by the company is depreciation at the rate of 10% of the cost of depreciable assets. The assumption of other expenses will not invalidate the conclusions reached.
3 The company is taxed at the rate of 50% of historical cost profit.
4 All sales and purchases are for cash.

Required:
Calculate cash flow and cash flow per share on the basis of the information provided. Consider the validity of the cash flow figure if between the time the inventory was acquired and sold its replacement cost increased by 20%.

[1026] Using generally accepted accounting principles, the profit of X Ltd is calculated as follows:

	$
Sales	210,000
Less cost of sales	150,000
	60,000
Less depreciation	5,000
Net profit before tax	55,000
Less tax	27,500
Net profit after tax	27,500

Cash flow and cash flow per share will then be calculated by adding back depreciation and dividing the resulting amount by the number of shares:

	$
Net profit after tax	27,500
Plus depreciation written off	5,000
Cash flow	32,500
Cash flow per share	16.25¢

[1027] If there was no change in price and the firm merely replaced the inventories sold (and paid its tax), the cash flow of $32,500 will represent in fact a cash surplus generated from operations as shown by the balance sheet below.

X Ltd
Balance sheet
(After replacement of inventories and payment of tax)

	$		$	$
Capital	200,000	Inventories		150,000
Retained profit	27,500	Depreciable assets, cost	50,000	
		Less depreciation	5,000	45,000
		Cash		32,500
	227,500			227,500

183

(It should be noted that the equality of the cash flow and cash surplus above is the result of the simplifying assumptions on which the example is based. Such direct correspondence between "cash flow" and cash surplus will not normally occur in real life.)

[1028] Assuming that between the time of acquisition and sale the replacement cost of the inventory increased by 20%, the profit and cash flow calculations will be the same as above. different as is shown in the following table:

	$
Sales	210,000
Less replacement cost of sales ($150,000 + 20%)	180,000
	30,000
Less depreciation	5,000
"Net profit" before tax	25,000
Less tax	27,500*
Deficiency after tax	2,500

*Tax is still 50% of historical cost profit as taxation rules do not recognize an increase in replacement cost for tax purposes.

Actual cash flow	$
Deficiency after tax	(2,500)
Add back depreciation	5,000
Cash flow	2,500

Actual cash flow per share = 1.25 cents

Balance sheet
(After replacement of inventories and payment of tax)

	$		$	$
Capital	200,000	Inventories		180,000
Retained profit	27,500	Depreciable assets, cost	50,000	
		Less depreciation	5,000	45,000
		Cash		2,500
	227,500			227,500

[1029] In circumstances such as these, it is misleading to show a cash flow of $32,500 or 16.25 cents a share. The difference between historical cost based profit and cash flow data and financial reality provide a strong argument for a replacement of historical cost accounting with an acceptable form of current cost accounting. Until that eventuates, one has to recognize the potential to mislead of indicators like "cash flow" per share.

[1030] The above simple example illustrates the financial effects of a price increase in relation to the replacement of inventories. The effect is important and is likely to be quickly felt. A firm carrying debtors will experience another immediate effect. As increases in selling prices normally follow increases in costs, a firm will need to finance an increased level of debtors. For example, a 20% increase in selling price will result in a 20% increase in debtors even if sales in terms of physical volume remain the same. Further, in the long run the firm may be faced with the financial consequence of having to replace productive resources in the form of fixed assets at prices much higher than their historical cost.

Net Assets per Share

[1031] Net assets per share is a ratio which is frequently included in financial reports and used by investors. The ratio may be calculated in relation to preference shares by dividing the total shareholders' equity by the number of preference shares, or it may be calculated in relation to ordinary shares by dividing the equity attributable to ordinary shareholders by the number of ordinary shares.

The implied significance of net assets per share relates to notions of security of investment and value per share. For example, a high ratio of net assets to preference shares implies a high level of security regarding the return of capital in the causes of liquidation. A similar notion of security is implied in the ratio of net assets per ordinary share.

[1032] Security in relation to the return of capital on liquidation, however, depends on the realizable value of assets, not on their book value. The balance sheet does show some assets, such as debtors, at estimated realizable value. Fixed assets are usually shown at historical cost less depreciation where appropriate. Such valuation reflects residuals of original investment. The current value of the assets on a going concern basis, however, would depend largely on the profitability of the business. The specialized assets of an unprofitable manufacturing enterprise may constitute a substantial proportion of the net asset backing (or net tangible assets per share), but have little value in a liquidation. When such a company seems likely to earn adequate *real* profits in the future (that is, after maintenance of its current operating capacity and gearing), then its specialized assets will have a value on the market as part of ongoing operational units of the total enterprise, or of the enterprise itself. Their contribution to net tangible assets per share may be meaningful, just as the debt/equity ratio may be meaningful. But if real profitability prospects are lost, then so is much of the value attached to such assets, and therefore the measure of shareholders' equity, net assets per share, and financial gearing. It is important, therefore, that the measure of net assets per share should be interpreted with considerable caution.

Some Ratios Based on Market Share Prices

[1033] The ratios discussed so far were based on data contained in the financial statements themselves. In this section we shall consider ratios which are based on data disclosed in the financial statements, such as dividends, earnings and net assets, but which involve the use of external data also, in particular the market value of the ordinary shares. The ratios are used to give an indication of the financial market's assessment of a firm as an avenue for investment. This assessment may be taken to be based on current profit levels, but with allowances considered to be appropriate for future growth in dividends per share and for the level of risk perceived, both business risk and financial risk.

Dividend yield; earnings yield (or price/earnings ratio)

[1034] *Dividend yield* measures the percentage return to an investor from shares in a particular company. The calculation is based on the latest annual dividend rate and the current market value per share:

$$\text{Dividend yield} = \frac{\text{Dividend per share}}{\text{Market value per share}}$$

Earnings yield is the rate of earnings to the market value of shares:

$$\text{Earnings yield} = \frac{\text{Earnings per share}}{\text{Market value per share}}$$

The relationship between the market value per share and earnings per share is frequently expressed in the form of a price/earnings ratio (P/E):

$$\text{P/E} = \frac{\text{Market value per share}}{\text{Earnings per share}}$$

[1035] The market indicates through the market price its assesment of the value of a share at a particular time. The market price fluctuates from day to day, in sympathy with variations in demand and supply, and under the influence of changing assessments of what the future holds for the enterprise. There are also fluctuations in the share market as a whole, as it reacts to changing economic conditions and expectations. For example, a change in the rates on interest-bearing investments is likely to affect share prices generally. Share prices over six months or a year can be expected to reflect the approach of a dividend payment, so that the price may be seen as consisting of a basic price plus an accumulation of expected dividend.

Assuming that the market behaves rationally, then the market price of a share may be conceived of as representing the present value of the expected stream of future dividends arising from ownership of the share. If growth in dividends is expected, then this will be built into the forecasted flow of future dividends. This flow will be reduced to present value by applying a discount rate made up of a market cost of equity capital, excluding the risk factor, plus an allowance made by the market for the risk attached to the particular share.

[1036] Now let us return to our ratios based on the market price of shares, to make some broad and, to a degree, questionable generalizations

(1) A high level of dividend yield (relative to the market) could be caused by:
 • a low market price; and/or
 • a dividend regarded as abnormally high.
 A low market price could be caused by:
 • low expectations of dividend flows, and of dividend growth in particular; and/or
 • a higher than average level of expected risk.

(2) A high level of earnings yield (relative to the market) could be caused by:
 • a low market price; and/or
 • earnings regarded as abnormally high. For example, earnings of the year may have been swelled by extraordinary and non-recurring profits.
 The factors causing the low market price would be the same as in (1) above. The benefit to the shareholder depends finally not on earnings but rather on dividend flows. Dividends have to be paid out in cash, and a company's financial position

may place restraints on its ability to pay dividends. This applies particularly where inflation affects the need to commit earnings, as traditionally measured, to aid in the financing of the extra investment in inventories, accounts receivable, and fixed assets that are necessary to maintain the present level of operations.

The price/earnings ratio is the reciprocal of the earnings yield. It is low when the earnings yield is high, and vice versa.

(3) A low level of dividend yield (relative to the market) could be caused by:
- a high market price; and/or
- a dividend regarded as abnormally low.

A high market price could be caused by:
- expectations of growth in dividend flows; and/or
- a lower than average level of expected risk.

(4) A low level of earnings yield (relative to the market) could be caused by:
- a high market price; and/or
- earnings regarded as abnormally low.

The same factors as in (3) would explain the high market price. The emphasis is not directly on the expectation of future profits but on the expectations of future dividends. There is a reatlionship between earnings and dividend potential, but it is not a direct relationship. There is a greater stability about dividends than there is about earnings. Dividends reflect the policy of the directors, a policy that may be explicit or merely inferred from the relationships between earnings and dividends in recent years.

A low earnings yield is reflected in a high price/earnings ratio.

[1037] Why are these relationships questionable, in the sense that they need careful interpretation? It is because market prices may be assumed to be based on changing *current* expectations of the *future*. *Past* earnings and dividends are not directly relevant to market prices, though the market needs this type of information to assist in its assessment of the future. The earnings and dividend data may be up to a year old as information. In the meantime the market has received new information influencing its estimates of the future and has been affected by changes in the environment affecting share prices generally. The influence of last year's dividends and earnings per share becomes less and less relevant to market value with the passage of time.

[1038] An indicator of the ability to pay dividends in the future is the *dividend cover* — the number of times the dividend per share is covered by the latest earnings per share. The actual ability of a company to pay dividends is dependent on its financial situation, however; they have to be paid in cash. The other determinant is the policy of the directors, who will have a concern to keep share prices up (and the cost of equity capital down) and also to please shareholders in the long as well as the short term. There is an assumption, sometimes supported by a statement of intention by the directors, that dividend rates will not be raised unless it is expected that the company can sustain the higher payout in future years.

[1039] The difference between earnings per share and dividend per share is the profit retention. The profit retention rate is: *Retained earnings per share divided by earnings per share, expressed as a percentage.*

The retention rate may be taken as an indicator, but by no means a reliable indicator, of the growth potential of a company. Growth in earnings is dependent on the use made of resources in the future as well as their absolute amount. One may distinguish also between the retention of disclosed dollar profits and the amount of real profits available for real growth after providing for the higher prices of the assets needed to merely maintain operations at their present level. In these real terms, profit retention may be an illusion. But while we account in dollars, and while cash flow is in dollars rather than purchasing power units, profit retention and dividend flows and growth in dollar terms are measures that we will continue to use.

The limitations introduced by our failure to account for price and price-level changes will be considered further in Chapter 19.

Net assets per share to market value of share

[1040] This ratio is calculated by relating the net assets, at book value, attributable to an ordinary share to the market value of the share. A high ratio (ie low market share value in relation to the assets attributable to the share) may indicate an inefficient utilization of resources and an under-utilized capacity to earn profits. As the book value of assets may be quite different from their current value in terms of, say, current replacement cost or realizable value, a more informative ratio may be calculated on the basis of the current value of assets and the market value of shares.

[1041] A high ratio of net assets per share to the market value of shares may indicate that conditions exist for a takeover bid. The following are some of the reasons why such a firm may be an attractive proposition for a takeover:
- the existence of under-utilized resources offers an opportunity for a more efficient firm to acquire the firm on favourable terms and reorganize its operations, and the combined operations of the enlarged group, on more profitable lines;
- with a low share price and current value of assets above book value, a firm effecting a takeover bid may acquire additional operating capacity at a price which may be well below the current acquisition cost of the separate assets;
- the opportunity may exist to acquire assets which have a substantial realizable value, which may then be sold at considerable profit. The "spin-off" from the sale of these disposable assets will serve to reduce the outlay required for acquisition of the shares in the new subsidiary.

[1042] Share prices are an important factor in the maintenance of the financial viability of a company. Under conditions of significant price increases and of inflation generally, a company has to either increase its level of investment or to reduce the scale of its operations so as to be able to operate within the resources available to it. Many enterprises would find it difficult to adopt the second alternative. To succeed in the first, the company has to maintain what is regarded as, and expected to be, a satisfactory financial structure. In particular, it has to avoid an overdependence on debt finance; and that calls for an increase in equity finance. New equity issues will succeed only where they are made at an attractive price — which is usually below the present market value. It is therefore vital for solvency that the share price be kept sufficiently above par to make an attractive offer possible. It is suggested that the relationship between the market price of a company's shares and their par value is information of considerable significance to investors, lenders, providers of credit, employees, and the society within which the business enterprise operates. Shares are kept above par by the prospect of the generation in future years of real profits which will enable the company to pay out dividends at the rate necessary to warrant the desired price per share. In theory, to justify continued investment, including the replacement of long-term productive capacity as it is used up, the rate of return and the dividend expectations should be such that the share price exceeds the net current cost of assets. In fact such replacement decisions are made in a relatively piecemeal fashion, and are likely to reflect managerial optimism and self interest to some extent at least.

Review questions

10.1 Discuss the uses and limitations of the earnings per share ratio in the evaluation of the relative performance of different business firms.

10.2 "Earnings per share may show a rising trend over time while, in fact, the rate of return on the shareholders' equity is falling."
Discuss.

10.3 Explain how the following situations may be dealt with in the calculation of earnings per share:
(a) An issue of ordinary shares during the period —
   (i) for cash;
   (ii) on a takeover of another company;
   (iii) a bonus issue.
(b) The split of $1 ordinary shares into 50c ordinary shares.
(c) The inclusion in the calculation of profit of material extraordinary items.

10.4 Explain the meaning of the term "diluted earnings per share".

10.5 From the following data of Aotea Ltd calculate the earnings per share for 19A1:

	$000
Ordinary capital in $1 shares	2,000
10% convertible notes of $1 each, convertible at the rate of 8 shares for 10 notes in 19A4	220
Net profit after tax	240
Marginal tax rate of Aotea Ltd	50%

10.6 " 'Cash flow' avoids some of the subjectivity associated with the measurement of profit, but suffers from loss of relevance for the evaluation of operating results and managerial performance."
Do you agree? Discuss.

10.7 "It is a dangerous misconception that depreciation is not an expense in the 'proper' sense of the word like materials used and labour, or other expenses requiring more or less immediate outlays of cash."
Discuss.

10.8 "Under conditions of rising prices, cash flow when measured by adding depreciation to reported profit can be particularly misleading."
Discuss.

10.9 X Company Ltd completed its first year of operations in 19A1. Shown below are the company's earnings per share and cash flow per share for the years 19A1 to 19A4:

	19A1	19A2	19A3	19A4
Earnings per share	(5¢)*	10¢	15¢	20¢
Cash flow per share	5¢	18¢	21.4¢	26.4¢

*The earnings per share figure for 19A1 is a negative amount as the company reported a loss of $50,000 that year.

What conclusions can you draw about the operations of the company from the above figures?

10.10 Discuss the uses and limitations of the net assets per share ratio.

10.11 Discuss the net assets per share as a measure of security of investment and value per share.

10.12 "A high ratio of net assets per share to the market value of shares may indicate that conditions exist for a takeover bid."
Discuss.

10.13 "It is important that the ratio of net assets per share should be interpreted with considerable caution."
Discuss.

10.14 Discuss dividend yield and earnings yield as indicators of the stock market assessment of a firm's future prospects.

10.15 "Share prices are an important factor in the maintenance of the financial viability of a company."
Discuss.

Chapter 11

Some Problem Areas in Financial Accounting and Reporting: The Allocation Problem

[1101] In this and the next six chapters we will consider some major problems associated with the measurement and reporting of the results and state of affairs of business enterprises. It is important that the analyst and interpreter of financial statements should understand the nature of these problems. Where alternatives are available, there should be awareness of the effect of the choice of accounting methods on what is reported as income and financial position.

[1102] The problems we will discuss arise primarily from the need to prepare periodic reports on the results and state of affairs of business enterprises. There is a normal expectation that a business enterprise will continue operations beyond one accounting period, and there may be an assumption, implicit in accounting, that the operations of an enterprise will continue indefinitely. In particular the problems relate to:

- the measurement of profit by a process of matching realized revenue with expired costs;
- the valuation of non-monetary assets on a going concern basis, primarily on the basis of historical costs or historical cost residuals;
- the uncertainty which permeates buisness operations and the role which judgment plays in the measurement of income and the values which are ultimately assigned to assets;
- the alternatives available for dealing with specific accounting problems, the degree of arbitrariness or bias which may effect the choice of accounting methods and procedures and the effect of the choice on the accounting numbers assigned to different accounting periods as revenues and expense, assets and liabilities, and residual shareholders' equity.

[1103] We will consider in particular inventory valuation, depreciation, accounting for income taxes, segment reporting, accounting for research and developments costs, leases, and foreign currency translation.

The Business Cycle and the Allocation Problem

[1104] In Chapters 1 and 5 and again in Chapter 7 we discussed the key role money plays in the operations of business enterprises and the importance of monetary measurement in accounting for such operations. The business cycle we considered began with investment of money for the purpose of earning income measured in monetary terms. Apart from lending money at interest, this cycle involves an intermediate investment in non-monetary assets destined for ultimate conversion into cash — by way of direct sale in the case of inventories, by way of regular charges to revenue in the case of depreciable assets, and, in the case of land, by ultimate sale, if such a sale was originally contemplated or eventually comes about. At the end of the cash → goods → cash earning cycle, income will be measured by the matching of two monetary amounts — monetary outlays and monetary inflows.

[1105] Continuing business operations require continuing investment in non-monetary assets as some cycles are completed and new cycles are initiated. At balance date, the need arises to measure the investment in the remaining non-monetary assets. This requires the allocation of the original cash outlays on non-monetary assets:

(a) to the period just ended — that portion of the investment which is considered to have been used up in operations and which is to be matched against the revenue of the period as expired costs (expenses); and

(b) to future periods — the balance of the investment to be carried forward as assets, to be recovered from the revenue expected to be generated by future operations.

[1106] The cycle we have described implies that the above allocations should be based on the historical (invested) cost of non-monetary assets. A major issue which arises in this respect is the effect of general and specific price changes on the results and state of firms and the need to reflect these in the measurement of their income and state of affairs:

(a) in relation to general price level changes, the issue is whether historical investment should be restated for changes in the purchasing power of money so that investment is measured and recovered from revenue in "real" terms (ie the purchasing power of the original investment) rather than in "nominal" terms (ie the number of dollars originally involved); and

(b) in relation to specific price changes, the question arises of whether investment in non-monetary assets should be measured on some basis other than historical cost ("nominal" or "real"), such as current replacement cost, and the implications of such alternative valuation on what is reported as income and state of affairs.

[1107] Accounting for changes in the general level of prices, and systematic accounting for specific price changes have yet to gain acceptance. On the other hand, some departures from the historical cost basis of valuation have become generally accepted, such as the writing down of inventories under the lower of cost or market value rule, and the revaluation of some fixed assets, in particular land and buildings, to some measure of their "current value". Where non-monetary assets have been revalued, allocation should be based on the value at which the assets are carried in the books of the enterprise.

[1108] Under current accounting practice, expenditure should be matched against the revenue of the period in which the benefit from the expenditure is derived and only costs which confer benefits to future periods should be carried forward for matching against the revenue of those future periods. For example, the New Zealand standard SSAP 11: *Expenditure Carried Forward to Future Periods* provides that expenditures may be deferred and allocated to future periods if they are expected with *reasonable certainty* to produce *identifiable benefits sufficient to cover the amount deferred.* The corresponding Australian standard (AAS9) lists a number of tests which must be met before expenditure can be deferred, among which are that the amounts must be material, that the expenditure must be clearly identified as contributing to the revenue earning capability of the business in the future, and that it must be reasonably expected that the business will obtain future revenue sufficient to absorb the expense carried forward.

[1109] Some writers have questioned the usefulness of accounting numbers produced by the periodic matching of revenue and expense. In his studies of the problem, Arthur L Thomas found allocations arbitrary and, in the context of formal logic, incorrigible in the sense that they can be neither refuted nor verified (Arthur L Thomas: "The Allocation Problem in Financial Accounting Theory", SAR No 3, American Accounting Association, 1969; "The Allocation Problem: Part Two", SAR No 9, American Accounting Association, 1974; "The FASB and the Allocation Fallacy", *The Journal of Accountancy*, November 1975, pp 65–8). He concluded that accounting allocations should cease.

[1110] The desire for precision and certainty in measurement in general, and accounting measurement in particular, is understandable, but the fact is that business operations are carried out on the basis of expectations in the face of uncertainty and risk.

[1111] Let us consider the relatively simple input/output relationship between cost of sales and sales. We cannot apportion the cost of inventory made available during a period (ie opening inventory plus purchases) between cost of sales and ending inventory at balance date without putting a value on the ending inventory which has regard to the future benefits embodied in that inventory. And this requires judgment about an uncertain future.

[1112] More realistically, output is the result of a number of inputs such as materials, plant and machinery, labour, production planning and control, general administration and various services, marketing, etc and also of the economic environment within which business operations take place. Since these inputs are joint to the output, there is no objective way one can assign actual or projected output to the individual elements of input. Any such allocation must of necessity rely on judgment and must be unavoidably "incorrigible" in the sense that neither the allocation made nor any alternative allocations can be verified or refuted. For example, in the case of depreciation, there is no way of verifying any of the alternatives available for the allocation of the cost or other value of depreciable assets over their estimated useful lives (eg straight line, diminishing balance, or some other method of depreciation).

[1113] Yet, despite the underlying problems, allocations are being made and there is little likelihood that they will be discontinued. In spite of their conceptual deficiencies and the arbitrary decisions and judgments involved, allocations are made because they are perceived to be useful. They are necessary for the measurement of periodic income and determination of end of period state of affairs of business enterprises. And the earning of income is the basic objective of business operations. The measurement and reporting of income is essential for the purpose of evaluation of results. The transaction basis of accounting and the matching approach to income measurement record the history of the firms' activities and enable the tracing of the sources of revenue and expense. By implication at least, the perceived disadvantages of allocation do not outweigh its perceived advantages to the end product of the financial accounting process.

[1114] The alternative to allocations is to move even closer to a system of accounting based strictly on cash flows, on the cash receipts and payments for a period. Yet, where business operations involve major investment in non-monetary assets, the cash receipts and payments of a period are inadequate indicators of performance and prospects.

For example, FASB Statement No 1, "The Objective of Financial Reporting by Business Enterprises" (1978) stated that the common interest of the diverse users of financial statements was in the ability of the enterprise to generate favourable cash flows (para 25). The statement added, however, that financial statements based on cash receipts and payments alone cannot, during a short period such as a year, indicate adequately whether the performance of the enterprise has been successful (para 43). The statement concluded that information about the earnings of an enterprise, based on accrual accounting (which requires allocations) provides a better indication of the ability of an enterprise to generate favourable cash flow than information limited to the financial effects of receipts and payments (para 44).

[1115] In the face of uncertainty, allocations cannot be verified or refuted. Yet allocations can be made with various degrees of arbitrariness. At one end of the scale they may reflect expediency, bias and, at worst, deliberate attempts to mislead; at the other end of the scale they may be the result of thoughtful study of all the factors which are perceived to be relevant to a particular accounting problem, and may reflect, therefore, what may be considered to be an informed decision.

[1116] Statements of Standard Accounting Practice (SSAPs) issued by professional accounting bodies attempt to define acceptable practices for dealing with accounting problems and to limit available alternatives. To that extent SSAPs may be said to limit the role of judgment in the preparation of financial statements. Given the subject matter of financial accounting, however, and the uncertainty which underlies the operations of business enterprises, SSAPs cannot overcome the need for judgment in the preparation of financial statements. In the final count, the quality of financial reports would depend to a very large extent on the honesty, skill, knowledge and responsible, informed judgment of the preparers of financial statements and the auditors who are required to express a professional opinion on them. Similarly, skill, knowledge and responsible, informed judgment is required of users of financial statements in their analysis and interpretation for decision-making.

Review questions

11.1 Discuss the connection between periodic reporting and accounting allocations.

11.2 Why allocate cost?

11.3 Discuss the jointness of inputs in business operations and its implications for accounting measurement.

11.4 "The alternative to allocations is to move closer to a system of accounting based strictly on cash flows."

Is this a viable alternative to accrual accounting?

11.5 "The allocation problem arises from the generally accepted accounting practice of measuring income by the matching of cost with revenue."

Why use matching in the measurement of income?

Chapter 12

Inventory Valuation

Inventories and the Allocation Problem

[1201] In Chapter 11 we discussed the general issues which underlie accounting allocations for the purpose of profit measurement by a process of matching period revenue with period expense, and for arriving at asset values in order to ascertain an enterprise's state of affairs at balance date. In this chapter we will consider the allocation problem as it relates to the specific area of inventory valuation.

[1202] The basic issues associated with inventory valuation are summarised in paras 6 and 7 of the Australian Statement of Accounting Standards AAS2, "Valuation and Presentation of Inventories in the Context of the Historical Cost System". The main points may be summarized as follows:

   (a) Inventories are acquired in the expectation of deriving revenue from their sale or use.

   (b) The results of a business are determined by an appropriate matching of revenues and expenses. To achieve such matching, it is necessary to carry forward the cost associated with the acquisition of inventories until the inventories are sold or used up.

   (c) In the context of historical cost accounting, the principal basis for the valuation of inventories at balance date is cost.

   (d) Where there is no reasonable expectation of future revenue associated with the sale or use of inventories sufficient to cover inventory cost, any irrecoverable cost should be charged against the revenue of the current period. In such cases, inventory should be valued at net realizable value if this is lower than cost.

[1203] In many business enterprises inventories represent a significant portion of total investment in assets. The value placed on inventories is important in the presentation in the balance sheet of the state of affairs of the enterprise. But that value is even more important in its effect on the income statement and on the measurement of net profit in particular. Every extra dollar in the value placed on inventory adds a dollar to the net profit before providing for taxation. This situation would not matter so much were there clear and straightforward methods to be applied in different circumstances to the valuation of inventories. But this is not the case.

   According to the Australian statement AAS2 referred to above:

> The determination of the amounts at which inventories are stated in financial statements has produced wider differences in practice than many other areas of accounting. Circumstances vary so greatly that no one method is suitable for all types of

business. The method adopted needs to be appropriate to the circumstances, consistently applied from period to period and adequately disclosed in the financial statements. [para 1]

[1204] The valuation of inventories is not a precise exercise. There is scope for the exercise of judgment, and bias, in the selection of methods from available alternatives and in the application of the method of valuation chosen. There may be wide variations in the value placed on inventory and therefore on reported income and state of affairs with differences in the methods of valuation applied by management. Further, circumstances in the market and industry do change over time, so that a basis of valuation which was appropriate last year may not be equally appropriate under the circumstances of this year.

[1205] One may think of the profit for the year as being dependent on the fairness of the value placed on inventory, as being "vulnerable" to inventory valuation. For example, the financial statements of a New Zealand trading company reported profit before tax of $478,000 and end-of-year inventory of $6,864,000. If inventory were valued only 5% lower, the profit before tax would be reduced by $343,200, a fall of 71.8%

[1206] A key point in understanding the nature of inventory valuation is that current accounting practice requires that it should be based on expectations about the future, hence the uncertainty which attaches to it. For example, under the lower of cost or market value rule, even when inventory is valued at what may be termed "cost", the valuation is based on the *expectation* that the inventories will realize an amount higher than cost in the future.

[1207] The analyst should be on guard in cases where there is a cricial relationship between the "value" of inventories and the disclosed profit before tax. For example, consider the following data for a manufacturing company operating currently in a depressed market:

	19A1 $000	19A2 $000
Inventory of finished goods	2,000	3,000
Net profit before tax	1,000	200

At the end of the 19A2 year the company could well be under financial stress. Competition on the market for available business could be very keen, with price cutting as a feature. Production volume could have been cut back producing idle capacity. Under circumstances like these, there would be a powerful incentive to show a favourable result in order to maintain the confidence of creditors and investors. As a result, values may be assigned to inventories which are designed more to avoid the showing of a loss than to express a true and fair view.

[1208] In a conversation with one of the authors some years ago, a prominent New Zealand accountant, then president of the New Zealand Society of Accountants, stated that in his entire career he had never seen a business facing difficulties which had its inventories undervalued. The statement is significant. Given the basic rule of inventory valuation at the lower of cost or market (net realizable) value, a firm in difficulties can show a better than true position by simply ignoring the need to review its inventory values with a view to writing down what may be a significant part of its inventories.

[1209] Further, it would be necessary for the analyst and interpreter of financial statements to consider the effects of any change in policy regarding inventory valuation. For example, the *Australian Financial Review* of 20 September 1982 described "a handy change in accounting policy" which enabled an agricultural machinery group to post a steady net profit instead of a 20% fall in the year to June 30:

> The group did not mention the change in policy when it released its final figures to stock exchanges, but it is evident from the annual report.
>
> [The group] reported a consolidated operating profit of $2.3 million, compared with $2.33 million (for the previous year).
>
> But a decision to change the way stocks were valued boosted net profit by $414,728. Without the change net profit would have slumped 20% to $1.88 million.

[1210] The basic principle of inventory valuation is that inventories should be valued at the lower of cost or market value. In Australia and New Zealand current accounting practice defines "market value" to mean "net realizable value". A third alternative, replacement cost, is acceptable as a basis of inventory valuation only to the extent that it represents a fair approximation of net realizable value.

In dealing with the valuation of inventories we are, therefore, faced with two problem areas:

(a) the determination of the cost of inventories; and

(b) the assessment of their net realizable value.

The Cost of Inventories

[1211] In the context of current accounting practice the cost of inventories means their historical cost.

In dealing with the problems associated with determining the historical cost of inventories we may distinguish between inventories purchased for own use or resale and inventories manufactured by the firm.

The cost of purchased inventories

[1212] Where inventories are purchased for resale, their cost, by convention, is assumed to consist of the purchase price plus duty and taxes, transport costs and other costs associated with the acquisition of the inventories and bringing them to their present location. Discounts, rebates and subsidies associated with the purchase of the inventories would normally be deducted from the cost.

When inventory purchases are made at different prices, the problem arises of assigning cost (value) to ending inventory. The value assigned to ending inventory affects the measure of the cost of goods sold and, therefore, reported profit.

[1213] The method selected for the valuation of ending inventory should be such as to permit a true and fair view to be given of the operating results and state of affairs of the business. The following methods are currently acceptable in Australia and New Zealand for measuring the cost of purchased inventories:

- actual cost (which requires the specific indentification of inventory items and their acquisition cost);
- weighted average cost;
- first in, first-out (FIFO);
- standard cost, if certain conditions are met.

The last-in, first-out (LIFO) method of inventory valuation which is popular in the United States is not commonly used in Australia and New Zealand. If applied in times of rising prices, LIFO may have a significant impact on reported profit and the balance sheet valuation of inventories. For example, reported profit would tend to reflect current costs but inventory valuation may be at historical costs which are far removed from current prices.

The cost of manufactured inventories

[1214] The problems associated with the valuation of purchased inventories apply also to the valuation of manufactured goods. In the case of manufactured goods, however, there are additional problems which arise from the nature of the costs incurred in manufacturing operations and in particular the problem of allocating joint manufacturing costs.

By convention, manufactured goods are valued at manufacturing cost — direct materials plus conversion costs necessarily incurred in the production of the finished products and any other costs incurred in placing the products in their present condition and location. Conversion costs comprise direct labour and an allocation of manufacturing overhead.

In most manufacturing situations the cost of raw materials and direct labour are charged directly to individual products as these costs are directly traceable to the products (at least in terms of quantity). This is not possible where the manufacturing process leads to the joint production of more than one product. In that case, more or less arbitrary methods have to be used to allocate the cost of the total inputs to the process, including overhead costs, to the joint products which comprise the output. One such method is to allocate total joint cost on the basis of the relative sales value of the joint products.

Manufacturing overhead costs are not directly traceable to specific products. They are normally allocated to production at a predetermined rate calculated on the basis of budgeted overhead expense and budgeted volume of production:

$$\text{Overhead recovery rate} = \frac{\text{Budgeted overhead}}{\text{Budgeted volume}}$$

In the setting of manufacturing overhead recovery rates the volume of production may be measured in terms of units of output or some other basis such as direct labour hours, machine hours, or direct labour cost.

In more sophisticated systems, manufacturing overhead may be divided into variable and fixed components. Variable overhead may be allocated to products using an appropriate output volume factor (for example, direct labour hours) recognizing a direct relationship between the volume of throughput and the variable overhead costs. Fixed overhead costs may be allocated to products systematically on the basis of the budgeted volume of throughput. There are significant differences of opinion regarding the inclusion of fixed manufacturing overheads in product costs.

[1215] Under the principles of *direct (variable) costing* only variable manufacturing overheads should be charged to production and included in the cost of manufactured goods. Fixed costs are treated as period costs and are charged against revenue in the period in which they are incurred. It has been argued in favour of direct costing that the valuation of production at variable cost is more objective because it avoids the largely arbitrary allocation of fixed manufacturing costs to final products. It has also been argued that under direct costing, reported profit is not distorted by fixed costs brought forward or carried forward in opening and closing inventory when inventory levels vary significantly from one period to another.

[1216] Under the principles of *full absorption costing* inventory is valued at full manufacturing cost — direct materials and direct labour plus a proportion of both variable and fixed manufacturing overhead. The arguments in favour of absorption costing centre on the relationship between the incurring of largely fixed manufacturing overheads such as production planning, supervision and depreciation of productive assets, and the creation of value in the form of saleable products. It has been claimed in favour of absorption costing that the input of fixed manufacturing costs associated, for example, with production planning, supervision and the use of plant and machinery are as instrumental to the creation of valuable goods as the inputs of raw materials and direct labour.

[1217] A third view known as *relevant costing* takes a position somewhat between those of direct and full absorption costing. Under relevant costing the extent to which fixed manufacturing overheads should be included in the value of inventories would depend on the circumstances of the firm at the time.

[1218] The viewpoints of direct, absorption, and relevant costing regarding the valuation of manufactured inventories will be illustrated and compared in Example 12.1.

Example 12.1

A firm manufactures a single product X. The following data relates to the manufacturing cost of the product:

	Cost per unit $
Raw materials	5.30
Direct labour	7.50
Manufacturing overhead:	
Variable	3.50
Fixed*	4.00

*The amount of fixed overhead per unit of X has been arrived at on the basis of budgeted fixed manufacturing overhead for the firm of $200,000 and budgeted volume of production of 50,000 units.

Given the above cost data, the manufacturing cost of product X can be calculated alternatively as follows:

Direct (variable) cost method

[1219] The cost of X and its end of period value, when X is valued at cost, will be based on variable manufacturing cost:

	$
Raw materials cost	5.30
Direct labour	7.50
Variable manufacturing overhead	3.50
Total cost per unit	16.30

Full absorption cost method

[1220] The cost of X will be based on full manufacturing cost, including a proportion of fixed manufacturing overheads:

	$	$
Raw materials cost		5.30
Direct labour		7.50
Manufacturing overheads:		
Variable	3.50	
Fixed	4.00	7.50
Total cost per unit		20.30

Relevant cost method

[1221] Under relevant costing, the valuation of inventory at "cost" is somewhat more complicated than under direct or absorption costing. For example, the extent to which fixed manufacturing overheads are included in ending inventory may be determined by comparing end-of-period inventory with the inventory required to service the expected level of sales at the start of the new period. Then the amount of inventory needed to service expected sales may be valued at full manufacturing cost, and any excess at variable cost. The idea underlying the relevant cost method is that the value assigned to inventory should not exceed the avoidable cost to the new period. The relevant costing of inventory valuation is illustrated in Example 12.2.

Example 12.2

Following Example 11.1, if we assume that the inventory required to service the expected sales in the next period is 8,000 units and that end of period inventory is 20,000 units, the end of period inventory may be valued as follows:

	$
8,000 units at full manufacturing cost of $20.30 per unit	162,400
12,000 units at variable manufacturing cost of $16.30 per unit	195,600
Total end of period value of inventory at "cost"	358,000

It should be noted in relation to Example 12.2, however, that as the end of period inventory is considerably higher than the inventory required to service expected sales, there may be a case for the writing down of the inventory to a figure below "cost".

In practice, effect may be given to the relevant cost concept by valuing the *whole* inventory at a figure below its absorption cost. It will be appreciated that decisions on what quantity was necessary to service sales and what quantity was temporary surplus would be subjective and would add materially to the practical problems of inventory valuation.

[1222] As stated earlier, one of the problems associated with the valuation of inventories at full absorption cost is the effect on reported profit of the fixed manufacturing overheads brought forward or carried forward as part of inventory values where inventory levels vary significantly from one period to another. This effect will be illustrated in Example 12.3.

Example 12.3

Following Examples 11.1 and 11.2, we will make the following assumptions:
(a) The average annual sales of product X in the past have averaged 50,000 units and annual production has been in line with sales at 50,000 units.
(b) The inventory level needed to service sales is 20% of sales.
(c) During the year just ended sales have dropped to 40,000 units. It is expected that sales will continue at the new lower level for the indefinite future.
(d) During the year just ended the company did not reduce the level of production and 50,000 units of X were produced as in previous years.
(e) No change in the amount of fixed manufacturing overhead has occurred since the previous year.

The effect on reported profit of the valuation of closing inventory in Example 12.3 at full absorption cost can be calculated as follows:

Fixed costs	$
Inventory brought forward 10,000 units @ $4.00	40,000
Charged to production — 50,000 units @ $4.00	200,000
	240,000
Less carried forward in ending inventory 20,000 units @ $4.00	80,000
Fixed costs charged to revenue	160,000
Fixed costs carried forward in ending inventory 20,000 units @ $4.00	80,000
Fixed costs included in inventory needed to service expected sales 8,000 units @ $4.00	32,000
Fixed costs carried forward in excess inventory	48,000

The effect of the valuation of the total inventory at full manufacturing cost is that only $160,000 of fixed manufacturing costs are charged against the revenue for the period, and $48,000 are carried forward into the next period as part of the value placed on excessive inventory. Reflecting the principles of relevant costing, the profit for the year has been overstated by $48,000 on account of the inventory valuation alone.

Absorption costing versus variable costing

[1223] The Australian and New Zealand standards on inventory valuation do not resolve the problem of what time related (fixed) overheads, if any, should be included in inventory values. The Australian Standard AAS2 notes (para 9) that in Australian accounting practice there is substantial support for both the absorption and variable costing methods of inventory valuation. The New Zealand Standard SSAP4 appears to favour the inclusion of at least some fixed manufacturing overheads in inventory values and states (para 5.2) that if fixed production overhead has been entirely or substantially excluded from the valuation of inventories, the fact should be disclosed.

Volume (capacity) considerations in equating cost with value

[1224] In the preceding section we pointed out that manufacturing overhead is charged to production and, therefore, included in the cost (value) of manufactured goods on the basis of a predetermined overhead recovery rate based on budgeted overhead expense and budgeted volume of production. A problem which arises in setting overhead recovery rates in this manner concerns the treatement of expected idle capacity and affects the recovery rate for fixed manufacturing overheads. For example, where overhead recovery rates are based on the *expected* volume of production, a fall in the volume of production would mean that a higher rate of manufacturing overhead will be charged against the reduced output resulting in a higher unit cost (and "value") being assigned to the goods produced. Following Example 12.1, if the expected volume of production falls from 50,000 units to 40,000 units, the overhead recovery rate for fixed overhead will increase from $4.00 per unit to

$5.00 per unit $(\frac{\$200,000}{40,000}$ units). It should be difficult to support a case that more value per unit was created by the production process when it was operating below capacity. In terms of selling value the reverse could well apply where the reduced output was not due to, say, scarcity of materials but to a fall-off in demand for the product.

[1225] Fixed manufacturing overhead should be allocated to production and included in inventory valuation on the basis of the "normal" capacity of production facilities. This means that the cost of idle capacity should be expensed as a period cost and not included in the cost (value) of inventories. The problem is to decide what is "normal" capacity under a given set of circumstances. "Normal" capacity might be interpreted in a number of ways, including:
• production expected to be achieved over a number of years;
• the maximum practical production capacity of the facilities;
• intended production by management (for example, one shift or two shifts).

In deciding what is "normal" capacity utilization in a particular case, some reference should be made to the level of capacity utilization achieved in the industry to which the firm belongs. For example, a firm may be operating at, say, 65% of practical capacity while, on the the average, the industry may be operating at, say, 80%. The issue is a difficult one, however. One may consider, for example, the problem of deciding what is normal capacity utilization in a depressed industry operating at, say, 65% of capacity or in a depressed economy operating at the same average level.

Efficiency considerations

[1226] The efficiency of production is another important consideration which arises from the attempt to value manufactured goods at cost. For example, an efficient firm may show lower manufacturing cost per unit of output in terms of raw materials usage, direct labour cost, manufacturing overhead, and utilization of productive capacity than an inefficient firm in the same industry. Yet, if manufacturing cost is automatically equated with the value of output the paradoxical situation will arise where the inefficient firm will assign a higher "value" to its output, simply because its production costs are higher than those of the efficient firm.

A concept of "normal" cost of production — standard cost

[1227] In order to overcome the problems which arise in equating "cost" with "value" in particular in relation to the efficiency and volume of production, inventories may be valued at "normal" cost — cost which is based on "normal" capacity utilization and excludes any cost of inefficiency in production. The valuation of inventory at "standard cost" is one such method.

Standard costs are predetermined costs in terms of the price and quantity of production inputs such as raw materials used, direct labour applied and budgeted overhead allocated to production facilities. Under a standard cost system the costs of inefficiency and idle capacity are treated as losses and charged against revenue rather than included in the value of inventories.

The major problem associated with the application of standard costs to production costing and inventory valuation is the setting of realistic standards regarding efficiency and capacity utilization.

Under current standard accounting practice, costs arising from excessive wastage (of materials, labour and other production expenses) or from excess idle capacity should be excluded from the cost of inventories. Standard costs are acceptable as a basis of inventory valuation if they realistically reflect current production costs. The standards used should be realistically attainable and should be regularly reviewed and, where necessary, revised in the light of current conditions (AAS2, para 29).

Replacement cost and inventory valuation

[1228] Current accounting standards preclude the use of replacement cost as a direct basis of inventory valuation. Replacement cost may be used in inventory valuation, however, where it represents a fair approximation of net realizable value. This may arise, for example, in relation to the valuation of raw materials and the raw materials content of work in progress and finished goods. In most cases the net realizable value of raw materials is likely to be less than cost. However, where the net realizable value of the final product is expected to be higher than cost, raw materials inventories should be valued at cost. Where replacement cost of raw materials has fallen below historical cost, this may indicate a decline in the net realizable value of materials and the finished product. In such a case, replacement cost may be taken to represent the best available measure of the net realizable value of the materials (AAS2, para 30; SSAP4, para 5.12).

The Valuation of Inventories at Net Realizable Value

[1229] Inventories are written down to net realizable value when net realizable value is estimated to be less than historical cost. Circumstances which may necessitate such a write-down include a fall in selling prices, deterioration or obsolescence of inventories, and inventory levels in excess of those considered necessary to service expected sales.

Related to inventory valuation, net realizable value is the estimated selling price in the ordinary course of business less any costs necessary to effect the sale. The estimation of the selling prices of damaged, obsolete, or excess stock items is a subjective exercise. Similarly, there is much room for argument about what constitutes the costs necessary to effect the sale of such items.

Inventories and security available to creditors

[1230] When inventories are considered from the viewpoint of the security available to creditors of the firm, it should be remembered that substantial difference can exist between the balance sheet valuation of inventories at "cost" and their realizable value on a forced sale. Let us illustrate the significance of this by looking at the case of a New Zealand company — Mosgiel Ltd of Dunedin.

Mosgiel Ltd was an old established New Zealand manufacturer of woollen goods which encountered trading and financial problems which led to the appointment of a receiver on 30 April 1980. In due course, the company filed a statement of affairs at the office of the Registrar of Companies. Among the lists attached was a summary of the inventory as at the date of the appointment of the receiver. It showed (in rounded figures):

	Book value $000	Expected to realize $000
Raw materials and yarns	3,102	1,241
Work in progress	4,633	463
Finished goods	5,517	1,207
Sample and sundry stocks	205	14
Consumable stores	Nil	300
	13,457	3,225

Note In the event that a sale of the company as a going concern can be successfully negotiated, the directors estimate the stocks and work in progress will realize $7,689,000.

The company had adopted an absorption cost basis of valuation of finished goods and work in progress. The industry generally was suffering from excess production capacity, and restructuring was envisaged. Some of the demand was seasonal, and the market limited. There was a high fixed cost element in the product costs. The heavy loss on work in progress in a shut-down situation is notable, and would account for part of the difference between the estimated break-up value and the estimated going concern value. This case illustrates quite well a number of important aspects of inventory valuation, including:

(a) the basis of valuation should be appropriate to the circumstances for which it is required;

(b) security value may be well below absorption cost, or even variable cost;

(c) in some industries, the treatment of fixed costs may affect inventory value materially;

(d) there may be significant differences between absorption cost, variable cost, and realizable value;

(e) incurring cost does not necessarily result in the creation of equivalent value.

Implications for Analysis and Interpretation

[1231] In the analysis and interpretation of financial statements, inventories would warrant a careful study, especially where reported profit is sensitive to inventory valuation. This will include the large number of cases where inventories represent a significant part of the firm's investment in assets.

In the analysis of inventory figures, the statement of accounting policies and other notes should be studied in order to determine the principles and methods used in the valuation of inventories and any changes in these principles and methods. Where information is available of the spread of inventory among such categories as raw materials, work in progress, and finished goods, then it is helpful to consider the significance of changes in the inventory mix as well as in the inventory total. A particular concern of the analyst and interpreter will be for those circumstances where full absorption costing has been applied and where more finished stock is held at the end of the year than at the beginning. In this situation the enterprise has produced more than it has sold. Had it matched production with sales, then the cost of idle capacity would have been borne by the past year. By producing in excess of sales, part of the idle capacity cost may have been carried forward in the "value" attached to inventory. That inventory may have to be sold in a depressed market, which makes the issue even more critical.

[1232] This leads us to the problem of inventory valuation at net realizable value. Where excess or slow inventories are held, net realizable value could well be below historical cost. Unavoidably, the measurement of inventories at net realizable value involves judgment and may be affected by bias. For example, the effect of a major write-down of inventories on reported profit could exert a strong influence on a decision whether or not to carry out such a write-down and its size. Consider for example the problem of inventory valuation faced by the directors of Mosgiel Ltd on the balance date immediately prior to liquidation assuming finished goods stocks well in excess of what was necessary to service the market, a year when production levels were low, and a tight financial position.

Special Valuation Cases

[1233] Under this heading we will consider the valuation of
• uncompleted construction contracts;

- forest assets;
- land under development.

Uncompleted construction contracts

[1234] Construction contracts typically involve major construction projects the completion of which extends over two or more accounting periods. Examples are contracts for the construction of buildings, roads, bridges, dams, major plant, ships, etc.

At balance date, uncompleted contracts represent the work in progress of the contracting firm.

Typically, the completion of construction contracts will occur irregularly over time. If profit were recognized on completion (ie realization), then one would expect wide variations in reported profit from year to year.

[1235] Current accounting practice favours the recognition of profit as the contract progresses: Australian Standards AAS11, ASRB 1009, and New Zealand SSAP No 14.

The progressive recognition of profit on contracts is usually referred to as the percentage of completion method.

The recognition of profit on contracts prior to completion carries risks and under current financial reporting standards is subject to certain restrictions. For example, profit should not be incorporated into the accounts of the contracting firm unless it can be reliably estimated in terms of total revenue to be received, cost to complete the contract and degree of completion at the point of time at which profit is recognized. In the case of cost plus contracts, cost attributable to the contract should be clearly identified and non-reimbursable costs reliably estimated.

[1236] In accounting for contracts, losses should be brought into account as soon as they become apparent. Claims or penalties payable by the conractor arising out of delays in completion or for other contract breaches should be provided for as costs attributable to the contract.

[1237] The costs assignable to a contract are costs which relate directly to the contract and costs which, although attributable to contract activity in general, can be allocated to specific contracts. The amount of profit taken on an incompleted contract is added to the value at which the contact is carried in the books of the contracting firm.

The valuation of forest assets

[1238] The valuation of forest assets creates some special problems. They may be regarded as inventory of raw materials of firms involved in forests and related industries, but they take a long time to mature. The question arises of what is the value of a growing forest — is it its cost or current market value? Then, what should one include in the cost of a forest? And should one ignore, for example, the effects of inflation over the many years it takes for a forest to come to maturity? No doubt problems would also arise in determining the current market value of a growing forest. There is no established market for such forests to which ready reference can be made in order to determine current market value at a point of time or changes in this value over time.

[1239] In Australia and New Zealand there are no accounting standards regarding the valuation of forests and practice varies across companies and over time. In the cases that follow, we will consider the valuation of forests in relation to the policies adopted by three New Zealand companies with substantial investment in forest assets.

Case Study 1
Carter Holt Harvey Limited

[1240] The 1987 financial report of this company disclosed forest assets valued at $101,460,000 ($77,160,000 in 1986).

The statement of accounting policies disclosed the following regarding the valuation of forest assets:

Forest Assets (other than land) are capitalised at cost which includes a proportion of interest at commercial rates, less cost of timber extracted.

Case Study 2
Fletcher Challenge Limited

[1241] The 1985 financial report of the company disclosed the following data regarding forest assets and forest land:

	North American Group		Central Group	
	1985	1984	1985	1984
	$000	$000	$000	$000
Forest and Mining assets	57,898	32,789	176,215	132,565
Forest land	136,843	125,463	120,046	110,523

[1242] The statement of accounting policies disclosed the following regarding the valuation of forest assets and forest land:

Forest assets:
Forest assets in New Zealand, which exclude land, are valued on the basis determined by the intended end use of the forest resource.

Where a forest block has been established to provide raw material to a major processing operation over a long period ... all costs associated with developing the first crop, including finance costs, are capitalized and the costs associated with developing the second and subsequent crops are written off against earnings. The initial costs of establishing the forest block will never be written off unless the growing of trees on the block on a constant rotation basis ceases.

Where the end use of a forest block has not been determined as being to supply a major processing operation ... all costs associated with forest crop development, including finance costs, are capitalized to forest units. The costs accumulated in each unit are amortized to earnings as depletions at the time of harvest of the unit.

The estimated market value of the forest crop is the upper limit to which finance costs are capitalized.

208

Forest assets in the North American Group, which include land, are included at the assigned cost of acquisition as at the date of acquisition less subsequent depletions. Amortization is based on the volume depleted as a proportion of the estimated volume available over 20 years.

Forest land:

In New Zealand fee simple forest land carrying value is increased by the capitalization of finance costs up to market value. Any excess over market value of the forest land is capitalized to the forest crop up to market value.

[1243] The following are some inferences which may be drawn from the above valuation policies:

(a) In the case of forest blocks established to provide raw materials for major processing operations, a kind of LIFO approach was used with the costs of developing the current crop being expensed to earnings as incurred and the initial costs of establishing the blocks being carried forward as balance sheet value. Under this method the current cost of forest development will be borne by current operations. Balance sheet values, however, are likely to be significantly understated. It is not indicated in the financial report the proportion of total forest assets which have been included under this classification; forest assets are shown as one total with mining assets, but it is reasonable to assume from the nature of the enterprise that mining assets are relatively insignificant.

(b) Regarding the valuation of forest land and forest assets the use of which has not been determined as that of supplying a major processing operation, the restriction that finance costs should be capitalized up to the market value of the land and forest assets implies that without this proviso the value assigned could exceed market value. This implies also that the reported value of some of these assets could be close to their assessed market value. Again, no indication is given regarding what proportion of the forest assets are included under this classification.

[1244] The 1986 financial report of Fletcher Challenge Limited reported a change in accounting policy regarding the valuation of New Zealand forest assets. The new policy was stated as follows:

Forest assets located in New Zealand, which exclude land, are valued on the basis of estimated market value of the forest assets taking into account age, condition, location and intended end use.

All costs incurred in the management, silviculture and ownership of the forest assets are written off to earnings at the time incurred.

All increments or reductions in the estimated market value of the forest assets are taken to earnings as they emerge.

All revenues related to forest asset harvesting are taken to earnings as realised.

[1245] A surplus of $21.9 million of estimated market value at the beginning of the financial year over the accumulated capital cost which resulted from the change in policy was credited to retained earnings as a prior period adjustment. The effect of the change in accounting policy on the net earnings after tax and minorities for the 1986 financial year amounted to $4,611,000.

[1246] There was no reported change in accounting policies regarding the valuation of forest assets in 1987.

Case Study 3
New Zealand Forest Products

[1247] The 1985 financial report of the company reported forest assets at cost (excluding land) of $85,785,000 ($73,943,000 in 1984). The statement of accounting policies disclosed the following regarding the valuation of forest assets:

Development forests are recorded at cost to date including financial charges. Productive forests being managed for a continuing supply of wood are recorded at the cost of the first crop.

The annual costs of maintenance, protection and management of the productive forest areas are treated as revenue expenditure and included in the cost of wood supplied to the mills each year.

[1248] A change in accounting policy was reported in the 1986 financial report. The new policy was stated as follows:

Development forests are recorded at replacement cost at 31 March 1985 increased by subsequent expenditure including holding costs.

Production costs are recorded at estimated market value as at 31 March 1985 adjusted for costs attributable to subsequent forest volume variations and holding costs. The annual costs of maintenance, protection and management attributable to the volume of wood extracted are treated as revenue expenditure and included in the cost of wood supplied to the mills each year.

The value of the forest asset is reviewed each year and changes are taken to the appropriate revaluation reserves.

As a result of the change, the consolidated net profit for the year was reported as having benefited by $11,912,000.

[1249] There was no reported change in accounting policy regarding the valuation of forest assets in 1987.

[1250] In 1986 NZ Forest Products became the target of a takeover bid by Fletcher Challenge. The bid was resisted by the directors of NZ Forest Products. An issue in the bid was the profitability of NZ Forest Products. The following excerpts are taken from a report entitled "NZFP Tries FCL Accounting" published in the business section of the *Otago Daily Times* on 6 December 1986:

Forest Products shareholders would be sent an alternative version of the company's results based on what NZ Forest Products' managing director, Mr Warren Hunt, described as "the application of Fletcher Challenge forestry accounting principles".

The use of FCL's forest accounting policies would have given NZFP a 79% higher after tax profit for the 1985–86 financial year, and 45% higher profit for the first half of this financial year than that which NZFP did report, according to Mr Hunt.

Bringing substantial unrealized profits into account provided "a much rosier picture of profit performance", he said.

Mr Hunt stressed that there was no criticism of the FCL accounting policies implied by his company.

"It is a simple fact that their policies are different from our own deliberately conservative policies, and those who wish to compare the two companies should understand the impact of those policies", he said.

"The application of FCL accounting policies to the NZFP accounts for the 1985–86 year would have increased pre-tax profit by $192 million (177%) to $300 million, increased tax provision by $107 million, and increased net profit after tax by $84.83 [million] to $191.137 million, a lift of 79%.

Had FCL policies been applied to the results of NZFP for the six months to September 30 1986, the company would have reported an after-tax profit of $87 million, rather than the $60 million announced", Mr Hunt said.

The valuation of development property

[1251] The problem we are faced with in the valuation of development land is the allocation of the original cost of the land and the costs associated with its development to the individual sections which are offered for sale. In particular it is important to allocate the joint costs of land acquisition and development between sold and unsold sections at the end of the period.

[1252] It would be reasonable to assume that the decision to acquire land for development would be based on the expected total cost associated with the acquisition and development of the land and the total amount expected to be received when the developed sections are sold. This being so, it would be reasonable to allocate the total cost of the developed land to individual sections on the basis of the originally expected selling prices of the sections;

$$\frac{\text{Estimated selling price of section}}{\text{Estimated selling price of all sections}} \times \text{Total cost}$$

It would be necessary then to compare the cost assigned to an individual section with the currently expected selling price. If the market drops, it would be necessary to ensure that the value assigned to sections does not exceed net realizable value after allowing for all expected expenses up to and including realization.

[1253] The question arises whether holding costs such as interest and rates should be capitalized. Prudence would suggest that such costs should be expensed. If they are capitalized, it would be necessary to ensure that the cost assigned to developed sections does not exceed the net realizable value of the sections.

An interesting sequel

[1254] An approach to the valuation of a growing forest is to forecast an expected net cash revenue at maturity, and the expected cash outflows in forest maintenance and other costs up to that point in time. These cash flows may be discounted at an appropriate rate of return to produce a present value of the forest. There will be allowance for income tax on expected net income included in this calculation.

The directors of NZFP thwarted the takeover offer from Fletcher Challenge through a related investment company, Rada Corporation, which acquired a significant holding of NZFP shares at what was shown later to be a very high price. The stock exchange crash of October 1987 brought a very large reduction in the market value of NZFP shares and a disastrous reduction in the value of Rada shares, NZFP being a major shareholder in that company. In the meantime Elders, an Australian group, acquired a controlling interest in the ailing NZFP, which became Elders Resources NZFP Ltd. An immediate problem was the need to provide to the stock exchange (along with other listed companies) a post-crash set of financial statements. A loss on investments, mainly in Rada Corporation, of $325.8 million would have made uncomfortable reading of the income statement. It must have been regarded as providential at the time that a change was made in the company tax rate from 48% to 28%. This provided the company with the opportunity to recalculate the value of its forests to allow for the much higher after-tax expected cash inflows on maturity. The loss on investments, treated as an extraordinary item, was offset by the write-up of forests by $295.5 million. The directors' report presented with the release to the stock exchange described the matter in these terms:

Aside from the difficult economic environment in which NZFP was operating throughout 1987–88, it was time for the company to recognize the true value of its assets and investments.

The potential strength of the company and its forest resource is proven in its ability to withstand the impact of the October 1987 crash on its investments together with a major restructuring and still increase its shareholders' funds.

Review questions

12.1 Examine the relationship between inventory valuation decisions and period profit.

12.2 Contrast the problems involved in inventory valuation with regard to:
(a) inventories purchased in saleable form; and
(b) manufactured inventories.

12.3 Discuss and contrast the direct (variable) costing, absorption costing and relevant costing methods of valuation of manufactured inventories.

12.4 Discuss the concept of "normal cost of production" in the valuation of manufactured inventories.

12.5 "The incurring of cost does not necessarily result in the creation of equivalent value."
Discuss in relation to the valuation of manufactured inventories at cost.

12.6 A manufacturing company produces four main products. Its normal profit margin is 30% of selling price, but the actual margin varies over the range of products. The following information applies to the units comprising its inventory at its balance date of 31 March 19A1:

Product	Units	Historical cost $	Cost to replace $	Cost to dispose $	Expected selling price $
A	2,000	35.	38.	8.	52
B	1,000	48.	46.	12.	75
C	1,600	24.	29.	7.	25
D	4,000	16.	18.	4.	23

What value would you place on the inventory for the purposes of financial reporting?

12.7 A capital intensive industry has operated for several years at close to capacity, but is now faced with the prospect of working to 65% capacity because of the loss of an important export market.

(a) What basis of valuation of its ending inventory should it have adopted in the past, so far as its plant related costs of conversion are concerned?

(b) Should this basis be changed in the current year?

(c) If the basis is changed, then how will this affect the financial report of the company for the year?

12.8 Discuss the basis of valuation that you would apply in the following cases:

(a) A line of seasonal fashion goods in a retail store:

Purchase was   50 units at $10.
Sales were   40 units at $18.
                 5 units at $15.

Value to be placed on end-of-season residue of 5 units.

(b) Bulk stocks of raw materials X and Y held by a manufacturer. Details are:

	X	Y
Ending stock (in units)	1,000	2,000
Average landed cost (per unit)	$10	$8
Standard cost, currently	$11	$8
Current replacement cost	$12	$7
Estimated usage in following year (units)	8,000	500

(c) 100 sheepskins held in a stock at balance date by a company operating a substantial butchery in a country centre.

(d) The five sections as yet unsold in the 40-section subdivision of Developers Ltd completed during the year. (The sections in the subdivision varied in market value according to location.)

12.9 Questions (a) to (d) below relate to inventory valuation. Answer each question briefly referring where appropriate to standard accounting practice.

(a) Discuss and contrast
  (i) the direct costing,
  (ii) the absorption costing, and
  (iii) the relevant costing
approaches to inventory valuation.

(b) At the end of 19A2 Company A has inventory comprising 34,000 units of product Z which has been valued at full absorption cost as follows:

	Cost per unit $
Materials	3.40
Labour	2.10
Manufacturing overhead:	
Variable	1.40
Fixed	3.70
	10.60

213

Required:
    (i) State the reporting implications, if any, if, at the end of 19A2, the company decides to change the method of inventory valu ation from an absorption to a variable (direct) cost basis.
    (ii) Assuming that the company did change to a variable cost basis of inventory valuation, what would the effect be on the reported profit for 19A2?

(c) Company B uses an important basic raw material X in the manufacture of product Y. Discuss the implications, if any, regarding the valuation of the ending inventories of raw material X and work in process and finished goods of Y if the current replacement cost of X has:
    (i) increased by 25%; or
    (ii) decreased by 25%.

(d) For the last five years XYZ Co Ltd has maintained its manufacturing operations at approximately 80% of total capacity. At the end of its current financial year, 19A2, the company's finished goods inventory was $4,800,000. The company's inventory at the end of the 19A1 financial year was $3,700,000. In both years the inventory was valued at full absorption cost.

    During 19A2 increasing competition had reduced the company's sales and its profit margins. As a result, production for 19A3 has been scheduled at 65% of total capacity.

Required:
    (i) Discuss the matters the company should have considered in deciding on an "appropriate" basis for the allocation of its fixed manufacturing overheads to production and their inclusion in the value of ending inventories in the past, including 19A2, and any problems associated with the decision.
    (ii) Should the basis of allocating fixed manufacturing overheads be changed in 19A3?
    (iii) Assume that you are the auditor of XYZ Co Ltd, how would you go about determining the fairness of the value placed on the ending inventory at the end of 19A2? State any matters that may be of special concern to you.

12.10 "A key point in understanding the nature of inventory valuation is that it should be based on expectations about the future."
Discuss.

Chapter 13
Depreciation

[1301] Accounting for depreciation poses some of the most difficult problems associated with the measurement of profit.

It is generally accepted that in the business context, physical assets (land being normally a notable exception) have limited useful lives. Accounting for depreciation aims to reflect this decline in service utility in the measurement of profit. Before we examine the problems of accounting for depreciation in the special context in which the term is used in current accounting practice, we will consider some of the meanings attached to the term. These include:
- (a) fall in resale value;
- (b) physical deterioration;
- (c) fall in economic utility.

Fall in resale value

[1302] Many long-term assets drop in resale value the moment they are purchased — motor cars, home appliances, plant and machinery — especially those of a specialized nature. The fall of resale value of such assets is, normally, expected by the purchaser. The reason such assets are acquired is their value in use. In the business context, such assets are acquired when their use promises to generate returns in excess of the outlays associated with their acquisition and operation.

Physical deterioration

[1303] The physical deterioration of assets results from wear and tear through use or deterioration through the passage of time. The extent of physical deterioration would be related to the extent of repairs and maintenance work carried out by the firm. Physical deterioration affects both the resale value of an asset and its economic utility.

Fall in economic utility

[1304] The economic utility of an asset is determined by its comparative ability to generate revenue in excess of cost. Physical deterioration and obsolescence will reduce the economic utility of assets.

The obsolescence factor

[1305] Obsolescence is an "event"-related cause in the fall of the economic utility of assets brought about by technological improvements in production processes

215

(technical obsolescence) and/or fall in the demand for the goods and services in the production of which depreciable assets are used (commercial obsolescence).

The variability of depreciation cost

[1306] In the business context, depreciation caused by wear and tear through use will be in the nature of a variable cost, while depreciation caused by deterioration and obsolescence will be in the nature of a "fixed" cost in the sense that it will not be related to the level of output (use). The cumulative effect of deterioration and obsolescence on the economic utility of depreciable assets, however, may not be strictly time-related in the sense that fixed costs are usually conceived to be.

The breaking down of depreciation cost into variable and fixed components is a very difficult task and is not usually attempted in practice.

An example of a motor car

[1307] Let us illustrate the preceding discussion with an example of a motor car.

When a new car is purchased, there will be an immediate fall in its resale value even though the car has not been affected by use or obsolescence. But cars are being purchased — the reason is their intended use and not their immediate resale value.

As the car is used, it will be affected by physical deterioration mainly in the form of wear and tear. Physical deterioration may be reduced by maintenance and part of the deterioration which has occurred may be made good by repairs. With the passage of time, the car will be affected by obsolescence on the market. The wear and tear which cannot be made good by repairs and the obsolescence will affect both the resale value of the car and its economic utility to the owner.

We will illustrate the variable and fixed components of depreciation by comparing the sales value of a last year's model unused car with the sales value of the same model car which has been driven for, say 20,000 kilometers. As the current year's models come on the market, the sales value of last year's unused car will drop. In this case we can say that the fall in market value is due to obsolescence caused by the availability of newer models. On the other hand, the same model car which has been driven for 20,000 kilometers would have dropped in value by a greater amount. We can say, therefore, that the difference in the value of the unused and used cars represents the, essentially, variable portion of depreciation.

[1308] Unfortunately, the breaking down of depreciation expense into fixed and variable components, is generally, much more difficult than may be suggested by the motor car example. In many cases, much of the effects of wear and tear can be removed by adequate maintenance and repairs. For most specialized assets there is no ready market which may be used as a reference to determine the amount of depreciation applicable to assets and provide a basis for the analysis of depreciation into fixed and variable components. Further, where a ready market does exist for some assets as is the case with motor cars, the effects of price changes (such as the significant price increases which occurred in many areas in the 1970s and 1980s) may obscure the fact that depreciation of assets does occur both through wear and tear and obsolescence. As a result, in practice, depreciation is usually regarded as a fixed cost allocated to different accounting periods in accordance with a preselected method, unrelated to short-term changes in the market value of the assets being depreciated.

Depreciation and Current Accounting Practice

[1309] Current accounting practice recognizes that the utility of physical assets declines over time. Accounting for depreciation attempts to reflect this decline in utility by allocating against revenue the cost less estimated residual value of depreciable assets over the assets' estimated useful lives.

The pattern of depreciation charges should reflect the expiration of utility and this is not necessarily related to short-term changes in the market value of the assets being depreciated. The utility of assets is normally reflected in their ability to generate revenue and the costs associated with using the assets in revenue-generating operations. In principle, therefore, the pattern of depreciation charges should reflect the patterns of expected revenue and costs over the estimated useful lives of the assets being depreciated. The practical application of such a principle of depreciation accounting, however, meets with insurmountable difficulties. The major cause of difficulties is the joint venture of both depreciation cost and revenue.

[1310] Depreciation over the life of an asset is a joint cost and, therefore, has no logical basis for distribution over the accounting periods which make up the estimated useful life of the asset. Further, revenue is the result of the interaction of a number of assets and other inputs; it is the joint product of a number of inputs and, therefore, it is impossible to determine what revenue arises from the use of a particular asset in a given accounting period or what pattern of revenue generation relates to the use of the asset over its estimated useful life. As a result, any pattern of depreciation cost allocation will be, of necessity, an arbitrary one; further, it will be impossible to show that the pattern chosen is the correct one.

Notwithstanding the above difficulties, accounting for depreciation is an established practice. It is accepted that total depreciation over the economic life of an asset is a joint cost so far as trading periods are concerned. It is also accepted that period income cannot be regarded as fairly measured without recognizing the fact of depreciation cost. There is uncertainty about the economic life of an asset and about the depreciation to be recovered over that life. That uncertainty has to be accepted; accounting is not an exact science.

We will consider next some of the problems associated with arriving at and implementing a policy of depreciation accounting.

Problems associated with the determination of depreciation charges

[1311] The problems associated with current accounting for depreciation expense include:

    (a) the estimation of the expected useful lives of assets;
    (b) the estimation of any residual value at the end of the assets' useful lives; and
    (c) the selection of an appropriate method of depreciation.

Traditionally, the total amount of depreciation to be recovered from revenue over the estimated useful life of an asset is the asset's historical cost less any estimated residual value. However, continuing rising prices and inflation have given rise to grave doubts above the relevance of depreciation based on historical cost for the evaluation of operating results and the measurement of profit. Proposals for accounting in terms of current value are discussed in Chapter 19.

Estimated useful life and residual value

[1312] In the face of an uncertain future, the estimation of the useful lives of depreciable assets is not an easy task. The concern is with the economic lives of assets, not their physical lives; it is not so much a question of how long an asset would "last" as it is a question of how long the use of the asset in operations will remain a viable business proposition. That the physical and useful lives of assets do not necessarily coincide is evidenced by the fact that depreciable assets are usually replaced or scrapped before they have fallen apart through wear, tear and decay.

The estimation of the useful lives of assets may be based on engineering studies and economic projections. Matters to be considered include:
- the potential physical life of the asset, projected usage, and expected maintenance over time;
- likelihood of technological advances which may render the asset technologically obsolete;
- expected trends in market demand for the goods or services in the production of which the asset is used; for example, an asset which is "technologically" up-to-date may be rendered "commercially" obsolete through a shift in market demand.

The estimation of residual value in determining the amount of depreciation to be charged against revenue is also a difficult task because of uncertainty and the specialized nature of many depreciable assets. As a result, residual value is usually ignored in the setting of depreciation charges.

Methods of Depreciation

[1313] Given the expected useful life of an asset, the amount of depreciation charged against revenue in different accounting periods will depend on the method of depreciation used. As pointed out earlier, the method applied will be of necessity an arbitrary one since there is no solution to the joint cost/joint revenue problem. The best that can be hoped for in dealing with the problem in practice is that the allocation of depreciation expense is based on understanding and commonsense.

The method chosen should result in systematic depreciation charges to revenue. The method should be appropriate to the nature of the assets. The choice should be based on a study of the physical and technical characteristics of assets and on projections of the commercial prospects of the goods and services to be produced. The method chosen should then be applied consistently from one period to another. When there has been a change in depreciation policy, the fact and the effect of the change should be disclosed.

[1314] The two most frequently used methods of depreciation are the straight-line and the reducing balance (diminishing value) methods. These will be considered in turn.

[1315] (a) *Straight-line method.* Under the straight-line method the total depreciable amount of an asset (for example, cost less salvage value) is divided by the number of years of the expected useful life of the asset giving a fixed annual depreciation charge.

The simplicity of the straight-line method is a major reason for its popularity. The following are some criticisms:

- the method assumes that both physical deterioration and osbolescence occur evenly over time — the assumption may be unrealistic regarding the incidence of obsolescence;
- the method ignores the decline in the relative productivity of the asset over time compared with new assets and the higher maintenance costs in later years.

A common application of the straight-line method is in accounting for the depreciation of buildings.

[1316] (b) *Reducing balance (diminishing value) method.* This method results in depreciation charges which decrease from period to period.

The following are some arguments in favour of the reducing balance method:

- the operating efficiency and productivity of an asset are likely to decline over time because of the cumulative effect of osbsolescence (ie more up-to-date assets in the hands of competitors). Depreciation policy, therefore, should reflect the likelihood of such decline in the value of assets by providing for higher deprecia-tion charges in the earlier years of asset use than in later years;
- depreciation charges should allow for the higher maintenance and repair costs expected to be incurred in the later years of asset use.

[1317] There are a number of methods for the calculation of reducing charges for depreciation. One method is to calculate depreciation charges as a fixed percentage of the reducing balance of the asset being depreciated. Given the estimated useful life of the asset, the depreciation rate to be aplied to the reducing balance may be calculated by the following formula:

$$\text{Annual depreciation rate} = \sqrt[n]{\frac{R}{c}}$$

where n = the number of years of estimated useful life of the asset;
R = the residual value of the asset at the end of its useful life;
c = the cost of the asset.

[1318] Under the double-declining balance method, the reducing balance depreciation rate is set at twice the straight-line rate. For example, if an asset has an estimated useful life of 10 years which would require an annual straight-line depreciation rate of 10%, the annual reducing balance depreciation rate will be set at 20%.

[1319] Under the declining balance method of depreciation an asset is never com-pletely written off. A depreciation method which will produce declining charges for depreciation and at the same time will result in the complete writing off of the depreciable value of an asset at the end of the asset's useful life is the sum-of-the-years'-digits method.

[1320] Under the sum-of-the-years'-digits method revenue is charged with a diminishing fraction of the total depreciable amount of the asset; the charge is calculated on the basis of the ratio of the number of years of remaining useful life at the beginning of the period to the sum of the digits of the years of total useful life. The application of the sum-of-the-years'-digits method is illustrated in Example 13.1.

Example 13.1

Cost of asset	$6,000
Estimated residual value	1,000
Total depreciation	$5,000

Estimated useful life 4 years
Sum-of-the-years'-digits $= 4 + 3 + 2 + 1 = 10$

Annual depreciation charges:

Year		Depreciation $
1	4/10 x $5,000 =	2,000
2	3/10 x $5,000 =	1,500
3	2/10 x $5,000 =	1,000
4	1/10 x $5,000 =	500
Total depreciation charged		5,000

Coping with Uncertainty and Complexity

[1321] Capital intensive industries operating in highly competitive markets, using high cost equipment subject to obsolescence, and engaging in periodic updating of facilities (rejuvenating maintenance), have a particular concern that depreciation expense be estimated fairly each period. For a particular asset or set of assets, a threshold period may be set of relatively certain economic life, and depreciation will be based initially on this period — say 10 years. After a set period of use, say five years, or in the event of a material change in expectations, a fresh assessment will be made of the relatively certain economic life, establishing a new threshold, and the asset balance, including upgrading costs, will be depreciated over this period. It is thus possible to cope with uncertainty through a process of systematic reviews.

Depreciation and Rising Prices

[1322] Experiences with continuing high levels of inflation have given rise to strong doubts about the adequacy of depreciation based on historical cost.

As we stated earlier, business operations involve the investment of money or money equivalent for the purpose of generating a monetary return in excess of monetary outlay. In this context, the allocation of the historical cost of depreciable assets against revenue over the useful lives of the assets provides for the recovery of the original monetary outlay before the recognition of profit. In times of inflation, however, it may be pointed out that the allocation of historical cost depreciation will recover from revenue only the number of dollars involved in the original outlay and not its purchasing power which is the real economic significance of monetary investment. A method of correcting this deficiency in traditional accounting for depreciation is to restate the historical cost of depreciable assets in dollars of constant purchasing power and to base depreciation charges on the restated historical cost.

[1323] Another approach to the problem of rising prices is to base depreciation on the replacement cost of depreciable assets. The purpose of this procedure is to maintain the operating capacity of the firm rather than the purchasing power of the shareholders' investment which is the objective of the purchasing power adjustment discussed in the preceding paragraph.

The question of accounting for the effects of price changes will be considered in greater detail in Chapter 19. At this stage we will illustrate some aspects of the problem with an example.

[1324] Let us assume that a contractor charges set hourly rates for the use of a front end loader. At expected usage the front end loader has an economic life of five years. The $50,000 cost of the loader is being depreciated at $10,000 per year. The revenue, less operating expense, has been steady at $15,000 per year. Net profit has been $5000 per year throughout the five years. An equivalent loader would now cost $90,000. Assuming replacement, an apparently profitable operation is now shown as producing a loss of $3000 per year — plus interest on the amount borrowed to finance the extra $40,000. But was the operation really profitable in the previous years?

Revaluation of Fixed Assets

[1325] The revaluation of fixed assets (land and buildings in particular) has become a common practice in Australia and New Zealand. The revaluations have usually involved the writing up of fixed assets to some estimate of current value such as replacement cost.

When assets are revalued, it will be necessary to make appropriate adjustments to depreciation charges. The review of depreciation policy should take into account the revised value of the assets, the assumed pattern regarding the using up of their service utility, and their estimated remaining useful lives. The new depreciation charges should result in the total depreciable amount of the revalued assets being written off over the assets' remaining estimated useful lives.

The procedures and some of the issues involved in assets revaluation will be illustrated in Example 13.2.

Example 13.2

Buildings which cost $500,000 20 years ago and have been depreciated at the rate of 2% per annum are written up to an estimated current value of $900,000. Their remaining expected useful life is 40 years.

The book value of the building at the time of valuation is:

	$
Cost	500,000
Less Depreciation (2% of $500,000 for 20 years)	200,000
Book value	300,000

[1326] In writing up the buildings, the depreciation written off will be transferred to the credit of the buildings account and then the balance of $300,000 will be written up to the current value of the buildings, the resulting surplus being credited to a reserve:

Provision for Depreciation — Buildings	$200,000	
Buildings		$200,000
Buildings	$600,000	
Buildings Revaluation Reserve		$600,000

Similar entries are made on the sale of depreciable assets: provision for depreciation and selling price are credited to the asset account and the surplus/loss on book value transferred to a reserve (or profit and loss account). In published financial statements such surpluses/losses should be disclosed as extraordinary items if material.

[1327] The manner in which the surplus on the revaluation or sale of fixed assets is treated in the books of the company may be affected by tax considerations. For example, in New Zealand, the recovery of depreciation on the sale of depreciable assets (except buildings) is assessable income. Depreciation written back or recovered on the writing up or sale of depreciable assets is treated as a revenue reserve. Cash distributions from such reserves are taxable in the hands of the shareholders, while distributions in the form of bonus shares are tax-free. Surpluses above historical cost on the sale of depreciable assets are regarded as capital reserves and are not taxable to the company or in the hands of the shareholders on distribution whether in cash or in the form of bonus shares. As a result, in the books of the company, recoveries of depreciation on the writing up or sale of assets may be credited to a revenue reserve and surpluses above historical cost to a capital reserve.

Following our example:

Buildings	$600,000	
General Reserve		$200,000
Buildings Revaluation Reserve		$400,000

[1328] After the revaluation, annual depreciation charges should be based on the written up value of the buildings and their remaining estimated useful life:

$$\frac{\$900,000}{40 \text{ years}} = \$22,500$$

For tax purposes, however, depreciation will continue to be based on historical cost at the rate specified by the tax regulations.

Analysis of Depreciation Expense

[1329] It should be apparent from the preceding discussion that accounting for depreciation is a highly subjective exercise. In the final count, the depreciation charge against revenue is very much the product of opinion — responsible opinion at best, a deliberately biased one at worst.

In the analysis of depreciation expense, a study should be made of the methods of depreciation used, any changes in depreciation policies, and the effect of such changes on reported profit at the present time and in the future. Consideration should be given also to the adequacy of depreciation charges based on historical cost or past revaluations of assets.

Where depreciation represents a significant proportion of the expenses incurred by a firm, the amount of reported profit may be very much dependent on the depreciation policy adopted by the firm and on any changes in this policy. Consider for example the case of a capital intensive company which reported profit before tax of $2,247,000 after charging $2,582,000 for depreciation!

[1330] As stated earlier, when fixed assets are revalued, depreciation should be based on the written up value of the assets. Even when this is stated to be the case, however, it may still be necessary to study the manner in which depreciation is charged to revenue. We will illustrate this point with an example from the 1981 financial statements of a New Zealand company:

> ... depreciation of buildings has been provided on the revalued amount. This policy results in an amount greater than cost being provided for depreciation, therefore an equivalent sum is transferred from revaluation reserves and is shown in the profit and loss account. Consequently, revaluation reserves are reduced over the lives of the buildings.

[1331] The effect of the policy described in the above statement is that only pre-revaluation historical cost depreciation is charged to the profit and loss account, the additional depreciation resulting from the written up value of the buildings being written off progressively against the surplus on revaluation. The reasoning behind this set of procedures reflects the present state of accounting measurement. While the income statement recognizes a more relevant charge for depreciation expense, it also brings into the income of the year the now "realized" portion of an earlier write up of the asset. One may well question whether the latter can be regarded fairly as income of the year we are studying.

[1332] In the analysis of financial statements a study of depreciation expense should be carried out with at least some reference to the level and accounting treatment of repairs and maintenance expenditure, in particular major rejuvenating expenditure. For example, rejuvenating expenditure may increase the economic value of plant by incorporating technological improvements. The manner in which such expenditure is treated in the books (that is, whether it is capitalized and depreciated over a number of periods or is expensed as incurred) will affect the total amount of plant-related expense charged against revenue in a particular period (that is, depreciation and maintenance expense).

Some Misconceptions about Depreciation

[1333] In this section we shall consider some possible misconceptions regarding the nature of depreciation:
  (a) that depreciation is a non-cash expense;
  (b) that depreciation is a source of funds for use in operations; and
  (c) that depreciation is concerned with the ultimate replacement of the assets being depreciated.

(a) Depreciation as a non-cash expense

[1334] The recording of depreciation in any one period involves a journal entry (debiting depreciation expense and crediting provision for depreciation), not directly related to any corresponding cash payment in the period. Further, the mechanics employed in the preparation of funds statements (statements of changes in financial position) require the adding back to profit of depreciation as a non-cash item.

In the long run, however, there is no such thing as a non-cash expense. If a business enterprise is to maintain its level of operations, it has, from time to time, to incur outlays for plant and buildings to replace assets reaching the end of their economic lives. Typically, these outlays occur at irregular intervals and in uneven amounts. It is very seldom that assets are replaced with identical assets. Fixed assets have relatively long lives, during which material price changes may take place.

[1335] The link between depreciation expense and cash flow can be best perceived through an example. If the plant owned by an enterprise consists of 10 equivalent units, has an economic life of 10 years and is at half life on average, with one unit being replaced each year, depreciation is straight-line, and there have been no price changes, then the depreciation expense each year would be matched by an equivalent cash outlay. It can be calculated, however, that if cost prices of the plant units rose over the 10 years by 4% per year, the cost of replacement would be 23.3% higher than the depreciation expense of the year. If the price increase were 15% per year, the cost of replacement would be no less than 99.3% higher than the depreciation expense of the year. See for example, T K Cowan, "Is Inflation All That Bad?", *The Accountants' Journal*, September 1983, pp 384–6. The cash outlay required is a fact. It is the adequacy of the depreciation expense measure that needs to be questioned.

(b) Depreciation as a source of funds

[1336] In the preparation of funds statements, the calculation of the amount of funds generated from operations is usually made by adding back to profit the amount of the depreciation expense for the period. This common practice may lead to the misconception that, somehow, depreciation is a source of funds to be used in operations.

Depreciation cannot be regarded as a source of funds in any direct sense. As stated earlier, the recording of depreciation expense involves a journal entry which is not directly related to any funds movements in the period. The reason why, in the calculation of funds inflow from operations, we add depreciation back to profit is that the relevant figure is profit before depreciation and not because depreciation as such is a source of funds.

Depreciation may be regarded as an indirect source of funds to the extent that it is allowable as a tax deduction and, therefore, reduces the amount of tax payable, and to the extent that, as a charge against profit, it actually reduces the amount of cash distributions to shareholders. On the other hand, this reasoning can be extended to include the writing down of inventories to a figure below cost, and finally to all expenses which are deductible for tax purposes or reduce the amount of profit regarded as available for distribution.

(c) Depreciation and the replacement of assets

[1337] Another misconception regarding depreciation is that the purpose of depreciation accounting is to provide for the replacement of assets.

As stated earlier, under present accounting practice, the objective of depreciation accounting is to allocate against revenue the cost of assets over the assets' estimated useful lives. As such, depreciation accounting is concerned with profit measurement and the residual amounts at which assets are shown in the balance sheet, and not with asset replacement.

Further, to the extent that depreciation accounting causes the retention of funds in the business, these funds will be absorbed in the continuing operations of the business and will not be held in the form of ready cash available for the replacement of the assets being depreciated.

While the objective of depreciation accounting is essentially the measurement of profit by the matching of expense with revenue, the replacement of depreciable assets involves capital investment decisions concerning the future operations of the firm. The kind of assets to be acquired will be determined not so much by the assets held in the past as by the kind of assets the firm needs in view of its plans for future operations. In fact there may be no need for a firm to replace some of its assets and, indeed, conditions may exist which make it economically undesirable to do so.

Depreciation and Taxation

[1338] To be allowed as a tax deduction, depreciation must be calculated on the basis of historical cost at the rates specified by current taxation rules. It should be stated, however, that as financial reporting objectives are different from taxation objectives, the depreciation methods and procedures adopted by a firm for its financial reporting need not coincide with the rules regarding tax allowances for depreciation. That is not to say that the choices may not be influenced by the rates set for taxation purposes. To adopt tax rates makes for convenience; and, at industry level, it probably reduces the risk of review of tax rates that are accepted as being favourable to the taxpayer.

[1339] An important consideration in the setting of taxation rules is practical application; hence the importance and convenience of historical cost as a basis for the measurement of taxable profit. In regards to depreciation, taxation rules specify standard allowances based on historical cost.

Taxation is also used by government as a means of effecting specific economic policies at the national level by encouraging some kinds of economic activity by providing tax incentives to firms investing in certain assets.

In the area of depreciation, tax incentives may be provided in the form of "special" depreciation allowances (over and above what may be termed "ordinary" depreciation) in respect of qualifying assets. It is normal accounting practice to claim the tax benefit from such special depreciation allowances but not to write off the additional amount of depreciation in the books of the company. In the analysis of financial statements a study should be made of any tax concessions relating to the year's profits, the manner in which the tax effect has been accounted for, and any effect on tax payable and profit after tax in future years. Some of the problems associated with accounting for taxation are discussed in Chapter 14.

Maintenance, Repairs and Renewals

[1340] Repairs and maintenance expense may be divided into:
  (a) routine recurring maintenance; and
  (b) major maintenance occurring at regular (and sometimes irregular) intervals.

To the extent that maintenance and repairs remove the effects of wear and tear, they form an integral part of any estimates of useful life and should be adequately reflected in a choice of depreciation rates. Sometimes, major repairs, maintainance and renewals may not only remove the effects of wear and tear on assets, but, by incorporating technological improvements increase their value to the firm and extend their economic lives.

As with other types of expense, accounting for the cost of repairs, maintenance and renewals is concerned with the "proper" matching of expense with revenue.

[1341] Strictly speaking, to the extent that reparis, maintenance and renewals make good the effects of wear and tear and have been allowed for in the asessment of economic life and in the selection of depreciation rates, their cost should be treated as being of a revenue nature and matched against revenue as such. This is a relatively straightforward matter as far as routine maintenance is concerned — the expense associated with routine maintenance will be matched against revenue in the period in which it is incurred. Matching problems may arise, however, with major maintenance, repairs and renewals expense which is not incurred evenly from one period to another. Such expenditure may significantly affect reported profit. As it is realistic to assume that the cost of such maintenance, repairs and renewals accrues from year to year rather than in the particular year in which the work is carried out, the proper matching of cost with revenue would require the creation of a provision for the annual accrual of major maintenance, repairs and renewals cost:

Maintenance expense account	$..........	
Provision for accrued maintenance account		$..........
Provision for accrued maintenance account	$..........	
Cash		$..........
Accounts payable		$..........

[1342] In some cases repairs and renewals may not only remove the effects of wear and tear but, by incorporating technological improvements in assets, may increase their economic value to the firm. The accounting problem of properly matching of expense with revenue in such cases is one of determining the part of expense which is properly chargeable to the current period and the amount which should be capitalized for recovery in the future by way of depreciation.

[1343] In practice, the accounting treatment of the cost of major maintenance and renewals is likely to be influenced by tax considerations; firms will tend to expense as much of such expenditure as they are able to claim as a tax deduction. This practice may have significant implications for the analysis and interpretation of depreciation expense and the reported value of depreciable assets in cases where depreciable assets and related expenses represent a significant part respectively of the firm's total investment and operating costs.

[1344] In times of rising prices and inflation, depreciation based on historical cost is usually criticized as being an inadequate measure of the cost associated with using depreciable assets in terms of either the purchasing power of the original investment or current replacement cost. Repairs and renewals of depreciable assets which increase the value of the assets to the firm but are expensed as they are incurred may offset, at least in part, the shortfall in depreciation based on historical cost. The book value at which such assets are reported may be well below what may be called their current value.

[1345] Within certain limits, the timing of some types of major maintenance, repairs and renewals is at the discretion of management. Such expenditure may be timed for periods when profit is expected to be high and, therefore, better able to absorb the impact. In the analysis of expenses an effort should be made to determine, as far as possible, the adequacy of the maintenance, repairs and renewals carried out. An analysis of past financial statements and the financial statements of other firms in the industry may provide some basis for comparison. Adequate maintenance is closely related to the useful life of assets. If adequate maintenance is not being carried out, both the results of the firm and the expected useful life of its assets may have to be reassessed.

Asset Valuation and Depreciation Policy: An Example of a Large Corporate Group

[1346] A large corporate group such as Fletcher Challenge encounters most if not all the problems in depreciation and depreciable asset accounting that have been discussed above.

[1347] An examination of the asset valuation and depreciation policies adopted by the Fletcher Challenge Group (as disclosed for example in the Group's 1987 financial statements) reveals that deliberate moves have been made from an historical cost basis of measuring depreciating assets in order to show what must be considered more relevant asset values and depreciation expense.

[1348] Under these policies, a distinction is made between "general purpose land and buildings" and "special purpose land and buildings". Each unit of the former is revalued to its estimated market value of 30 June each year. The net gain arising on revaluation is credited to a fixed asset revaluation reserve. There is a market for general purpose buildings such as office blocks and warehouses, so that reasonably objective valuation is posible. On the other hand, there would be an unacceptable level of subjectivity in establishing separate market values for "special purpose" land and buildings at, say, pulp and paper mill locations. Such buildings are valued at the lower of:
   (a) "estimated replacement value less allowance for wear and tear and technological obsolescence" (a subjective exercise certainly, but a relevant one to current decisions as well as for reporting purposes); and
   (b) "the value at which reasonable earnings can be achieved, or net realizable value in an alternative use, whichever is the greater."

[1349] The approach adopted to the valuation of special purpose land and buildings reflects the concept of "value to the business" ("value to the owner") which is discussed in greater length in Chapter 19. If (a) exceeds (b), then the inference is that the particular asset would not be worth replacing, under conditions then prevailing.

[1350] Properties rated as "investment properties" are valued at net realizable value each year, recognizing that the return on these investments is a sum of net rentals and change in value. In that situation depreciation becomes irrelevant and has not been provided for.

[1351] Ships, plant, motor vehicles and office equipment are valued at cost less accumulated depreciation.

[1352] Major New Zealand-based pulp and paper manufacturing plant and structures were revalued on 31 December 1981 to depreciated replacement cost but the write up was limited to 55% of the excess valuation over book value, presumably in recognition that at the then current tax rate of 45%, 45% of the extra depreciation would constitute tax on a non-deductible item.

So much for the asset bases on which depreciation is calculated.

[1353] The following is the rather simple statement of the group's accounting policy on depreciation:

> Depreciation of fixed assets is calculated on the most appropriate method that would allocate as fairly as possible the depreciable amount over its useful life and after due allowance has been made for the expected residual value. The expected useful lives, which are regularly reviewed are (on a weighted average basis across the Fletcher Challenge Limited Group):

buildings	40 years
pulp and paper mills	27 years
ships, plant, equipment	13 years
motor vehicles	5 years
office equipment	6 years

> Where it is considered that past depreciation has been inadequate due to technological change or market conditions, additional depreciation is provided to write down the value of the affected assets to the current value to the business. Land is not depreciated.

[1354] The above statement of accounting policy on depreciation of fixed assets will be backed by a large manual of detailed applications. In a capital intensive exercise such as pulp and paper manufacture, the regular review of economic lives and related maintenance, renewals and updating programs, consititutes a vital part of the process of accounting for major assets and their depreciation.

[1355] The 1987 financial statements of Fletcher Challenge Limited we have referred to in this discussion disclosed that the depreciation charged against revenue was $177,386,000 and that total earnings before tax were $508,488,000. In the capital intensive sections of the Group's operations the relative significance of depreciation would be even greater. The earnings statement shows an initial balance "net earnings under historical cost" and a final balance "net earnings under modified historical cost". The emphasis is on the latter balance, which is arrived at by adjusting the former by adding the year's increment on revaluation of investment properties and deducting depreciation on asset revaluations.

Review questions

13.1 " ... depreciation charges against revenue tend to lack objectivity."
Discuss.

13.2 Discuss briefly the following propositions regarding depreciation written off
in the accounts:
(a) depreciation provides the business with cash;
(b) depreciation provides for the replacement of assets;
(c) depreciation writes off losses due to use;
(d) depreciation retains capital intact;
(e) depreciation is an allocation of cost.

13.3 (a) What are causes of depreciation?
(b) To what extent is it practicable to allocate the estimated overall depreciation cost to accounting periods, having regard to these causative factors? For
example, is it practicable to assess and separate with reasonable accuracy:
    (1) depreciation through use; and
    (2) depreciation through obsolescence?
(c) In the context of the matching concept, discuss the relationship between
depreciation and major maintenance work.

13.4 The following remarks have been made by the directors of two different
companies:
(a) "We have not charged any amount for depreciation of plant during the
year because the value at which it is shown in the books is much lower than
its current market value as a result of price changes since its date of acquisition."
(b) "We consider that the depreciation charge for this year should be increased because of increases in the cost of replacement of the plant. If we
continue to charge depreciation on the original cost we will not have sufficient funds on hand when it is necessary to replace worn-out plant."
Comment on the different interpretation of the nature of depreciation, and
of the purpose of the depreciation charge implied in the above quotations.
What do you consider the nature of the depreciation charge to be, and what
effect should a period of rising prices have on the depreciation policy?

13.5 In what circumstances is repairs and maintenance expense an important
item to consider in the analysis and interpretation of financial statements?

13.6 The balance sheet of Apex Ltd shows land and buildings as follows:

	$	$
Land (cost)		20,000
Buildings (cost)	120,000	
Less prov for depreciation	30,000	
		$90,000

The directors have decided to write up the land and buildings to government valuation:

	$
Land	35,000
Buildings	145,000

Instructions:

(a) Give the journal entries (without narrations) necessary to record the revaluation.

(b) Explain how you will arrive at the new charge for depreciation of buildings.

(c) State where you will show the surplus resulting from the revaluation in the Balance Sheet of Apex Ltd.

Chapter 14

Accounting for Income Tax and Interperiod Income Tax Allocation

[1401] The major problems associated with accounting for income tax and, in particular, with the interperiod allocation of income tax, arise when the principles and methods used to arrive at the accounting profit before tax of a year differ significantly from the principles and methods used to dĕtermine the taxable income of the year.

The question of whether or not income tax should be allocated to different accounting periods has caused considerable controversy in accounting circles in the past. The controversy has been caused largely by different views regarding the nature of income tax. For example, people who have held the view that income tax is not an expense of operations but a distribution of profit have argued against interperiod allocation of income tax. On the other hand, people of the view that income tax is an expense have argued that income tax should be properly matched with pre-tax profit by making use of the accounting processes of accrual and deferral where necessary.

[1402] Further argument has developed over the status of the provision for deferred taxation (whether it is really a liability), and of the accrual of future tax benefit (whether it is really an asset). It is pointed out forcefully by opponents of tax allocation that a provision for deferred tax is not currently owing to anyone, and that a future tax benefit is not owing by anyone, but is only a contingent benefit — contingent on the earning of taxable profit in future years, and that it is not normal accounting practice to recognize contingencies otherwise than by way of notes to the accounts. Proponents of tax allocation claim that a broader view than this of liabilities and assets is necessary if the state of affairs of an enterprise is to be presented fairly.

The predominant view at this time is that income tax is an expense and that, as such, it should be properly matched with pre-tax income. This attitude reflects the view that, ultimately, it is profit after tax (rather than profit before tax) which is the significant figure for shareholders, investors and others with vested interest in the operations of business enterprises.

Some Reasons for Differences between Accounting Income and Taxable Income

[1403] One of the basic objectives of accounting is the truthful measurement and fair reporting of the income of business enterprises. To the extent that the objective of government is the fair taxation of income, then we can say that the measurement of income which is appropriate for accounting purposes would be appropriate also for the purposes of taxation. There are two main reasons, however, why usually, accounting income and taxable income do not coincide:

(a) The measurement of accounting income reflects to a large extent expectations about the future and, within certain limits, depends on estimates, judgment and choice from available accounting alternatives. On the other hand, rules for determining taxable income must be capable of objective application (ie taxpayers should be given minimum discretion in determining the amount of tax they should pay — for obvious reasons) and they must also be practicable in their application to a very large number of taxpayers.

(b) Governments use taxation to achieve certain fiscal aims such as to encourage some types of economic activities and discourage others. Special tax allowances aimed to achieve such fiscal aims would cause the tax payable to diverge from that which would have resulted by the application to income of the normal rate of taxation, and so cause further differences from accounting income. Such use of taxation has, at different times, included tax incentives to encourage exports, special depreciation and investment allowances to stimulate investment in particular types of capital asset or investment in particular geographical locations, incentives and subsidies to encourage farm development and increases in farm production, etc.

[1404] The measurement of both accounting and taxable income is based on matching revenue and expense. In the case of accounting income, the matching is carried out in the context of generally accepted accounting principles which allow alternatives and a certain degree of flexibility. In the measurement of taxable income, the matching process is effected within the framework of rather rigid taxation rules. For example, in New Zealand, under existing taxation rules, depreciation claimed for tax purposes must be calculated on the basis of historical cost at the tax allowable rates, even though the tax-paying firm may, in its own books, write off depreciation on the basis of, say, a written up value of the assets at rates different from those specified for determining taxable income. On the other hand, provision is made for a taxpayer to apply to the Commissioner of Taxes for special depreciation rates to be allowed, if justified by the circumstances of the case.

[1405] The need for objectivity (and also relevance) has made historical cost and realization key principles in the determination of taxable income, while in the measurement of accounting income the application of the two related principles has been to some extent relaxed and modified.

[1406] Viewed broadly, accounting and taxable income have a strong common characteristic. In both cases the capital of a business enterprise is perceived, by implication at least, as monetary investment, the maintenance of which is regarded as a precondition for the recognition of income. In both cases capital is measured in terms of the number of dollars invested regardless of changes in purchasing power. A notable move away from the last rule is the use of an indexed cost base in the calculation of taxable capital gains in Australia. Some of the general rules applicable to the taxation of capital gains in Australia are discussed in paras [1421] to [1428].

[1407] Taxation policies change over time. Sometimes major changes take place over relatively short periods of time. In this chapter we discuss some basic characteristics of taxation as they affect the analysis and interpretation of financial statements in general. In the analysis and interpretation of specific financial statements it would be necessary to consider taxation in the context of the taxation rules and policies applicable at the time and in particular as affecting the companies the financial statements of which are being studied. In making projections, due consideration should be given to any potential changes in taxation policies by present and prospective governments.

[1408] Some of the reporting issues associated with income tax will be illustrated in Example 14.1. The figures are taken from the 1968 financial statements of a New Zealand fertilizer company. This rather early example has been chosen because, at the time, accounting for income tax had not become a major issue in New Zealand company reporting and the example illustrates the kind of situations which led to the recognition that a reporting problem did in fact exist.

In the example, taxation for 1967 represents 49.3% of profit before tax. As the rate of company taxation at the time was 50%, the reported profit before tax indicates that in 1967 there were no significant differences between the principles applied in the measurement of accounting profit before taxation and taxable income.

The situation is quite different in 1968. The reported drop in profit is approximately 50%. However, if the normal rate of taxation is deducted from the 1968 profit figure, the drop will be 75%. The interpretation of the 1968 result requires an understanding of the factors which have contributed to the differences between disclosed profit before tax and taxable profit:

Example 14.1

Reported profit:	1968 $	1967 $
Profit before taxation	116,967	462,126
Provision for taxation (Note 1)	—	228,000
Net profit for year	116,967	234,126

Notes to the accounts:
Note 1 Investment allowances of $187,105 and special depreciation of $128,762 have been taken into account as a deduction for taxation purposes but have not been written off in the books of account. No taxes are payable on the current year's profits. $198,000 will be carried forward for taxation purposes against next year's profits.

Investment allowances, $187,105

These represented a deduction from taxable income of a specified percentage of the cost of qualifying assets acquired during the year. They did not affect future tax claims for depreciation and therefore, resulted in a permanent saving of tax.

Special depreciation, $128,762

This was a depreciation allowance, for tax purposes, (over and above what could be called "ordinary" depreciation) in the first year or early years of asset use. However, as the total amount which could be claimed for depreciation on the assets over their economic lives was limited to their historical cost, the special depreciation allowance resulted in a postponement of tax rather than a tax saving. For example, the higher depreciation claimed for tax purposes in the early years of asset use meant that lower depreciation claims would be allowed in later years.

There is the further significant fact that, as these allowances exceeded the profit before taxation by $198,900, this amount was available for carrying forward and offsetting against the taxable income for 1969 (or subsequent years). The taxation payable on this income would be $99,450 lower as a result, and the net profit after tax correspondingly higher.

[1409] If income tax is to be treated as an expense to be matched against the income on which it is based, then there is a case for going beyond disclosure (as in Note 1) and actually incorporating in the accounts and financial statements the accrual and deferral of income tax expense where this is necessry. In accounting for income tax, standard practice in Australia (AAS 3) and New Zealand (SSAP 12) distinguishes between "permanent differences" and "timing differences" between disclosed profit before taxation and profit assessable for income tax in a particular year. In our Example 14.1 for instance, the tax saving from the investment allowance is a permanent difference, because claiming it in 1968 had no effect on the tax payable on the income of future years; whereas the reduction in the tax assessed on the 1968 income through the claiming as a deduction of special depreciation may be regarded not as a saving but merely as a postponement of tax. The claiming of more depreciation for tax purposes than is written off in the accounts is compensated for later by being able to claim less for tax purposes than is written off in the accounts.

To summarize the position:

Permanent differences — these alter the amount of tax payable in the period in which they occur but do not affect the computation of tax in subsequent periods.

Timing differences — these affect the amount of tax payable in the period in which they occur but reverse (and, therefore, affect the computation of tax) in subsequent periods.

Shown below are some examples of permanent and timing differences between accounting profit and taxable income and the manner in which they may currently be accounted for.

Accounting for permanent differences

[1410] Current accounting practice favours the recognition of the tax effect of permanent differences in the period in which the differences occur, with disclosure by way of a note to the financial statements if reported profit after tax is materially affected. Let us look at investment allowances.

[1411] From the viewpoint of government fiscal policy, the purpose of the investment allowance is to encourage certain kinds of capital investment such as plant and machinery either generally or in particular geographical areas. The allowance is at a stated percentage of the cost of qualifying assets and is deducted from the taxable income of the firm in the year in which the assets are acquired or first put into use. The allowance does not affect the tax claims for depreciation and, therefore, results in a saving of tax.

For example, if a firm invests a substantial sum in qualifying assets and the investment allowance is 20% of cost, with a tax rate of 50%, the tax saving will result in an increase in profit after tax equivalent to 10% of the cost of the qualifying assets; or to put it differently, in the period the tax advantage is taken, the firm will report a 10% tax paid "return" on its investment in qualifying assets merely as a result of the acquisition of the assets and unrelated to their use.

[1412] Permanent differences may arise through revenue not assessable for income tax (for example, company dividends received by New Zealand companies, or where capital profits on the sale of fixed assets are not taxable or are subject to tax at a different rate from the "normal" rate of taxation, through concessions such as export tax incentives, through development expenditure of a capital nature which may be allowable as a deduction (for example, farm development expenditure), and through expenses which may not be deductible for tax purposes because of their nature (for example, certain types of legal expenses, the amortization of goodwill, etc).

If the permanent difference arising from the acquisition of productive assets is material and significant in assessing the adequacy of the return on investment from the relevant operations, then there seems to be a case for treating the tax effect as a reduction in the cost of the asset. Such circumstances would be unusual.

Accounting for timing differences

[1413] Current accounting practice favours the interperiod allocation of income tax in relation to timing differences. There are two main methods to achieve this:
   (a) the liability (accrual) method; and
   (b) the deferral method.

The liability (or accrual) method involves the recording and reporting of timing differences either as liabilities for tax payable in the future, or as tax benefits (for example, prepayments of tax) realizable in the future. Under the liability method, accruals of future tax payments or tax benefits are adjusted for subsequent changes in the rates of taxation.

The deferral method for interperiod tax allocation operates in a manner similar to the liability method except that any liability for future taxation (deferred taxation) and any future tax benefits recorded in the books are not adjusted for subsequent changes in the rates of taxation.

[1414] The method for interperiod income tax allocation currently preferred (in Australia and New Zealand at least) is the liability (accrual) method.

Examples of situations which give rise to timing differences include:
• different rates or methods of depreciation used for tax and accounting purposes;
• differences in inventory valuation for tax and accounting purposes;
• exchange gains and losses on foreign currency loans recognized at different times for financial reporting and tax purposes. For example, a company may record an "unrealized" loss on foreign currency loans if exchange rates have moved against it. (On the other hand, tax rules may provide for such losses to be allowed as tax

deductions on "realization" — when the loans are actually repaid, as is the case in Australia. In contrast, in New Zealand since July 1988 tax rules dealing with foreign exchange differences have been brought closer to accounting practice with the progressive recognition in the determination of taxable income of exchange gains and losses as they occur);
• differences between accounting and tax methods for recognizing profit from hire purchase sales; etc.

[1415] Accounting for timing differences in the interperiod allocation of income tax will be illustrated by examples dealing with special depreciation allowances and exchange losses on foreign currency loans.

Example 14.2

Income tax allocation and special depreciation allowances

X Co Ltd acquired plant at the cost of $100,000. The company's policy is to depreciate such plant at 10% reducing balance. The tax allowances for depreciation on the plant are:

Ordinary depreciation   10% on reducing balance
Special depreciation (to be claimed
   in the first year of plant use)   20% on cost.

Shown below is a table of the amounts of depreciation written off for accounting purposes and claimed for taxation in the first three years of the use of the plant and the differences between tax depreciation and accounting depreciation:

Depreciation written off

Year	Books of account $	Tax depreciation $	Differences between tax and accounting depreciation $
1	10,000	30,000*	+20,000
2	9,000	7,000**	− 2,000
3	8,100	6,300	− 1,800

* Ordinary depreciation	$10,000
Special depreciation	20,000
	$30,000

**10% of $70,000

The figures in Example 14.2 show that while in year 1 $20,000 more depreciation is claimed for tax purposes than written off in the books of the company, the position is reversed in the following years when the amount of depreciation allowed as a tax deduction is less than the amount written off in the company's books. The effect of the special depreciation allowance, therefore, is to postpone taxation.

The tax effect of the special depreciation allowance may be accounted for by means of deferred tax provision created in year 1 to be used to provide for the additional tax payable in subsequent years. Assuming that the company is taxed at the rate of 50%, the journal entries will be as shown opposite.

The exchange loss of $500,000 suffered by Y Co Ltd may be accounted for by debiting the profit and loss account with $500,000 and crediting the loan account. The exchange loss, however, is "unrealized" and (under current Australian tax rules) will not be allowed as a deduction from revenue for income tax purposes

Year 1

Tax expense }	$10,000	
(Profit and loss account) }		
Provision for deferred taxation		$10,000
being future tax liability 50% of		
$20,000		

Year 2

Provision for deferred taxation	$1,000	
Provision for taxation payable		$1,000
being tax on depreciation written off		
in the books but disallowed for tax		
purposes, 50% of $2000		

Year 3

Provision for deferred taxation	$900	
Provision for taxation payable		$900
(50% of $1,800) etc		

Example 14.3

Income tax allocation and foreign exchange losses

Y Co Ltd acquired plant from Germany and raised a $5 million loan in German marks to pay for it. Because the exchange rate between the dollar and the mark has moved against the dollar by 10%, the dollar value of the loan is now $5,500,000.

until "realization" (that is until the loan is repaid). At a tax rate of 50%, however, the loss carries a potential future tax saving of $250,000. This potential tax benefit may be recognized in the books of Y Co Ltd as an asset and be used to reduce the exchange loss accordingly. The journal entry will be:

Profit and loss account	$250,000	
Future tax saving	$250,000	
Loan account		$500,000

[1416] Current accounting practice, however, does not adhere to strict tax allocation procedures. For example, accounting standards impose certain restrictions on the recognition of future tax benefits and allow exemptions from the requirement that deferred taxation should be provided for in regards to timing differences, in the latter case if it can be demonstrated that there is a reasonable probability that the liability will not be paid in the foreseeable future (SSAP 12, para 5.3).

Tax deductible losses

[1417] When a firm incurs tax-deductible losses, the realization of the associated tax benefit depends on the firm's making taxable profits in the future against which such losses can be charged. The recognition of future tax benefits arising from tax-deductible losses is a matter of prudence in the face of uncertainty. While the past performance of the firm may provide a guide regarding future profits, the crucial factor is the expected performance of the firm in the future in view of projected business conditions.

The need to exercise prudence in the recognition of future tax benefits arising from tax-deductible losses becomes obvious when one considers a firm which incurs losses for a number of accounting periods and then goes into liquidation.

Under current accounting standards, tax benefits arising from tax-deductible losses should not be recognized unless there is virtual certainty of realization.

Where a provision for deferred income tax account exists, future tax benefits from income tax losses may be recognized even if the criterion of virtual certainty of realization is not met. The recognition of such tax benefits, however, is limited to the amount of the net credits from timing differences accumulated in the deferred tax account. The rationale for this position is that the provision for deferred income tax will not become payable while the tax loss remains available as a deduction.

Taxation and the writing up of depreciable assets

[1418] When depreciable assets such as plant and buildings are written up, the depreciation written off on them in the books of the firm should be based on the written up value of the assets so that they are completely written off by the end of their expected useful lives. For taxation purposes, however, depreciation will continue to be based on historical cost at the rates specified by the tax rules. If there are significant differences between accounting and taxable profit on account of these depreciation differences, the question arises of whether the tax effect should be formally accounted for.

[1419] One may argue that because the difference arising from the writing up is a "permanent" one (one which does not reverse in the future), no formal recognition in the accounts (for example, beyond the disclosure of accounting policies regarding depreciation) is necessary. One may look at the position in another way, however. If the differences between accounting and taxable profit on account of depreciation are significant, they must be taken into account in the analysis and interpretation of financial statements. Further, the surplus on the writing up of assets will be credited to a reserve. This surplus, however, is not tax paid and is not the same as, say, retained earnings from operations. For example, each accounting period, there will be a difference between accounting and taxable profit equivalent to the depreciation on the amount of the revaluation surplus. For tax purposes, this difference is added back to taxable profit and is taxed. As a result, during the depreciable life of the asset, the total surplus on the writing up will be added back to taxable profit and will be taxed. Finally, a depreciable assset which has been written up to current value is not as valuable to a firm as an identical asset acquired now and paid for at current price simply because of the different amounts the firm will be able to recover by way of tax allowable depreciation in respect of the two assets. See for example B Popoff, "The Incidence of Capital Gains Tax in New Zealand", *The Accountants' Journal*, June 1980, pp 167–70.

The above points are illustrated in Example 14.4.

Example 14.4

Z Co Ltd owns buildings which it acquired 20 years ago at a cost of $100,000. The buildings have been depreciated on a straight-line basis at an annual rate of 2½% on cost for both accounting and taxation purposes. The position at present is as follows:

Buildings, at cost	$100,000
Less depreciation (20 years at 2½% pa)	50,000
Book value	$50,000

The company writes up the buildings to their estimated current value of $200,000. The original estimation of useful life has remained unchanged and the new depreciation charge is calculated at $10,000 per annum.

(ie $\frac{\$200,000}{20 \text{ years}}$).

Using the data in Example 14.4, the following comments can be made:

(a) The surplus on writing up of $150,000 is not tax paid. Each year there will be a difference between accounting depreciation and tax depreciation of $7500:

Accounting depreciation	$10,000
Tax depreciation (2½ % of $100,000)	2,500
	$ 7,500

The difference of $7500 represents the depreciation on the amount by which the buldings have been written up ($\frac{\$150,000}{20 \text{ years}}$). As a result, over the next 20 years the total surplus on the writing up will be added back to profit and will be taxed.

(b) Let us assume that Z Co Ltd has just acquried identical buildings and paid for them their current cost of $200,000. Although both buildings will be carried in the books at the same amount ($200,000), other things being equal, the buildings just acquired will have a greater economic value to the company because for tax purposes the company will be able to claim a total of $200,000 by way of depreciation compared with $50,000 in regards to the buildings purchased 20 years ago.

The tax liability on the surplus on writing up may be accounted for by the creation of a provision for deferred taxation at the time of writing up. Assuming a tax rate of 50%, the journal entries will be:

Provision for depreciation of buildings	$50,000	
Buildings		$50,000
Buildings	$150,000	
Surplus on the revaluation of		
buildings		$75,000
Provision for deferred taxation		$75,000

The provision for deferred taxation will then be used to provide for the tax on the revaluation surplus each year:

Provision for deferred taxation	$3,750	
Provision for taxation payable		$3,750
(ie 50% of $7,500)		

The tax charged in the proft and loss account will be calculated on the amount of accounting profit as far as depreciation expense is concerned. It should be noted, however, that providing for deferred taxation on the writing up of depreciable assets is not a generally accepted practice.

The reporting of tax differences

[1420] It should be apparent that tax differences can arise for a number of reasons and may have a significant impact on current reported profit and profit reported in the future. The tax expense charged against profit, therefore, should be carefully analyzed. Current accounting practice requires the notes to the financial statements to include an explanation and reconciliation of any difference between the income tax expense shown in the profit and loss account and the tax calculated at the current rate on the accounting profit before tax. A good example of disclosure taken from the 1979 financial statements of Wattie Industries Ltd is shown in Example 14.5. In the example the amount of tax at the normal rate of 45% is reconciled with the actual tax shown in the profit statement.

Example 14.5

Wattie Industries Ltd

From the notes to the profit and appropriation statement
for year ended 31 July 1979:

Income tax expense	1979 $000	1978 $000
Earnings before tax per accounts	23,307	17,448
Income tax on this profit at 45¢	10,488	7,852
Less tax savings from permanent differences between earnings and assessable income:		
Export incentives	1,406	1,418
Investment allowances	442	555
Trading stock adjustment	—	1,455
Specified preference dividend	322	107
Non-taxable dividends received	640	259
Other	(35)	(71)
	2,755	3,723
Tax in respect of current year	7,733	4,129
Under (over) provided in previous years	26	(32)
Income tax expense	7,759	4,097
Comprising		
Income tax payable	7,430	3,823
Deferred tax	303	306
Under (over) provided in previous years	26	(32)
	7,759	4,097
Effective rate (cents in the $)	33.3	23.5

Australian Capital Gains Tax

[1421] In this section we will consider some of the general provisions regarding the taxation of capital gains in Australia.

[1422]   General capital gains tax has been applicable in Australia since 19

September 1985. The effect of the legislation is that capital gains made on the disposal (realization) of assets are subject to capital gains tax. For the purpose of taxation, capital gains are calcualted by deducting from the proceeds of disposal the assets' indexed cost.

[1423] For the purposes of capital gains tax, disposal is defined broadly as a change in ownership in any manner whatsoever eg by sale, gift or exchange. Disposal also includes the destruction or loss of assets which result in the receipt of compensation, for example, under an insurance policy or otherwise.

[1424] The amount of consideration (proceeds) received on the disposal of assets is determined as follows:

(a) Where assets are sold, the consideration is represented by the sales prices less expenses associated with the sale.

(b) Where assets are sold jointly without allocation of selling price to individual assets, the consideration assumed to have been received in respect of individual assets is determined by the Commissioner.

(c) Where assets are disposed of otherwise than by way of sale (eg by way of gift or exchange) the consideration received is taken to be the value of the assets at the date of disposal.

(d) In the case of loss or destruction of assets, the consideration is represented by the amount received or receivable under an insurance policy or otherwise.

[1425] The cost base used in the calculation of capital gains includes capital expenditures associated with the acquisition, improvement and disposal of assets. Expenses of a revenue nature which are tax-deductible under other tax provisions do not form part of an asset's cost base for the purpose of determining capital gains. However, capital expenditure on the acquisition of assets such as plant and equipment and expenditure on income-producing buildings in respect of which depreciation deductions have been allowed for tax purposes are included in the cost base of assets.

[1426] In determining capital gains on the disposal of assets which have been held for a period longer than 12 months, the assets' cost base is adjusted for inflation on the basis of the consumer price index. Only gains in excess of the rate of inflation are subject to capital gains tax. The inflation adjustment is not available where assets are disposed of within 12 months of acquisition. In such cases, the taxable gain is represented by the excess of proceeds over cost, without adjusting cost for inflation.

In contrast to capital gains, capital losses are determined without deduction for the effects of inflation.

[1427] The following adjustments are made on the disposal of assets in relation to which depreciation deductions have been allowed for tax purposes:

(a) Where cost less depreciation is greater than disposal value, the difference is allowed as a tax deduction.

(b) Where cost less depreciation is less than the disposal value, the recovery of tax depreciation is called a "balancing charge" which is added to assessable income or which the taxpayer has the option to set off against the cost or value of a replacement asset or other assets which are subject to tax-allowable depreciation. The latter option will result in a deferment of tax rather than a tax saving

[1428] The general provisions regarding the taxation of capital gains in Australia reflect the importance of cost (investment) and realization as bases for determining taxable capital gains as well as measuring taxable income in general. Very importantly, the provision for the indexation of cost in the measurement of taxable capital gains is a recognition, limited as it may be, of the need to measure tax-deductibe costs and taxable gains in real rather than nominal terms.

Taxation and the Analysis and Interpretation of Financial Statements

[1429] The analyst and interpreter of financial statements should be concerned with the impact of taxation on reported profit and its implications for profit projections. The analyst and interpreter should also be concerned with the relative size and nature of the provision for deferred taxation and its effect on reported balance sheet relationships.

[1430] Where timing differences have been accounted for by way of tax allocation, the reported result would be the same as if there had been no such differences between accounting and taxable income. Regarding timing differences, the concern will be with those which have not been allocated, the impact of this on reported profit, and its bearing on projections of profit and future tax liability. Such concern was illustrated in Example 14.1.

[1431] Under generally accepted accounting practice, permanent differences will be reflected in the period in which they occur. The concern again would be with the impact on reported profit and profit projections. A case in point are the export tax incentives which were available to New Zealand companies until the end of 1987. A study of the impact of these incentives on tax-paid profit was important because of their size in the case of some companies, the manner in which they were sometimes reported, and the growing public criticism of some companies for paying little or no tax as a result of these and other tax incentives and concessions.

[1432] We will illustrate this state of affairs in Example 14.6.

Example 14.6

The 1983 financial statements of a New Zealand company disclosed the following information about its treatment of taxation in relation to its reported profit for the year: "The tax charged in the Consolidated Statement of Profit is the estimated liability in respect of profit for the year excluding export incentives which are included in Other Income."

"The value of tax credits for incentive allowances amounting to $12,028,000 to encourage increased performance in the export field is classified as Other Income."

The financial statements disclosed the following amounts for profit before and after tax:

	($000)
Net profit before tax	34,541
Tax (credit)	(+8,047)
Net profit after tax	42,588

If the tax incentives had been reported as an offset against tax payable, net profit before tax would have been $12,028,000 less and the tax credit added to profit would have been higher by the same amount:

	($000)
Net profit before tax	22,513
Tax (credit)	(+20,075)
Net profit after tax	42,588

[1433] Regarding the above example, one could argue that since the objective of export tax incentives was to encourage sales by making such sales more profitable, the tax effect of the incentives could properly be added to income. On the other hand one could conjecture that adding the tax effect of export (and other) incentives to income and so reducing the reported amount of tax credits added to profit before tax (or increasing the reported tax payable) was motivated in part at least by actual or potential criticism of companies for paying little or no tax or, as in the case in this example, having a negative liability for tax.

Be that as it may, from the viewpoint of analysis and interpretation, the relevant considerations are the size of the tax and after-tax incentives and concessions, the dependence of export sales on these, and the effect of possible changes in government policies regarding such incentives and concessions. In fact, a general election in 1984 brought about change of government in New Zealand. The economic policies of the new government included the removal of tax concessions and subsidies from the economy. As a result, export tax incentives were phased out and completely removed by the end of 1987.

Balance Sheet Relationships

[1434] The provision for deferred tax is not a legal liability, but is regarded as an accounting liability by those who follow tax allocation procedures. Provided that the firm's level of new investment in qualifying depreciating assets, and of business done in the relevant areas (for example, hire purchase), continues at least up to past limits, and the relevant tax concessions and rates cointinue also, then the provisions for deferred tax "liability" will not require reduction. Each year, there will be new credits to offset the debit transfers to provision for tax payable. If the enterprise became insolvent, then there would almost certainly be losses from operations more than sufficient to preclude any payment of deferred tax on realization of the relevant assets. For these reasons, it can be argued with some force that provision for deferred tax is not a liability that is relevant to the calculation of a meaningful equity/debt ratio. If it is included as debt, then this introduces a quality factor into the ratio which may be significant if the proportion of the provision to total debt is significant.

Review questions

14.1 Why the need to account for income tax otherwise than by recognizing as an expense the income tax on the assessable income of the accounting period?

14.2 In the interpretation of financial statements consider the implications of the following tax-related items:

(a) past losses set off against the income of the current period;

(b) trading losses of the current period;

(c) investment allowances and "special" depreciation claimed for tax purposes but not charged in the accounts of the firm;

(d) substantial tax savings because of tax incentives in relation to export sales.

14.3 Should the amount of the write up of a depreciating asset be credited in full to a reserve account, and be available in full for backing a bonus issue?

14.4 Assuming that income tax is levied on company income (excluding dividends) at 50%, list and discuss briefly the possible factors which might explain the departures from this norm, and your views regarding disclosure:

		$
(a)	In the case of A Ltd, which showed:	
	Net Profit before providing for Tax	200,000
	Provision for Income Tax	10,000
	Net Profit after providing for Tax	190,000
(b)	In the case of B Ltd, which showed:	
	Net Profit before providing for Tax	3,000,000
	Provision for Income Tax	1,600,000
	Net Profit after providing for Tax	1,400,000

14.5 The following figures have been extracted from the 19A2 financial statements of ABC Ltd:

	($000)
Profit before Taxation	4,880
Taxation	1,050
Profit after Taxation	3,830

The following additional information is provided:

(i) Profit before taxation includes non-assessable income of $900,000.

(ii) Investment allowances of $720,000 were claimed during the year.

(iii) Dividends paid on specified preference shares amounted to $240,000.

(iv) Deferred taxation was provided in regards to timing differences due to differences in depreciation and inventory valuation methods. Depreciation in the financial statements was calculated on a straight-line basis and amounted to $2,850,000, while for taxation purposes the maximum allowable of $3,630,000 was claimed. Inventory write-downs of $340,000 were made in the financial statements; these write-downs were not allowed for taxation purposes.

(v) No deferred taxation was provided for additional timing differences of $480,000 which were expected to continue indefinitely into the future. The effect of these timing differences was to reduce taxable income.

(vi) The figure for profit before tax included tourist promotion expendi-

244

tures of $560,000. Tourist promotin expenditures are claimed at a rate of 150% for taxation purposes.

(vii) Discussion with the Inland Revenue Department revealed that there was an underprovision for taxation of $33,000 in the previous year.

Required:

(a) Prepare a reconciliation between the normal taxation at 45% on the company's reported profit before taxation of $4,880,000 and the income tax expense of $1,050,000.

(b) Show the journal entry necessary to record the deferred tax liability and provision for tax payable arising in 19A2.

14.6   Shown below is the tax reconciliation included in the notes to the 1987 financial statements of Fletcher Challenge Limited:

	Fletcher Challenge Group	
	1987	1986
	$000	$000
Taxation		
Adjustments were made to accounting income to recognise non-taxable income, Government incentives and other permanent adjustments required under local taxation legislation.		
Total operating and investment earnings	508,488	258,837
Non-deductible expenses		
fringe benefit tax, legal expenses and depreciation	2,208	9,470
	510,696	268,307
Non-assessable Income		
dividends and investment gains	62,358	8,060
gains on disposal of fixed assets	23,435	42,552
equity in retained earnings of associate companies	24,790	938–
export incentives included in net income	12,436	19,544
investment allowances and other incentives	2,862	180
income of foreign subsidiaries recovering tax benefits	101,329	104,283
capitalised interest and other costs	1,623	
other items	15,869	12,884
Taxable earnings	265,994	81,742
Taxation at 48c per dollar	127,677	36,784
Adjustment for foreign rates other than 48c	5,274–	2,036–
Taxation at rate of country of residence	122,403	34,748
Adjustment in respect of deferred taxation liabilities accrued in previous years	21,502–	19,343–
Taxation expense	100,901	15,405

Required:

Explain the nature of the items shown in the tax reconciliation.

14.7 "The fact that income taxation is often modified in an attempt to bring about certain social or economic effects perhaps makes it hopeless that tax and accounting income will ever be identical."

"In any event, it seems clear that insofar as we wish simply to tax income, the same need for soundness of concept and objectivity of measurement exists both for taxation and accounting."

Discuss the above statements in relation to differences and similarities which exist between accounting and taxable income.

Chapter 15
Financial Reporting by Segments

[1501] The diversification of business enterprises across industry, geographical and national boundaries is typical of the business environment today. It adds to the complexity of accounting for the results and state of affairs of business enterprises and the analysis and interpretation of their financial statements.

For example, according to the annual report of Fletcher Challenge Limited for the 1986–87 year, tax-paid earnings increased from $240.7 million in 1985–86 to $355.1 million in 1986–87, an increase of 47.5%. That would be good news for shareholders but it leaves them with a lot of questions requiring answers. What caused the big rise in profit? What are the profit prospects for 1987–88 and subsequent years? The company derives its income from subsidiary companies operating in the forest industry, in the building industry and in primary industries such as fishing and meat processing. These include major companies operating in North America in forestry-related enterprises. To really understand why profit has increased, and to make a fair projection of what the future holds, one needs a great deal of information about the results and prospects of the various operations that make up the total enterprise.

[1502] In a company group like Fletcher Challenge, timber may be produced, milled, manufactured into diverse products, used in building operations, all by different companies dependent on one another for supplies. Some company accounts will be in different currencies. And there are other accounting problems too. It all adds to the problems of those engaged in the analysis and interpretation of the results and state of affairs of company groups and in seeking to make projections regarding the future of the total enterprise.

[1503] In order to report more adequately, company groups like Fletcher Challenge Limited may produce data and other information about the operation of significant segments of their total enterprises. This may include information about such matters as:
• the relative profitability of the various segments, in terms of rates of return on net assets;
• the relative growth prospects of the different sections of the total enterprise;
• the expected financing requirements in the near future for each segment;
• the relative risks related to the various segments;
• matters affecting top level management and administration where this is expected to have material effects on the results of particular enterprises.

[1504] The preparation of reports by segments is not without its special problems. In particular:
• segment boundaries have to be defined;
• the revenue, expenses, and net earnings of each segment have to be determined;

247

• the net investment of group resources in each segment has to be measured, in order to provide fair measures of the relative rates of return of all the segments of the total enterprise.

[1505] In some countries, guidance has been given and standards on segment reporting by company groups have been established by or for the accounting profession.

In Australia, Approved Accounting Standard ASRB 1005: "Financial Reporting by Segments" requires the disclosure of information about material industry and geographical segments in which a company or company group operates. The stated objective of the standard is to provide users entitled to rely on published accounts with information necessary for an understanding of the risks and conditions which have affected or may affect the operations and financial position of such companies or company groups.

[1506] Those involved in the interpretation of the data provided regarding significant segments of company group operations need to be aware of the problems involved in seeking to develop this information. How these problems are dealt with may affect the fairness of the information provided. Some of these problems are discussed below.

Definition of Segment Boundaries

[1507] Segments may be defined in terms of industry (products and services), markets (domestic and export) and geographic location (domestic and overseas). In some countries, sales to governments are very important (eg US defence contracts).

The segmentation of financial reports may also be designed to reflect the performance of individual companies within a group, since the performance of profitable and unprofitable subsidiaries may be obscured in the aggregate figure reported in consolidated financial statements.

A general guide on starting point in the process of segmentation may be provided by profit centres within a company or company group defined by management for the purpose of planning and control. Such profit centres may reflect industry, product, market or geographical divisions.

(a) Segmentation by industry

[1508] When company operations are diversified across industry lines, it would be necessary to disaggregate overall results into significant industry segments in order to evaluate performance by industry in terms of profitability and profit prospects and associated risk.

In some cases industry boundaries would be relatively easy to discern. In other cases considerable difficulties may exist. For example, the operation of some New Zealand breweries involve the brewing of beer, the ownership of hotels and taverns, and participation in the production of wine. In such cases the definition of industry boundaries would be relatively easy as would be the determination of segment assets. Intersegment transfer pricing, such as relating to beer supplied to own hotels and taverns, also should not create serious problems as prices for beer supplied to "outsiders" would be readily available. On the other hand, as we shall see later, the allocation of debt and the cost of debt finance may create considerable problems.

[1509] In many cases, segmentation along industry/product lines will create considerable difficulties as, for example, where operations involve the common use of production facilities, or common raw materials, or partly completed production from other segments of company or group operations. Difficult decisions have to be made as to how far it is useful to carry the process of segmentation. Segmentation along broad industry/product lines may result in segments which are themselves conglomerates, while segmentation in "excessive" detail will add to the difficulties associated with determining segment revenue and expenses and rates of return and would reduce the decision usefulness of the segmented figures. Some of these and other problems associated with segment reporting discussed below will be illustrated by means of two case studies at the end of this chapter.

(b) Segmentation by markets

[1510] Where domestic production is sold on both domestic and overseas markets, segmentation of sales into domestic and export would be necessary in order to assess the relative importance of export sales to the overall performance of the enterprise. Geographical segmentation of export sales would also be useful for assessing export performance, trends and prospects.

[1511] In evaluating export performance important matters to consider include:
• the volatility of export markets in term of prices and competition;
• exchange rates fluctuation and the impact of these on export sales;
• protectionist policies in export markets and the prospects and effects of possible changes in such policies;
• the level of export subsidies and export tax incentives and likely effect of any changes in these;
• domestic inflation compared to the inflation of the countries which are the target of export sales.

[1512] The foregoing discussion can be related to the experiences during the late 1970s and early and mid 1980s of some New Zealand companies with significant export sales, experiences which would be similar to those of exporting companies in other countries operating under similar circumstances.

By 1984 the New Zealand government had built up a system of encouraging the growth of exports in the form of substantial tax incentives related to export sales and export markets development. The extent of these subsidies to exports in some cases can be gauged from the following figures extracted from the annual accounts of a New Zealand company during this period:

	19A3 ($ millions)	19A2 ($ millions)
Total net profit before tax	85.40	43.80
Export tax incentives included	16.00	12.00
Tax incentives as % of net profit before tax	23%	38%

[1513] In 1984 there was a change in government in New Zealand following a snap election. By this time there was general recognition that subsidy support in the New Zealand economy in general and in exporting industries in particular was excessive and that it should be reduced or removed. There was also a widely held view that in terms of foreign exchange rates the New Zealand dollar was overvalued and that a major devaluation should be brought about to bring the dollar down to a more realistic level and so improve the international trading position of New Zealand exporting companies. The same year the new Labour government devalued the dollar by 20% and stated its intention to phase out export subsidies by the end of 1987. Restrictions on overseas exchange dealings were removed and subsequently the New Zealand dollar was floated.

As an immediate result of the substantial devaluation, the earnings of New Zealand exporting companies improved. However, in a relatively short time, high interest rates in New Zealand brought up the value of the New Zealand dollar to a higher level than existed immediately prior to devaluation while inflation much higher than that of New Zealand's major trading partners further eroded the competitive position of New Zealand exporters. These developments adversely affected the exports of New Zealand companies and as a result some companies pulled out of export markets.

[1514] The above example taken from a period of rapid change illustrates both the importance of separating export and domestic sales and the need to have regard for environmental factors affecting specific markets before forming opinions about past performance and projecting future results.

[1515] The above discussion has been concerned with segmentation of markets into domestic and export. A segmentation of the domestic market of companies could also provide useful information by indicating trends and changes in marketing methods and patterns and may assist in projections and assesement of prospects.

(c) Geographical segmentation

[1516] A major development in recent years has been the expansion of business operations across national or geographic boundaries. We are concerned here not so much with the export of domestic production and with facilities such as offices, agencies or storage facilities established in other countries to facilitate such exports. The concern is with companies operating manufacturing and trading enterprises in other countries usually with separate financial structures and corporate identity.

[1517] Where domestic and foreign operations involve the same industry, it may be appealing to segment reports on operations along industry lines across national or geographical boundaries. Foreign operations, however, take place in different economic and political environments and segmentation along geographical rather than industry lines would be necessary to provide more useful information about results, risks and prospects. For example, some New Zealand companies involved in forestry have expanded their forestry operations overseas to countries such as Canada and Chile. A geographical segmentation of the reports on forestry operations of such companies would be necessary because of differences in efficiency/profitability of operations, associated prospects for growth and risks related to economic and political stability.

Segment Reporting and the Allocation Problem

[1518] The evaluation of performance by segments would require the determination of segment revenue and expenses for the purpose of determining profit and of investment in segment operations for the purpose of calculating segment rates of return.

[1519] All the allocation problems associated with the measurement of profit by the process of matching revenue and expense apply to the determination of segment results. These problems are further aggravated by the need to consider the matters of intersegment sales and transfers and the allocation of expense items such as general administration and service costs, the cost of integrated marketing activities, financial costs and taxation. Further complications arise from the need to determine investment in segments, for example, the value of assets used in segment operations, especially where these are shared, and the extent to which such assets may be considered to be financed by way of shareholders' equity and debt. These problems will be discussed further below.

(a) The determination of segment revenue

[1520] When the end product of a segment is sold outside the company or company group, it is likely that few, if any, problems will be created in addition to those generally associated with the recognition of revenue. Problems arise, however, where operations involve intersegment transfers and sales, in particular in relation to transfer pricing as this would affect the reported results of both the segment making the transfers and the segment receiving these.

　ASRB 1005 includes in its definition of "segment revenue" sales to customers outside the company or company group and intersegment sales and transfers of products and services, other than charges for the cost of shared facilities or other jointly incurred costs. Paragraph .26 of the standard states that in the preparation of segment information, intersegment transactions which have been eliminated in the preparation of the company or group accounts should be reinstated if material. It is important, therefore, that where significant intersegment sales and transfers take place, the transfer pricing policies followed in the preparation of segment reports should be disclosed.

(b) The determination of segment expenses

[1521] The allocation to segments of expenses other than those directly associated with the operation of the segments would require the exercise of judgment and would, therefore, be to varying degrees arbitrary in nature which would in turn reduce the interpretative value of the resulting figures for segment profit and rate of return.

　ASRB 1005 (para .06) defines "segment expense" as an operating expense which is directly attributable to a segment, or the relevant portion of an operating expense which can be allocated on a reasonable basis to a segment for the benefit of which the expense was incurred.

[1522] A way around the problem of allocating joint expense would be to base segment reports on contributions to total profit. For example, the commentary to

ASRB 1005 states that where allocation of an item of expense (or revenue) cannot be made to segments on a reasonable basis, no allocation is to be made and the allocated amount is to be adjusted against the total result of all segments in determining group operating profit. Problem items of expense include general corporate expenses, the cost of integrated marketing activities, taxation applicable to operating profit, and financial costs except to the extent that segments have responsibility for financing their operations.

(c) The determination of investment in segments

[1523] In the evaluation of segment performance it is necessary to determine corporate investment in individual segments for the purpose of calculating rates of return. The problem involves the identification and valuation of the assets used in segment operations and related debt finance for the purpose of determining net investment.

The general problems of asset valuation apply equally to the valuation of segment assets. A major problem of asset allocation to segments arises where assets are used jointly in the operations of more than one segments. The commentary to ASRB 1005 states that in identifying assets with segments, the procedures used should parallel those employed in allocating common operating expenses to segments and that general corporate assets not used in the operations of any particular segments should not be allocated. The problem with using the allocation of common operating expenses as a basis for allocating commonly used assets to segments is that the allocation would reflect the degree of arbitrariness embodied in the allocation of common expense.

[1524] The allocation of debt finance to segments for the purpose of determining net investment also creates difficult problems. For example, financing policies regarding the use of debt finance would normally be formulated from the viewpoint of the company or company group as a whole and its allocation (and the allocation of related expense) to segments could be arbitrary. To circumvent the problem, performance of segments could be evaluated on the basis of return on the total assets employed by segments with financing expense and total debt being related to the total operating results and overall state of affairs of the company or company group.

Segment Reporting and Materiality

[1525] It would be fairly evident that materiality would play an important role in considering the degree of segmentation to be applied to the financial reports of companies or company groups. The general notion of materiality used in accounting may also be applied to the segmentation of company reports. This is the notion embodied in ASRB 1005 that information related to industry or geographical segments is material if its omission, non-disclosure or mis-statement is likely to affect economic decisions or other evaluations made by users entitled to rely on company or group accounts. The commentary to ASRB 1005 provides some general guidelines for dealing with the question of materiality in relation to segments reporting in terms of relative size of segment revenue, profits/losses and assets employed.

Segment Reports, Accounting Principles, Disclosure and Comparability

[1526] As the segmentation of company reports involves the breaking down of aggregated reported figures for results and assets into segments, the accounting principles used in the preparation of the overall financial statements should also be used in arriving at the segmented figures. Where segmented figures include intersegment sales and transfers which have been eliminated in the preparation of the principal published company reports, the accounting policies used in determining segment revenues and costs resulting from such intersegment sales and transfers should be disclosed.

[1527] The general accounting problems associated with attaining intercompany comparability in published reports apply also to attaining intercompany comparability in reported segment performance. For fair comparisons there has to be intercompany comparability in the definition of segments, in the allocation of costs and investment to segments and in the determination of segment revenue. This may not be the case.

[1528] It should be apparent that from the viewpoint of accounting standards, the attainment of intercompany comparability in segment reports would require detailed prescription of rules regarding the definition of industry and geographical segments, the allocation of costs and investment and the measurement of segment revenue. No such prescriptions exist at present. The difficulties associated with making such prescriptions and their likely restrictive nature with individual and complex business operations cast doubt on their practicality or even desirability. It follows that, in considering the relative performance of segments of different enterprises, due recognition should be given to the definition of segments and the accounting policies followed by each enterprise. There may be differences which are sufficient to invalidate the comparison.

[1529] In general, disclosures regarding segment operations should include:
• description of industry and geographical segments including the location of geographical segments, and of the products and services from which sale revenue has been derived;
• segment revenue from sales to outside customers and from intersegment sales and transfers, including the basis for pricing intersegment sales and transfers;
• changes in the definition of segment boundaries and in accounting policies if the effect of such changes on reported segment performance is material, together with appropriate adjustments to comparative figures for previous periods.

[1530] As segment reporting requires the disaggregation of overall results, it should be possible from the disclosed data, to reconcile the reported figures of segment performance with the reported figures of overall performance. Paragraph .25 of ASRB 1005 requires the inclusion in published company reports of a reconciliation of aggregated segment information with related information in the published reports.

Summary:

[1531] It will be clear from the above discussion that the analyst and interpreter of financial statements has to be aware of the problems involved in the segmented reporting of a diversified enterprise. It is necessary to have regard to the statement of accounting policies, including in particular those applied in the evaluation of the results by segments and any changes in those policies. Careful study should be made of the information about individual segments provided by the directors and management as part of the total report, in order to obtain an appreciation of the factors responsible for the results of each segment and of management perception of the future prospects for each segment in terms of turnover, costs, profits, risk and growth. The overall analysis, interpretation, and projection then becomes the sum of the insights obtained from the study of the individual segments of the enterprise.

Two Cases of Segment Reporting

[1532] This section discusses two examples of segment reporting taken from the published reports of Fletcher Challenge Limited and Wattie Industries Limited. At the time of the reports there was no accounting standard in New Zealand dealing with segment reporting. The examples are interesting in that they are voluntary disclosures of information on segment operations and illustrate attempts to deal with a difficult problem in the absence of formal accounting guidelines or constraints.

Case 1

Segment Reporting: Fletcher Challenge Limited

[1533] Fletcher Challenge Limited is the largest New Zealand Company Group operating both in New Zealand and overseas. Its operations are highly diversified. The 1987 published report of the group included an "operating summary by sector" which is reproduced below as Figure 15.1.

The operating summary by sector breaks down the operations of the group into eight segments which are grouped under four broad headings:
  (1) *forestry industry*, which includes North America and Tasman Pulp and Paper as separate geographical segments, and forestry and wood products;
  (2) *building industry* which includes three segments: construction and property; building materials; and steel;
  (3) *primary industry and trading*; and
  (4) *corporate and investment*.

Figure 15.1
Operating Summary by Sector

Fletcher Challenge operates in three main lines of business and the operating summary groups the seven sectors with the addition of the corporate and investment sector.

Forestry Industry	Key figures	1986/87	1985/86
North America	Turnover	$1912.7 m	$1246.8 m
	Tax-paid earnings	$147.0 m	$50.1 m
	Shareholders' funds	$694.1 m	$321.0 m
	Return on s/funds	21.2%	15.6%
Tasman Pulp and Paper	Turnover	$287.3 m	$296.1 m
	Tax-paid earnings	–$12.4. m	–$15.2 m
	Shareholders' funds	$148.0 m	$141.9 m
	Return on s/funds	–8.4%	–10.7 m
	Exports	$176.2 m	$192.1 m
Forestry and Wood Products	Turnover	$289.9 m	$262.8 m
	Tax-paid earnings	$58.0 m	$61.8 m
	Shareholders' funds	$162.4 m	$161.6 m
	Return on s/funds	35.7%	38.3 m
	Exports	$49.5 m	$40.7 m
Building Industry			
Construction and Property	Turnover	$568.9 m	$387.6 m
	Tax-paid earnings	$51.8 m	$58.6 m
	Shareholders' funds	$103.9 m	$118.8 m
	Return on s/funds	49.9%	49.3 m
	Exports	$3.6 m	$4.8 m
Building materials	Turnover	$615.1 m	$515.4 m
	Tax-paid earnings	$19.1. m	$22.2 m
	Shareholders' funds	$82.5 m	$67.1 m
	Return on s/funds	23.2%	33.1 m
	Exports	$0.3 m	$4.0m
Steel	Turnover	$433.7 m	$282.6 m
	Tax-paid earnings	$15.6 m	$14.3 m
	Shareholders' funds	$79.7 m	$78.3 m
	Return on s/funds	19.6%	18.3%
	Exports	$22.1 m	$7.0 m
Primary Industries and Trading			
Fishing	Turnover	$4242.8 m[1]	$2644.0 m[1]
Rural servicing	Tax-paid earnings	$39.7 m	$17.1 m
Meat	Shareholders' funds	$279.1 m	$166.6 m
Consumer products	Return on s/funds	14.2%	10.3%
	Exports	$408.9 m	$202.8 m
Corporate and Investment			
	Turnover	$19.5 m	$21.6 m
	Tax-paid earnings	$36.3 m	$31.8 m[2]
Total Group			
	Turnover (trading sales)	$5822.4 m	$4268.1 m

Continued p 256

Turnover (total)	$8369.9 m	$5656.9 m
Tax-paid earnings	$355.1 m	$240.7 m
Exports	$660.6 m	$451.4 m

(1) *Includes commission sales of wool, livestock and real estate $2548 m (last year $1389).*

(2) *Includes $4.5 m for financial services.*

[1534] The review of operation in the published report of the group reveals considerable diversification of activities within the reported segments:

Forestry industry

North America. Operations involve lumber, newsprint, market pulp, lightweight coated paper. Reference is made to Norsk Pacific Shipping which had increased its earnings by 18% in a generally depressed and competitive shipping market.

New Zealand operations. These involve forestry, saw milling and the timber processing industries producing in particular wood panels, and pulp and newsprint for export and the New Zealand market. For reporting purposes Tasman Pulp and Paper results are shown separately, the remainder being aggregated into the Forestry and Wood Products segment which includes also a joint venture Chilean operation, Tasman Forestal. The report elaborates on the performance of the Tasman Pulp and Paper segment. An eleven week total plant shutdown due to industrial dispute was the main factor behind the company losing $12.4 million. Without the disruption the company would have returned a profit of $10 million.

Building industry

Construction and property. Included in this segment are construction activities in New Zealand and overseas. The report refers to the acquisition of 80% interest in Hawaii's second largest construction company with operations extending across the North Pacific. Included in this segment is investment in properties including shopping centres. The reported $51.8 million tax paid profit of this segment includes $18 million of investment property revaluation.

Building materials. The operations of this segment involve the manufacture of some building materials such as ready-mixed concrete and concrete products and the merchandising of building materials and products. The report advises the formation of separate divisions to cater for specialised customer requirements — the building and allied trades, the home handyman, and the rural sector.

Primary industries and trading

This is a widely diversified segment the operations of which include:

Fishing. The report speaks of major structural changes as a result of the government introducing a totally new form of catch licensing, of charter arrangements with Japanese firms and the USSR and a joint venture with an Australian firm.

Rural servicing. The report speaks of positive but inadequate returns in this sector as a result of merger expenses and the downturn in farmer spending. Expectations of a substantial improvement in profitability is indicated as a result of restructuring of the farming industry and the company's operations.

Meat. The report refers to improved but still inadequate earnings in an industry which has excess capacity and during the year has experienced a 10% decline in New Zealand lamb kill; of some restructuring of operations; and of the company's strategy to take operations out of the commodity carcass business and into consumer food manufacturing and marketing using sheep meat as the prime input.

Consumer products. Operations include retailing, consumer credit, retailing of home appliances, motor vehicles sales and rentals.

Corporate and investment

This is a segment established in 1987. The establishment of the segment, according to the report, "is a reflection of both the group's financial capability and its information bases in both domestic and offshore operations". The report speaks of the group's intention to "take advantage of this financial strength and knowledge by investing in those operations which have sound long-term growth potential", etc.

As shown in Figure 15.1, the published segment report discloses for all segments except corporate and investment, the following figures:

Turnover
Tax-paid earnings
Shareholders' funds
Returns on shareholders' funds
Exports

For the corporate and investment segment the disclosed figures are:
Turnover
Tax-paid earnings

In addition to the segmented figures the following figures relating to the total operations of the group are included:

Turnover (trading sales)
Turnover (total)
Tax-paid earnings
Exports

[1535] Relating the aggregate of the segmented figures to the total reported figures of the group, the following reconciliations can be made:

(1) *Segment sales — total and export.* Allocated to segments are the total sales of the group of $8,399.9 million including commission sales of wool, livestock and real estate and total export sales of $660.6 million (see Figure 15.2 for a further breakdown of sales).

(2) *Tax-paid earnings.* The tax-paid earnings allocated to segments are the net earnings after allowing for minority interest and extraordinary items net of tax and investment earnings (which include equity in the retained earnings of associated companies).

(3) *Shareholders' funds.* The aggregate of the shareholders' funds allocated to segments (excluding "corporate and investment") is $1,549.7 million. This is $895.3 million short of the figure shown in the balance sheet at 30 June 1987 for shareholders' funds net of minority interests. No figure is shown in the table for the total of shareholders' funds invested in all the segments, nor for the investment in the "corporate and investment" segment of the total enterprise.

257

[1536] The purpose of the presentation by segments is to indicate the relative importance and profitability of the various segments. To do this fairly, it is necessary to base rate of return calculations on fair measures of net capital investment. During the 1986–87 year, shareholders' funds net of minority interests increased from $1,285.4 million to $2,445 million (=90%). The financial highlights statement in the report shows:

	1987	1986
Average shareholders' equity	$1,845.1 m	$1,145.5 m (up 61.1%)
Net earnings	$355.1 m	$240.7 m (up 47.5%)
Return on shareholders' funds	19.2%	20.8%

It seems clear that the aggregate of shareholders' funds shown in the segmented results reflects an averaging process in the individual segments. No explanation is provided for the difference between $1,845.1 million and $1,549.7 million ($295.4 million). Had it been regarded as fair to relate it to the "corporate and investment" segment profit of $36.3 million, presumably this would have been done, to produce a return of 12.3%.

[1537] Earlier in this chapter we considered some of the allocation problems which arise in the preparation of segment reports and the evaluation of segment performance. In this respect the following points may be made in relation to this example:

Net tax-paid profit. The determination of segment tax-paid profit would have required the allocation to segments of funding costs which for 1987 were reported at $238.8 million (193.8 million for 1986) and taxation of $100.9 million ($15.4 million in 1986). There is no indication in the published report of the company regarding how these allocations were made. The profit allocated to segments would also have been affected by the policies followed in the pricing of intercompany transfers. The extent of intercompany trading is evident from the breakdown of group turnover included in the Notes to the accounts and shown here as Figure 15.2.

Figure 15.2

Turnover	1986–87 $000	1985–86 $000
Trading sales		
Exports from New Zealand		
• to external customers	658,658	448,461
• to companies within the group	1,892	2,905
Sales by non-New Zealand companies	2,119,758	1,311,201
Other sales		
• to external customers	2,388,386	2,014,592
• to companies within the group	421,179	282,320
Commissions, rentals and fees	232,515	208,608
Total turnover	5,822,388	4,268,087

Turnover	1986–87 $000	1985–86 $000
Sales of wool, livestock and real estate on behalf of clients	2,547,515	1,388,788

[1538] Intercompany pricing is of material importance and the following extract from the 1987 statement of accounting policies is helpful:

> The earnings statement ... excludes unrealized earnings on material intercompany transactions. Earnings include earnings on self-constructed real assets or major plant and the earnings of any company on its sales of finished product that has been further processed by another group company.

[1539] *Shareholders' funds.* The allocation to segments of profit net of funding costs would presuppose the allocation to segments of debt finance which, when related to segment assets would give the amount of shareholders' funds invested in segments. The 1987 report does not refer to the manner in which shareholders' investment in segments has been arrived at. The discussion of group performance in the 1986 report contained the following statement (p 6):

> To allow the measurement of the performance of its individual business units, the company allocates each of them a notional equity funds base which would be considered appropriate in an independent company operating in the same business.

It is evident from the example that the preparation of segmented data is likely to require the establishment of commonsense policies and procedures and the application of some subjective judgments. It is clear also that segmentation adds greatly to the information value of the total financial reports of enterprises like this one.

Case 2
Segment Reporting: Wattie Industries Limited

[1540] Shown below as Figure 15.3 is a segment summary included in the 1985 financial report of Wattie Industries Limited. The segment summary is an interesting attempt to deal, among other things, with the complexities of allocation in reporting on segement results and performance.

Figure 15.3
Segment Summary

	Sales				Operating Earnings				Funds employed			
	1985 $000	%	1984 $000	%	1985 $000	%	1984 $000	%	1985 $000	%	1984 $000	%
Consumer foods	495,202	55.6	406,699	53.3	38,450	40.5	30,353	46.7	265,567	36.8	219,969	41.2
Cereal milling and poultry	289,707	32.5	250,769	32.9	13,981	14.8	12,001	18.4	87,418	12.1	86,162	16.2
Diversified activities	105,876	11.9	105,216	13.8	2,661	2.8	1,354	2.1	32,738	4.6	28,689	5.4
Investments					39,730	41.9	21,324	32.8	335,513	46.5	198,301	37.2
Total operations	890,785	100.0	762,684	100.0	94,822	100.0	65,032	100.0	721,236	100.0	533,121	100.0

			Borrowing costs			
Borrowing costs			(28,380)	(15,947)		
Corporate and inter-national			(4,504)	(2,696)	23,759	14,804
Share of associates' sales	(142,965)	(120,239)				
	747,820	642,445	61,938	46,389	744,995	547,925

Definitions
(1) Sales for operations include share of associated companies' sales except those of public companies. These associates' sales are then deducted to agree with the statutory accounts.
(2) Operating earnings are before borrowing and corporate costs and after tax.
(3) Borrowing costs are after tax.
(4) Funds employed are shareholders' funds plus interest-bearing debt.

[1541] The accompanying discussion on segment performance discloses figures summaries for all segments, except "investments", for:
Sales
Operating earnings
Return on sales
Funds employed
The figures provided for "investments" are:
Operating earnings
Funds employed
Return on funds employed

[1542] The percentages shown in the segment summary indicate the relative importance of the segments to total sales, earnings, and investment in assets. Further information was provided showing return on sales and return on funds employed:

Segment	Return on sales		Return on "Funds employed"	
	1985	1984	1985	1984
Consumer foods	7.8%	7.5%	14.5%	13.8%
Cereal milling and poultry	4.8%	4.8%	16.0%	13.9%
Diversified activities	2.5%	1.3%	8.1%	4.7%
Investments	—	—	11.9%	10.8%

[1543] It is clear that there have been four special problems in the segment analysis (discussed below):
(1) the treatment of borrowing costs;
(2) the treatment of interests in associated companies operating in the various segment areas;
(3) profits and losses and funds included under "corporate and international";
(4) the treatment of income tax.

Borrowing costs

Interest-bearing liabilities have been added to shareholders' funds to give totals of "funds employed" (=assets). Interest expense has been added back to earnings and tax assessed on the total, to give "operating earnings" for each segment. The borrowing costs, less tax, are then shown as a deduction from total segment earnings. The alternative (adopted in Case 1) of spreading total borrowing among segments, and the related interest cost, has not been followed.

Interests in associated companies

In view of the relative importance of interest in associated companies, it was considered useful to include the shares of sales, earnings, and funds, and, presumably of liabilities and borrowing costs, in the segmented results.

Profits and losses

It was considered wise not to allocate corporate costs to segments, but to show them as a deduction from total segment earnings. The assets under this category have been added to the total of segment "funds employed".

Income tax

Taxation has been allocated to each segment and to borrowing costs. Presumably the earnings of segments entitled to tax concessions would reflect this fact.

[1544] When total costs are not allocated to segments, care should be taken not to equate segment profitability with the overall profitability of the firm. In the case we are considering, the rate of return for 1985 given by the aggregate of the profit and funds employed allocated to segments is 13.1% ($\frac{\$ 94,822}{\$721,236} \times 100$) while the overall rate of return is 8.3% ($\frac{\$ 61,938}{\$744,995} \times 100$).

[1545] It will be noted also that the earnings of associated companies form a substantial part of the total earnings of the Wattie Group. This affects the "quality" of the reported total earnings as the retained earnings of associated companies are not really under the control of the group. The reported figures were:

	1985 $000	1984 $000
Dividends received from associated companies	16,353	5,956
Share in the retained earnings after tax of associated companies	30,501	21,812
Earnings from interests in associated companies	46,854	27,768
Total earnings after tax, including share of earnings of associated companies	61,938	46,389
Percentage of earnings from associated companies	75.6	59.9

Review questions

15.1 "The analysis of aggregated reported results of diversified companies or company groups provides limited scope for informed evaluation and projection of operating results."
Discuss.

15.2 Define and discuss some of the problems associated with accounting for and analysis of operating results of diversified companies or company groups by segments.

15.3 "In the analysis and interpretation of financial statements it should be kept in mind that a significant difference exists between an associated company and a subsidiary company."
Discuss.

15.4 The main activity of ABC Breweries is the production of a number of popular brands of beer. In addition, the company has a major investment in hotels and taverns and owns a subsidiary, Northern Winery Limited, involved in the production of wine for the domestic market. Recent successes of Northern Wines in international competitions have resulted in a number of large overseas orders and the company is currently exploring the possibility of developing overseas export markets for its wines.

Required:

Discuss the need for ABC Breweries Limited to prepare segmented reports on its operations and the nature and extent of the problems which may be encountered in the preparation of such segmented reports.

Chapter 16
Research and Development Expenditure; Exploration Costs; Leases

Research and Development Expenditure

[1601] Research may be defined, generally, as a systematic inquiry or investigation for the purpose of acquiring new knowledge.

Research activities may be divided into two classes — basic research and applied research:

- *basic research* is generally undertaken for the purpose of advancing knowledge without specific practical aims or applications;
- *applied research* is primarily directed at providing solutions to recognized practical problems.

[1602] Business firms may undertake research for a number of reasons:

- to develop new products and services or improve existing products and services;
- to develop new production methods and techniques or improve existing ones;
- to study existing or new markets for the firm's products or services;
- to study organizational and behavioural aspects of the firm's operations, in order to increase work satisfaction and the level of efficiency and effectiveness of the human contribution to the enterprise.

[1603] Development is the intermediate stage between research and the full application of decisions made on the basis of new information — it is the translation of research findings or other knowledge into the design of new products or services or plans for the application of improved production techniques of commercial production.

Development costs may range from costs incurred in the development and proving of new technology in production (say through a pilot plan) to the development of new markets with the aid of initial advertizing campaigns and product demonstrations.

[1604] Since research and development expenditure is undertaken essentially with the future in mind, it follows that, in accounting for such expenditure, we are faced with the problem of its proper matching with the revenue to which it is related.

The major principles underlying the matching process, as discussed in Chapter 11 are that the expenditure should be matched against the revenue of the periods in which the benefit from the expenditure is derived, and that only costs which confer benefits to future periods should be carried forwards for matching against the revenue of those future periods (see [1108]–[1115]).

[1605] Australian Accounting standards AAS 13 "Accounting for Research and Development Costs" requires that research and development costs should be deferred to future periods only to the extent that future benefits arising from the expenditure are expected, beyond any reasonable doubt, to equal or exceed the sum of
* the costs deferred this period;
* any previously deferred costs; and
* any future deferred costs.

A similar requirement is reflected in Approved Accounting Standard ASRB 1011 of the same title. Both standards favour the expensing as incurred of the costs associated with basic and applied research. They allow, however, that, in the case of applied research, there may be, on rare occasions, a discernible relationship between expenditure on research projects and probable future benefits. In such cases, there may be grounds for the deferral of the resarch expenditure if the prescribed criteria for deferral are met.

[1606] The New Zealand Standard SSAP 13, "Accounting for Research and Development Activities" requires research costs to be expensed in the period in which they are incurred. Development costs may be deferred to the extent that they, together with further development costs, related production costs, and selling and administrative costs directly incurred in marketing the product, can be reasonably expected to be recovered from related future revenues. Some additional criteria must be met, however, before such a deferral may be regarded as acceptable:
* the product or process must be clearly defined and the cost attributable to it separately identified;
* the technical feasibility of the product or process must have been demonstrated;
* the management of the enterprise must have indicated its intention to produce and market, or use, the product or process;
* there must be clear indication that a future market for the product or process exists or, if the product or process is to be used internally, its usefulness to the firm must have been demonstrated;
* adequate resources must exist or must reasonably be expected to be available to complete the project and to market the product or process.

[1607] Deferred research and development expenditure should be amortized over future accounting periods in order to match such expenditure with related benefits. Any unamortized amounts should be reviewed at the end of each period; if necesary, deferred expenditure brought forward should be partly or entirely written off against profit in order to ensure compliance with the criteria for deferral.

[1608] The New Zealand standard SSAP 13 requires the disclosure of the policies adopted for accounting for the cost of research and development activity and, where development costs have been deferred, the basis of amortization. In Australia, the Approved Standard ASRB 1011 requires the disclosure of the amount of research and development costs charged to the profit and loss account during the financial years, the amount of research and development costs incurred during the year and deferred, the gross amount of deferred research and development costs at balance date with accummulated amortization shown as a deduction, and the basis used for the amortization of deferred costs.

[1609] In the analysis and interpretation of financial statements, a study of research and development costs may be useful for making projections about the future performance of an enterprise. In this regard it would be necessary to consider the importance of research and development expenditure to the operations of the enterprise and the amount of such expenditure incurred in a particular period and over time; it would be necessary to make valid comparisons with the research and development expenditure undertaken by other firms. Consideration shoud be given to the amount of research and development costs deferred and the manner in which these are being amortized.

[1610] It should be readily apparent that judgment and managerial policy will play an important role in accounting for research and development costs. The assessment of future benefits associated with research and development expenditure is likely to be a highly subjective exercise in view of the uncertainty which surrounds future operations. Consider for example the problem of assessing the future benefits from the results, of technological research in a highly competitive and fast developing field, and the future benefits of market research and development in a competitive field where action by one firm is likely to provoke counteraction from competitors. In addition, the policy of management may be motivated by considerations other than the "proper" matching of expense with revenue, subjective as the exercise may be. A strong motivating factor may be the size of reportable profit before the charging of research and development expenditure and the impact of alternative treatments on the profit which is finally reported.

[1611] The anlayst and interpreter of financial statements should be concerned both with research and development costs carried forward and the possibility of manipulation of reported profit on the one hand, and, on the other, with the effect on reported profit of possibly, over-conservative accounting standards, and play-safe attitudes which go beyond the constraints imposed by prudence. A further concern is with the establishing enterprise which may expense research and development costs in the establishment period and show poor results, but come later to profitable operations.

There is another matter which must also be considered — that of the adequacy in a competitive environment of the expenditure on research and development for the year and over time. In a real sense research and development outlays are an investment in the future whether deferred or not, and current "savings" in research and development may well indicate an erosion of the ability of an enterprise to maintain its competitive position in the future.

[1612] We will conclude this section on accounting for research and development costs and their relevance to the analysis and interpretation of financial statements with the following example which has some bearing on the matter under discussion.

The accounts of a large United Kingdom manufacturing enterprise had been showing apparently, increasing profits year by year, to the satisfaction of directors and shareholders. But when a critical study was made by a young and keen senior executive brought in from an overseas subsidiary of the parent company, it was found that the UK company's market share in its major products had fallen seriously during the previous 10 years from over 40% to 22%. Among the explanations of the maintenance of profit were the savings that had been made in advertizing expense and material reductions that had been affected in the costs of product research and development. Further, depreciation expense was kept well down by the continued use of outdated plant.

265

Accounting for Exploration Costs

[1613] What is usually regarded as a special case of accounting for research and development expenditure arises in relation to the operations of firms in extractive industries — firms engaged in the search for and commercial exploitation of oil, natural gas and minerals. The problem relates to accounting for the pre-production costs arising from:

- exploration activities — the search for commercially viable deposits of ore, natural gas or minerals;
- the evaluation of the commercial viability of reserves;
- development up to the commencement of commercial production.

[1614] As in the case with other research and development costs, the basic accounting principle involved is that costs should be matched fairly with associated revenue. There are no major difficulties of principle regarding the carrying forward of development costs as these would normally relate to the bringing into production of proven reserves. The major problem relates to the accounting treatment of unsuccessful exploration efforts. Accounting alternatives cover a very wide range of possible practices including:

(a) the writing off of exploration and evaluation costs as incurred;

(b) the writing off of costs but reinstating those costs associated with the discovery and evaluation of reserves which subsequently prove to be commercially viable;

(c) the carrying forward only of the costs associated with the discovery and evaluation of commercially viable reserves and the writing off as incurred of the cost of unsuccessful efforts;

(d) the allocation of total exploration and evaluation costs to commercially viable reserves;

(e) the allocation of costs to promising "areas of interest" and the carrying forward of such costs to the extent that reasonable probability of success exists.

[1615] The methods which advocate the writing off of all exploration and evaluation costs or the carrying forward of the costs associated only with successful efforts may be defended on the grounds of the need to exercise prudence in the face of the uncertainty and high level of risk associated with exploration. On the other hand, one may argue for the "full cost" method on the grounds that the nature of exploration is such that unsuccessful efforts will inevitably occur, that their cost is an unavoidable and integral part of the total cost of exploration and that as such it should be included in the costs carried forward.

[1616] The Australian Standard AAS7, "Accounting for the Extractive Industries" recommends the use of the "area of interest method" which it describes as an approach part way between the "full cost" and the "total write off" methods.

[1617] Exploration, evaluation and development costs which have been carried forward should be amortized during the production period by appropriate charges to revenue. AAS7 discusses two bases of amortization — "production output" and

266

"time" bases and recommends the use of the "production output" base unless special circumstances make the "time" base more appropriate. According to AAS7, the rate of amortization should not lag behind the depletion of economically recoverable reserves and should be treated as forming part of the cost of production.

[1618] AAS7 requires that provision should be made for restoration costs when an obligation or intention exists to restore an area of exploration or production. Restoration costs associated with exploration should be provided for and included in exploration costs, and restoration costs associated with production should be provided for during the production period and included in the cost of production.

[1619] According to AAS7, the high level of risk and uncertainty associated with extractive operations requires a high standard of disclosure. In particular, the standard requires the separate disclosure of the amount of exploration, evaluation and development costs written off during a period and the amount charged in the period for the amortization of such costs. The standard requires the separate disclosure of costs carried forward in respect of areas of interest which are still subject of exploration and evaluation, areas of interest where production has not yet commenced, and areas of interest where producton has commenced. Separate disclosure is also required of government royalties paid and payable on sales or production, and of government subsidies received or receivable brought into account in the period and the circumstances, if any, in which such subsidies may become repayable.

Leases

[1620] A lease is an agreement under which a lessor conveys to a lessee the right to use property for a stated period of time in return for a series of payment by the lessee to the lessor.

Leasing is an important means of financing business assets such as plant, equipment and property. In some cases it may be the only way of obtaining the use of some assets; in other cases leasing may provide the means to acquire the use of assets without major investment outlays. An arrangement to sell and lease back long-term assets already owned by a firm (such as property) may be used to obtain working capital for the day-to-day operations of the firm.

When lease arrangements are of a long-term nature, are non-cancellable, and involve significant amounts of rental payments, their current and potential impact on the operating results and state of affairs of the firm should be taken into account in the analysis and interpretation of financial statements.

Let us take an example:
A trading firm builds a retail store to its needs and sells it to an investment company with a 30-year non-cancellable leaseback and an option to purchase the store at the end of the lease. The objective of such an arrangement is to enable the trading company to acquire the store without having to obtain, and commit long term, the funds necessary to acquire the property outright. On the other hand, the sale–leaseback arrangement may provide the purchasing company with a desirable avenue for investment. From the viewpoint of the investment company, the calculation of the rental charges to be paid by the trading company will include elements of both interest and principal repayments.

[1621] The reporting problems associated with lease arrangements include the extent and manner of disclosure of the lease commitments entered into by a firm. The financial analyst's concern is with the effect of lease arrangements on the operating and financial relationships disclosed in the financial statments of the lessee firm.

[1622] Let us return to the sale and 30-year non-cancellable leaseback example referred to above. From the viewpoint of the lessee, the lease arrangements may be regarded as a purchase of equivalent property with a useful service life of 30 years, the acquistion to be paid for by a series of instalments equivalent to the lease rentals over the period of the lease. In this context, the purchase of the property will be financed entirely by debt and each lease rental payment will consist of an interest charge and repayment of principal.

From the viewpoint of financial reporting, if the property had been acquired by an outright purchase, the balance sheet would have incorporated the asset acquired and the liability incurred at equivalent amounts and in a subsequent analysis these would have been reflected in balance sheet relationships such as debt to equity. Similarly, the profit and loss statement would have shown the financial charges associated with servicing the debt and depreciation charges made to recover from revenue the value of the asset over the asset's estimated useful life. The profit and loss statement would have then been used to evaluate the financial leverage of the enterprise from an income statement point of view by examining, for example, the relationship between finance charges and the income before finance charges and tax.

[1623] Since the acquisition of a right to use an asset by way of a long-term non-cancellable lease is not in substance different from the purchase of the assets, it may be argued with considerable force that long-term non-cancellable leases should be accounted for in a manner similar to that used in the case of a purchase of the asset.

Finance leases and operating leases

[1624] Suggestions on accounting for lease commitments have ranged from disclosure by way of a note to the accounts of details regarding the nature, amount, and time period of the leasehold obligations undertaken, to the formal incorporation in the financial statements of the lessee company of the assessment of the rights to property use as an asset and of the related obligations under the lease as a liability.

[1625] Recommendations on standard accounting practice for accounting for leases require that a distinction be made between "operating" leases and "finance" leases.

[1626] An operating lease is one where the lessor effectively retains the risks and benefits associated with the ownership of the leased property.

[1627] A finance lease is one which effectively transfers the risks and benefits associated with the ownership of the property from the lessor to the lessee.

Finance leases are normally non-cancellable. Approved Accounting Standard ASRB 1008, "Accounting for Leases" defines a non-cancellable lease among other things as one which can be cancelled only with the permission of the lessor or on the occurrence of some remote contingency, or where the lessee is subject to penalties on cancellation of a magnitude which would discourage cancellation. In adition to being non-cancellable, the term of a finance lease should cover the larger part of the expected useful life of the property (for example 75% or more) or, alternatively, the present value of the minimum lease payments, discounted at the rate of interest implicit in the lease, should be equal to the bulk of the fair value of the property, for example, 90% or more.

[1628] Recommended standard practice of accounting for leases favours the capitalization of finance leases and the disclosure of rental expense associated with operating leases.

Accounting for finance leases

[1629] The capitalization of a finance lease involves the calculation of the present value of the minimum lease payments and the recording of the amount as an asset and a liability.

[1630] In the capitalization of a lease, the minimum lease payments are represented by the rental payments over the term of the lease (but excluding payments related to the operation and maintenance of the leased property such as insurance, property taxes and repairs) plus any guaranteed residual value of the property by the lessee to the lessor on the expiry of the lease. The discount rate used is the interest rate implicit in the lease — this is the rate of interest which, at the inception of the lease, will equate the minimum lease payments and any unguaranteed residual value to the fair value of the leased assets. The determination of the interest rate implicit in the lease would require an assessment of the fair value of the assets subject to a lease agreement.

[1631] At the outset of the lease, the asset and liability arising from the capitalization of the lease will be recorded in the books of the lessee at equal amounts. Thereafter, the asset will be depreciated at an appropriate rate (in accordance with existing standards regarding the depreciation of fixed assets) and the liability will be reduced by that part of the rentals of the period which represents a reduction of the principal of the lease liability.

[1632] An elementary method of accounting for a lease by way of capitalization is illustrated in Example 16.1.

Example 16.1
Capitalization of a lease

A company has acquired a 5 year property lease at $10,000 per annum (plus property taxes and insurance) payable at the beginning of each year. There is no right to purchase at the end of the lease. The company wants to account for the lease by the capitalization method and considers the appropriate rate of interest to be 10%.

Accounting for the lease by the capitalization method will involve the following:

(a) the calculation of the present value of the five net rental payments of $10,000 at 10% and the recording of the lease in the books of the lessee company as an asset and a liability at that value;

(b) the calculation of the present value of the obligations under the lease in terms of outstanding rental payments at the beginning of each of the five years;

(c) the amortization of the leasehold asset over the term of the lease.

The calculation of the present value of the obligations under the lease at the beginning of the lease period is as follows:

Start of year	Lease rental $	Discount factor at 10%	Present value $
1	10,000	1.0000	10,000
2	10,000	0.9091	9,091
3	10,000	0.8284	8,284
4	10,000	0.7513	7,513
5	10,000	0.6873	6,873
Total capital value of obligations under lease			41,761

The journal entry to record the lease will be:

Leasehold property	$41,761	
Liability under lease		$41,761

The present value of the obligations under the lease at the end of the first year (beginning of the second year) will be $34,888 (that is, $10,000 + $9091 + $8284 + $7513). The difference between the present value of the obligations under the lease at the beginning and end of the first year of $6873 represents the repayment of principal and will be used to apportion the first annual rental payment:

Principal	$6,873
Interest	3,127
	$10,000

The journal entries to account for the accrual and payment of the obligation under the lease at the end of the first year will be:

Interest expense	$3,127	
Liability under lease	6,873	
Rentals on leasehold property		$10,000
Rentals on leasehold property	10,000	
Bank		$10,000

A policy will have to be decided upon regarding the amortization of the lease. For example, if straight-line amortization is adopted, the annual charges will be $8352 (that is, $41,761 ÷ 5). The journal entry to record the amortization charge at the end of each year will be:

Amortization of leasehold property	$8,352	
Provision for amortization of leasehold property		$8,352

At the end of the first year, the profit and loss account will be debited with $8352 for amortization of the leasehold property (an expense) and $3127 for interest expense. The provision for amortization of the leasehold property will be deducted from the balance sheet (asset) value of the lease. The liability under the lease will be reduced by the amount of principal repayment ($6873).

The calculations and entries will be repeated at the end of each of the remaining years in the lease period. For example, the apportionment of the rental payment at the end of each of the five years will be as follows:

Year	Interest $	Principal $	Total $
1	3,127	6,873	10,000
2	2,487	7,513	10,000
3	1,716	8,284	10,000
4	909	9,091	10,000
5	—	10,000	10,000
	8,239	41,761	50,000

[1633] During the term of a lease, differences may emerge between the rental payable under the lease and a current market rental for the property. The capitalized difference between rentals payable under the lease and the expected market rental rates up to termination of the lease consititutes a lessee's interest in the property, where market rates are higher, and a decline in the value of the leasehold asset where they are lower. Under an historical cost accounting system, the former would not be recognized (unless and to the extent that it had been paid for by the present tenant), and the latter, if material, should lead to an additional writing down of the leasehold asset. Under a comprehensive current cost system, both gain and loss should be recognized, subject to an acceptable level of objectivity in the estimates of value.

It should be fairly evident that lease commitments have important short- and long-term effects on the operating results and state of affairs of business firms. For that reason, information about existing lease commitments should be fully taken into account in the analysis of financial statements and any projections which result from such analysis.

[1634] In the study of the financial gearing of an enterprise the analysis may be extended to cover all rental payments including those under operating leases. In a broad sense one may regard all rental payments as related to the acquisition of the services of assets as an alternative to purchase.

Review questions

16.1 "... judgment and managerial policy will play an important role in accounting for research and development costs ... the interperiod allocation of such costs is likely to be open to manipulation and abuse."
Discuss.

16.2 During the year just ended the Zenith Co Ltd (a progressive marketing organization) carried out a major expansion of its operations aimed at giving its operations a nationwide coverage.

The major costs of the expansion consisted of the following:

(a) extensive market research into existing and proposed new territories;

(b) a major nationwide advertizing campaign;

(c) a major staff recruitment and training program aimed to ensure a continued high standard of service;

(d) the expansion of existing premises and the acquisition of new premises.

Discuss the treatment of the above costs in the accounts of the company with a particular view to the profit to be reported for the year.

16.3 "The high level of risk and uncertainty associated with extractive operations requires a high standard of disclosure."
Discuss.

16.4 Compare the successful effort and full cost method of accounting for exploration costs. What arguments may be put forward in favour of and against each?

16.5 How do lease arrangements affect the operations and state of affairs of lessee firms?

16.6 Why the need to distinguish between the interest and principal components in the rentals of finance leases?

16.7 Discuss some of the problems associated with the capitalization of a company's obligation under long-term leases.

16.8 Should commitments under operating leases be taken into account in determining the financial gearing of an enterprise?

Chapter 17

Foreign Currencies Translation

[1701] In financial accounting and reporting, the need for foreign currencies translation arises when firms extend their operations across national boundaries. Such expansion of operations typically involves:

- the raising of debt finance overseas;
- making sales and purchases denominated in foreign currencies;
- establishing foreign based operations by way of branches, subsidiaries or associated companies, etc.

[1702] If a company's financial statements are to provide useful information to financial statement users, primarily shareholders and investors, the transactions incorporated in the reports should be expressed in a common unit of measurement, usually the "domestic" currency of the reporting business firm.

The need for currency translations is as old as accounting itself. In his historic treatise on double entry accounting Pacioli (1494) stated about making entries in the journal of a merchant:

> In the columns for the amounts, only one kind of money should appear, as it would not be proper to have appear in this column different kinds of money. [Chapter 12, translation by J B Geijsbeek, "Ancient Double-Entry Bookkeeping", Denver, 1914]

[1703] Foreign currency translation is an issue of growing importance in present day financial accounting and reporting because of the extent of international financing and trade involved in business operations, the volatility of exchange rates, the divergent views regarding how to deal with the problem of currency translation, and the variety of methods employed in the preparation of financial statements.

[1704] Accounting for foreign based operations involves all the problems associated with accounting for domestic operations plus some additional problems related to currency translation. The problem may be further complicated by differences in accounting and reporting practices in countries where foreign subsidiaries are located as well as differences in the social, economic and political environment. The principal objective of currency translation is to so incorporate amounts and accounts expressed in foreign currencies in the financial statements of an enterprise as to show a true and fair view of the overall profit or loss and the state of affairs of the total enterprise. Subsidiary objectives may be to disclose company policy regarding exposure to the risk of exchange fluctuations, the effects on income, debt and investment of fluctuations in the current year, and the nature and extent of exposure to exchange rate fluctuations as perceived at balanced date. The overall objective has to be the presentation to decision-makers of "a true and fair view" of managerial performance and enterprise position.

The following are cases where a need for currency translations arises:

(1) debt denominated in foreign currencies;

(2) sales and purchases denominated in foreign currencies;
(3) foreign based operations.

Foreign Currency Translation and Accounting Practice

[1705] Requirements of practice in Australia are reflected in ASRB 1012 "Foreign Currency Translation", October 87. The corresponding standard in New Zealand is SSAP 21, "Accounting for the Effects of Changes in Foreign Currency Exchange Rates", April 1988.

Opinions on how to account for exchange variations have concentrated on the effects such variations have on the reporting entity. In considering the problem, distinction has generally been made between "integrated foreign operations" and "self-sustaining foreign operations" (ASRB 1012, para .06).

Integrated foreign operations

[1706] These are defined as operations which are financially and operationally interdependent with those of the reporting entity and which directly or indirectly expose the reporting entity to exchange gains or losses. Examples of integrated operations are loans, sales and purchases, debtors and creditors denominated in foreign currencies entered into or made by the reporting entity. Operations through foreign branches or through subsidiaries intended to function as branch extensions of the operations of a parent company would fall under this heading also.

Self-sustaining foreign operations

[1707] These are operations which are financially and operationally independent of those of the reporting entity. In such cases the exposure of the reporting entity to exchange gains and losses is perceived to affect primarily the reporting entity's net investment in foreign operations.

Methods of Translation, Accounting Treatment and Interpretation

[1708] What may be deemed an "appropriate method of translation" would depend on the nature of the items being translated and the circumstances of the case. There are differences of views also regarding the accounting treatment and interpretation of any resulting exchange gains and losses.

Foreign Currency Loans

[1709] Recent years have seen an increase in the proportion of loan finance raised by business enterprises from foreign sources and expressed in foreign currencies. Such loans have to be accounted for by the borrowing company in its domestic currency, but interest and repayments have to be made in the foreign currency at the time when due.

[1710] The problems associated with accounting for foreign currency loans arise from movements in the exchange rate between the currency in which the loan was raised and is repayable, and the domestic currency of the borrowing company in which the loan is recorded and reported on. These matters are illustrated in Example 17.1.

Example 17.1

A loan of US$1 million is raised by a New Zealand company at the end of 19A0. Shown below are the exchange rates of the NZ$ to the US$ at the end of the years 19A0 to 19A3:

	NZ$ = US$
19A0	0.62
19A1	0.52
19A2	0.44
19A3	0.53

The translation procedure to be used at the end of each of the three years following the raising of the loan will be as follows:

(a) At the end of 19A0 the US amount of the loan will be converted into New Zealand currency at the exchange rate ruling at the time the loan was raised and will be recorded in the books of the borrowing company at its New Zealand dollar equivalent.

(b) At each subsequent balance date (eg the end of each year) the loan will be recalculated in terms of New Zealand dollars using the exchange rate in effect at balance date. The new amount of the loan will be compared with the New Zealand equivalent at the end of the previous year in order to determine the exchange gain or loss.

(c) If the exchange rate between the US dollar and NZ dollar has moved against the New Zealand dollar, an exchange loss will result. If the exchange rate has moved in favour of the New Zealand dollar, the recalculation will show an exchange gain.

[1711] The translation of the loan into New Zealand currency in order to effect the original recording of the transaction and subsequent exchange rate movements will be as follows:

End of year			Restated amount $NZ	Gain/loss + / –
19A0	$\dfrac{US\$1,000,000}{0.62}$	=	1,612,903	
19A1	$\dfrac{US\$1,000,000}{0.52}$	=	1,923,077	– 310,174
19A2	$\dfrac{US\$1,000,000}{0.44}$	=	2,272,727	– 349,650
19A3	$\dfrac{US\$1,000,000}{0.53}$	=	1,886,792	+ 385,935
Total (net) exchange difference for period (loss)				– 273,889

[1712] Having calculated the exchange differences at the end of 19A1, 19A2 and

19A3, the question now arises regarding how to account for them, ie record them in the books. A number of alternatives exist:

(a) Exchange differences may be recognized on "realization", that is, when the loan is repaid. The problem with this approach is the distortion of reported profit in the year of repayment if a loan is repaid at a significant exchange loss or gain.

(b) Exchange differences may be accrued as they occur and may be written off against the profit and loss account over the remaining term of the loan. The problem with this method is that the charges in the profit and loss account would not relate to exchange differences which have occurred during the period; further, there is the possibility that with a continuing adverse trend in exchange rates, an increasing amount of exchange losses will be accumulated to be written off against the reducing number of years remaining in the term of the loan.

(c) To write off as expense exchange losses as they occur but to recognize as income exchange gains only to the extent of unamortized losses. The justification for this inconsistent treatment is prudence — gain may not be "realized" and is held in a provision (or reserve) for exchange fluctuation until offset by losses or realized on payment. An argument against this method is that exchange gains can be calculated with the same objectivity as exchange losses and there should be no difference in the treatment of the two.

(d) Exchange differences may be regarded as arising from the ordinary activities of a firm and that all such differences should be accounted for in the profit and loss account with appropriate disclosure.

[1713] The weight of opinion appears to favour alternative (d), at least where exchange differences relating to monetary accounts are concerned (eg ASRB 1012, para .12).

In Example 17.1, the journal entries to record the loan and subsequent exchange differences, following alternative (d), will be as follows:

19A0	Bank	1,612,903	
	Loan a/c		1,612,903
	To record the loan		
19A1	Profit and loss a/c	310,174	
	Loan a/c		310,174
	To restate loan and record exchange loss		
19A2	Profit and loss a/c	349,650	
	Loan a/c		349,650
	To restate loan and record exchange loss		
19A3	Loan a/c	385,935	
	Profit and loss a/c		385,935
	To restate loan and record exchange gain		

Realized and Unrealized Exchange Differences

Realized exchange differences

[1714] A realized exchange difference is the difference between the amount of a loan at the time it was raised and the amount of the loan at the time it was repaired, both in the borrower's domestic currency.

Unrealized exchange differences

[1715] An unrealized exchange difference is the difference between the amount of the loan at the end of a period, converted to domestic currency at the end-of-year exchange rate, and the amount of the loan at the end of the period converted to domestic currency at the start-of-the-year exchange rate or at the date during the year when the loan was raised.

[1716] In Example 17.1, if we assume that the loan was repaid at the end of 19A3 the realized exchange difference of the loan (a loss) will be calculated as follows:

	NZ$
Amount of loan raised, 19A0	1,612,903
Less amount of loan repaid, 19A3	1,886,792
Realized Loss	273,889

The realized exchange loss on the loan is equal to the net amount of the unrealized exchange differences during the term of the loan.

[1717] Exchange gains/losses prior to realization have no direct monetary impact on the firm as far as the principal of the loan is concerned. The recognition of such gains and losses involves a journal entry only although reported financial relationships will be affected. The only direct monetary effect exchange rate variations have prior to repayment relates to interest payments — as these are denominated in the foreign currency, an adverse movement in the exchange rate will increase the amount of interest payable in the domestic currency. The reverse will be the case where favourable changes in the exchange rate occur. In the case of the principal of a loan, the tangible effect of exchange rate variations relates to the realized difference on repayment. In Example 17.1, assuming the loan was repaid at the end of 19A3, this would amount to NZ$273,889.

Exchange Differences and Taxation

[1718] In Chapter 14 we saw that in taxation the general rule is that gains become taxable and losses tax-deductible on realization. In a departure from this rule, in New Zealand, since July 1988, for tax purposes, gains and losses on foreign exchange transactions may be accounted for on an accrual basis — ie they may be brought into the calculation of taxable income prior to realization. In Australia such gains and losses are still subject to the realization rule.

[1719] Where, for reporting purposes, exchange losses are brought into account before realization, but are deferred until realization for tax purposes, they may be recorded and reported net of tax — ie reduced by the amount of the potential future tax saving on realization. Financial reporting standards normally impose restrictions on the recognition of future tax benefits associated with losses carried forward. For example, they may require virtual certainty of realization or may restrict the recognition to the amount of any credit balance in a deferred taxation account. For accounting for exchange losses net of tax and associated restrictions see Example 14.3 and [1417].

[1720] To be consistent with the accounting treatment of exchange losses, exchange gains should also be recorded and reported net of tax.

Foreign Sales and Purchases

[1721] A firm may make sales to foreign customers or purchases from foreign suppliers expressed in fixed amounts of foreign currencies. For the purpose of the initial recording of the transactions, the amounts will be translated into domestic currency at the exchange rate applicable at the time of the transactions. If the transactions are for cash, the translated amounts will equal the translated amount of the cash received/paid in settlement and no exchange differences would occur. The problem of exchange differences arises in the case of foreign sales and purchases made on credit when, between the time of sale or purchase and the time of settlement, changes occur in the exchange rate between the foreign and domestic currencies.

Foreign sales

[1722] We will assume that a New Zealand firm makes a credit sale to an Australian customer for A$20,000 with setlement in, say, 40 days. At the time of sale the exchange rate of the Australian dollar to the New Zealand dollar was A$0.85 for NZ$1 and at the time of settlement the rate had moved against the Australian dollar to A$0.95 for NZ$1.

The currency translations at the time of sale and settlement will be as follows:

At time of sale	$\dfrac{\text{Aust } \$20,000}{0.85} =$	NZ \$23,529.41
At time of settlement	$\dfrac{\text{Aust } \$20,000}{0.95} =$	NZ \$21,052.63

The resulting exchange difference
is a loss of   NZ $2,476.78

The above transactions may be recorded in the books of the New Zealand company as follows:

Customer	$23,529.41	
Sales		$23,529.41
to record the sale		
Bank	$21,052.63	

278

Exchange variation $ 2,476.78
a/c
Customer $23,529.41
    to record the settlement

In the above example, if the company's balance date falls between the times of sale and settlement, the outstanding amount will be translated at balance date to determine and record an unrealized exchange difference for the purpose of preparing the company's financial statements, and a further translation will be made at the time of settlement of the account.

Foreign purchases

[1723] In the above example we may assume that, instead of making a sale of A$20,000 to an Australian customer, the New Zealand company made a purchase of the same amount from an Australian supplier. In this case an exchange gain of NZ$2,476.78 will occur and the journal entries to record the transaction will generally be a reversal of those used to record the sale:

Purchases $23,529.41
Supplier $23,529.41
    to record the purchase

Supplier $23,529.41
Bank $21,052.63
Exchange variation a/c $ 2,476.78
    to record the settlement

As in the case of sales, if the company's balance date falls between the times of purchase and settlement, the outstanding amount will be translated at balance date to determine and record an unrealized exchange difference for the purpose of preparing the company's financial statements, and a further translation will be made at the time of settlement of the account.

Interpretation and Accounting Treatment of Exchange Gains and Losses

[1724] The predominant view is that exchange gains and losses on monetary items (money held and items to be received or paid in money) should be shown in the profit and loss account in the year which they occur (eg ASRB 1012, para .12).

A common practice is to show exchange gains and losses as part of the financing (funding) costs of the company. Discussed below is the rationale for such interpretation and accounting treatment.

[1725] Borrowing in foreign currencies has been increasing in importance as a means of financing the operations of business firms. It has advantages and carries potential risks. For example, a hard currency loan, say in Swiss francs, is likely to be made at a rate of interest which is very much lower than the domestic rate; on the other hand, such a loan is likely to involve a high risk of exchange loss on repayment.

[1726] If the results of the borrowing company, including the financing of its operations, are to be fairly presented, exchange gains and losses should be reflected in the financial statements of the company as they occur rather than on realization, as in the latter case there may be significant distortions of reported profit in the year of realization, the likelihood of which has not been reflected in preceding financial statements of the company.

[1727] In the case of foreign sales and purchases, the use of credit may be regarded as a means of financing the relevant transactions and that, therefore, any resulting exchange differences should be treated as part of the financing (funding) costs of the companies concerned.

[1728] In published financial statements, exchange gains and losses should be disclosed separately and adequately explained. Such differences should not be classified as extraordinary unless the items to which they relate are themselves extraordinary.

[1729] If the exchange difference in a particular year is a major one, it could be embarrassing to treat it as a financing expense of that year. For example, during the year ended 31 March 1976 Air New Zealand had a $27.8 million exchange loss on borrowing in United States dollars. Air New Zealand had borrowed the money in order to purchase new American aircraft and spares. The net profit of the company for the year was $5.6 million. The "unrealized loss" of $27.8 million was left in an exchange fluctuation reserve account which went heavily into debit. The directors must have been made rudely aware of the inadequacies of accounting for such transactions at the time. After all, the relationship in US dollar terms between the cost of the aircraft and the loans raised to finance the purchase would be more or less the same as at the time of purchase. There would have been little if any change in the capacity of the planes to produce revenue denominated in US dollars. In a real sense the loss was unreal. On the other hand, if forward exchange contracts had been entered into when the loans were raised, the loss would have been avoided. In the event, it was recognized that some of the company's properties were significantly undervalued. With the help of a $14 million "gain" on revaluation of properties, and the elimination of most of the accumulated reserves, it was possible to offset the $27.8 million exchange "loss" and still to end the year with some $3 million credit in overall reserves.

This example underlines the importance of protecting the enterprise from the adverse effects of exchange fluctuations by a process of "hedging".

Hedging Foreign Currencies Transactions

[1730] Companies engage in hedging in order to avoid or minimize possible adverse effects of exchange rates movements. Hedging may take a number of forms.

[1731] A company may obtain cover in the form of a forward exchange contract. This is a contract with a bank to exchange, for example, domestic currency with the currency of another country at a stated time in the future at an agreed rate called the "forward exchange rate". For example, a trader selling products to regular customers in a foreign market at prices denominated in the foreign currency may protect the profitability of this business from the risk of exchange fluctuations by entering into forward exchange contracts to sell the expected flow of receipts from foreign sales. Similarly, a manufacturer dependent of the supply of raw materials or components from another country may set his prices with some confidence if he enters into forward exchange contracts for the purchase of foreign currency at the dates he expects to pay for his supplies. In both cases, the risk involved in exchange fluctuations, and the relevant gain or loss, are transferred to the dealer in foreign exchange. This kind of transaction is entered into at a cost. Unless a material change is expected by the market in the particular currency, the rate for buying a currency forward can be expected to be higher than the current buying rate, and the rate for selling a currency forward can be expected to be lower than the current market rate. The difference reflects the market's perception of the risk, and of the margin necessary to cover the operating costs and profit requirements of foreign exchange operations. Major customers may obtain favourable rates by negotiation.

[1732] Another form of hedging against exchange losses on a loan may, in some cases, be perceived to be provided by assets for the acquistion of which the loan was originally raised. The example of Air New Zealand quoted earlier in the chapter is a case in point.

From a business viewpoint, Air New Zealand might have maintained that the US dollar loan obtained to acquire the new aircraft for use in its international operations was hedged by the aircraft, and their undiminished capacity to produce a flow of revenue denominated in US dollars. The current replacement costs of the aircraft would be increased significantly by the decline in value of the NZ dollar. If the international airline operation were conducted through a subsidiary company domiciled in the United States, then no loss would be recognized, and, in fact, the net assets would be consolidated in New Zealand at an exchange rate favourable to the US dollar, probably producing a gain from exchange fluctuations. But there is another viewpoint. In essence, Air New Zealand entered into two transactions — one based on the decision to acquire a certain type of aircraft, and the other based on a decision on a particular method of financing the purchase. Had the loan finance been raised in domestic currency, then the exchange loss would not have occurred. There are good grounds for arguing that any loss incurred as a result of the latter decision should be recognized and reported.

[1733] This discussion points the way to additional ways of hedging against the risks of loss or embarrassment through exchange fluctuations. If an enterprise operating in a foreign market is able to maintian some balance between cash assets and liabilities in the foriegn currency, then it is hedged against loss. Operation in a foreign market may involve less risk of embarrassment if it is carried on through a subsidiary, as the fixed assets held overseas may be converted into domestic currency in a consolidation at end of year exchange rates.

Accounting for the cost of hedging foreign currency transactions

[1734] The cost of hedging by way of forward exchange contracts can be calculated as the difference between the amount subject to the contract at the spot rate at the time the contract was entered into and the amount payble or receivable in the future under the contract.

[1735] The following is the recommened practice of accounting for the cost of hedged transactions:

(a) Apart from hedged transactions entered into in order to establish the price of particular goods and services, costs and gains arising at the time of entering into hedged transactions should be accounted for separately from the exchange differences on the hedged transactions and should be brought into the profit and loss account over the lives of the hedged transactions.

(b) Where hedged transactions relate to the establishment of the price of particular goods and services, the gains or losses on such transactions up to the date of purchase or sale, and any costs or gains arising at the time of entering into the hedged transactions are to be deferred and included in the amount of purchase or sale.

(c) Under New Zealand SSAP No 21 (para 4.19) where a short-term foreign currency transaction is hedged by a forward contract, the forward rate specified in the contract should be used as the basis for measuring and reporting the transaction.

Foreign Based Operations

[1736] In addition to entering directly in transactions denominated in foreign currencies such as foreign sales, purchases and loans, which have been discussed in the preceding pages, a firm may establish foreign bases of operations for example in the form of branches and subsidairies. The financial statements of such branches and subsidiaries will be prepared in the relevant foreign currencies and will need to be translated into the domestic currency in order to be incorporated into the financial statements of the parent company for reporting purposes.

[1737] The generally prevailing view is that, for the purpose of translation, foreign based operations should be broadly classified into:

(a) integratd foreign operations; and

(b) self-sustaining foreign operations.

Integrated foreign based operations

[1738] These are operations through branches and subsidiaries which are intended or perceived to function as extentions of the operations of the parent company. Such foreign based operations are regarded as exposing the parent company, directly or indirectly, to exchange gains and losses.

Self-sustaining foreign operations

[1739] These are operations which are financially and operationally independent of those of the parent company. In such cases, the exposure of the parent company to exchange gains and losses is perceived to affect primarily the parent company's net investment in foreign operations.

Methods for Translating the Results and State of Affairs of Foreign Based Operations

[1740] Present thinking and financial reporting standards tend to favour two broad methods for translating the financial statements of foreign based operations:

(a) the temporal method; and

(b) the current rate method.

The temporal method is generally recommended for use in the case of integrated foreign operations.

The current rate method is generally recommended for use in the case of self-sustaining foreign operations.

The temporal method

[1741] The temporal method of translation requires distinction to be made between monetary and non-monetary items in the accounts to be translated. The procedure then is as follows:

(a) Monetary assets will be translated at the effective rate at balance date.

(b) Non-monetary assets will be translated at the rate which was effective on the date of the transaction which gave rise to the asset. In the case of assets carried at historical cost, the relevant translation rate will be the historical rate. In the case of assets carried at valuation, the relevant translation rate will be the effective rate at the date of valuation.

(c) Revenue and expense items will be translated at the rate applicable at the time of the transaction except for non-monetary items. In the case of non-monetary items, the relevant rate is the one used to translate the non-monetary items themselves. For example, in the case of depreciation, if the depreciable assets are carried at historical cost, both the assets and related depreciation charges for the period will be translated at the historical exchange rates. If depreciable assets are carried at valuation, the translation of the assets and the related depreciation charges will be at the rate applicable at the date of the valuation.

[1742] The temporal method translates foreign based operations as if the operations of the group were those of a single enterprise. This is the reason why it is perceived as the appropriate method to apply in the case of integrated foreign operations.

The current rate method

[1743] The curent rate method of translation is applied as follows:

(a) Assets and liabilites are translated at the exchange rate applicable at balance date.

(b) Revenue and expense items (including depreciation) are translated at the exchange rates applicable on the dates such items are recognized in the income for the period.

[1744] A comparison of the translation of depreciation charges under the temporal and current rate methods may be helpful at this stage:

• Under the temporal method depreciation is translated at the historical exchange rate where depreciable assets are carried at historical cost, or, where depreciable assets are carried at valuation, at the rate applicable at the date of valuation.

• Under the current rate method, depreciation is translated at the exchange rate applicable at the time depreciation is brought into the measurement of the income for the period. For example, if depreciation is assumed to have occurred evenly during the period, it will be translated at the average exchange rate for the period.

[1745] The application of the current rate method will result in non-monetary items being revalued in the books of the parent company every time the relevant exchange rates change.

Under the current rate method, the foreign currency unit is the basic unit of measure. Translations under this method generally do not disturb the relationships, such as ratios, in the foreign currency accounts. For the above reasons, the current rate method is perceived as the appropriate method to apply in translating statements dealing with self-sustaining foreign operations.

When the accounts of self-sustaining foreign operations are translated using the current rate method, any exchange differences should be taken directly to a foreign currency translation reserve (ASRB 1012, para .20).

Translation of the Shareholders' Equity

[1746] The following is the general approach to translating the shareholders' equity favoured by ASRB 1012 under both the temporal and current rate methods of foreign currency translation:

(a) The shareholders' equity at the date of investment (ie share capital and reserves of a subsidiary at the date of acquisition, adjusted for any revaluations by the acquiring company where applicable) is translated at the exchange rate current at the date of investment.

(b) Post-acquisition movements in the shareholders' equity, other than retained profits or accumulated losses or transfers between items within the shareholders' equity, are translated at the exchange rates current at the dates of the movements. Transfers between items within the shareholders' equity are translated at the exchange rate current at the date that the amount transferred was first included in the shareholders' equity.

(c) Post-acquisition movements in reserves which have been processed in the profit and loss account will be dealt with in the translation of profit and loss account and no further translation is necessary in the year in which they are determined and included in the shareholders' equity. In subsequent years such retained profits or accumulated losses will be translated as part of the normal translation of capital and reserves.

(d) Dividend distributions (paid or proposed) are translated at the exchange rates current at the dates when the distributions were proposed or, where the approval of shareholders is necessary, at the dates when the dividends were declared.

Functional Currency

[1747] A variation of the methods of foreign currency translation discussed above is introduced by the notion of "functional currency". Functional currency is the currency of the primary environment in which business operations take place. For example, in the case of relatively independent operations taking place in a particular country, the functional currency would be the currency of that particular country. On the other hand, in the case of integrated foreign operations (ie where foreign operations represent an extension of the parent company's operations) the functional currency would normally be the domestic currency of the parent company.

[1748] Foreign currency translations which incorporate the notion of functional currency would require the preparation of the financial statements dealing with foreign centred activities in the functional currency and their translation into the domestic currency of the parent company.

[1749] An illustration of the application of the notion of functional currency is found in the following explanatory statement of accounting policy in the 1988 report of the directors of Fletcher Challenge Limited:

> Functional currency is an accounting term used where the accounting records are not kept in the domestic currency of the business but in the dominant currency of its operations.
>
> Each significant business unit wherever domiciled is evaluated by reference to the currency of its cashflow, sales prices, sales market, expenses and finance to determine its dominant functional currency. Non-monetary assets of the business are expressed in the functional currency rather than the currency of domicile and translated to New Zealand dollars in accordance with normal currency translation policy. As a result of the adoption of this policy, previously recorded revaluation of major New Zealand based pulp and paper manufacturing plant is considered inappropriate and has been reversed.

Use of Average Exchange Rates

[1750] For reasons of practical convenience, average rather than actual exchange rates may be used to translate some transactions such as sales, purchases and expenses. For example, monthly sales, purchases and expenses may be translated at the average monthly exchange rates, or the translation may be carried out by using the annual figures for sales, purchases and expenses and an annual average exchange rate on the assumption that such a rate reasonably represents the exchange rates at which the total volume of transactions took place.

ASRB 1012, para .50, provides for the use of average or standard rates of exchange provided that their application does not result in material differences in amounts or in the non-disclosure of material information.

Foreign Currency Translation and the Analysis and Interpretation of Financial Statements

[1751] Foreign currency translation for the purpose of preparing financial statements creates some complex problems; the manner in which these problems should be handled is a matter of controversy.

For example, it could be argued that exchange rates are translation rates for cash and cash equivalents and that their application to arrive at values for non-cash items for the purpose of financial reporting is generally inappropriate.

[1752] Judgment and opinion are likely to play an important part in foreign currency translation, for example, regarding the method of translation to employ and underlying considerations such as:
- the organizational structure within which foreign operations take place, eg whether they are integrated with or independent of the operations of the parent company;
- the method of translation to be applied given the assumed nature of foreign operations;
- the accounting treatment of translation gains or losses, ie whether they are treated as special component of income or as movements in reserves, or a combination of both.

[1753] In the analysis and interpretation of financial statements which incorporate foreign currency translations it is important to determine the nature and extent of the enterprise's activities denominated in foreign currencies in relation to the total business of the enterprise, the translation policies adopted and their implication for the reported results and state of affairs.

The policies regarding the translation of foreign currencies are likely to be stated in general terms and details disclosed may be limited. The translation method employed may obscure the facts underlying foreign operations. For example, the application of the temporal method in the translation of the financial statements of a foreign subsidiary will alter the internal relationships in the translated statements and may make the evaluation of the operations of the foreign subsidiary difficult even if the information were provided. In such cases, it may be more useful to evaluate the performance of foreign operations on the basis of the financial statements prepared in the respective foreign currencies. This may create its own problems. Further, it is very unlikely that such foreign currency financial statements would be available to domestic users of published company reports.

[1754] Foreign currency translation should reflect the economic nature of the events and facts which underlie the operations and state of affairs of foreign subsidiaries and the company groups to which such foreign subsidiaries belong. The economic environment within which foreign operations take place will vary between firms and for the same firm over time and would not necessarily be effectively reflected in any general model of foreign currency translation.

We may consider the example of a property investment company, with substantial property investments overseas, operated and managed through foreign based subsidiaries. The parent company and its subsidiaries carry out annual revaluations of their investment properties to current market (net realizable) value. Reported annual income consists of operating income represented by rentals received for rented and leased properties, and changes during the year in the market value of properties included as a separate component of income. In translating the financial statements of the foreign subsidiaries for the purpose of consolidation, the current rate method is used on the grounds that foreign operations are independent of those of the parent company. In such a case, translation differences would be reported as movements in reserves rather than as components of income. On the other hand, it may be argued with some force that exchange differences related to investment properties should be reported as components of income on the grounds that they arise from the translation of net realizable values (current cash equivalents) which determine both the income and state of affairs of the group.

Review questions

17.1 Why the need for foreign currencies translation?

17.2 In relation to foreign currencies translation define and contrast:
(a) integrated foreign operations;
(b) self-sustaining foreign operations.
What methods may be used in accounting for each? Give reasons.

17.3 How "real" is an exchange loss on a foreign currency loan if the loan is repayable in five years?

17.4 Explain and contrast the temporal and current rate methods of translating financial statements dealing with foreign currency operations.

17.5 Should exchange gains or losses on foreign currency debt be reported net of tax?

17.6 With reference to Example 17.1:
(a) Show the journal entries to record the exchange differences on the loan for 19A1, 19A2 and 19A3 net of tax.
(b) What conditions normally apply in reporting such exchange differences net of tax?

17.7 " ... exchange rates are translation rates for cash or cash equivalents and ... their application to arrive at values for non-cash items for the purpose of financial reporting is generally inappropriate."
Discuss.

17.8 "Judgment and opinion are likely to play an important part in foreign currency translation ... "
Discuss with particular reference to the anaslysis and interpretation of financial statements.

17.9 The ABC group of companies acquired a foreign subsidiary company D on 30 September 19A1, the group's balance date.

Required:

With reference to the translation of the financial statements of company D for the purpose of preparing consolidated accounts for the ABC group, explain briefly the following, assuming, alternatively, an application of (a) the temporal, and (b) current rate methods of foreign currency translation:
(1) The translation of the financial statements of company D as at the date of acquisition (30 September 19A1).
(2) The translation of the following items appearing in the financial statements of company D for the year ended 30 September 19A2:
(i) Land and buildings — these were revalued as at 30 June 19A2.
(ii) The shareholders' equity of company D assuming that the only movements in share capital and reserves consisted of the revaluation of land and buildings and the retained profit for the year referred to under (i) above.

    (iii) The following profit and loss account items:
- sales;
- purchases;
- expenses;
- taxation.

    (iv) The following balance sheet items:
- plant and machinery (carried at historical cost less accumulated depreciation);
- inventories (valued on a first-in, first-out basis, assumed to have been acquired during the last quarter of the group's finan cial year);
- bank balance, trade creditors and trade debtors;
- long-term debt.

(3) The translation of the following items appearing in the 19A3 financial statements of company D, for the purpose of preparing the consolidated accounts of the group for the year ended 30 September 19A3:
- depreciation expense;
- plant and machinery;
- land and buildings;
- shareholders' equity (the only movements in the shareholders' equity were retained earning and a transfer of $500,000 from the profit and loss appropriation account to general reserve).

(4) How should the exchange differences arising from the above translations be reported in the consolidated financial statements of the ABC group?

Chapter 18
Consolidated Financial Statements—Accounting for Associated Companies

Company Groups

[1801] Growth and diversification of business operations through mergers, take-overs, or the establishment of subsidiaries has caused the company group to become the predominant form of business organization. As a result, the majority of published financial statements are the consolidated financial statements of company groups.

[1802] The factors which have led to the development of company groups include:

Growth

The achievement of growth, including entry into new geographic areas by takeover or merger rather than by the slower and more costly process of competitive attrition. This process is one of horizontal combination — the joining together of similar enterprises to form a larger group.

Security and control

The linking together in a consolidated group of a set of enterprises so as to control operations in a field from the provision of raw materials to the marketing of finished products. This is vertical integration.

Economies of scale

An endeavour to increase the market standing and competitiveness of the total enterprise through the better utilization of production facilities (which may require rationalization), the consolidation of research and development efforts, the achievement of more effective planning and performance in marketing, improved access to sources of finance, and a higher overall standard of management.

Reduction in risk

The incorporation into a business group of enterprises providing different products or services may reduce the level of risk inherent in the separate enterprises. The process of diversification calls for high levels of managerial expertise at group level.

Effective management

Some company groups may be designed with the objective of maximizing the effectiveness of the management of each business sector through a degree of decentralization while retaining the level of group control considered to be desirable.

Joint ventures

Investments may be made in enterprises where it is considered to be necessary or wise to share control with other companies or company groups. Examples may be enterprises in foriegn countries and enterprises (like oil exploration) involving high levels of risk.

[1803] It should be evident from the above discussion that a company group consisting of a holding company and its subsidiaries may be regarded as a single economic (business) unit because it is designed to operàte as such, with the ultimate control of the group's operations resting with the board of directors of the holding company. The perception of a company group as an economic entity is also reflected in the preparation of consolidated financial statements which report on the operations and state of affairs of the group as if the group were a single business unit.

It should be noted, however, that even though from the viewpoints of control and of reporting on results and state of affairs a company group may be regarded as a single business unit, the group is not a single entity at law. Rather, each company in the group is a legal entity, with its own directors, management, assets, liabilities, and legal responsibilities. Typically, the analyst and interpreter does not have access to the financial statements of the individual companies in the group, but only to those of the holding company and the consolidated statements for the group as an entity.

[1804] The essential feature which makes a group of companies an economic entity is the fact of control through the board of directors of the holding company. In practice the business interests of company groups may include less than controlling interests in associated companies. In such cases the feature of control may be widened to include the ability to exercise "significant influence". In many cases, interests in associated companies constitute a material share of total investment and produce a significant proportion of profits or losses of the group as a whole.

In the discussion which follows, we will deal first with the more narrow concept of a company group, and will extend this later to include accounting for interests in associated companies.

A Holding Company and Its Subsidiaries

[1805] Company legislation (Companies Acts: Aust, s 7; NZ, s 158) defines the holding company of a subsidiary as one which:
(a) controls the composition of the board of directors of the latter company; or
(b) controls more than half of its voting power; or
(c) holds more than half of its issued capital (excluding capital which carries a

right to participate in the distribution of profit or capital only up to a specified fixed amount).

[1806] In addition to "subsidiary" as defined by company legislation, New Zealand Standard SSAP No 8, "Accounting for Business Combinations" (October 1987) (para 3.14) defines an "in-substance subsidiary" as a company in which another company,

(a) controls directly, indirectly, or beneficially: the majority of equity capital or voting rights, or the majority of voting rights of the board of directors, or the right to in excess of 50% of earnings or dividends or other distributions of the company; or

(b) where the other company obtains under any other scheme, arrangement or device, in substance, the benefits or risks of majority ownership or control.

Normally, a holding company–subsidiary company relationship is established by the holding company acquiring more than half of the issued ordinary shares of another company or by itself forming a company and providing more than half of its ordinary share capital.

[1807] As stated earlier, from the viewpoint of company law, a holding company and its subsidiaries are separate legal entities, each responsible for its own debts, unless one company in the group has guaranteed the debts of another. However, the creditors of a holding company have an indirect access to the assets of subsidiary companies by way of the controlling interest of the holding company in its subsidiaries.

Financial Reporting for Company Groups

[1808] Although a company group is not a legal entity, it is the economic entity of primary interest to the shareholders of the holding company. For this reason company legislation requires the directors of a holding company to present to shareholders at annual general meetings group accounts dealing with the profit and loss and state of affairs of the group. The group accounts must give a true and fair view of the profit and loss and state of affairs of the group so far as they concern the members of the holding company (Companies Acts: Aust, s 269; NZ, s 156).

[1809] The group accounts presented to shareholders of the holding company consist normally of a consolidated balance sheet and consolidated profit and loss account dealing with the state of affairs and profit or loss of the holding company and its subsidiaries. In addition, Australian company legislation requires the directors of a holding company to provide a consolidated cash statement which gives a true and fair view of the cash movements of the company and its subsidiaries during their respective last financial years (s 269(3A)).

[1810] The following alternatives to presenting a single set of consolidated accounts are available to the directors if they are of the opinion that the same or equivalent information can be better presented in another form (Aust, s 266; NZ, s 155):

(a) two or more sets of consolidated accounts covering the group; or

(b) separate accounts for each company in the group; or

(c) a combination of these.

The presentation of group accounts in a form other than a single set of consolidated accounts is the exception rather than the rule.

[1811] There may be good reasons for departing from the normal practice of producing a single set of consolidated financial statements. For example, in its 1987 report Fletcher Challenge Limited produced two sets of consolidated financial statements: one for the holding company and the subsidiary companies included in what was described as the "central group", and one for the subsidiary companies in the "finance and investment group". The net investment in the "finance and investment group" was added to the total "central group" assets to arrive at the total assets shown in the holding company and central group balance sheet. Separate earnings statements were not provided, but separate statements of changes in financial position were shown. Among the reasons for providing separate statements for the set of subsidiaries involved in investment and financial operations were the specialized nature of the assets held by such enterprises and the different factors determining the appropriate financing of these assets.

The need for consolidated financial statements

[1812] An investor acquiring shares in a holding company acquires indirectly an interest in its subsidiaries. From the viewpoint of a shareholder or an investor, therefore, an investment in a holding company has to be evaluated in terms of the operating results and state of affairs of the group as a whole. The purpose of consolidated financial statements is to present the revenues, expenses and profit, and the assets, liabilities and owners' equity of a company group as though it were a single enterprise.

The following are some of the reasons why the financial statements of the holding company alone may not meet the information needs of readers of financial statements, in general, and of shareholders and investors in particular:

Profitability

The profit and loss statement of the holding company will show the results of operations of the holding company itself and the amount of dividend received from its subsidiaries. The dividends received from subsidiaries, however, may not reflect, fairly, the profits of the subsidiaries for the period. There is no necessary relationship between the profit of the year and the dividend of the year. Retention rates tend to vary more than dividend rates. The subsidiary may even operate at a loss but still pay a dividend from retained earnings. Dividends may be paid from capital profits. In the case of a subsidiary acquired during the year, the dividends may have been paid wholly or in part from pre-acquisition profits.

Net asset backing

In the balance sheet of the holding company the investment of the holding company in a subsidiary will be shown as:

> Shares in subsidiary company (at cost) $xxx

The cost of shares in subsidiary figure may not be very informative because:

(i) substantial losses may have accumulated in the subsidiary company for which no provision has been made in the accounts of the holding company; or

(ii) substantial profits may have accumulated in a subsidiary as a result of which the current value of the subsidiary's shares may be materially higher than the figure recorded in the books of the holding company.

The consolidation of financial statements

[1813] The consolidation process involves the combining of the financial statements of the holding company and its subsidiaries on a line-by-line basis, by adding corresponding revenues and expenses and assets and liabilities, after making certain adjustments.

Adjustments required on consolidation include:
(a) The elimination of
  • intercompany balances such as intercompany indebtedness;
  • unrealized intercompany profits on inventories and fixed assets;
  • intercompany sales and purchases;
  • intercompany charges;
  • intercompany dividends.
(b) The calculation and recording of goodwill or surplus (discount) on acquisition.
(c) The recording, where subsidiaries are not fully owned, of minority interest in the profits for the period and in the net assets of subsidiaries.

The net effect of consolidation is to present, from the viewpoint of the shareholders of the holding company, the group results and state of affairs in relation to interests outside the group.

The two main methods of consolidating the financial statements of a holding company and its subsidiaries are the purchase method and the pooling of interests method.

The purchase method of consolidation

[1814] The purchase method of consolidation conceives the creation of a holding company–subsidiary company relationship as one involving the purchase by the holding company of a controlling interest in a subsidiary. The purchase may be for cash, loan securities, or shares in the holding company or a mix of these, and will be recorded in the books of the holding company at "cost":

Shares in subsidiary		$
Cash		$
Debentures		$
Unallotted shares		$
Share premium (if applicable)		$

A major problem of accounting for the purchase of a controlling interest in a subsidiary is the measurement of cost where the consideration includes shares and/or other securities in the acquiring company, and the determination of a fair value of the assets (and liabilities) of the subsidiaries acquired.

[1815] The recording of the acquisition of controlling interest at cost should reflect the economic substance of the transaction. To achieve this, it would be necessary to determine the fair values, at the date of acquisition, of the various forms of purchase consideration given. There are no major problems in arriving at the amount of considerations to the extent that it consists of cash or monetary assets and/or liabilities of readily determinable cash value. Where the consideration includes non-monetary assets, its amount would have to be determined by reference to the fair values of those non-monetary assets. Where the purchase consideration comprises shares or other securities of the acquiring company, their fair value may be estimated as the price at which they would have been placed on the market at the time of issue. According to the New Zealand Standard SSAP No 8, cost is determined by the fair value of the consideration given or, if this is not clearly evident, by the fair value of the property or right acquired (para 4.19).

[1816] According to NZ SSAP8, the total purchase consideration should be assigned to the underlying tangible and intangible assets on the basis of fair value of the acquired net assets as at acquistion. If this is not done in the books of the acquired company, it should be done on consolidation (para 4.47). Australian Standard AAS21, "Accounting for the Acquisition of Assets (Including Business Entities)" provides similarly for the recording of the identifiable net assets at their cost of acquisition, measured by reference to their individual fair values (para 19).

Goodwill or discount on acquisition

[1817] Where the cost of acquisition exceeds the fair value of the identifiable net assets acquired, the balance represents goodwill. Where the fair value of the identifiable net assets acquired exceeds the cost of acquisition, the balance represents discount on acquisition.

Approved Australian Standard ASRB 1013, "Accounting for Goodwill" provides that purchased goodwill should be brought to account as a non-current asset at acquisition. Such goodwill should be systematically amortized to the profit and loss account over the period during which the benefits associated with the goodwill are expected to arise, such period not to exceed 20 years. At each balance date unamortized goodwill should be reviewed and written off to the profit and loss account to the extent that future benefit associated with it are no longer probable. Discount on acquisition should be accounted for by reducing proportionately the fair values of the non-monetary assets acquired. Similar provisions are made in the New Zealand Standard SSAP8.

According to ASRB 1013 goodwill or discount on the acquisition of a subsidiary should be accounted for as adjustments in the group accounts and not in the subsidiary's or holding company's accounts.

[1818] The aim of the above recommendations for accounting for goodwill is to avoid the recording of meaningless figures for goodwill on consolidation. For example, the commentary to ASRB 1013 refers to goodwill as comprising the future benefits from unidentifiable assets which, because of their nature, are not normally recorded individually in the books. Examples of such asets are stated to include market penetration, effective advertising, good labour relations and a superior management and operating team.

[1819] It should be noted, however, that accounting for goodwill in general and on the acquisition of a subsidiary in particular creates some very complex problems.

For example, when the consideration paid on the acquisition of controlling interest consists wholly or partly of securities, the asessment of the amount of the consideration would require a reference to be made to market conditions to determine the amount that could have been obtained from a hypothetical issue of the securities to the public. Obviously that amount is a matter of opinion. If the issue is large relative to the capital pre-merger, then the value becomes very subjective indeed because there will have been a significant change in the business operations and assets of the group. The allocation of this subjectively determined value to the underlying net tangible and intangible assets introduces further subjectivity and, indeed, borders on the impossible as there is no logical basis for making the allocation.

There is also a further problem. One could expect the value of the shares in the subsidiary to reflect the present value of the resulting increment to the net cash flows of the enlarged group. This increase will relate in part only to the pre-acquisition earnings or even projected earnings of the subsidiary and to the assets which generate these earnings. It follows that the goodwill on consolidation relates not so much to the acquired company as such as to the enlarged group. So far as tangible assets are concerned, it can be argued that values that are to be regarded as "fair" must have some relationship to current market prices — replacement cost or net realizable value. The former basis involves subjectivity, particularly if the assets are specialized and on the way to obsolescence; and the latter measure may be very subjective indeed. Finally there is the fact that the purchase price for the shares may not reflect the market price. There may have been few potential buyers at the time, and the circumstnaces of the sellers may have affected what they were willing to accept at the time. In the acquisition of a company making losses, the price may have allowed for an expectation of losses to be incurred and profits to be foregone until adequate profitability of operations is reached. It may be argued that this is not a case of lower asset values but rather one where an overall undervaluation should be brought back to group revenue over the planned recovery period.

[1820] The last issue referred to above arose when Fletcher Challenge Limited acquired in 1983 a controlling interest in Crown Forest Industries, a large Canadian timber processing enterprise which was operating relatively unprofitably under depressed conditions in the industry. The large cost of acquisition was considered to be well below the medium- to long-term worth of the investment. Substantial servicing costs were to be incurred during the few years required to achieve adequate profitability and these would have depressed the overall earnings of the enlarged group. Following the takeover, and not without criticism from some quarters, Fletcher Challenge revalued its share of the net assets of Crown Forest Industries to $194 million above the purchase price. The surplus on revaluation was credited to a deferred income account and was to be "amortized" to the profit and loss account over five years. This writing up of assets enabled Fletcher Challenge to transfer to profit $15.2 million to report a profit of $9.9 million for the three months in 1983 on its North American operations and $55.5 million in 1984 to report a profit of $24.2 million. The 1985 report of the Fletcher Challenge Group stated that the considerable turnaround that had occurred had justified the move to accounting for North America from 1 July 1984 on a "normal operations basis".

Pre-acquisition profits; dividends from pre-acquisition profits

[1821] Under the purchase method, the pre-acquisition profits of a subsidiary are treated as part of the net assets taken over at the time of acquisition and are, therefore, not regarded as distributable to the shareholders of the holding company. On consolidation, the holding company's share of the pre-acquisition profits of a subsidiary company is set off against the cost of the shares in the subsidiary and is, therefore, not included in the reported consolidated reserves of the group. A minority share in pre-acquisition profits is included in minority interest.

In the books of the holding company, dividends received from pre–acquisition profits are treated as a return of purchase price; as such they are credited to the "share in subsidiaries account" and not to the profit and loss account as dividend income.

Unrealized intercompany profits: subsidiaries and associated companies

[1822] An unrealized intercompany profit exists where one member of a company group holds assets transfered to it by another member of the group at a value higher than that recorded in the books of the transferor (eg purchase price, manufacturing cost, or some other value).

Standard accounting practice requires that unrealized intercompany profits be eliminated in the preparation and presentation of consolidated financial statements. Where the asset transfer is from the holding company or from a wholly owned subsidiary, the total amount of the unrealized profit should be eliminated. Where the transfer of assets is from a partly owned subsidiary, there are two views regarding the accounting treatment of unrealized profit:
  (a) elimination of total unrealized profit on assets on hand at balance date; and
  (b) elimination of only the group portion of the unrealized profit on assets acquired from partly owned subsidiaries.

New Zealand Standard SSAP8 recommends the elimination of total unrealized profit in both cases (para 4.64).

[1823] In the case of associated companies, SSAP8 states that, in the case of sales from the investor company to an associated company, unrealized gains or losses should be eliminated at a percentage equal to the investor's interest in the associate. In the case of sales from associated companies, unrealized profits should be completely eliminated before the calculation of the investor's share in the profits of the associated companies (para 4.64).

Australian Standard AAS 14: "Equity Method of Accounting" requires the elimination of unrealized gains and losses on transactions between an associated company and any other company within the economic entity in porportion to the investor's ownership interests in the transacting companies. The adjustment is to be made to the particular aggregated balances for the economic entity in which the effects of the unrealized profits or losses are recorded (paras 22–5).

The pooling of interests method

[1824] The pooling of interests method accounts for a company combination, not as a purchase of a controlling interest by one company in another, but as the merging of the assets, liabilities and ownership interests of two or more companies by the exchange of shares. The merger may be consumated either by one company taking over the other (usually on terms agreed on by the two boards of directors and acceptable to the shareholders of the company acquired), or by a new company being formed to take over both the merging companies on mutually acceptable terms.

The following are the main features of accounting for business combinations by means of the pooling of interests method:

(a) The holding company records the shares issued at their nominal value.

(b) On consolidation, the reserves, assets, and liabilities of the companies in the group are combined at book value.

(c) Where the nominal value of the shares issued is less than the nominal value of the shares received in exchange, the difference is treated as an undistributable reserve. Where the nominal value of the shares issued is greater than that of the shares received, the difference is treated as a reduction in reserves, applied first against undistributable reserves and second against distributable reserves.

(d) The net distributable reserves of subsidiaries are treated by the holding company as distributable to its shareholders.

(e) Assets and liabilites are aggregated at their book values.

[1825] The purchase/pooling of interests approaches to consolidation are generally regarded as mutually exclusive and not as alternatives. The Australian Standard AAS 21 precludes the use of the pooling of interests method in accounting for acquisitions. The New Zealand Standard SSAP No 8 provides that where two or more companies are joined together through an exchange of shares in circumstances where none of the companies can be identified as an acquirer, the combination may be regarded as a pooling of interests. It considers, however, that such combinations are rare (para 4.24). The standard then sets a number of conditions which would need to be met before it could be said that no party to a combination can be identified as an acquirer.

Basic Consolidation Techniques

[1826] The analysis and interpretation of financial statements requires at least some knowledge of basic consolidation techniques. The basic techniques of consolidation using the purchase and pooling of interests methods are illustrated in Examples 18.1 and 18.2.

The purchase method

Example 18.1

On 31 March 19A1 H Ltd acquired 80% of the ordinary shares of S Ltd for a cash payment of $1,400,000. The abbreviated balance sheets of the two companies immediately prior to the takeover were as follows;

	H Ltd $000	S Ltd $000
Capital in $1 fully paid shares	4,500	1,000
Retained profits	3,000	500
Shareholders' funds	7,500	1,500
Liabilities	6,500	1,000
	14,000	2,500

Continued p 298

Fixed assets	6,000	1,200
Current assets	8,000	1,300
	14,000	2,500

The balance sheets of the two companies immediately after the takeover are shown below:

	H Ltd $000	S Ltd $000
Capital	4,500	1,000
Retained profits	3,000	500
Shareholders' funds	7,500	1,500
Liabilities	6,500	1,000
	14,000	2,500
Fixed assets	6,000	1,200
Shares in S Ltd	1,400	
Current assets	6,600	1,300
	14,000	2,500

After the takeover, there is no change in the balance sheet of the subsidiary S Ltd. This is so because there is no change in the assets and liabilites or the amount of the shareholders' equity of S Ltd as a result of the takeover. What has changed is the composition of the shareholders.

The only changes in the balance sheet of H Ltd are a reduction of current assets of $1.4 million, the amount of cash paid for the acquisition of the 80% controlling interest in S Ltd, and the recording of the investment in shares in S Ltd of the same amount:

Shares in S Ltd	1,400,000	
Cash		1,400,000

If the consideration had included the allotment of shares at a stated premium as well as a payment of cash, the journal entry recording the transaction would have been:

Shares in S Ltd	$	
Unallotted shares		$
Share premium		$
Cash		$

The profit and loss and appropriation statements of H Ltd and S Ltd for the year ended 31 March 19A2, the first year after the takeover, and the balance sheets of the two companies at 31 March 19A2 are given on p 299.

During the year ended 31 March 19A2 S Ltd sold $50,000 of goods to H Ltd. The mark up by S Ltd included in the price was 25% on cost. The stock of H Ltd at 31 March 19A2 included $10,000 of goods purchased from S Ltd.

As the takeover of S Ltd was effected by the payment of cash, the question of determining fair value of the consideration given does not arise — the value of the

Profit and loss and appropriation statements for year ended 31/3/19A2

	H Ltd $000	S Ltd $000
Sales	12,000	3,500
Cost of sales:		
Opening inventory	4,500	800
Purchases	9,300	2,900
	13,800	3,700
Closing inventory	6,000	1,500
Cost of sales	7,800	2,200
Gross profit	4,200	1,300
Expenses	2,250	700
Trading profit	1,950	600
Plus charges to S Ltd	50	—
Profit before tax	2,000	600
Provision for tax	900	270
Profit after tax	1,100	330
Unappropriated profit brought forward	3,000	500
	4,100	830
Provision for dividend	450	100
Unappropriated profit carried forward	3,650	730

Balance Sheets as at 31 March 19A2

	H Ltd $000	S Ltd $000
Capital in $1 fully paid shares	4,500	1,000
Retained earnings	3,650	730
Shareholders' funds	8,150	1,730
Term liabilities	4,800	800
Current liabilities:		
Creditors	1,200	340
Bank	500	260
Prov for taxation	900	270
Prov for dividend	450	100
	16,000	3,500
Fixed assets	6,400	1,400
Shares in S Ltd	1,400	
Current assets:		
Debtors	2,200	600
Stocks	6,000	1,500
	16,000	3,500

consideration is represented by the amount of the cash payment. A question which does arise is that of allocating the purchase consideration to the underlying net tangible and intangible assets on the basis of their fair value. For the sake of simplicity we shall assume that the book value of the assets of S Ltd represents their fair value and that, therefore, no adjustment to asset values is necessary.

The consolidation of the balance sheets of H Ltd and S Ltd immediately after the takeover will involve the following adjustments shown below in the form of journal entries and a consolidation worksheet.

(1) The setting off of the cost of shares in S Ltd against the H Ltd's share in the net assets of S Ltd and the recording of any difference between cost and the assets taken over as goodwill or capital surplus on consolidation:

	$000	$000
Capital — S Ltd	800	
Retained earnings — S Ltd	400	
Goodwill on consolidation	200	
Shares in S Ltd		1,400

Net assets takeon over (80% of the capital and retained earnings of S Ltd) and goodwill on consolidation — the excess of the consideration over the relevant share of the net assets at the date of acquisition of the shares.

(2) The recording of the minority interest in the net assets of S Ltd:

	$000	$000
Capital — S Ltd	200	
Retained earnings — S Ltd	100	
Minority interest		300

Minority interest 20% of the net assets (capital and retained earnings) of S Ltd

Consolidation work sheet

	H Ltd $000	S Ltd $000	Adjustments Dr $000	Adjustments Cr $000	Consolidated $000
Capital	4,500	1,000	800(1) 200(2)		4,500
Retained earnings	3,000	500	400(1) 100(2)		3,000
Shareholders' funds	7,500	1,500			7,500
Minority interest				300(2)	300
Liabilities	6,500	1,000			7,500
	14,000	2,500			15,300
Fixed assets	6,000	1,200			7,200
Shares in S Ltd	1,400			1,400(1)	
Current assets	6,600	1,300			7,900
Goodwill on consolidation			200(1)		200
	14,000	2,500	1,700	1,700	15,300

Consolidated balance sheet as at 31/3/19A1

	$000		$000
Capital	4,500	Fixed assets	7,200
Retained earnings	3,000	Goodwill on consolidation	200
Shareholders' funds	7,500	Current assets	7,900
Minority interest	300		
Liabilities	7,500		
	15,300		15,300

The adjustments to consolidate the financial statements of H Ltd and S Ltd at 31 March 19A2, are illustrated below:

Adjustments to profit and loss and appropriation statements

(1) To eliminate intercompany sales and purchases:

Sales	50,000	
Purchases		50,000

(2) To eliminate unrealized profit on ending inventory:

Reduce the value of ending inventory (and profit) by $2000.

(3) To eliminate intercompany charges:

Charges to S Ltd	50,000	
Expenses (S Ltd)		50,000

(4) To record the minority interest in the year's profit of S Ltd:

Net profit after tax	$330,000
Less unearned profit on ending inventory	2,000
	$328,000

Minority interest 20% of $328,000 = $65,600.

(5) To eliminate the pre-acquisition retained earnings of S Ltd:

Reduce retained earnings by $500,000
A similar adjustment will apply to all reserves of the subsidiary company.

(6) To eliminate intercompany dividends:

Remove S Ltd's provision for dividend of $100,000.

Consolidation work sheet
Profit and loss and appropriation statements

	H Ltd $000	S Ltd $000	Adjustments Dr $000	Cr $000	Consoli- dated $000
Sales	12,000	3,500	50(1)		15,450
Cost of sales:					
Opening inventory	4,500	800			5,300
Purchases	9,300	2,900		50(1)	12,150
	13,800	3,700			17,450
Closing inventory	6,000	1,500		2(2)	7,498
Cost of sales	7,800	2,200			9,952
Gross profit	4,200	1,300			5,498
Expenses	2,250	700		50(3)	2,900
Trading profit	1,950	600			2,598
Charges to S Ltd	50	—	50(3)		—
Profit before tax	2,000	600			2,598
Provision for tax	900	270			1,170
Profit after tax	1,100	330			1,428
Minority interest					65.6
Profit after tax attributable to H Ltd shareholders					1,362.4
Unappropriated profit brought forward	3,000	500	500(5)		3,000
	4,100	830			4,362.4
Provision for dividend	450	100	100(6)		450.0
Unappropriated profit carried forward	3,650	730			3,912.4

Adjustments to balance sheets

The adjustments on the consolidation of the balance sheets of H Ltd and S Ltd as at 31 March 19A2 are illustrated below in the form of journal entries and consolidation work sheet.

(1) To record goodwill on consolidation:

Capital — S Ltd	800,000	
Retained earnings — S Ltd	400,000	
Goodwill on consolidation	200,000	
Shares in S Ltd		1,400,000

Net assets taken over (80% of the capital and retained earnings of S Ltd) and goodwill on consolidation — calculated as at the time of the takeover.

(2) To eliminate the unrealized profit on ending inventory:

$$
\begin{array}{llr}
\text{Retained earnings} & 2,000 & \\
\text{Stocks} & & 2,000 \\
\end{array}
$$

(3) To record minority interest in the net assets of S Ltd:

Capital	200,000	
Retained earnings	145,600	
Minority interest		345,600

Minority interest in the net assets of S Ltd as at 31/3/ 19A2 (ie 20% of capital and retained earnings after reducing earnings by $2,000 for unearned profit on stock)

(4) To eliminate the provision for dividend of S Ltd:

Provision for dividend	100,000	
Retained earnings		80,000
Minority interest		20,000

Being elimination of the provision for dividend of S Ltd — 80% written back to retained earnings and 20% to minority interest.

Consolidation work sheet

	H Ltd	S Ltd	Adjustments Dr	Adjustments Cr	Consolidated
Capital	4,500,000	1,000,000	800,000(1) 200,000(3)		4,500,000
Retained earnings	3,650,000	730,000	400,000(1) 2,000(2) 145,600(3)	80,000(5)	3,912,400
Shareholders' funds	8,150,000	1,730,000			8,412,400
Minority interest				345,600(3) 20,000(4)	365,000
Term liabilities	4,800,000	800,000			5,600,000
Current liabilities:					
Creditors	1,200,000	340,000			1,540,000
Bank	500,000	260,000			760,000
Prov for taxation	900,000	270,000			1,170,000
Prov for dividend	450,000	100,000	100,000(4)		450,000
	16,000,000	3,500,000			18,298,000
Fixed assets	6,400,000	1,400,000			7,800,000
Shares in S Ltd	1,400,000			1,400,000(1)	—
Current assets:					
Debtors	2,200,000	600,000			2,800,000
Stocks	6,000,000	1,500,000		2,000(2)	7,498,000
Goodwill on consolidation			200,000(1)		200,000
	16,000,000	3,500,000	1,847,600	1,847,600	18,298,000

The consolidated profit and loss and appropriation statements and balance sheets of H Ltd and S Ltd may then be presented as follows:

Consolidated profit and loss and appropriation statement year ended 31/3/19A2

	$000	$000
Sales		15,450
Cost of sales:		
Opening inventory	5,300	
Purchases	12,150	
	17,450	
Closing inventory	7,498	
Cost of sales		9,952
Gross profit		5,498
Expenses		2,900
Profit before tax		2,598
Provision for tax		1,170
Profit after tax		1,428
Less minority interest		65.6
Profit after tax attributable to shareholders of H Ltd		1,362.4
Unappropriated profit brought forward		3,000
		4,362.4
Provision for dividend		450
Unappropriated profit carried forward		3,912.4

Consolidated balance sheet as at 31/3/19A2

	$		$
Capital	4,500,000	Fixed assets	7,800,000
Retained earnings	3,912,400	Goodwill on consolidation	200,000
Shareholders' funds	8,412,400		
Minority interest	365,600	Current assets:	
Term liabilities	5,600,000	Debtors	2,800,000
Current liabilities:		Stocks	7,498,000
Creditors	1,540,000		
Bank	760,000		
Prov for taxation	1,170,000		
Prov for dividend	450,000		
	18,298,000		18,298,000

Consolidation under the pooling of interests method

Example 18.2

Using the basic figures in Example 18.1 we will assume that H Ltd acquired all the shares of S Ltd by an issue of 900,000 $1 shares at par, having increased its authorized capital by the same amount for the purpose of effecting the merger. We will assume also that all other figures in the profit and loss statements and balance sheets of H Ltd and S Ltd at 31/3/19A2 have remained the same.

The effect of the consolidation of the shareholders' equities of the two companies at 31 March 19A2 under the pooling of interests method is illustrated by means of consolidation journal entries and work sheets as follows:

	$	$
(1) Capital — S Ltd	1,000,000	
Shares in S Ltd		900,000
Capital reserve		100,000
(2) Retained earnings — S Ltd	2,000	
Stocks		2,000
To eliminate unrealized profit on ending stocks.		

Consolidation work sheet

	H Ltd $	S Ltd $	Adjustments Dr $	Adjustments Cr $	Consoli- dated $
Capital	5,400,000	1,000,000	1,000,000(1)		5,400,000
Retained earnings	3,650,000	730,000	2,000(2)		4,378,000
Capital reserve				100,000(1)	100,000
	9,050,000	1,730,000			9,878,000

The consolidation of the profit and loss and appropriation statements and balance sheets of the two companies will involve the aggregation at book value of the revenues and expenses and assets and liabilites of the two companies after eliminating the intercompany purchases, the unrealized profit on ending inventories and intercompany indebtedness. It should be noted, however, that, as shown above, there will be no elimination of the pre-acquisition accumulated earnings of S Ltd — these will be shown as part of the consolidated retained earnings of the group.

Finally, it should be noted that the adjustments and aggregations on consolidation are carried out outside the double entry accounting systems of the individual companies in the group. As such they do not affect the books or financial statements of the individual companies.

Associated Companies

[1827] An associated company is a company, called "investee", in which another company, called "investor", has a "substantial" though not controlling interest. The key requirement for a company to be classified as an associate is the ability of the investor company to exercise "significant influence" over its decisions. As a general guide, 20% of equity voting rights is regarded prima facie as representing substantial interest allowing significant influence to be exercized over the decisions of the investee.

[1828] The question of significant influence in the absence of assured control is a complex one and cannot be decided on the basis of percentages alone. Significant influence does not necessarily begin at 20% of shareholding, nor does it necessarily stop imediately below that. For example, a 25% shareholding in an investee company built up by an investor as a preliminary to a takeover bid could have very little direct influence on the decisions of the target company if the takeover bid meets with a determined resistance by the directors of the target company with the support of the majority of shareholders. On the other hand, the same level of shareholding could give effective control over an investee company in which the balance of equity (voting) capital is widely held by largely passive shareholders.

The question of whether an investor company has significant influence over an investee is a matter which will have to be decided in light of the circumstances of each case. Significant influence normally stems from the voting power of the investor. In this regard it would be necessary to consider the distribution of the balance of voting power, eg whether it is concentrated in the hands of a small number of large shareholders or a large number of small shareholders.

[1829] Accounting practice requires the coverage of financial statements to be extended to include an investor company's share in the profits and increase in the net assets of associated companies by the application of the "equity method" of accounting.

The following are the main characteristics of the equity method in its application to accounting for investment in associated companies:

(a) An investment in the shares of an associated company is recorded initially at cost.

(b) Subsequent to acquisition and initial recording, the investment in associated companies is increased or decreased by the investor company's share of post-acquisition profits or losses of the associated company, subject to adjustments to eliminate the effects of intercompany transactions. The investor company's share of the profit or loss is then shown separately in its profit and loss account.

(c) The amount of the investment in associated companies is decreased by the amount of dividends received by the investor company from the associated company.

(d) The amount of the investment in associated companies should be adjusted for post-acquisition changes in the reserves of the associated company other than retained earnings.

The question of eliminating unrealized gains or losses on intercompany transactions involving associated companies was discussed in [1822].

[1830] In the analysis of financial statements it should be kept in mind that a significant difference exists between an associated company and a subsidiary company. A holding company has a direct control over the activities and dividend policies of a subsidiary. In the case of an associated company this control is shared with others so that the ability of an investing company to control for example the dividend policies of an associated company may be limited. These considerations become important if reported profit contains material amounts of profits by associated companies, as illustrated in Example 18.3 (see also example in [1546]).

Example 18.3

The following figures have been extracted from the 1978 consolidated financial statements of a New Zealand company group:

	1978	1977
	$000	$000
Turnover	363,984	365,333
Consolidated profit before equity in retained earnings of associated companies	9,860	12,681
Equity in retained earnings of associated companies	5,391	2,566
Total consolidated net profit	15,251	15,247

In Example 18.3 the reported total consolidated net profit for 1978 and for 1977 are very much the same. There is an important qualitative difference between the two profit figures, however, in that in 1978 one-third of the profit is represented by retained earnings of associated companies; these earnings are not under the direct control of the investing company.

[1831] Example 18.3 illustrates effectively one of the reasons why equity accounting is considered by most accountants to be desirable and is criticized and opposed by others. Without it, the $5,391,000 would have been excluded from group income altogether. With it, a significant item is included in income which may be regarded as unrealized so far as the holding company is concerned. With the increasing use of the joint venture type enterprise, and of share exchanges as an alternative to acquisition, the associated company relationship has become a more common feature of company groups, and the need to account for it more relevant. Behind equity accounting is an extended concept of the economic entity to be accounted for — extended from "control" to "significant influence". The analyst and interpreter has to be fully aware of the significance of the extension. His appreciation of the facts may be enlarged when he is able to study the reports of the associated company, and to examine the extent of interdependence between the associated company and the group. Without this study, there is a need for caution in interpretation where the relationship with the associated company is expected to have a material effect on group profits and position in the future.

[1832] There are some intriguing aspects of accounting for equity interests in other companies which are 50% or less.

It would be evident from the preceding discussion that the problems associated with determining significant influence provide room for judgment and choice regarding when to treat an investment as involving an associated company. An associated company status may be assumed in order to present a better picture of profitability. It is also possible to switch to and from an associate status to suit circumstances.

A company "entrepreneur" may acquire a significant interest in another company primarily as an investment because of either its potential for sale at a profit in an anticipated takeover or in the belief that the share price does not reflect fairly the long-term prospects of the enterprise. A group specializing in business reconstruction through more effective management may exercise significant influence through representation and action on the board of directors, and move to a position either of takeover or of a profitable sale of shareholding. An insurance company holding over 20% of the shares in a trading enterprise may have a policy of not exercising "significant influence" on the management of that enterprise.

[1833] A problem may develop where the market value of shares in associates diverges materially from their purchase price. At what point should profit or loss be recognized? It may be held with some justification that the current market price of shares is not a fair basis of valuation of a major shareholding; but determination of what does constitute a fair valuation will be inevitably a subjective exercise.

[1834] Some property companies have a policy of revaluing their properties each year, and recognizing increases in value as income, albeit unrealized. No provision is made for depreciation on the buildings component of these properties. To foil a takeover bid from a property company, a large department store enterprise arranged with some corporate investors to form a property company (with the department store holding 50% interest) which acquired its land and buildings at market prices well in excess of book value, then leased them back to the original owner. The store was then able to include in its income statement for the year the profit from the sale of its properties and its 50% share of the write-up of those properties during the year.

It is clear from the above that the analyst/interpreter of financial statements of enterprises which have significant investments in company equities needs to be aware of the underlying facts and to walk with care.

Cross Shareholdings

[1835] A reciprocal or cross shareholding occurs when two companies hold shares in each other.

In Australia and New Zealand, company legislation prohibits a subsidiary (as defined by company law) from holding shares in its holding company. Crossholdings may occur, however, between associated and investor companies and between a holding company and an in-substance subsidiary as defined by New Zealand Standard SSAP8 and referred to earlier: [1806].

Where a cross shareholding exists between an investor and an investee and is to be accounted for by the investor as involving an associated company by the equity method, Australian Standard AAS14 requires the investor's share in the income of the associated company to be calculated excluding any dividend received or receivable from the investor. When the investee company also uses the equity method to account for its investment in the investor, the investor's share in the income of the investee should be calculated excluding the investee's share in the retained earnings of the investor. This is what is referred to as the treasury stock method and is the method favoured also by the New Zealand Standard SSAP8.

[1836] The application of the treasury stock method will be illustrated with a simple example. Company A (with capital in $1 shares of $1 million holds 40% interest in company B. Company B (with capital in $1 shares of $700,000) holds

20% percent interest in company A. The unadjusted profit statements of the two companies prior to accounting for the cross holding are:

Company A	$		Company B	$
Operating income	200,000	Operating income		150,000
Dividend from B	30,000	Dividend from A		20,000
	230,000			170,000
Dividend paid	100,000	Dividend paid		75,000
	130,000			95,000

If both companies were to apply the equity method of accounting and the treasury stock method in dealing with the cross shareholding, the results may be presented as follows:

Company A	$		Company B	$
Operating income	200,000	Operating income		150,000
Plus 40% share of income		Plus 20% share of income		
of B $150,000 =	60,000	of B $200,000 =		40,000
Total income	260,00	Total income		190,00
Less dividend paid	100,000	Less dividend paid		75,000
Retained income	160,000	Retained income		115,000

The income from the associated company in each case can be presented alternatively as follows:

	Company A $	Company B $
Income from associated company:		
Dividend received	30,000	20,000
Share of retained earnings in		
associated company	30,000	20,000
	60,000	40,000

[1837] A crossholding of shares may be viewed as resulting in each company owning a certain portion of itself. In the above example, company B owns 20% or 200,000 shares in A. Since A owns 40% of the shares of company B, company A may be said to own 80,000 of its own shares (ie 40% of the 200,000 company A shares held by company B). Similarly company B could be said to own 56,000 of its own shares ie 20% of the 280,000 company B shares held by company A (40% of 700,000 company B shares) on account of company B holding 20% of the shares of company A.

[1838] The above interpretation of the nature of cross shareholdings may be used in the calculation of the earnings per share (EPS) of the two companies by using the number of shares held by "outsiders":

Company A:

Total number of shares	1,000,000
Less held indirectly by Company A	80,000
Shares held by "outsiders"	920,000

$$EPS = \frac{\$260,000}{920,000} = 28.26c$$

Company B:

Total number of shares	700,000
Less held indirectly by Company B	56,000
Shares held by "outsiders"	644,000

$$EPS = \frac{\$190,000}{644,000} = 29.5c$$

For a more extensive discussion on equity accounting for cross shareholdings readers are referred to Michael E Bradbury and Shirley C Calderwood, "Equity Accounting for Reciprocal Stockholdings", *The Accounting Review*, April 1988, pp 330–45.

Equity Supplementary Financial Statements

[1839] In Australia, the National Companies and Securities Commission has formed the view that consolidated accounts which incorporate equity accounting financial information by way of consolidation adjustment do not comply with the company legislation on the grounds that, by definition, a set of consolidated accounts must not include accounts other than those of the holding company and its subsidiaries (NCSC 600A, 340, Practice Note: "Companies Act and Codes, Equity Supplementary Financial Statements", June 1987). As a result, in Australia, the recommended practice to account for associated companies is by way of supplementary equity financial statements (AAS14, paras 51–3).

In New Zealand associated companies are normally accounted for in the consolidated accounts of company groups.

Some Problems of Analysis of Consolidated Financial Statements

[1840] As stated earlier, the purpose of consolidation is to produce financial statements which present the results and state of affairs of a company group as though it were a single enterprise. The need for such consolidated statements arises from the inability in many instances of the financial statements of the holding company to present an adequate view of the results and state of affairs of the group as a whole.

However, consolidation, while overcoming some of the problems of reporting for company groups, creates its own problems for the analysis and interpretation of financial statements. The following are some of these problems:

(a) Uniformity of accounting principles

[1841] The information value of consolidated financial statements will be enhanced if the financial statements of the individual companies in the group are prepared on the basis of uniform classification and uniform, and relevant accounting principles for the determiantion of profit and state of affairs. New Zealand Standard SSAP No 8 requires uniform accounting policies to be followed, where practical, by all companies in a group. There should be disclosure of any differences in accounting policies used and the extent to which they have been applied to assets and liabilities which have been included in a single classification in the consolidated balance sheet (para 4.63).

(b) Lack of detail regarding companies' performance

[1842] Another problem is the lack of detail regarding the performance and state of affairs of individual companies and company subgroups (divisions) within a company group. The reporting of the results and state of affairs of a group as a single enterprise may cover up poor performance and unfavourable financial position of some companies or divisions within the group. An analysis of the financial statements of a group, therefore, may need to be extended to incorporate an analysis of the results and state of affairs of individual member companies or divisions. Many company groups are involved in widely diverse areas of commercial activities. In such cases, the analysis of performance by segments may be necessary for evaluation and projections. Where the concern of the analyst and his principals is with a subsidiary company, it should be recognized that a subsidiary may fail even though the group appears to be solvent and profitable. Each company in a group is a separate legal entity. The need for and problems associated with segment reporting are discussed in Chapter 15.

(c) Overall cost determination and allocation

[1843] Problems of determining the overall cost to the acquiring company of the shares in the subsidiary, and of allocating total cost to specific assets under the purchase method may also arise. The assessment of cost when a controlling interest is acquired by an issue of shares leaves considerable room for judgment. The merger creates a new combined enterprise, so that past market prices per share may not be relevant to the share issue made to consummate the merger. A public issue would be made below market price so as to ensure that all would be taken up. How much below? Presumably issue costs should be deducted also. The alternative is to place a fair value on the enterprise as a going concern and that is a very subjective exercise.

Considerable room for judgment also exists when "total cost" is assigned to the individual assets of a subsidiary for the purposes of consolidation. There are serious problems where the purchase consideration, or the assessed value to the group of the business as a going concern, is significantly less than the sum of the book or other values of the separate assets, including specialized assets. In such circumstances a capital surplus on consolidation may well be regarded as unrealistic. There is a strong case for writing down the assets, particularly the specialized and sunk assets, and for making provision for the expected costs of the restructuring and rehabilitation of the enterprise. On the other hand, a matter of concern is the possible creation of secret reserves by the undervaluation of assets or overprovision for liabilites (such as redundancy pay), or estimated costs of rationalization. The result may be a distortion of the earnings of the group in the year of acquisition and the following year or years. Undervalued inventories may swell trading profits and understated fixed assets may produce future profits on realization of surplus land, buildings and equipment.

Current value of assets versus book value

[1844] Under the pooling of interests method group assets are consolidated at book value. This may lead to a material understatement of fixed assets and depreciation expense and to overstatement of profit and the rate of return. There is the possibility of "instant profits" on the sale of surplus fixed assets, and these may distort the profits of the following period or periods. It should be noted also that the purchase method of consolidation only partly overcomes the problem of asset valuation — revaluation of assets (with its inherent problems) is required only in regard to subsidiaries and only at the time of the takeover.

Review questions

18.1 Explain the nature of the following items which appear in a consolidated balance sheet, and indicate the section of the balance sheet in which each would appear:
  • goodwill on consolidation;
  • capital reserve;
  • provision for proposed dividend;
  • minority interest.

18.2 Write short notes on the following matters:
  (a) the problem of determining the purchase price to be recorded in the holding company's accounts for the shares in a subsidiary taken over by means of an exchange of shares — three $1 shares in the holding company for every four $1 shares of the subsidiary's capital of $500,000;
  (b) goodwill on consolidation and discount on consolidation as related to the valuation of the assets of the subsidiary company in question and of the shares given in exchange for the shares in the subsidiary company;
  (c) the recognition in the holding company and group accounts of:
    (i) dividends from pre-acquisition profits;
    (ii) losses incurred by a wholly owned subsidiary after acquisition;
    (iii) profits accumulated by a subsidiary after acquisition.

18.3 "The recording of the acquisition of controlling interest at cost should reflect the economic substance of the transaction."
Discuss.

18.4 Explain and contrast the purchase and pooling of interests methods of consolidation of financial statements.

18.5 Discuss some of the problems that may arise in determining goodwill or discount on consolidation. Once determined, how should these be accounted for?

18.6 "As a general rule, 20% of equity voting rights is regarded prima facie as representing substantial interest allowing significant influence to be exercised over the decisions of the investee."

Discuss the above guideline as a basis for classifying an investee company as an associated company.

18.7 "In the analysis and interpretation of financial statements it shoud be kept in mind that a significant difference exists between an associated company and a subsidiary company."

Discuss.

18.8 Holdings Ltd acquired 75% of the shares of Subsidiary Ltd some years ago at the cost of $100,000. At the time of the takeover the capital and reserves of Subsidiary Ltd were as follows:

Capital	80,000
General reserve	32,000
P & L appropriation a/c	8,480

The following are the balance sheets of Holdings Ltd and Subsidiary Ltd as at 31 December 19A8:

		Holdings Ltd $		Subsidiary Ltd $
Capital		300,000		80,000
Share premium a/c.		30,000		—
General reserve		85,000		41,500
P & L appropriation a/c.		21,350		10,520
		436,350		132,020
Sundry creditors		61,500		22,600
Prov for dividends		30,000		5,000
Prov for taxation		36,150		8,500
		564,000		168,120
Fixed assets (cost)	202,100		76,250	
Less prov for depn	41,550	160,550	11,600	64,650
Shares in S Ltd (cost)		100,000		—
Stocks		174,500		60,450
Debtors		120,050		41,020
Bank		8,900		2,000
		564,000		168,120

The stock of Holdings Ltd as at 31 December 19A8 included $10,000 of stock purchased from Subsidiary Ltd on which Subsidiary Ltd had made a profit of $4000.

You are required to show:

(a) the consolidation journal entries as at 31 December 19A8; and
(b) a work sheet showing the adjustments necessary to the assets and equities

313

of the two companies on consolidation as at 31 December 19A8.

18.9 Provide *brief* answers to the following unrelated cases of accounting for company groups:

(a) At balance date H Ltd and its 70% owned subsidiary S Ltd had the following provisions for dividend: H Ltd $30,000, S Ltd $20,000.

Required:

Illustrate by means of a journal entry (or entries) the adjustments (if any) which would be necessary in regard to the dividend provisions of the two companies in the consolidation of their accounts.

(b) An 80% owned subsidiary company declared $40,000 cash dividend from pre-acquisition profits.

Required:

Explain how the receipt of the dividend should be treated in the books of the holding company. Illustrate your answer with a journal entry.

(c) A Ltd acquired 80% of the ordinary shares of B Ltd in 19A5 for the consideration of 100,000 $1 shares issued at a premium of 25% and the payment of $45,000 in cash. At the time of the takeover the capital and reserves of B Ltd were as follows:

	$
Capital (ordinary shares)	100,000
Reserves	80,000

Required:

(i) Give the journal entry (or entries) necessary to record the consolidation adjustments in relation to the goodwill or discount on consolidation as at 30 September 19A8 when the capital and reserves of B Ltd stood as follows:

	$
Capital	100,000
Reserves	115,000

(ii) Give the journal entry (or entries) in the books of A Ltd which was necessary to record the takeover of B Ltd in 19A5. Cash transactions may be journalized.

(d) X Ltd acquired 75% interest in Y Ltd some years ago. At the time of the takeover the reserves of Y Ltd were as follows:

	$
General reserve	220,000
P & L appropriation a/c	70,000

Required:

Calculate the amount of reserves as they would appear in the consolidated balance sheet of X Ltd and Y Ltd as at 30 September 19A8 when the reserves of the two companies were as follows:

	X Ltd $	Y Ltd $
General reserve	450,000	310,000
P & L appropriation a/c	170,000	120,000

18.10 Millers Ltd, a private company, take over Retailers Ltd on 30 June 19A3. Millers Ltd acquire 80% of the share capital of Retailers Ltd for which they pay $60,000 in cash and issue 30,000 $1 shares. The value of these shares is estimated to be $2 per share.

At the date of acquisition the shareholders' funds section of Retailers Ltd balance sheet was as follows:

	$
Ordinary shares ($1 fully paid)	100,000
Share premium	15,000
General reserve	35,000
Profit and loss appropriation	20,000
	$170,000

At 31 December 19A3 the balance sheets of the two companies were as follows:

	Millers Ltd $	Retailers Ltd $
Ordinary shares ($1 fully paid)	230,000	100,000
Share premium	—	15,000
Property revaluation reserve	40,000	6,000
General reserve	12,500	37,500
Profit and loss appropriation	50,400	16,600
Shareholders' funds	332,900	175,100
Loan from Retailers Ltd	12,200	—
Current liabilities		
Provision for dividend	15,500	2,500
Creditors	53,400	23,100
Bank	—	3,000
Total shareholders' funds and liabilities	$414,000	$203,700
Fixed Assets (written down values)		
Land and buildings	145,700	135,900
Plant and machinery	56,800	27,400
	202,500	163,300
Investment in Retailers Ltd	116,000	—
Loan to Millers Ltd	—	12,200

Continued p 316

	Millers Ltd $	Retailers Ltd $
Current assets		
Inventories		
Dividends receivable		
Debtors		
Bank	95,500	28,200
Total assets	$414,000	$203,700

Additional information
(a) Between 30 June and 31 December 19A3 Retailers Ltd sold Millers Ltd $28,700 of goods with a 25% mark-up on cost. At 31 December 19A3 Millers Ltd hold $3000 of these goods in inventory and they owe Retailers Ltd $1950 in respect of these purchases.
(b) At 31 December 19A3 Retailers Ltd transferred $2500 from profit and loss account to general reserve.
(c) Immediately after acquisition Retailers Ltd paid a dividend of $5000.
(d) A property revaluation was conducted by Retailers Ltd at acquisition date.

Required:
(a) Show, *without* narration, the journal entries including cash transactions required, at date of acquisition, to record the events at that date.
(b) Show the consolidation worksheet as at 31 December 19A3.

18.11 On 30 June 19A2 Eastman Holdings Ltd purchased 48,750 ordinary $1 shares in Smithstone Plumbing Ltd. At 30 June 19A2 the shareholders' funds section of Smithstone Plumbing Ltd was as follows:

	$
Ordinary shares ($1 fully paid)	65,000
Share premium	11,240
General reserve	5,500
Profit and loss appropriation	6,760
	$88,500

The consideration for this purchase was satisfied by the issue of 16,250 ordinary Eastman Holdings Ltd shares and cash of $28,465.

Immediately on acquisition the properties of Smithstone Plumbing were revalued by $6260 in the books of Smithstone Plumbing Ltd. Also Smithstone Plumbing Ltd paid a dividend out of pre-acquisition profits of $6500.

The market value of Eastman Holdings Ltd shares at 30 June 19A2 was $3.30 each.

The balance sheets of the two companies as at 31 December 19A2 were:

	Eastman Holdings Ltd	Smithstone Plumbing Ltd
	$	$
Ordinary shares		
($1 fully paid)	110,000	65,000
Share premium	17,750	11,240
Property revaluation reserve	—	6,260
General reserve	5,400	5,500
Profit and loss appropriation	78,030	3,980
Shareholders' funds	211,180	91,980
Loan from Eastman Holding Ltd	—	7,500
Current liabilities		
Provision for dividend	11,000	720
Creditors	14,700	2,740
Bank	—	3,750
Total shareholders' funds		
and liabilities	$236,880	$106,690
Fixed Assets (written down		
values)		
Land and buildings	73,000	38,260
Plant and machinery	33,400	27,230
	106,400	65,490
Investment in Smithstone	77,215	—
Loan to Smithstone	7,500	—
Current assets		
Stock	20,410	12,570
Dividends receivable	540	—
Debtors	22,715	28,630
Bank	2,100	—
	$236,880	$106,690

Additional information obtained:
(a) During the period 1 July 19A2 to 31 December 19A2 Smithstone Plumbing Ltd sold to Eastman Holdings Ltd $23,100 of goods. At 31 December 19A2 Eastman Holdings Ltd had $5400 of these goods in stock. Smithstone Plumbing Ltd made a 25% mark-up on cost in respect of these.
(b) At 31 December 19A2 Eastman Holdings Ltd owe $2130 in respect of stock purchased from Smithstone Plumbing Ltd.

Required:
(i) Show, *without* narration, the journal entries including cash transactions required in Eastman Holdings Ltd's books and Smithstone Plumbing Ltd's books in respect of the above mentioned property revaluation and dividend out of pre-acquisition profits.

317

(ii) Show the consolidation worksheet in respect of this group as at 31 December 19A2.

18.12 On 1 July 19A1, H Ltd acquired an 80% interest in S Ltd for $10 million. At the time of acquisition the shareholders' equity of S Ltd comprised: paid up capital $6 million; profit and loss appropriation $4,800,000. Immediately after acquisition S Ltd paid a dividend of $400,000. On 1 July 19A2 S Ltd acquired a 60% interest in X Ltd for $3,400,000. The shareholders equity of X Ltd at the time of acquisition comprised: paid up capital $4 million; profit and loss appropriation $200,000.

The income statements of the three companies for the year ended 30 June 19A4 are as follows:

	H Ltd $000s	S Ltd $000s	X Ltd $000s
Sales	50,000	40,000	30,000
Cost of sales	43,000	37,000	27,000
Gross margin	7,000	3,000	3,000
Dividend income	640	240	—
	7,640	3,240	3,000
Sundry expenses	3,000	1,000	1,200
Net profit before tax	4,640	2,240	1,800
Tax (50%)	2,000	1,000	900
Net profit after tax	2,640	1,240	900
Profit and loss appropriation:			
brought forward	9,000	5,200	500
Total available for appropriation	11,640	6,440	1,400
Less dividends • interim paid	1,000	400	400
• final payable	1,000	400	—
Profit and loss appropriation carried forward	$9,640	$5,640	$1,000

Additional information:

(a) H Ltd purchased goods from S Ltd for $8 million.
(b) S Ltd purchased goods from X Ltd for $2 million.
(c) Unrealized profits in the stocks of H Ltd (purchased from S Ltd) at 1 July 19A3, $400,000; at 30 June 19A4 $800,000.
(d) Unrealized profits in the stocks of S Ltd were at 30 June 19A4, $400,000.

Required:

Prepare a consolidated income statement for H Ltd and its subsidiaries for the year ended 30 June 19A4. Show all workings.

Chapter 19
Financial Statements and Price Changes

[1901] The development of accounting standards and guidelines dealing with specific problem areas, and improvements in the presentation and disclosure of accounting information, have done a great deal to improve the overall standard of financial reporting. At the same time, changing prices and changes in the value of the monetary unit have severely limited the usefulness of financial statements prepared in the traditional manner from historical cost and realized revenue data. In fact, it has been claimed that these statements present misleading measures of profit, assets and owner's equity; and of trends over a series of accounting periods.

The development of modifications to traditional accounting to deal with the complexities introduced by material price changes has not yet reached the stage of general acceptance. This is not surprising because the problem concerns the central issue of accounting, the measurement of profit, and typically involves material changes in the profit disclosed, the measurement of assets and rates of return, and the level of subjectivity required in the measurement process. It is therefore important that those engaged in the analysis and interpretation of financial statements should be aware also of the nature, objectives and limitation of the main alternatives put forward for modification of the traditional historical cost based accounting model.

Profit Measurement and Capital Maintenance

[1902] The concept of profit is linked with the concept of capital maintenance — profit is seen as a surplus after providing for the maintenance of capital.

A major source of problems in financial accounting and reporting is the lack of agreement among accountants regarding the nature of business profit and the concept of capital maintenance which should underlie its measurement.

While there is currently a general acceptance of the view that, in times of high inflation, profit, as measured by traditional accounting methods and procedures, is subject to severe limitations as a fair portrayal of the operating results of business enterprises, there is a considerable divergence of opinion regarding how a more useful measurement of profit is to be achieved.

Before we move on to a more detailed discussion of the problems associated with the measurement of profit in times of significant prices changes, we shall take a closer look at the nature of accounting profit as implied by traditional accounting practice.

The Accounting "Model" for Profit Measurement

[1903] The following are the main characteristics of accounting profit:

(a) Accounting profit is measured in terms of money; no provision is made, however, for changes in the purchasing power of the monetary unit.

(b) The concept of capital maintenance implied is the maintenance of the shareholders' investment (subscribed capital and retained profit) in terms of the *number* of dollars involved regardless of their purchasing power.

(c) The basis of asset valuation and expense measurement is largely historical cost. Net realizable value is used in the valuation of debtors and in the case of inventories 'where net realizable value is estimated to be less than cost.

(d) Under the historical cost and realization conventions, gains are not recognized until realized by way of sale. There is an implicit linking of accounting profit with objectivity, through adherence to historical cost in asset measurement, and with distributability through the postponement of profit recognition until a sale has taken place. It should be noted, however, that the revaluation of fixed assets, in particular land and buildings, is an accepted practice both in Australia and New Zealand. Where depreciable assets have been written up, depreciation expense should be based on the written up value and a reassessment of economic life.

(e) The profit shown is dependent not only on actual transactions, which are objective in nature, but also on a set of judgments based on approximations of facts and forecasts of the future. These judgments are applied in the measurement of the cost of assets, the value of inventories, the depreciation expense of the period, provisions for bad debts and cash discounts, the extent of expensing of research and development costs, and other problem areas discussed earlier in this text.

(f) Profit is measured by matching expense with realized revenue. Revenue is measured in terms of the principles which define the accounting conception of realization, for example, on sale but prior to debt collection. There are a number of special cases in connection with the recognition of revenue, however. For example, in the case of major contracts some revenue (profit) may be recognized prior to completion; revenue from farm produce (conservatively estimated) is normally recognized when severed; revenue from the mining of precious metals, such as gold, is frequently recognized on production. The adoption of different policies in the assessment of debt balances under hire purchase and time payment contracts can have material effects on period income.

(g) To the extent that existing accounting practice offers alternatives for the measurement of revenue and expense, accounting measurement of profit requires the exercise of choice and judgment in the selection of accounting principles, methods and procedures for the measurement of profit and the disclosure of these principles, methods and procedures in published financial statements.

[1904] It should be apparent from the above descriptive "definition" of accounting profit that:

• to obtain an understanding of the significance of the profit figure disclosed by an enterprise, the analyst should be aware of the nature and limitations of the accounting profit and the procedures applied to its measurement;

• the amounts of profit reported by different firms may not be comparable because different accounting policies and procedures may have been used;

• the data of a series of periods may not be comparable because of the policies applied in profit measurement, and of changes in these policies and their application over time;

• accounting profit measured in the traditional way is seldom if ever fully objective, and indeed the whole concept of an historical cost based system of asset and profit measurement involves a set of implicit judgments regarding the function of accounting measurement and the reporting of assets and profit.

The last point is of considerable importance in an era of significant price and price level changes which has led to a questioning of the continued adequacy and even usefulness of traditional historical cost-based accounting. The analyst needs an understanding of the nature of these criticisms, and a broad appreciation of alternative proposals which have been advanced in order to meet them.

The Problem of Accounting for Price Changes

[1905] There are two aspects to the problem of accounting for price changes:
  (a) accounting for changes in the general level of prices (these affect the purchasing power of money); and
  (b) accounting for changes in the prices of the specific commodities which a firm holds and deals in.

We shall examine these in turn.

The nature and effect of general price level changes

[1906] The term "changes in the general level of prices" refers to the *trend* in the movement of the prices of commodities and services over time. For example, if we plot the prices of different commodities over time we will notice that the prices of some commodities have tended to increase, the prices of other commodities have tended to fluctuate, while the prices of still other commodities have remained relatively stable or have shown a falling trend. In studying these changes in prices, we will also discern an overall trend — we can say that, over a period of time, prices *in general*, or, *on the average*, have been rising, or falling, or tended to remain stable.

When the general level of prices is rising, we say that we are having a period of *inflation*; when the general level of prices is falling, we say that we are having a period of *deflation*.

Price level changes affect the purchasing power of money. As prices, on the average, increase, we can buy, on the average, less with a given number of monetary units (that is, dollars).

Let us take an example, If the index used to measure the general price level increases from, say 124 at the beginning of a given period to 136 at the end of the period, the rate of inflation will be 9.7% (that is, $\frac{136 - 124}{124}$). The change in the general purchasing power of the monetary unit will then be given by the ratio $\frac{124}{136} = 0.912$, which means that at the end of the period the purchasing power of \$1, as measured by the index, is equivalent to the purchasing power of \$0.912 at the beginning of the period. This represents a fall in purchasing power of 8.8% (that is, $\frac{1 - 0.912}{1}$).

[1907] Accounting uses the monetary unit, the dollar, as a basis of measurement — a common denominator under which accounting transactions are expressed, recorded, analyzed and ultimately interrelated in financial statements such as the profit and loss statement and the balance sheet. However, since the economic significance of the dollar (its size) is represented by its purchasing power, and since the dollar has no stable purchasing power, traditional accounting may be criticized on the grounds that, in times of general price level changes, it involves the recording, classification and interrelation of accounting transactions in dollars of different sizes, dollars which are not comparable and are, therefore, not properly additive. Preparing financial statements on this basis, therefore, can be said to be as illogical as preparing statements on the basis of a mixture of, say, New Zealand, American and Hong Kong dollars.

Accounting for specific price changes (accounting for current value)

[1908] The accounting conventions of historical cost and realization require assets to be recorded and valued at original cost, gains being recognized on realization by way of sale. On the other hand, accounting conservatism requiries the recognition of losses due to a fall in prices, as soon as such losses become apparent. As a result, in times of significant price rises, assets may be carried in the books of a firm and reported in its balance sheet at amounts far below what may be termed their current value. In addition, in times of rising prices, the measurement of expenses (such as the cost of sales and depreciation) on the basis of historical cost may well be regarded as leading to an overstatement of profits by the difference between the historical cost and the current value measures of these expenses. It may be argued that to the extent of this difference the accounting profit shown is not distributable by an ongoing business which has to replace what it sells or uses at current prices. Such overstated profit when related to undervalued assets will produce an overstated rate of return which may mislead the readers of financial statements regarding the profitability of a business enterprise. A growing appreciation of these shortcomings of established accounting practice has led to attempts to develop methods of accounting for profit and state of affairs in terms of "current value".

[1909] "Current value", however, is a concept which is easier to state than to define and easier to define than to apply in practice.

For example, the current value of assets may be measured in terms of their net realizable value or their current replacement cost. In the case of many assets such as specialized plant and buildings, there may be a significant difference between the two figures. The choice between replacement cost and net realizable value as the relevant measure of the current economic value of the asset may have a material effect on the state of affairs shown in the balance sheet of the enterprise. Indeed the difference for an enterprise in an uncertain financial position may be of crucial importance. In order to deal with the problem, the notion of "value to the owner" has been developed and has achieved a considerable level of acceptance.

Value to the owner (business)

[1910] The value of an asset to business operations depends on its expected use, since it is expected use which determines whether a firm will acquire an asset, or retain or dispose of an asset it already owns. This value may be formally quantified in terms of the present value of the net receipts expected to arise from the asset's use. Present value, however, is too subjective to provide a basis for accounting measurement. Accounting measures of current value, therefore, will have to be sought in current market prices. However, to the extent that current market buying and selling prices for the same asset differ, a choice would have to be made between the current buying price and the current (net) selling price as the appropriate measure of current value.

The notion of value to the owner aims to provide a basis for such a choice (see for example D Solomons, "Economic and Accounting Concepts of Cost and Value", in Morton Backer's *Modern Accounting Theory*, Prentice-Hall Inc, 1966).

In the business context any rational decision regarding the buying, holding or of selling an asset must be closely related to the expected use of the asset. Put more formally, such a decision should be based on the present value of the future net receipts expected to arise from the ownership and use of the asset.

For replacement cost to represent a measure of economic value to a firm, the present value of the net receipts associated with the assets ownership and use must equal or exceed the asset's replacement cost (ie $PV > RC$). When this condition holds, the use of replacement cost in asset valuation can be justified on the basis of "deprival value" — replacement cost represents the maximum amount which would be necessary to restore the firm to its original position if it were deprived of the asset.

[1911] If we take replacement cost to represent the *upper limit* of market price based value of an asset to a firm, net realizable value should be taken to represent the *lower limit* on the grounds that the value of an asset to a firm cannot be less than the net amount which can be realized by selling the asset.

The range of values between replacement cost and net realizable value as representing respectively the upper and lower limits of current value has been referred to as "value in use" or "recoverable amount".

In the above context, the notion of value to the owner as a basis for arriving at the "current value" of assets may be illustrated as follows:

$$
\begin{aligned}
\text{RC} \quad &= \text{upper limit of current value} \\
\updownarrow &= \text{value in use (recoverable amount)} \\
\text{NRV} \quad &= \text{lower limit of current value}
\end{aligned}
$$

In the above scheme, the current value assigned to an asset should not exceed its current replacement cost or be less than its net realizable value. Assets should be assigned "value in use" where

$$PV > NRV \text{ but}$$
$$RC > PV$$

or, to combine the two expressions, where

$$RC > PV > NRV$$

[1912] An illustration of the application of the notion of value to the owner in practice is found in the financial statements of Fletcher Challenge Limited. For example, the 1987 report of the company disclosed the following policy regarding the valuation of special purpose land and buildings:

Special Purpose Land and Buildings, except for those in North America which are valued at historical cost, are valued at the lesser of:

(a) estimated replacement value less allowance for wear and tear and technological obsolescence; or

(b) the value at which reasonable earnings can be achieved or net realisable value, whichever is the greater.

The range of "value in use" implied in the above policy of Fletcher Challenge Limited is the same as defined earlier and falls between replacement cost and net realizable value as respectively the upper and lower limits of current value.

It should be evident from the above discussion that the notion of value to the owner provides a wide range of "current values" which may be assigned to an asset. This is especially true in the case of specialized fixed assets, where replacement cost may be very high, net realizable value very low, giving a wide range of values which fall within the notion of "value in use". As "value in use" is essentially the present value of an asset (eg in the case of Fletcher Challenge the "value at which reasonable earnings can be achieved"), valuation on the basis of value in use will be a highly subjective exercise.

[1913] The subjectivity and some problems involved in the application of value to the owner approach to asset valuation have been demonstrated in New Zealand in a somewhat vivid way. In its restructuring of the New Zealand economy in the 1980s the government converted a number of government departments into state-owned corporations which were expected to operate on a profitable commercial basis. One of these enterprises, Electricity Corporation Ltd (Electricorp) had protracted negotiations with the New Zealand Government over the value to be placed on the assets previously held by a government department (Electricity Department). At the time, the marginal cost of supply was materially in excess of the market price and the position was one of oversupply. In such circumstances replacement cost would not be appropriate as a basis of asset valuation and "value in use" should be applied. It was here that the views of the parties diverged with Treasury arguing for asset value double that calculated by Electricorp. Presumably the differences were in the calculation of future net cash flows and in the discount rate applied to these. Treasury had assumed a progressive increase in real selling prices (above the rate of inflation) to a figure closer to marginal cost. One could surmise that, given over-supply, the position of Electricorp was that it may not be realistic or necessary in the public interest to increase real prices to equate marginal cost and selling price at least in the short to medium term. It is also likely that the position taken by Electricorp was motivated in part at least by political considerations, for example, public reaction to major price increases given the corporation's monopoly position in the supply of electricity. It is clear that objective resolution of such differences would be extremely difficult, to say the least.

[1914] It should be noted that, under the concept of value to the owner, even when the actual values assigned to assets reflect current market prices or some derivative of current market prices (RC or NRV) the choice of valuation base depends on the *expected* use of the assets. This subjectivity in asset valuation is present in traditional accounting, where the carrying forward of historical costs and historical cost residuals is justified on the basis of benefits expected to be derived in the future. It cannot be avoided in any relevant accounting for price changes for the reason that operating assets are acquired and held by firms for future use.

The concept of value to the owner as a basis for choosing among alternatives in asset valuation has not been free of criticism. Value to the owner, based on deprival value, has been developed from the work of Bonbright on the valuation of properties in litigation for indemnity in case of actual loss: J C Bonbright, *The Valuation of Property*, New York, 1937. Chambers has argued that the concept of value to the owner lacks clear guidance on asset valuation for balance sheet and related purposes. As, in accounting, we are concerned with the valuation of property which owners possess and do not expected to lose, the valuation of assets reflecting deprival value has little relevance to the valuation problem in accounting: R J Chambers, "Value to the Owner", *Abacus*, June, 1971, pp 62–72.

[1915] In this chapter we shall define an approach to the use of replacement cost as a measure of the value of assets to the owner which moves away from the notion of deprival value. It will be pointed out that for replacement cost to represent a market price based measure of economic value, the replacement of the asset must be an economically feasible investment alternative at the time of valuation: B Popoff, "The Informational Value of Replacement Cost Accounting for External Company Reports", *Accounting and Business Research*, Winter, 1974, pp 61–70, and B Popoff, "Replacement Cost and Asset Measurement: The Interpretability of Current Value Aggregates", *Working Paper Series No 38*, School of Accountancy, University of New South Wales, October 1983.

[1916] The question of the economic value of an asset to the owner will be discussed on the basis of the following two criteria:

(a) the condition for holding an asset, and

(b) the condition for replacement cost to represent a measure of the economic value of an asset to the owner.

The condition for holding an asset

[1917] The condition for holding an asset is that the present value (PV) of holding the asset is higher than its net realizable value:

$$PV > NRV$$

If NRV is higher than PV, the firm will sell the asset regardless of its replacement cost (RC). For example, if

$$NRV > PV > RC$$

the firm will sell the asset and replacement will be one of the investment alternatives available to the firm for the proceeds. If

$$RC > NRV > PV$$

the firm can sell the asset but, under these circumstances, replacement cannot normally be contemplated.

It should be noted that in the above examples PV means the present value of *holding* the asset. Otherwise the expression NRV > PV will be contradictory in the sense that present value cannot be less than net realizable value. This is so because, to the extent to which NRV represents a notional receipt now associated with the disposal of the asset, PV cannot be less than NRV.

The condition for replacement cost to represent a measure of the economic value of asset to an owner

[1918] The condition is that

$$PV > RC$$

In other words, in the context of business operations, RC cannot be regarded as representing economic value if the replacement of the asset cannot be considered to be an economically feasible investment opportunity open to the firm, given current expectations.

It should be noted, however,that even when the condition $PV > RC$ holds, it does not necessarily mean that the asset will be replaced. Whether actual replacement takes place would depend on the array of investment opportunities open to the firm at the time replacement is considered. What the condition $PV > RC$ does stress, however, is that RC cannot be taken to represent a relevant measure of economic value if the replacement is not an economically feasible proposition.

Accounting for General Price Level Changes

[1919] The defect of traditional accounting, that it uses a measuring unit of unstable purchasing power, can be remedied by restating the financial statements in dollars of comparable purchasing power, using for the purpose an appropriate general price level index.

A number of advantages are claimed for this common dollar, or current purchasing power (CPP) accounting:

(a) It does not require a change in existing accounting procedures; for example, it can be applied as an end-of-period restatement of the figures produced by the existing accounting system of a firm.

(b) It does not add to the subjectivity of existing accounting measurement since the accounting procedures need not be affected, and the price level adjustment itself can be objectively applied on the basis of an externally prepared index.

(c) Price level adjustments are relatively easy to apply in practice and are verifiable by the auditor.

[1920] The concept of capital maintenance which underlies the general price level adjustment is the maintenance of the general purchasing power of the shareholders' investment in the firm.

A general price level adjustment also measures purchasing power gains and losses on monetary accounts. The amount of a monetary account is fixed by contract or otherwise in terms of a set number of dollars regardless of changes in the purchasing power of money. Examples of monetary accounts are assets such as cash, bank deposits, accounts and notes receivable, mortgages receivable and other similar items; and liabilities such as bank overdraft, accounts payable, mortgages and debentures payable. In times of inflation a firm suffers purchasing power losses on its monetary assets and makes purchasing power gains on monetary liabilities. As a result, in times of inflation, there is a powerful incentive for firms to utilize borrowed funds in the financing of their operations. Let us take a simple case of a farmer who purchases the neighbour's farm property for $300,000, borrowing $250,000 on mortgage at an average rate of 16%. His interest expense of the year is

$40,000, and he is able to deduct this from his farm revenue for income tax purposes, saving (say) $20,000 in tax as a result. If inflation for the year was 12%, then his mortgagee has suffered a loss during the year of 12% of $250,000 = $30,000, and this loss is non-deductible to the mortgagee but represents a gain to the mortgagor, who has profited through the debt contract alone to the extent of $30,000 − $20,000 net interest = $10,000. It may be argued that the purchaser's profit or loss is dependent on changes in the value of the farm property acquired. This argument disregards the fact that we have to account for the results of two decisions — a purchase decision and a financing decision.

Price level adjustments and the index problem

[1921] A problem associated with price level accounting is the measurement of changes in the general level of prices. The best available method for measuring changes in the general level of prices is by means of index numbers.

Ideally, a general price level index should incorporate changes in the prices of all commodities and services. For reasons of practicality, however, changes in the general level of prices are measured on the basis of the average change in the prices of a sample of commodities and services selected and weighted in order to fairly represent the movement of prices in general.

One of the best known measures of general price level changes is the consumer price index. It is calculated on the basis of a selected number of consumer commodities which are assumed to represent the spending pattern of a "typical" consumer, with weights assigned to the various commodities to reflect their relative importance to consumer spending. It may be argued, however, that the consumer price index is "specialized" in the sense that it deals with commodity prices from a consumer point of view and that therefore, it is of limited relevance when considering the effects of general price level changes on particular business enterprises.

The question regarding the kind of index to use in accounting for the effects of general price level changes on the operations of business enterprises is beyond the scope of this book. However, the folowing arguments can be put forward in favour of using a price level index based on consumer prices:

• consumer prices reflect what most people understand as the purchasing power of money — the consumer price index, therefore, is a generally accepted measure of what people have in mind when they speak of changes in the value of the monetary unit;

• from an investor's point of view the sacrifice of consumer purchasing power measures the cost of investment in business operations against which should be related the consumer purchasing power of the return;

• command over consumer goods and services is the context in which the wealth of people is conceived.

For a further discussion of the problems associated with the preparation of a general price level index readers are referred to Cecilia Tierney, "The Index Number Problem", Appendix A, *Accounting Research Study No 6*, "Reporting the Effects of Price-Level Changes", AICPA, New York, 1963, pp 61–117. For a discussion on the consumer price index as a basis for restating financial statements for changes in the purchasing power of money, readers are referred to R C Jones, "Effects of Price-level Changes on Business Income, Capital and Taxes", *American Accounting Association*, 1956, pp 179–81.

Some limitations of the general price level adjustment

[1922] The practicality and convenience of the price level adjustment led to considerable interest on the part of the accounting profession in price level adjusted accounts. It was soon realized, however, that, taken on its own, the price level adjustment fell far short of producing financial statements which portrayed in current terms the results of operations and state of affairs of business enterprises in times of significant price changes.

Current purchasing power accounting still has its advocates; but a strong body of opinion has developed which holds that realism in accounting requires profit measurement and asset valuation in terms of current costs and values. To reflect current costs and values in financial statements, it is necessary to consider, among other things, the current prices of the commodities a firm holds and deals in.

Some writers have argued that changes in the general level of prices are irrelevant in accounting for the operations of business firms which deal in a limited number of specific commodities, see for example R S Gynther, "Why Use General Purchasing Power?", *Accounting and Business Research*, Spring 1974, pp 141–57. On the other hand, business operations are initiated and maintained through investment of money on the basis of expected return on monetary outlays. Since investment is an economic activity and the economic value of money is general purchasing power, it is difficult to envisage a realistic system of accounting for the results of business operations which did not take into account changes in the purchasing power of money from the viewpoint of accounting measurement in general and return on investment in particular.

[1923] The need to reflect current values in accounting even when historical costs are restated for changes in the purchasing power of money will be illustrated with a simple example.

Example 19.1

A firm acquired adjacent land some years ago for $30,000 which it has been using as a parking site. Since then the general price level has doubled.
Consider the problem regarding the figure at which the land should be reported in the financial statements of the firm if its current value is, alternatively:
(a) $50,000; and
(b) $90,000.

Under current purchasing power accounting, if the price level adjusted cost of the asset exceeds its current value, then the asset is to be shown at current value ($50,000 in case (a)); but if the current value of the asset is higher than the adjusted cost, the asset is to be shown at adjusted cost ($60,000 in case (b)). Under current purchasing power acounting, therefore, "real" (though unrealized) gains on assets will not be reported in the financial statements of firms ($30,000 in case (b)).

The interpretative uses of a general price level adjustment

[1924] The general price level adjustment removes one of the two distortions in accounting measurement caused by price changes. It enables the measurement of the capital investment in a business enterprise in terms of current purchasing power and is, therefore, an important first step in the maintenance of the purchasing power of this investment as a precondition for the recognition of profit.

Further, a price level adjustment allows an assessment to be made of purchasing power gains and losses on monetary accounts. In times of inflation, an appreciation of these gains and losses is important for the evaluation of the performance of a business enterprise and the manner in which its management has handled the inflation factor in financing business operations. Related to this is the recognition of the true cost of debt finance. In times of inflation, the market interest rate includes some allowance for the expected reduction in the purchasing power of the principal of the debt. It is important to recognize that the real cost of servicing debt is not the interest charge, shown in traditional accounting as an expense to its full amount, but rather the difference between the after tax interest expense and the inflation rate of the period; and this may yield a greatly reduced and even negative true servicing cost for the debt.

[1925] Common dollar presentation is useful in the comparison of data covering a series of years. Unadjusted financial data in trend statements are not without value in making monetary projections, but may be quite misleading in the assessment of real changes in such items as income and sales.

Accounting for Specific Price Changes (Current Value Accounting)

[1926] As stated earlier in this chapter, accounting measures of current value would need to be sought largely in current market prices.

There has been a considerable debate regarding whether market selling prices (realizable value) or market buying prices (replacement cost) should be the basis for accounting in terms of current value, and whether such current value accounting should also incorporate a recognition of general price level changes. Two Australian names have featured large in the debate — Profesor R J Chambers with his proposal for accounting in terms of the net realizable value of assets and Professor R S Gynther with his proposal for replacement cost accounting based on the maintenance of the operating capacity of the firm. Both views have recceived support and have been subjected to criticism.

The rather rigid position adopted by Chambers and Gynther on the question of accounting for price changes and their determined defence of their views have stimulated considerable debate and have contributed greatly to understanding the nature of price changes, and the nature of the problems that price changes create in accounting for the operating results and state of affairs of business enterprises.

We shall examine briefly the Chambers and Gynther proposals.

Continuously contemporary accounting (CoCoA)

[1927] Professor Chambers' proposal for accounting for price changes which he calls continuously contemporary accounting (CoCoA) is based on net realizable value as a single measurement concept for all assets. The proposal has been expounded in Professor Chambers' numerous publications; for a concise summary readers are referred to "Accounting for Inflation", Exposure Draft published by

Chambers, Department of Accounting, The University of Sydney, 1975.

The CoCoA proposal is based on the argument that only like magnitudes may be properly added, subtracted, or related. Since only current prices are relevant to current decisions, the chocie is one of accounting in terms of selling price (current cash equivalent) or buying price (current replacement cost). Chambers argues that by valuing assets at their net realizable value, one arrives at a "dated financial position" in terms of ability to buy goods, pay debts, secure loans, or make other changes.

[1928] The capital maintenance concept embodied in the CoCoA model is the maintenance of the general purchasing power of the shareholders' equity — the shareholders' equity and changes in it being measured in terms of the net realizable value of the firm's assets. For example, in the absence of changes in the general level of prices, profit for a period under CoCoA will be represented by the increase in net assets after adjusting for any contributions to capital or dividend payments during the period. If there have been changes in the general level of prices, such as inflation, provision is made to maintain the general purchasing power of the net assets at the beginning of the period by restating them in end-of-period dollars and recognizing as profit the increment to net assets over and above that value.

The CoCoA model for profit measurement will produce valid results where business operations involve the acquisition of assets such as company shares, bonds, or property held for the purpose of earning income through an increase in the realizable market value of the assets. This is so because the objective of the business undertaking is to earn income through changes in the realizable value of assets and the model measures income on the basis of the realizable value of assets. Further, the net realizable value of assets represents a measure of the ability of the firm to provide security for loans and the amount of funds available for payment of trade creditors, dividends, and loans, for redeployment within the firm, and, in a potential liquidation, the surplus available to shareholders.

There are several typical business situations, however, where the CoCoA system may be held to fail to provide relevant information. A typical example is where assets are acquired for the purpose of producing goods and services and the earning of income by the sale of these goods and services at a price above cost. In such cases, the evaluation of the ongoing operations of a firm may be held to require the assessment of results in terms of current costs and prices. Further, while such firms may borrow on the security provided by the realizable value of their assets, repayment of loans in the normal course of business is from cash flows generated by operations, or from refinancing of loans, or from further subscriptions to capital, rather than from the realization of the firm's assets, including assets needed for the continuation of the firm's operations.

Replacement cost accounting

[1929] If we place the CoCoA system of Professor Chambers at one end of the range of proposals for accounting for price changes, we should place at the other end of the range the proposal of Professor Gynther for replacement cost accounting based on the maintenance of the operating capacity of the firm: R S Gynther, *Accounting for Price-level Changes: Theory and Procedures*, Pergamon Press Ltd, Oxford, 1966.

Central to Gynther's system is the use of replacement cost in the calculation of what we shall call "current operating profit" — sales less current replacement cost of sales. Gynther has argued that current operating profit is the maximum amount a firm can distribute and still be able to maintain its operating capacity. In this context "operating capacity" is conceived in physical terms — in terms of inventory levels and output capacity of production facilities. Holding gains or losses (differences between the historical cost and current replacement cost of assets) are treated as restatements of capital rather than as adjustments to profit.

[1930] As we shall see later, the calculation of operating profit on the basis of current replacement cost can be of great value in the analysis and evaluation of operating results in times of significant price changes. As a system of accounting for capital and profit, however, replacement cost accounting in the narrow context suggested by Gynther has been the subject of considerable controversy and criticism (for a more deailed discussion of Gynther's proposal, readers are referred to B Popoff, "Holding Gains as Components of Business Income", *The Australian Accountant*, November 1977, pp 611–19). The following are some specific points of criticism:

(a) Replacement cost accounting is based on costs which are specific to the firm. As such it does not account for inflation in the context in which the term is usually understood. As a result, replacement cost accounting will report the same amount of profit regardless of the level of inflation.

(b) Purchasing power gains and losses on monetary accounts are ignored.

(c) Replacement cost accounting concentrates on the assets side of the balance sheet and pays only cursory attention to the equities side which reflects the financing of the firm's assets. As a consequence we have the disputable claim that, from the viewpoint of the firm, there is no difference between equity finance and long-term borrowing.

(d) The contention that current operating profit is the maximum amount which can be distributed if the firm is to maintain its operating capacity can also be disputed. For example, in times of rising prices, a firm may, by judicious use of borrowing, distribute more than its replacement cost profit and still maintain both its operating capacity and what it considers to be a "sound" financial structure in terms of a satisfactory equity/debt ratio.

(e) Increases in the current cost of assets required for the continuing operations of the firm increase the economic value of the assets and, therefore, the value of the economic resources under the firm's control. To report such increases as capital adjustments would tend to conceal accretions to the wealth of the firm and may be criticized on the grounds that it does not amount to fair reporting.

(f) Replacement cost accounting is based on a concept of capital concerned with maintaining physical operating capacity, yet the maintenance of physical operating capacity as such cannot be taken to be objective of a business firm.

(g) There may be an unacceptable degree of subjectivity involved in the measurement of replacement cost, where continuity is uncertain, where normal capacity has to be defined, and where there are significant changes in technology, products, markets and competition.

Financial Analysis and Price Changes

[1931] The problem of accounting for price changes has yet to be resolved in a generally acceptable manner. In this chapter so far we have discussed some of the major issues involved as a preliminary to illustrating some of the effects of price changes on the operations of business enterprises and the need to take price changes into account in the analysis and interpretation of financial statements.

The discussion which follows is based on some very simple numerical examples. The simplicity of the examples is intended to highlight the issues being discussed. The issues themselves are relatively straightforward, but the moves towards an accounting remedy are hampered by a failure to appreciate the seriousness of the problems, a natural opposition to major changes in the basis of accounting, vested inverests in the status quo, a lack of agreement on basic issues such as the concepts of capital and income to be applied in accounting, and the complexity and added subjectivity introduced by a move from traditional accounting to accounting in terms of current costs and values.

[1932] Without general agreement on the concept of capital which should underlie the measurement of profit, we lack clearly defined and generally accepted criteria on the basis of which to evaluate the shortcomings of existing accounting practice and the advantages of proposed alternatives.

In such circumstances, it is important that the analyst and interpreter of accounting statements have a proper appreciation of the extent to which existing accounting practice may be regarded as failing to make good business sense under conditions of material price and price level changes.

[1933] For the sake of simplicity, in the examples which follow operations are assumed to involve trading in only one commodity. It is further assumed that the business firm does not have fixed assets and that the only expense it incurs is the cost of goods sold. The examples can be extended to cover fixed assets and a range of expenses. Such expansion of the examples, however, will not invalidate the conclusions reached.

It should be noted, however, that when the replacement cost of fixed assets is considered, the concern is not with the current cost of identical assets, but with the replacement cost of the business utility of assets in terms of assets currently available. For example, in the case of business premises the concern is with the current cost of obtaining equivalent facilities in terms of operational floor space; in regards to plant the concern is with the current cost of obtaining equivalent production capacity in terms of plant current available, etc.

The evaluation of operating results in times of stable prices

Example 19.2

A firm has capital of $100,000 invested in 10,000 units of trading inventory which was acquired at the cost of $10 per unit. The inventory is sold at a 40% mark up on cost or $14 per unit. The firm is taxed at the rate of 50% of historical cost profit.
In what sense can we say that the historical cost profit of this firm is "real" if there has been no change in the current replacement cost of the inventory sold and the general level of prices has remained stable?

[1934] Shown below are the balance sheet of the firm prior to the sale of inventory, a profit and loss satement showing the result of the sale, and a balance sheet immediately after the sale but before replacement of the inventory sold.

Balance sheet
(Prior to sale)

	$		$
Capital	100,000	Inventory (10,000 units)	100,000

Profit and loss statement

	$
Sales (10,000 units @ $14)	140,000
Less cost of sales (10,000 units @ $10)	100,000
Profit before tax	40,000
Less tax (50%)	20,000
Profit after tax	20,000

Balance sheet
(After sale)

	$		$
Capital	100,000	Debtors/Cash	140,000
Retained profit	20,000		
Shareholders' funds	120,000		
Provision for taxation	20,000		
	140,000		140,000

In Example 19.2 the profit after tax of $20,000 is "real" in the sense that the firm began with an investment of $100,000 and ended, (after the payment of taxation) with resources of $120,000. As we have assumed a stable general level of prices, the profit represents an increase in the purchasing power under the control of the firm. Further, if the firm decides to continue in the same line of business, it can replace the inventory sold for $100,000 (maintain its level of operations) and be left with a surplus of $20,000. The profit of $20,000, therefore, has a "tangible" reality in that the firm began with 10,000 units of inventory and after the sale and replacement it ended up with 10,000 units of inventory plus $20,000 in cash which it can use to expand the level of operations (increase the level of inventory) or to pay dividends, or a combination of both.

The effect of an increase in replacement cost

Example 19.3

Following Example 19.2, re-examine the results of operations assuming that there was a 20% increase in the replacement cost of the inventory between the time the inventory was acquired and sold. Assume again a stable general level of prices.

[1935] In Example 19.3 the historical cost profit will be $20,000 as calculated in

Example 19.2. The operating results, however, can be evaluated in terms of replacement cost as follows:

	$
Sales	140,000
Less replacement cost of sales (10,000 units @ $12)	120,000
"Profit" before tax	20,000
Less tax*	20,000
"Profit" after tax	NIL

*As current tax regulations do not allow an increase in replacement cost as a tax deduction, tax will be assessed on the historical cost profit of $40,000 as in Example 19.2.

In Example 19.3 some doubt could be thrown on the reality of the tax-paid profit of $20,000 calculated under the historical cost method. After the firm pays its tax and replaces the inventories sold it is left with no surplus to pay dividend or to expand its operations. For example, if the firm wanted to pay a dividend it would have to borrow the money to do so.

In Example 19.3 the firm was assumed to have sold its inventory at the old price of $14 per unit even though the replacement cost had increased to $12 per unit. This is what firms seem to be expected to do by society in times of price rises — ie to sell old stock at old prices so that there is no profiteering at the expense of consumers. Let us assume, however, that the firm was not under price control and its management was not motivated by lofty ideals such as fairness to consumers, so that the firm increased the unit selling price to $16.80 (that is 40% mark-up on the replacement cost of $12 per unit) as soon as replacement cost increased. Let us also assume that the firm's competitors acted in the same way, and that the total market for the product was not affected by the price increase.

Example 19.4

Following Example 19.3, evaluate the operating results if the firm sold its inventory at $16.80 (40% mark-up on replacement cost).

The operating results in Example 19.4 may be calculated in terms of historical cost and replacement cost as follows:

	Historical cost $	Replacement cost $
Sales	168,000	168,000
Less cost of sales	100,000	120,000
Profit before tax	68,000	48,000
Less tax	34,000	34,000
Profit after tax	34,000	14,000

In Example 19.4 the firm will report a "record" profit of $34,000 which is 70% higher than the $20,000 profit it would have reported if prices had not increased (see Example 19.2). Yet, after paying its tax and replacing the inventory sold, the company would be left with a cash surplus of $14,000 which is $6,000 or 30% less than the surplus which would have resulted if prices had not increased.

[1936] Example 19.4 illustrates much of what happens to business firms in times of rising prices. While reported profits are at record levels, businesses are faced with liquidity problems and shortage of funds for maintaining or expanding the level of their operations. In fact the consequences of price rises for the financing of business operations will be worse than indicated in the above example. An increase in selling prices will require the financing of an increase in the level of debtors; for example, a 20% increase in selling price would result in a 20% increase in the level of debtors, given no change in the physical level of sales and in credit policies. In the long run, firms will also be faced with the need to replace fixed assets at prices which may be very much higher than their historical cost.

[1937] The relative difference between historic cost based depreciation and the average investment required each year to maintain the operating capability of the firm is likely to be material because the price changes which are relevant have been compounded over the average age of the fixed assets concerned. For example, if the average age of a class of plant items is 7½ years and the replacement cost has risen on average 10% each year, then the depreciation expense (straight line) calculated on an historic cost basis will be just below half of the outlay required to replace the productive capacity used up during the period.

The nature of "holding gains"

[1938] The difference between the historical cost and the higher replacement cost of assets is called a "holding gain". In the absence of price constraints, holdings gains on assets required for the continuing operations of the firm may be regarded as being in the nature of "profit" in the sense of "cost savings" — in the sense that the firm acquired the asset at a lower cost (monetary outlay) than would be incurred if the asset were to be acquired now. Following the last example:

	$
Replacement cost of inventories	120,000
Historical cost of inventories	100,000
Holding gain (cost saving)	20,000

As for tax purposes deductions are allowed only at historical cost, the above holding gain of $20,000 is not taxpaid. At 50% tax rate, the tax paid holding gain would be $10,000 (that is $20,000 less tax on realization of $10,000).

[1939] In the examples so far we have assumed a stable general price level. If general price level changes are assumed, it will be necessary to adjust historical costs for changes in the purchasing power of money before making comparisons. If in the last example we assume inflation of 10% since the acquisition of the inventory, the assessment of the holding gain will be as follows:

	$	$
Replacement cost of inventory		120,000
Historical cost of inventory	100,000	
Purchasing power adjustment 10%	10,000	110,000
"Real" holding gain before tax		10,000
Less tax		10,000*
"Real" holding gain after tax		NIL

*50% of $20,000 as current tax rules do not recognize the effects of price level changes.

Reflecting the combined effects of general and specific price changes, holdings gains treated as accretions to profit

Example 19.5

Following Example 16.4, assume that in addition to the 20% increase in the replacement cost of inventories, there was an increase of 10% in the general level of prices.
Prepare a profit and loss statement and balance sheet which incorporate the effects of the increase in the replacement cost of the inventory and the general level of prices, and treating the holding gain on inventories as an accretion to profit.

[1940] The effect of the increase in the general level of prices can be accounted for by charging the profit and loss statement with the amount necessary to maintain the purchasing power of the shareholders' investment at the beginning of the period (10% of $100,000).

Assuming that the specific price changes are recognized in the books of the firm as they occur and general price level changes are adjusted for at the end of a period, the journal entries to record the effects would be as follows:

(a) to record the increase in the replacement cost of inventories at the time the increase occurs:

    Inventory $20,000
        Inventory revaluation account $20,000;

(b) the inventory revaluation account is a revenue account; it represents the holding gain on inventories and at the end of the period will be transferred to the profit and loss account:

    Inventory valuation account $20,000
        Profit and loss account $20,000;

(c) the general price level adjustment to maintain the purchasing power of the shareholders' investment may be recorded at the end of the period as follows:

    Profit and loss account $10,000
        Purchasing power maintenance
        adjustment $10,000;

Profit and loss statement

	$
Sales	168,000
Less replacement cost of sales	120,000
Current operating profit	48,000
Add holding gain	20,000
	68,000
Less adjustment necessary to maintain the purchasing power of the shareholders' investment — 10% of $100,000	10,000
Profit before tax	58,000
Less tax	34,000
Profit after tax	24,000

Balance sheet

	$		$
Capital	100,000	Inventories	120,000
Purchasing power adjustment	10,000	Cash/Debtors	48,000
	110,000		
Retained profit	24,000		
Shareholders' funds	134,000		
Provision for taxation	34,000		
	168,000		168,000

Financial statements restated for specific and general price changes as in Example 19.5 may be interpreted as follows:

[1941] (a) *Current operating profit.* This is sales less cost of sales and expenses measured in terms of current buying prices. Current operating profit is an indication of the continuing economic viability of the operations of the firm. If a firm cannot produce sufficient revenue to replace the inventories and plant used up in generating that revenue, and a surplus to cover the cost of capital, then its operations seem to have no long-term future. If current costs and prices persist, it will not pay the firm to replace its assets once they are used up. An operating statement showing current operating profit and a balance sheet showing the shareholders' investment in terms of the current replacement cost of assets provide the basis for the calculation of a rate of return to be used for assessing long term economic viability.

[1942] (b) *Holding gains.* These are represented by the increase during the period in current replacement cost over the historical cost of assets. For depreciating assets and inventories required for the continuing operations of the firm, an increase in current replacement cost may be said to represent a gain in the sense of a "cost saving": that the firm acquired the asset at a lower monetary outlay than would be needed if the asset were to be acquired now. In times of inflation, a firm cannot be said to have made a "real" holding gain unless the "value" of its assets has increased at a rate higher than the rate of inflation. In Example 19.5 the holding gain has been included in the profit and loss statement to reflect the cost saving through the increase in the price of inventories.

[1943] (c) *Purchasing power adjustment.* The general price level adjustment to maintain the pruchasing power of the shareholders' investment reflects the view that business operations are launched and maintained through the investment of money. Therefore, no profit should be recognized unless the purchasing power of the shareholders' investment has been maintained.

[1944] (d) *Taxation.* In the example, taxation has been calculated on the basis of historical cost profit. In Example 19.5 it was assumed that the total inventory was sold and that, therefore, the total holding gain was "realized". When "unrealized" holding gains are included in end-of-period inventory value, a provision for deferred taxation may be created to allow for the tax which will be payable on these holdings gains on realization: See Example 19.6.

[1945] (e) *Profit after tax.* The profit figure incorporates profit from operations and from changes in the value of assets, after provision has been made for the maintenance of the purchasing power of the shareholders' investment. It should be pointed out, however, that the cash surplus after the replacement of the inventory sold will still be only $14,000 as in Example 19.4

[1946] It should be noted regarding Example 19.5 that the conditions under which the firm is assumed to have operated are particularly favourable. For example, it was assumed that:
• the value of the firm's inventory increased at twice the rate of inflation;
• the firm was not under price control;
• the firm was able to increase its selling price immediately after the increase in the replacement cost of inventory;
• sales were not affected by the increase in selling price.

Replacement Cost and Intercompany Comparability of Financial Statements

[1947] Asset valuation and profit measurement in terms of current replacement cost would greatly enhance the intercompany comparability of financial statements. This is so because, in principle at least, both current operating profit and the investment base (shareholders' equity) will be measured on a comparable basis (current replacement cost), one which is currently relevant for assessing the performance of different firms.

Adjustments for general and specific price changes including purchasing power gains and losses on monetary accounts and deferred tax on unrealized holding gains

[1948] The procedures of accounting for purchasing power gains and losses on monetary accounts and for providing for deferred taxation on unrealized holding gains are illustrated in Example 19.6. The example deals with deferred tax on the writing up of inventories. Accounting for deferred taxation on the writing up of depreciable assets is illustrated in Chapter 14.

Example 19.6

A firm is established with a capital of $100,000. It acquires 15,000 units of trading inventory at $10 per unit financed as follows:

Subscribed capital	$100,000
Borrowing	$ 50,000
	$150,000

The replacement cost of the inventory increases by 20% to $12 per unit. 10,000 units are sold for $16.80 per unit (40% mark up on replacement cost) and are replaced at $12 per unit. The only cost incurred is the cost of goods sold. Sales and purchases are for cash. Between the time the firm is established and the inventory is sold the general level of prices increases by 10%. The company is taxed at the rate of 50% of historical cost profit.

Required:

(a) Prepare an operating statement and a balance sheet to show the results of operations and state of affairs of the firm using the principles of historical cost.

(b) Restate the historical cost statements for the increase in the general level of prices.

(c) Prepare an operating statement and balance sheet which incorporate the effects of the changes in both the general level of prices and the replacement cost of inventory. The answer should allow for the tax effect on holding gains recognized as a result of the price changes.

Note:

Assume that the sale and replacement of inventory sold took place at the end of the accounting period and that both sales and replacement were for cash.

[1949] (a) *Operating results and position on the basis of historical cost.*

Operating results	
	$
Sales, 10,000 units @ $16.80	168,000
Cost of goods sold	100,000
Profit before tax	68,000
Tax	34,000
Profit after tax	34,000

Balance sheet

	$		$
Capital	100,000	*Inventory*	
Retained profit	34,000	5,000u @ $10	50,000
Shareholders'		10,000u @ $12	120,000
funds	134,000		170,000
Borrowing	50,000	Cash	48,000
Provision for taxation	34,000		
	218,000		218,000

[1950] (b) *Operating results and position on the basis of historical cost adjusted for general price level changes.*

Operating results

	$
Sales, 10,000 units	168,000
Cost of goods sold (100,000 x 1.1)	110,000
Profit before tax	58,000
Tax	34,000
Profit after tax	24,000

Balance sheet

	$		$
Capital		Inventories:	
($100,000 x 1.1)	110,000	5,000u x ($10 x 1.1)	55,000
Retained profit	24,000	10,000u x $1.20	120,000
Gain on monetary accounts	5,000		175,000
Shareholders' funds	139,000	Cash	48,000
Borrowing	50,000		
Provision for taxation	34,000		
	223,000		223,000

The purchasing power gain on monetary accounts of $5000 is calcualted on 10% of borrowing. No purchasing power gain/loss has been calculated on the ending cash balance and provision for taxation as the sales and hence liability for taxation are assumed to have taken place at the end of the accounting period.

The purchasing power gain on monetary accounts could be shown separately in the operating statement above after the operating profit after tax of $24,000, bringing the total profit after tax to $29,000.

[1951] (c) *Operating results and position on the basis of both general and specific price changes.*

The restatements necessary to incorporate the effects of both general and specific price changes can be illustrated in the form of journal entries as follows:

Inventory Account	$30,000	
Inventory Revaluation Account		$30,000

To record the revaluation of inventory
to replacement cost and holding gain:
15,000 units at $2 per unit.

The general price level adjustment can be made through a capital adjustment account:

Inventory Revaluation Account	$15,000	
Capital Adjustment Account		$15,000

10% of the historical cost of inventories of $150,000. Restates the historical cost in current dollars and leaves "real" holding gain in the Inventory Revaluation Account.

Capital Adjustment Account	$10,000	
Capital Account		$10,000

10% of $100,000. Restates capital in dollars of current purchasing power.

At this point the balance of the capital adjustment account is $5000 credit which represents the purchasing power gain on net monetary accounts:

Capital Adjustment Account	$5,000	
Purchasing Power Gain on		
Monetary Accounts		$5,000

Operating statement

	$
Sales	168,000
Replacement cost of goods sold	120,000
Current operating profit	48,000
Plus Inventory revaluation account	15,000
Profit before tax	63,000
Tax*	39,000
Profit after tax	24,000
Add Purchasing power gains on	
monetary accounts	5,000
Profit after tax and purchasing power	
gains on monetary accounts	29,000

*Calculation of the provision for taxation:

Historical cost profit	$68,000
Tax 50% of $68,000 =	$34,000
Deferred tax on unrealized holding	
gain on inventories:	
5,000u @ $2 = 50% of $10,000	5,000
	$39,000

Journal entry to record tax:

Profit and Loss Account (Tax Expense)	$39,000	
Provision for Taxation		$34,000
Provision for Deferred Taxation		5,000

Balance sheet

	$		$
Capital	110,000	Inventories:	
Retained earnings	29,000	15,000 units @ $12	180,000
Shareholders' funds	139,000	Cash	48,000
Borrowing	50,000		
Provision for deferred taxation	5,000		
Provision for taxation	34,000		
	228,000		228,000

[1952] In Example 19.6 we have been able to calculate the purchasing power gain on monetary accounts because of an important simplifying assumption. We assumed that all receipts and payments associated with the sales and the replacement of inventory sold took place at the end of the period and that, therefore, the only monetary account of the company during the period was the fixed amount of borrowing of $50,000. Such a simple state of affairs is very unlikely to arise in real life. Rather the level of monetary accounts, both assets and liabilities, is likely to vary over time so that a "precise" calculation of gains/losses such as shown in Example 19.6 will not be possible: any calculation would have to be made on the basis of an assumption regarding how monetary accounts have varied during the period.

[1953] Chambers has argued that purchasing power gains and losses on monetary accounts cannot be effectively and meaningfully separated from other gains and losses: R J Chambers, "A Study of a Price Level Study", *Abacus*, vol 2, No 2, December 1966. In a case where financial statements have been expressed in "current values" an adjustment which will reflect the effects of inflation, including gains and losses on monetary accounts, will be to restate the opening shareholders' equity in end of period dollars. Applying this adjustment to Example 19.6:

Operating statement

	$
Sales	168,000
Replacement cost of goods sold	120,000
Current operating profit	48,000
Plus inventory revaluation account	30,000
	78,000

Continued p 343

Less purchasing power adjustment (10% of $100,000)	10,000
Profit before tax	68,000
Tax	39,000
Profit after tax	29,000

The $29,000 profit after tax shown above includes the $5000 purchasing power gain on monetary accounts which was calculated separately in the previous operating statement.

The effects of falling prices

[1954] In the examples so far we have considered the effects of specific and general price level rises. In this section we will examine briefly the effects of falling prices by way of a simple example.

Example 19.7

Referring to the figures in Example 19.2 we will assume that between the time the firm acquired and sold its inventory of 10,000 units of X, the replacement cost of X fell by 20% from $10 to $8 per unti and that the firm had to sell its inventory at $11.20 per unit (ie at 40% mark up on replacement cost) instead of $14 per unit (ie at 40% mark up on historical cost).

The operating results of the firm may be evaluated in terms of historical and replacement cost as follows:

	Historical cost $	Replacement cost $
Sales 10,000u @ $11.20	112,000	112,000
Less cost of sales	100,000	80,000
	12,000	32,000
Less tax	6,000	6,000
Profit after tax	6,000	26,000

The above figures show that while the profit figure calculated on the basis of historical cost is $6000, compared with an expected profit figure of $20,000 if prices had not changed, the replacement cost calculation reveals a surplus of $26,000. Further, if the fall in the replacement cost of X was the result of a general fall in prices, the $26,000 will have a greater per dollar general purchasing power than the purchasing power per the dollar if prices had not fallen.

In Example 19.7 we have assumed that no debt was used in the operations of the firm. If debt had been used and there had been a fall in the general level of prices, the firm would have suffered a general purchasing power loss on the debt.

Professional Reaction to Price and Price Level Changes

[1955] The reaction of the accounting profession to the challenge of price and price level changes has been slow, indecisive and inconclusive. To begin with there was reluctance to recognize that a problem existed which needed to be tackled at the practical level. At the same time the considerable amount of work by academics on the subject had failed to produce a convincing consensus on the nature of business capital and income, on the effects of price and price level changes on capital and income and on how to account for these at the financial reporting level.

[1956] Under the stimulus of the high inflation of the 1970s there was a large measure of acceptance by the accounting profession of the need to account for the effects of price and price level changes. The emphasis was on current cost models which accounted for specific price changes rather than on general price level changes, and on supplementary presentations rather than the amendment of the primary financial statements.

[1957] Recommendations on accounting for price changes in Australia and New Zealand are contained in the Australian Statement of Accounting Practice SAP1, "Current Cost Accounting" (November 1983) and the New Zealand Statement of Standard Accounting Price CCA-1, "Information Reflecting the Effects of Changing Prices" (April 1982).

[1958] The recommendations failed to gain general acceptance and with lower inflation rates and expectations of further falls in the level of inflation, it appears that the issue has been relegated by the profession to a position of considerably less than primary importance. Yet the issue is one of continuing importance. For example, the cumulative effect of a "low" rate of price rises of, say 5% would be significant over time. Even the immediate effect of such price rises would be significant. In this respect it is suggested that readers rework the preceding numerical examples in this chapter assuming price rises of, say, 5%.

Shown below is a summary of the Australian and New Zealand recommendations on accounting for price changes. While, as stated above, interest in the subject has recently waned, in professional circlces at least, it is considered that a brief summary of the proposals would be of interest, at least from an "historical" point of view.

[1959] *Two professional recommendations.* As stated earlier, recommendations on accounting for price changes in Australia were contained in Statement of Accounting Practice SAP1, "Current Cost Accounting" (November 1983) and in New Zealand in Statement of Standard Accounting Practice CCA-1, "Information Reflecting the Effects of Changing Prices" (April 1982).

Both statements recommended a method of current cost accounting based on the concept of maintaining the operating capacity of the firm. Operating capability was conceived in phsyical terms as results and resources were measured primarily on the basis of replacement cost. Under the New Zealand standard, alternative methods, including the financial concept of capital, were acceptable, provided certain minimum disclosure requirements specified in the standard were met.

Both standards recommended CCA profit and loss statements which began with historical cost profit before interest and tax, followed by adjustments for cost of goods sold and depreciation to restate the two expense items to current cost or recoverable amount if lower. The statements then required adjustments in relation to monetary items in order to arrive at "current cost accounting profit". The aim of the adjustments was to reflect losses/gains in purchasing power calculated on the basis of specific price changes as they affected the operations of the business. In the case of the New Zealand statement, the adjustment related to monetary working capital; in the case of the Australian statement the adjustment related to monetary items excluding loan capital.

The New Zealand statement then recommended a "gearing adjustment" which added to current cost operating profit the proportion of asset revaluations during the period, net of monetary working capital adjustment and backlog depreciation, which was financed by net borrowing. After interest expense and taxation, the CCA operating statement arrived at "profit attributable to shareholders".

The Australian statement recommended the calculation of *CCA entity net profit attributable to members of the holding company* by deducting from current cost operating profit tax, interest expense and, where applicable, minority interest. For readers who wish to see a proprietary result, the statement recommended the adding to entity CCA profit of gains on loan capital. Under the Australian statement, loan capital consisted mainly of long-term borrowing including redeemable preference shares. The adjustment can be calculated on the basis of a general price index.

[1960] While the CCA recommendations failed to gain general acceptance, some companies did publish supplementary CCA statements. Summarized below in Table 19.1 are effects of the CCA adjustments on the reported profit figures of four New Zealand companies. For more detailed figures and discussion of these examples see Popoff and Cowan, "Analysis and Interpretation of Financial Statements", Second Edition, Butterworths, 1985, pp 242–247.

[1961] The figures shown in Table 19.1 relate to the following New Zealand companies:

Company A: Ivon Watkins Dow Ltd: manufacturers and distributors of chemical products;

Company B: Freightways Holdings Ltd: engaged mainly in road transport operations;

Company C: TNL Holdings Limited: engaged mainly in road transport operations;

Company D: Firestone NZ Ltd: tyre manufacturers.

The following matters may be noted regarding the CCA adjustments as they applied to the above companies:

Table 19.1

The Effects of CCA Adjustments on the 1981
Reported Profit Figures
of Four New Zealand Companies

	Company A	Company B	Company C	Company D
	$000	$000	$000	$000
Reported profit before tax	7,239	12,606	6,225	4,874
CCA Adjustments:				
Cost of sales	1,376	267	984	2,194
Depreciation	712	3,286	4,486	2,471
Circulating monetary assets	1,202	986	(4)	240
Extraordinary items	29	—	658	—
	3,319	4,539	6,124	4,905
Less gearing adjustment	1,852	2,322	2,107	4,408
Total net adjustments	1,467	2,207	4,017	497
CCA profit before tax	5,772	10,399	2,208	4,377
Provision for taxation	2,268	5,159	522*	1,836
CCA profit after tax	3,504	5,240	1,686	2,541
Reported figures (in primary statements) for:				
Depreciation	1,353	4,164	2,536	1,324
Interest expense	433	1,685	2,450	1,412
Shareholders' funds				
Primary statements	20,396	35,503	34,535	17,785
Adjusted (CCA)	26,294	52,350	58,745	40,212
Net profit after tax:				
Primary statements	4,971	7,447	5,703	3,038
Adjusted (CCA) before gearing adjustment	1,652	2,908	(421)	(1,867)
Rate of return:				
Primary figures	24.4%	21.0%	16.5%	17.1%
CCA adjusted figures	6.3%	5.6%	(-0.7%)	(-4.7%)
*After tax concessions				

(a) The relative impact of the CCA adjustments for cost of sales and depreciation on companies which have different levels of investment in inventories and fixed assets.

(b) The gearing adjustment which has cushioned the impact of the CCA restatement on the final profit figure relates to "unrealized" gains. In this respect, of particular interest is the depreciation adjustment (see for example Company C), especially where the adjustment relates to specialized assets. In the final count, the current value of specialized assets depends on their use in the context of the overall operations of a profitable enterprise.

(c) The impact of the CCA adjustment on the profit figures and rates of return. As stated earlier in this chapter, profit measurement, asset valuation and the calculation of rate of return on the basis of current cost provide an indication of the continuing viability of operations given current costs and prices. In the examples, Companies A and B show substantial reductions in adjusted profit figures and rates of return and Companies C and D negative adjusted profit figures and rates of return. In the calculations the net profit figures used exclude the gearing adjustment as this would indicate the rate of return the company would have earned if it had acquired its assets at current prices.

Price Changes, Behavioural Effects and Social, Economic and Political Implications: A Case Study of Two New Zealand Meat Processing Companies

[1962] The experiences with continuing price rises in the 1970s and early 1980s have brought about a general recognition of the disruptive economic social and political effects of inflation and have made the control of inflation a major issue for governments around the world. What is probably inadequately appreciated is the potential contribution to economic and social concern and unrest of the failure to account, in realistic terms, for the effects of price and price level changes. Some of the major issues will be illustrated by way of the following case study of two New Zealand meat processing companies. The case study is relevant because of the vital importance of the meat processing industry to the New Zealand economy and its history of turbulent industrial relations. The case study is based on statements made respectively in the 1972 and 1973 reports of the first and second company.

First company

The annual review of the board of directors of the 1972 operations of the first company began with the following statement:

> Your company has vastly improved results in all spheres in the 1971/72 financial year, and the forecast of a record consolidated tax-paid profit has been realized. The net profit and the return on shareholders funds are at new levels and all concerned in the welfare of the company — directors, employees, clients, shareholders and executives — will be pleased after the previous year's results.

In this case the rate of return earned by the company on its investment at book value was reported as 13.3%. The fixed assets of the company were shown in its balance sheet at a net figure of just over $6 million. They were valued at book value as at 1 January 1957 plus additions at cost less disposals.

347

Second company

In moving for the adoption of the 1973 accounts at the annual general meeting of this company, the chairman noted an increase in net profit of some 65%. He noted also, however, that while operating costs had been quite satisfactory (based on the historic cost of buildings and plant) had these assets been related to 1973 prices an entirely different picture would have emerged. The replacement value of the firm's assets at that time had been estimated at something like $25 million compared to a written down book value of $7 million. Had the assets been written up to their replacement cost, the earning rate on the resulting shareholders' funds even in that record year would have been slightly in excess of 3%.

The seconder of the motion to adopt the annual accounts made the following interpretation of the operating results for the year:

The profit achieved is an excellent one... The earnings rate for the year is a significant 55 cents per share compared with 33 cents per share last year. At first glance, this year's earnings rate and increase in profit appears high and comparable increases shown by other companies have led to adverse comments from government ministers. However, as illustrated in the chairman's address, the profit represents a return of about 3.5% on the current cost of replacing the assets of the company. A return of 3.5% is less than is paid on government loans and would not encourage an investor to sink funds in a freezing works — all this in a year in which favourable factors have produced good profits.

The facts quoted above also illustrate the limitations of accounting reports in times of rapid inflation such as we have experienced in recent years. A balance sheet does not purport to show the current value of the enterprise. However, if those in employment are entitled (as they should be) to current wage rates, surely investors are entitled to a return on the current value of their investment.

The first matter that comes to mind from the above quotations are the attempts by the managements of the two companies to portray their (and their companies') performances in a favourable light and, when faced with a dilemma, as in the case of the second company, to make the best of a difficult situation.

Regarding the first company, it should be fairly apparent that the reported rate of return of 13.3% was overstated in the face of undervalued assets and prevailing inflationary conditions. Even taken at face value the rate of return could have hardly been considered excessive.

In 1972 New Zealand had elected a Labour government. One of the major concerns of the new government was to fight inflation, in particular by the control of profits and price rises. An attempt to control price rises was reflected in the requirement that goods should be labeled with the maximum retail price, a move which, given the inflationary conditions of the time, (and these were to get worse in the years that followed) was particularly unsuccessful. At the time, labour unions in general and meat workers' unions in particular were pressing for an even higher share of what was perceived to be a rich economic cake.

What happened in the next 12 months or so and how the management of at least one New Zealand meat processing company attempted to deal with developments may be gauged from the quotations from the 1973 report of the second company. The quotations appear to be an attempt by the management to perform a delicate balancing act between a desire to impress shareholders and investors with the profitability and success of the company on the one hand and to pre-empt government criticism and union action on wage demands on the other.

The statements that the "profit achieved is an excellent one" and that the "earnings rate for the year is a significant 55 cents per share compared with 33 cents per share last year" (an increase of 66%!) was presumably to impress shareholders and investors. The emphasis is on "earnings rate" but on per share basis, not on investment measured on the current value of assets (or even historical cost). One wonders what effect such claims of profitability had on labour unions determined to increase members' income in a vital and "profitable" industry. To the casual reader an earnings rate of 55 cents per share could easily imply a rate of return on shareholders' investment of 55%. This compared at the time with interest on savings bank accounts, where most workers were likely to hold their savings, of about 5%. The statements which follow presumably aim to forestall adverse reaction to the claimed company profitability. While the profit appeared to be high "at first glance" and "comparable" increases had lead to adverse comments from government ministers, given a return of about 3.5% on the current cost of the investment, presumably, only uninformed investors would "sink" funds in meat works. Then, finally, as if to reassure shareholders and investors about the profits of the company "...all that in a year in which favourable factors have produced good profits". One would be excused for asking whether the results for the year in question were "good" or "bad"!

What happened in the New Zealand meat processing industry in the years that followed is a matter of history. Continuing demands for higher wages backed up by crippling strikes cost the meat industry, farmers and the New Zealand economy many millions of dollars. The meat industry continued to operate under these conditions by passing its cost increases to farmers in the form of higher killing and processing charges. In the meantime farmers were able to absorb such increases in processing charges because of massive farm subsidies on the part of the governemnt in the form of various tax concessions and supplementary minimum prices. While on the face of it the subsidies were being paid to farmers and were coming increasingly under critical scrutiny, much of them in effect went to support the New Zealand meat processing industry. It was generally felt at the time that the respite was only temporary, not only because of the high cost of subsidies but also because of growing criticisms and pressure from farm lobbies overseas against imports of farm products from New Zealand on the grounds that such New Zealand exports were heavily subsidised. The meat proceing industry made attempts to cut costs and improve its profitability by labour replacement technology, moves which were strongly resisted by the meat workers' unions. Yet the inevitable had to come. There was the closure of uneconomic meat works in which shocked communities saw their major source of income disappear overnight.

The real "shocks" to farmers, the meat industry and the meat workers' unions, however, came after 1984. In 1984 a Labour government was again elected to power. The new government was determined to restructure the economy and to remove subsidies from farming and the export sector of the New Zealand economy. The removal of subsidies, continuing high level of inflation, high interest rates and the resulting high value of the new Zealand dollar seriously affected the ability of farmers to meet high operating costs and to maintain, let alone increase stock numbers. As farmers began fighting for survival, so did the meat workers faced with the closure of meat works and redundancies. In moves which were inconceivable a few years earlier, meat workers chose to forego wage increases and even in some cases offered to accept wages cuts in order to prevent some meat works from closing.

Could the developments in the New Zealand meat processing industry have been foreseen in 1972 or 1973? They should have been foreseen. The management of the industry must have had some inkling regarding what the true state of the industry's profitability was.

One can only conjecture that matters would have been different if management had chosen to place before shareholders, investors, organized labour and the government the state of the industry in plain unambiguous terms. The matter would have been aided further by a clear and more decisive policy on the part of the accounting profession in New Zealand on accounting for and reporting of the true effects of price level changes. We can say with some degree of assurance, however, that the failure to do the above could not but have aggravated the situation.

Review questions

19.1 The following statement has been made by the directors of a listed public company:
"During the year the company has increased its sales by 15% to a new record level of $135 million, and net profit has been lifted by 17%. It is proposed that dividend be increased from 18% to 20%." Consider the statement of the directors in view of an 18% inflation which has taken place during the period.

19.2 Explain the nature of:
  • general price level changes; and
  • specific price changes;
and their effect on the operations and state of affairs of business enterprises. In what respects would financial statements adjusted for general and specific price changes be more informative than those prepared on the basis of traditional accounting methods?

19.3 Consider the index problem in accounting for general price level changes.

19.4 Why are financial statements adjusted only for general price level changes of limited usefulness?

19.5 Discuss the usefulness for the analysis and interpretation of financial statements of information regarding:
  • the net realizable value, and
  • the current replacement cost
of business assets.

19.6 In relation to accounting for price changes, explain the significance of:
  (a) holding gains;
  (b) current operating profit;
  (c) maintaining the operating capacity of the firm;
  (d) maintaining the purchasing power of investment.

19.7 Consider the claim that current operating profit (sales less current replacement cost of sales) is the maximum amount a firm may distribute if it is to maintain its operating capacity.

19.8 ABC Ltd, an old established trading company, has reported what its directors have described as "very satisfactory profit" for the financial year just ended. This profit has been measured by the use of traditional accounting methods and procedures.

Required:

   (a) Discuss the reality of the profit reported by ABC Ltd if during the period the replacement cost of the inventories in which ABC Ltd deals increased on the average by 20% and if, in addition, the general level of prices increased by 15%.

   (b) Describe a method of accounting which you believe will better reflect the "real" profit made by the firm.

19.9 The following statement regarding the decision of the New Zealand Government to discontinue the 5% tax allowance on inventory valuation was included in the chairman's review of the 1978 financial year of a New Zealand trading company. "It has largely been overlooked that this measure, which has been described as crude and inequitable, nevertheless has acted as a kind of hedge against the possible introduction of inflation accounting, which will be a trader's nightmare. The stock valuation allowance as a form of relief is simple and understandable, which may be far from the case of any substitute which may have to be considered should inflation accounting come to be used as a yardstick. WE EARNESTLY HOPE THAT THE GOVERNMENT WILL RECONSIDER ITS STANCE" (emphasis original).

Consider possible reasons for the chairman's description of inflation accounting as a "trader's nightmare" and the attractiveness of the stock valuation allowance as an alternative. (*Note:* Under the stock allowance companies were allowed a deduction from their taxable income equal to 5% of the book value of starting inventory.)

19.10 A firm deals in commodity X which it normally sells at a 20% mark-up on cost. During an accounting period the firm sold 10,000 units of X at $12 per unit. The historical cost of sales was $10 per unit. The firm is taxed at the rate of 50% on its historical cost profit.

Required:

   (a) Calculate the historical cost profit of the firm.

   (b) Evaluate the historical cost profit of the firm under (a) if, between the time the inventory of X was acquired and sold, the replacement cost of X increased by 8% and there was inflation of 16%.

   (c) Calculate the historical cost profit of the firm if it had increased the selling price of X to $12.96 (ie 20% mark-up on replacement cost) as soon as replacement cost increased, and evaluate the historical cost profit in view of the increase in replacement cost and the 16% inflation.

   (d) Would the company have been better off than shown under (c) if there had been no increase in the replacement cost of X and no inflation and if sales had been at $12 per unit?

19.11 The following information has been extracted from the annual financial statements of a trading company, XYZ Ltd for years ended 30 September 19A2 and 19A1:

	19A2 $000	19A1 $000
Sales	34,950	31,450
Stocks at 30 September		8,580
Debtors at 30 September		3,990

Required:

Consider the effect of 16% inflation in 19A2 on the operations of XYZ Ltd for the year. You may assume that the costs and selling prices of XYZ Ltd moved more or less in line with the rate of inflation.

19.12 The following figures (all at historical amounts) relate to the operations of the ABC Ltd for the two years ended 31 March 19A2 and 19A1:

	19A2 ($000)	19A1 ($000)
Sales	9,000	7,500
Cost of goods sold	6,000	5,000
Gross profit	3,000	2,500
Expenses	1,800	1,500
Net profit before tax	1,200	1,000
Tax (at 50%)	600	500
Net profit after tax	600	500
Provision for dividend	300	250
Retained in business *to finance growth*	300	250

Inventories and debtors at 31 March 19A1 were:

        Inventories $1,500,000

        Debtors $1,000,000

The physical quantities of inventories at the end of 19A1 and 19A2 were virtually the same.

In his address to the shareholders, the chairman of ABC Ltd made the following comments about the results of the year ended 31 March 19A2:

"Although there was no increase in the quantity sold and the company had to face an average increase of 20% in the cost of goods sold and expenses in a year when general inflation was 18%, the company has lifted its profit by 20% from $500,000 to a new record of $600,000.

"In view of the very satisfactory results for the year and following the established policy of the company to retain 50% of tax-paid profit for growth, the directors propose a significant 20% increase in dividend.

"A continuing major concern for the company are the high interest rates it has to pay on its loan finance. The current average interest rate on the company's borrowing is 15%."

Required:

In view of the 20% increase in the cost of goods sold and expenses incurred by ABC Ltd in 19A2 and general inflation of 18%, comment briefly on the following matters:

(a) The record profit reported by the company.

(b) The profit retention by the company of $300,000 for growth.

(c) The proposed dividend for 19A2.

(d) The concern by the company about the high cost of the loan finance the company uses in its operations.

(e) Would the company have been better off if, in 19A2, its costs and expenses and selling prices had not increased and there had not been general inflation?

In providing your answers to questions (a) to (e) above, use figures and comparisons as far as is possible with the information provided.

19.13 The figures shown below have been extracted from the financial statements of Greedy Traders Limited for the year ended 30 September 19A5:

	$
Sales	15,000,000
Cost of goods sold	12,000,000
Gross profit	3,000,000
Expenses	2,000,000
Net profit before tax	1,000,000
Tax (45%)	450,000
Net profit after tax	550,000
Dividends (40% of net profit after tax)	220,000
Profit retained for expansion	330,000

Debtors at 30 September 19A5	$1,700,000
Stocks at 30 September 19A5	$4,000,000

Mr Roger Black, managing director of the company, is discussing the prospects of the company in the new financial year. In the process of the discussion he makes the folowing claim:

"It is not really inflation that is killing business but high interest rates. With the lifting of price controls business can not only recover its costs but also improve its profit margins."

To make his point he provides you with the following projections regarding the operations of the company in the coming year:

(1) The cost of purchases and cost of goods sold is expected to increase by 15%.

(2) The company expects to increase its selling prices by 20%. The physical volume of sales is expected to remain at the same level as in 19A5.

(3) Improved cost control is expected to keep the increase in expenses to 12%.

(4) The rate of tax is expected to increase to 48%.

(5) The physical level of stocks and the collection period for debtors are expected to be the same as in 19A5.

(6) General inflation for the year is expected to be 17%.

Given these projections, Mr Black expects that in the new financial year his company will almost double its after-tax profit and profit retention for the expansion of operations. To support his views he gives you the following estimates:

	$
Sales	18,000,000
Cost of goods sold	13,800,000
Gross profit	4,200,000
Expenses	2,240,000
Net profit before tax	1,960,000
Tax (48%)	940,800
Net profit after tax	1,019,200
Dividend (40%)	407,600
Profit retained for expansion	611,600

Required:

Using appropriate figures and comparisons from the data provided, answer the following questions:

(a) Comment on Mr Black's claim that in the coming year the company will almost double its profit and profit retention for expansion of its operations.

(b) Would the company be better off if in the new financial year all prices remained at their 19A5 level and there was no general inflation?

(c) Comment on Mr Black's complaint about the high rate of interest of borrowed funds. The company uses $5 million of borrowed funds on which it pays interest at the rate of 20% p.a.

19.14 (a) "Replacement cost does not automatically measure current value." What condition(s), if any, must be present before replacement cost can be regarded as a measure of the current economic value of assets used in income generation?

(b) "To value at replacement cost an asset which a firm does not need to replace because it already has it and may not want to replace in the future, goes against basic commonsense and logic."

Discuss.

19.15 The following figures relate to specialized plant operated by the XYZ Company in one of its departments:

Historical cost	$600,000
Depreciation to date	$200,000
Book value	$400,000
Replacement cost	$1,400,000
Net realizable value	$180,000

Required:

Explain *briefly* how the notion of "value to the owner" may be used in arriving at the current value of assets and ilustrate your answer by using the figures provided above.

Chapter 20

Case Studies in Analysis and Interpretation

[2001] In this chapter we shall consider five case studies in analysis and interpretation of financial statements based on published company reports. The studies cover an example of misinterpretation (Case 1); a company failure in hindsight (Case 2); a case of company survival (Case 3); the importance of analysis (Case 4); and historical costs, current cost accounting and purchasing power gains and losses on monetary accounts (Case 5). A number of case studies are included at the end of the chapter for class assignment and discussion.

Case Study 1

The Case of the Excessive Company Profits Which Caused a Housewives' Boycott

[2002] An interesting approach to a study of interpretation of financial statements is by way of a study of cases which demonstrate the effects of misinterpretation. Let us take as an example a controversy which arose in 1977 regarding the profits of Wattie Industries Ltd.

Wattie Industries Ltd was a large New Zealand enterprise engaged in the production of a wide range of processed foods. A material proportion of the output of this group was seasonal, and was also affected by variations in crop yields each year. This applied particularly to the production of canned and frozen fruit and vegetables. The group was a major producer of flour, ice-cream and poultry.

The controversy about the profits of Wattie Industries arose when the company, then operating under price control, obtained approval to increase prices. The result was an organized housewives' boycott of Wattie retail products, an exchange between the Minister of Trade and Industry and the opposition spokesman on consumer affairs, and considerable publicity in the news media.

For example, under a heading "MP accuses accountants over profits", *The Otago Daily Times* reported on 30 May 1977 that the opposition spokesman on consumer affairs had said that the latest annual report showed that Watties had revalued their land and buildings by $16 million. He was further quoted as saying: "Now they demand what they describe as an adequate financial return on those book-keeping-created assets. That is $4 million profit before tax. Not only have they exploited inflation by writing up their assets by $16 million and profited that way, but they are also demanding from the public an additional $4 million in every year in increased sales profits".

The following day the same paper reported the reply of the Minister of Trade and Industry to the effect that, in approving the price increases for Watties, the standard practice had been followed of deducting the revaluation for assets from the shareholders' funds, and that the comments of the opposition MP had been motivated by political considerations.

Yet the housewives' boycott of Wattie products was not just an understandable emotional reaction against constantly rising prices, nor were the comments of the opposition spokesman on consumer affairs just politically motivated. They were based to an important extent on a misinterpretation of accounting data.

Some of the figures disclosed in the then latest annual report of the company are shown in Figure 20.1.

Figure 20.1

	1976 $000	1975 $000	1974 $000
Sales and commissions	227,435	199,508	181,787
Earnings before taxation	17,998	9,508	14,279
Taxation (note 1)	7,074	3,255	5,540
Net earnings (note 2)	10,940	6,623	9,051
Ordinary shareholders' funds	88,343	80,873(3)	61,590
Preference share capital	1,600	1,600	1,600
Total shareholders' funds	89,943	82,473	63,190
Earnings rates:			
On ordinary paid up capital	43.2%	26.2%	36.1%
Net earnings per 50¢ ordinary share	21.6¢	13.1¢	18.1¢
On shareholders' funds	12.2%	8.0%(3)	14.3%
On total assets	6.6%	4.2%	7.5%
Dividend distributions:			
On $2 preference share	12¢	12¢	12¢
	6%	6%	6%
On 50¢ ordinary share	6.25¢	6.25¢	6.25¢
	12½%	12½%	12½%
Ordinary dividend cover	3.4	2.1	2.9

Note 1 After savings in tax payable from tax concessions, the principal ones (in 1976 year) being:

> Export incentives $722,446
> Investment allowance $481,223

Note 2 Excluding extraordinary items and prior period adjustments.
Note 3 Including a surplus arising from the revaluation of land and buildings of $15.9 million.

The following comments were made in the chariman's review:

Consolidated net profit before tax was $17,998,307 and the equity tax-paid profit before extraordinary items $10,940,446, an increase of 65%. It must be remembered that this increase is compared with the depressed results of 1974–75 and that on a comparison with 1973–74 the increase is 21% only which does not fully compensate for inflation and increased investment in the intervening two years. The group tax-paid profit percentage to turnover is 4.8% which is identical with the percentage obtained in the 1973–74 year, a welcome return to a more stable situation.

The liquidity situation at 31 July 1976 was favourable due mainly to tight inventory and cost control. For the first time in many years the value of inventories has reduced in the face of severe inflationary conditions.

In common with other enterprises in New Zealand and indeed elsewhere, we have been faced with the need to cope with rapidly escalating costs on the one hand and controls of selling prices on the other. The situation has been a spur to improve operations and management controls but problems remain, not the least of which is the necessity to weigh up very carefully the viability of investment in new projects.

What were some of the misconceptions at the root of the 1977 criticisms of Wattie Industries?

Above all there was the attaching of significance to *absolute* rather than *relative* data. The company had reported $11 million profit, an increase of 65% over the previous year, and wanted more!!! This view of the firm's profits raises a number of questions including:

(a) the validity of the reported profit figure (though one can hardly blame the housewives for taking it seriously since that was the profit figure reported by the company itself);

(b) the drawing of conclusions from a base (the 1974–75 profit) which may not have been a fair standard for comparisons (in fact 1974–75 was a difficult year for Wattie Industries, especially because of delays in the recognition of cost increases in prices);

(c) the issue of how much profit Watties should be allowed to make and in particular whether this profit should be held at an absolute figure regardless of how efficiently the company operates and how much more it invests in assets aimed at increasing productivity.

Evaluation of relative data would have been more relevant to people concerned about prices and profits. Let us look at some of the reported figures.

Net profit to sales

The rate of profit on sales for 1975–76 was:

After tax	4.88%
Before tax	7.91%

*Part of the difference from the norm before and after tax profit is due to tax savings because of investment allowances and tax incentives on export sales.

Are these rates of profit to sales excessive regarding, say, the canned and frozen seasonal products which were the principal subject of the boycott?

Totals of data drawn from a diverse enterprise and a set of relationships calculated from these totals (such as rate of return on sales) are of limited value only. In the Watties case, totals and averages across a non-homogeneous mix of activities from processing peas to producing poultry, and from operating flour mills to producing and marketing ice-cream will tend to lack meaning. Indeed in a multi-product enterprise there is a strong case for different rates of net profit to sales, according to the turnover rate of the relevant assets. For example, a desired rate of return on investment in assets which have a high turnover rate can be achieved at a lower rate of turnover. A way by which a business firm may (within limits) absorb increasing costs is by increasing inventory turnover through control over inventory levels. The company did achieve a reduction in inventory levels from $57 million at 31 July 1975 to $55.7 million at 31 July 1976, an event which was stated in the chairman's review to have contributed to the favourable liquidity position of the company at the end of its 1976 financial year. There is not enough information, however, to determine the remaining capacity of the company to absorb increased costs and the consequent reduced profit margins by further increasing the stockturn rate. There would seem to be little opportunity for this in the seasonal products side of the enterprise.

Rate of return on funds

Earnings per 50c share for the three years 1974 to 1976 were as folows:

1974	17.95c
1975	13.22c
1976	21.94c

For the year ended 31 July 1976 reported profit represented 43.88% of the share capital of the company. Was this rate of profit coupled with the 65% increase over the previous year excessive?

At 31 July 1976 net tangible assets per 50c share (due mainly to profit retention) were $1.76:

	$
Paid up capital	0.50
Writing up of assets (land and buildings)	0.24
Retained profits	1.02
	1.76

The rate of return on shareholders' funds in 1976 was 12.49%.

$$(\text{ie } \frac{0.50}{1.76} \times 43.88\%).$$

Was the net profit after tax excessive?

It is a fact of history that quite a large number of people thought that the 1976 profit of Wattie Industries was excessive, and they expresed their strong feelings on the subject by organizing and participating in a boycott of Wattie products. Certainly a rate of return of 43.8% on share capital and an increase of profit over the previous year of 65% *seem* exorbitant to one who does not understand how to interpret accounting data fairly, and to make use of the helpful information provided in the chairman's review.

As the chairman of directors pointed out, the 1974–75 year did not provide a fair basis for comparison. Compared with the more normal year of 1973–74, sales were up 25% in two years, earnings 21%, and shareholders' funds (excluding the write-up) 17%. The increase in earnings of 21% was well below the inflation rate of the two years.

One is left with the question, is a rate of return on shareholders' funds of 12.49% excessive? The figure itself is derived mainly from historical cost data, which made no allowance for the differences between historical cost and current cost measures of fixed assets, cost of sales, and depreciation. Part of the after-tax profit was due to a tax saving from an investment allowance. Anyway, one might well ask how a

12.49% return could be excessive when the inflation of the year was around 15%. Comparisons with other companies could be useful, but an objective guide on whether the rate of return was excessive or not is provided by the share market.

How did the share market assess the profitability prospects of the company?

If the share market at the time rated the profitability of Wattie Industries very highly, one would have expected a share price which showed a high premium over net tangible assets. In fact, at the time of boycott the price of a 50c Wattie share was around $1 compared with net tangible assets (before revaluation of plant) of $1.76. At market expectation of future profitability, therefore, capital investment in Wattie Industries to expand production and job opportunities was unwarranted. The profitability expectation of the market would need to be $\frac{1.76}{1.00}$ higher to equate market price with net tangible assets per share. If the market expectation was for continuance of the 1975–76 rate of return on the net tangible assets of 12.49%, then the company would have needed a 22% (ie $\frac{1.76}{1.00}$ x 12.49%) rate of return after tax on the equity financed portion of any additional investment to justify expansion. One may well ask why the rate was so high.

Case Study 2

A Company Failure in Hindsight

[2003] Mosgiel Ltd had a long history of successful operation in the woollen industry in New Zealand. On 23 October 1979 the company's annual report for the year ended 30 June 1979 was presented at the 106th annual general meeting. The directors' report to the annual accounts indicated that there was $2,525,933 "available for distribution". An interim dividend of 5% had been paid in April 1979, and the directors recommended the payment of a further 8% as a final dividend, making 13% for the year. Of the tax-paid profit (including special items) of $953,249, a total of $618,751 was being paid out in dividends. The funds statement showed that there had been a material increase in net working capital during the year. The statistical summary for 1979 showed earnings per ordinary share at 26.18 cents, net asset backing per $1 ordinary share at a high of $4.04, the current ratio at its highest level for the period of 2.2:1, and a proprietary ratio some 2% down on the previous year. The meeting approved the payment of the final dividend. The directors acknowledged that it had been a difficult year, but a fair though superficial view would be that the company had operated profitably and had been able to meet a dividend on ordinary shares at the same rate as for the previous year.

It must have come as a shock to the shareholders to learn from an interim report issued by the directors on 11 March 1980 that the company had made a $1.5 million loss for the six months ended 31 December 1979. Seven weeks later, receivers were appointed by the first ranking debenture holders. It soon became apparent that there was a strong posibility that the company's business would not be saleable as a unit, and that the second ranking secured creditors might well not be paid in full, while unsecured creditors stood to receive nothing at all in an eventual liquidation. The ordinary shares, which had been ranging from around 80 cents to $1.05, quickly fell away to 10 cents or less on the share market. Well over a thousand employees were likely to be left without a job.

Hindsight is a great help in the interpretation of financial statements; but a critical study in the light of hindsight may well be useful in the assessment of what the future may hold for other enterprises. There was evidence in the financial statements (and the chairman's review) of potential problems for Mosgiel Ltd. Shown below are:

- excerpts from the chairman's review;
- the group consolidated profit and loss statement;
- the consolidated balance sheet;
- the statement of source and application of funds;
- the financial summary showing comparative data and ratios for the five years 1975–79.

Excerpts from chairman's review

The results of the year's trading are disapointing to your board . . . the final quarter of the year produced sales well below our expectations. The main cause of this was undoubtedly the comparatively mild (albeit very wet) winter experienced during those months. Fresh competition in a fairly static domestic market also played a part in the result, as did earlier action taken to reduce our holding of blanket stocks.

Sales for the year amounted to $28.54 million which was an increase of $2.37 million or 9.1% over the previous year. Obviously there was some reduction in volume as this increase would not equal inflationary trends. However, we were pleased by our export sales which increased by 81.8% to a total of $1.22 million or 4.27% of our total sales. In 1977 export sales were 1.67% of the total and in 1978 they were 2.56% so that we continue to make progress in this field. Indications are that in the current year exports will again represent a larger proportion of our sales. I must assure you that in working to improve our export position we are conscious of the perils of neglecting our domestic market.

Profit from trading before tax was $1,165,802 in addition to which we made a capital profit on the sale of some surplus property of $36,982. The amount to be provided for tax from this year's profit is $249,535 leaving us with a profit after tax and special items of $953,249. This compares with $1,230,398 a year ago. It is something of a commentary upon the taxation situation that although our pre-tax profits were $195,745 less than a year ago we paid $60,500 more tax. This of course was principally due to the fact that there was no stock valuation adjustment for tax purposes this year. Net profit from trading amounted to 19.25% of our subscribed share capital, 5.95% of our shareholders' funds and 3.21% on sales. These returns to a business whose main purpose is the processing of raw materials produced in New Zealand can only be described as sadly inadequate.

Your board recommends a final dividend of 8 cents per share on ordinary shares which together with the interim dividend of 5 cents paid in April makes a total of 13 cents per share (unchanged from last year).

Dividends of 13% on ordinary and specified preference shares amount to $545,041 net of tax and are covered 1.75 times by total tax paid profits. Under today's conditions this dividend cover is insufficient.

It will be noted that the consolidated balance sheet again shows increases in both term and current liabilities. These liabilities have been incurred mainly in connection with the increase in stocks and work in progress amounting to $2.155 million. The figure for these assets is too high and we are concentrating on a reduction. Some raw material stocks have been disposed of at a profit since balance date.

Group consolidated profit and loss statement 12 months to 30 June 1979

		1979 $	1978 $
Sales		28,540,369	26,165,592
Profit from manufacturing and trading after deducting the following items:		1,165,802	1,308,226
Depreciation	568,477		586,572
Interest on loans — fixed	806,859		366,579
— other	701,769		707,664
Plant leasing costs	207,382		139,193
Directors' fees	17,500		17,500
Audit fees	20,000		18,000
Profit from exchange variation		—	53,321
Profit before tax		1,165,802	1,361,547
Tax provision		249,535	189,035
Profit after tax		916,267	1,172,512
Capital profits		36,982	57,886
Profit after tax and special items		953,249	1,230,398
Add retained earnings brought forward		1,179,954	1,157,943
Transfer from share premium account		392,730	153,638
Available for distribution		2,525,933	2,541,979
Less appropriations for year:			
Transfer to capital profits reserve	36,982		57,886
Transfer to capital replacement reserve	392,730		153,638
Transfer to general reserve	—		600,000
		429,712	811,524
		2,096,221	1,730,455
Dividends:			
Specified preference shares:			
10 months to 30 April (1978 —			
5 months)	136,500		68,250
Accrual 2 months to 30 June	27,300		27,300
	163,800		95,550
Ordinary shares:			
Interim paid April	174,981		174,981
Proposed final	279,970		279,970
	454,951		454,951
Total dividend appropriation		618,751	550,501
Retained earnings carried forward		1,477,470	1,179,954

Group consolidated balance sheet as at 30 June 1979

	1979 $	1979 $	1978 $	1978 $
Authorized capital		12,000,000		12,000,000
Issued and paid up capital				
3,499,623 ordinary shares of $1 each fully paid	3,499,623		3,499,623	
1,260,000 specified preference shares of $1 each fully paid	1,260,000		1,260,000	
Total issued and paid up capital		4,759,623		4,759,623
Reserves and retained earnings				
Statutory capital reserves	648,711		255,981	
Property revaluation reserves	3,967,521		3,971,842	
Capital reserves available for tax free distribution	955,429		1,311,177	
Retained earnings	5,077,470		4,879,954	
	10,649,131		10,418,954	
Total shareholders' funds		15,408,754		15,178,577
Deferred taxation provision		260,419		274,750
Term liabilities:				
Mortgage finance	792,932		803,040	
Bank of New Zealand	2,200,000		—	
Debenture finance — NZ domiciled	2,377,200		2,641,200	
Debenture finance — Overseas currencies	1,963,094		1,963,094	
NZ Government suspensory loans	365,935		326,400	
Capital lease commitments	869,311		678,452	
	8,568,472		6,412,186	
Less Repayments due within 12 months	1,250,734		389,467	
		7,317,738		6,022,719
Current liabilities:				
Bank of New Zealand	3,460,437		4,459,125	
Short term borrowings	1,959,331		1,356,845	
Trade creditors and accruals	2,788,431		2,846,345	
Bills payable	406,457		433,811	
Provision for taxation	74,849		27,368	
Provision for dividend	307,270		307,270	
	8,996,775		9,430,764	
Add term liabilities repayable within 12 months	1,250,734		389,467	
		10,247,509		9,820,231
		33,234,420		31,296,277

	1979 $	1979 $	1978 $	1978 $
Fixed assets				
Land and buildings	6,526,875		6,558,635	
Plant, machinery, vehicles, etc.	4,020,031		4,097,126	
		10,546,906		10,655,761
Employee share purchase scheme				
Loans to employees	247,357		251,758	
Advances to trustees	23,046		77,714	
		270,403		329,472
Investments				
Sundry		1,434		25,192
Current assets				
Cash and bank imprest accounts	14,101		19,395	
Debtors and prepayments	5,480,379		5,520,503	
Stocks and work in progress	16,900,947		14,745,954	
Livestock	20,250		—	
		22,415,677		20,285,852
		33,234,420		31,296,277

363

Statement of source and application of funds
12 months to 30 June 1979

	1979 $	1979 $	1978 $
Source of funds			
From operations:			
Net profit before taxation		1,165,802	1,361,547
Capital profits		36,982	57,886
Adjustment for items not involving movement of funds:			
Depreciation		568,477	586,572
Total funds from operations		1,771,261	2,006,005
From other sources:			
New share issue			1,260,000
Realization of investments		23,758	239,635
Reduction in staff share scheme advances		59,069	148,499
Increase in long term debt		1,295,019	2,381,746
		3,149,107	6,035,885
Application of funds			
Increase in fixed assets	463,943		1,885,725
Taxation paid	216,385		251,338
Dividend paid	618,751		523,201
Rationalization losses	—		75,530
		1,299,079	2,735,794
Increase in working capital		1,850,028	3,300,091
Details of increases (decreases) in working capital			
Accounts receivable	59,876		1,304,644
Stocks	2,154,993		4,298,810
Accounts payable	(775,999)		(662,499)
Cash and bank	993,394		(284,019)
Short term borrowing	(602,486)		(1,356,845)
Livestock	20,250		—
	1,850,028		3,300,091

Financial summary

	1979 $000	1978 $000	1977 $000	1976 $000	1975 $000
Sales	28,540	26,166	22,885	20,080	19,378
Trading profits	1,166	1,308	1,279	1,214	971
Extraordinary items	—	53	—	—	146
	1,166	1,361	1,279	1,214	1,117
Taxation	250	189	408	426	404
	916	1,172	871	788	713
Transfers from capital profits	37	58	200	67	201
	953	1,230	1,071	855	914
Dividends	619	551	420	369	336
Retained earnings	334	679	651	486	578
Assets					
Current assets	22,416	20,286	14,677	13,364	12,566
Less current liabilities	10,248	9,820	7,575	7,544	7,473
Working capital	12,168	10,466	7,102	5,820	5,093
Fixed assets	10,547	10,656	7,618	6,610	6,644
Investments (including share					
purchase scheme)	272	355	743	976	7
	22,987	21,477	15,463	13,406	11,744
Less long term liabilities	7,318	6,023	3,641	3,583	2,423
	15,669	15,454	11,822	9,823	9,321
Less deferred taxation	260	275	246	260	—
Net shareholders' equity	15,409	15,179	11,576	9,563	9,321
Derived from —					
Ordinary capital	3,500	3,500	3,500	3,355	3,354
Specified preference capital	1,260	1,260	—	—	—
Preference capital	—	—	—	—	9
Total paid up capital	4,760	4,760	3,500	3,355	3,363
Capital reserves	5,572	5,539	3,818	2,464	2,494
Revenue reserves	5,077	4,880	4,258	3,744	3,464
	15,409	15,179	11,576	9,563	9,321
Statistical summary					
Net profit —					
To ordinary capital	26.18%	33.49%	24.88%	23.51%	21.25%
To subscribed capital	19.25%	24.62%	24.88%	23.51%	21.20%
To shareholders' funds	5.95%	7.72%	7.52%	8.24%	7.65%
Net asset backing per $1					
ordinary share	$4.04	$3.97	$3.31	$2.85	$2.77
Ratio — current assets to					
current liabilities	2.2 to 1	2.1 to 1	1.9 to 1	1.8 to 1	1.7 to 1
Shareholders' funds as					
percentage total assets	46.36%	48.50%	50.25%	45.65%	48.50%
Dividend on ordinary shares	13%	13%	12%	11%	10%

Let us now review the 1979 financial statements of Mosgiel Ltd and, with the benefit of hindsight, look for signs of the unhappy outcome:

(a) Sales

Sales were up by 9%. Sales are the result of three factors — quantity, price, and sales mix. There is some information in the chairman's review, but one is unable to draw conclusions from it regarding the relative significance of the quantity and price factors. Some enquiry in the market place could have produced approximate price information. For example, if selling prices were up by around 20%, then the sales at 1977–78 levels would have been approximately $31.4 million. Physical sales in 1978–79 would then have been down by 9.1% on the previous year. In an undertaking with high fixed costs and a stable labour force, a major fall in physical sales volume must have serious effects on profitability and finance.

(b) Profit from operations

	1979 $000	1978 $000
Profit from manufacturing and trading as disclosed in profit and loss statement	1,166	1,308
Add back disclosed fixed costs (eg depreciation, interest on loans, plant leasing costs, directors' fees and audit fees)	2,322	1,836
	3,488	3,144
Percentage to sales	12.22	12.02
If operating profit after depreciation:		
Adjusted profit as above	3,488	3,144
Less depreciation	568	587
	2,920	2,557
Percentage to sales	10.23	9.77

The result is not what one would have expected after reading in the chairman's review of keen competition, some shedding of stocks, and a drop in physical sales volume. There may well be scope for enquiry regarding the value placed on the ending inventory, and into the fairness for comparison in the 1978 data.

(c) Fixed charges cover

	1979 $000	1978 $000
Fixed charges:		
Interest on loans — fixed	807	367
other	702	708
Plant leasing costs	207	139
Total "fixed charges"	1,716	1,214
Plus profit before tax	1,166	1,362
Profit before tax and "fixed charges"	2,882	2,576
"Fixed charges" cover	1.68	2.12

One notes the increase in the absolute sum of "fixed charges" of $502,000, the decline in the cover, and the fact that these charges have to be met in cash from an operating net cash inflow if the company is to stay solvent. The increase in interest on fixed loans would seem to relate to the Bank of New Zealand's overdraft being converted in part into a term liability. From a study of the balance sheet, it can be seen that total indebtedness to the Bank of New Zealand rose during the year from $4.5 million to $5.7 million. The conversion of part to term liability will have improved the current ratio but done little if anything to improve the overall financial situation of the company.

It is noted in passing that liability under "capital" leases has been capitalized and shown under "term liabilities" in the balance sheet. There is no need to adjust the gearing for an unquantified debt.

Perhaps the most serious aspect of this analysis is the volatility of profit as a result of the high fixed charges.

(d) Profitability

One notes a fall in the net profit to sales ratio, as a result of the rise in fixed charges. There would seem to be a case for enquiring further into the reliability of the disclosed profit, with inventory valuation as the most likely source of potential doubt.

The statistical summary shows percentages of net profit to ordinary capital for 1979 (and 1978) which disregard the dividend rights of preference shareholders, and which are therefore misleading even though they are literaly what is described. The earnings per ordinary share are 22.56 cents, not 26.18 cents.

The earnings rate to shareholders' funds of 5.95% is very low. With debenture interest around 15% and a matching inflation level, there was good reason for the shares of the company to be priced down on the market. For the future, one recognized that the company would have a serious problem if it required additional equity capital, unless it could achieve a much higher rate of return on funds. A 20% fall in the profit before tax and fixed charges would reduce profit before tax by 49.4%. It is noted that it would take only a 3.4% reduction in the value placed on inventories to cause this 20% fall in profit before tax and fixed charges.

(e) Net asset backing

The net asset backing of $4.04 per ordinary share included $10.5 million (= $3 per share) of land, buildings, plant, machinery and vehicles. With such low earning rates, there is a real threat to the business as a going concern. For security purposes, these assets are worth what can be obtained for them in a forced sale. It is just possible that some sections of the operation may be saleable as profitable independent units, but it is by no means certain; others may have a low potential sale value. Partial sale could be very difficult to achieve. It follows that the providers of debt finance to such an enterprise will be most concerned about any erosion of the current assets, being the main realizable portion of the company's assets. In a case like this, net asset backing lacks significance as a total, and the extent of sunk cost in fixed assets makes the equity/debt relationship of little significance also. One notes in passing that increases in net asset backing resulting from the revaluation of specialized assets may well lead to an inadequate appreciation of the changes in financial leverage over the period of years covered by the trend statement.

(f) Debt finance

There has been an increase in debt of $1,722,297, and this has been classified mainly as "term liabilities". The notable transfer of $2.2 million of the Bank of New Zealand debt to the long term category, and the increase in short term borrowings of $603,000, are the most important differences. However, if the cost inputs of the year, for example wool, are up in price significantly (and information to estimate this effect could have been obtained), then the slight reduction in trade creditors and accruals could indicate a pre-balance date reduction in purchasing.

Information regarding the terms and repayment dates of the various secured loans could have been obtained from the company files, in order to form a better judgment of the financial situation of the company.

The general impression is that there has been a significant increase in the vulnerability of the company, arising from both the extent and sources of its debt, and probably given added emphasis by its debt repayment schedules.

(g) The current ratio

The current ratio in 1979 was 2.19:1 and this appears to be an improvement on the 2.07:1 ratio for 1978. Further study suggests that there may have been a decline in solvency, however.

The "debtors and prepayments" show little change, yet prices rose materially during the period (probably over 20% — an approximate figure could have been obtained through research). The chairman's review confirms that sales in the last quarter of the year were well below expectations. The sitaution is clarified further in the notes to the accounts:

	1979 $	1978 $
Stock and work in progress Inventory sub-classifications were:		
Raw materials	3,447,852	3,818,579
Work in progress	5,529,397	5,068,135
Finished goods	7,923,698	5,859,240
	16,900,947	14,745,954

It seems that there has been a severe trimming back of materials stocks prior to balance date, and that there is a substantial carryover of as yet unsold winter stocks. There is every indication of a cash flow problem unless this apparant surplus is sold. The chairman's review dated 3 September 1979 gave no indication of a potential loss on such a clearance. This raises the question of the basis of inventory valuation; and the accounting policies statement includes this note: "*Valuation of stocks* Raw materials are valued at the lower of cost or market value. Work in progress is valued on the basis of standard direct cost plus departmental overheads and finished goods are valued on the basis of the lower of absorbed standard cost or net realizable value. Due allowance for obsolescence has been made where appropriate. In determining stock values the principle of FIFO has been observed".

The setting of normal capacity for the purposes of overhead absorption is a subjective exercise, as is the decision on net realizable value. One can only note that there is the possibility of overvaluation, leading to a potential loss on sales in the ensuing period. If climatic conditions have affected the recent sales of this company, they will have affected its competitors also, creating a buyers' market.

(h) Solvency

Solvency is the ability of the company to meet its debts as they fall due. It is concerned not with the past but with the future cash inflows and outflows. It would not have been very difficult to forecast at 30 June 1979 that the company would need a substantially higher investment in inventories and debtors in order to sustain the present level of operations in the face of rising input costs and selling prices. For example, at say 20% overall increase an extra $4 million would have been required. Where could it be obtained? It is clear that the company must have been operating up to if not beyond safe debt limits. If its ordinary shares are in the 80 cents to $1.05 range on the market, then its propsects of raising additional equity capital are small. Its immediate prospects of raising profitability and, with this, the share price, would appear to be very small indeed. Its only option would seem to be the cutting back of the scale of its operations by the sale of selected sections of the enterprise — if it can find a buyer, and that may not be easy as similar problems may be facing other companies in the relevant aspects of the trade.

Could the Mosgiel Outcome have been Foreseen?

There is little doubt that the Mosgiel outcome could have been foreseen as a distinct possibility. This conclusion would have been reached on the basis of a study of the company's own statements supplemented by other relevant information which could have been obtained by the analyst/interpreter. It would have been more difficult to assess the degree of probability of insolvency, and even more difficult to assess the potential loss on a receivership or forced liquidation; yet both assessments would be necessary if one were to obtain a measure of financial risk involved in share investment, secured debt, and the granting of trade credit. Once a business ceases to be a going concern, realization values of assets, including inventories, may be only a fraction of their book values — as proved to be so in the case of Mosgiel Ltd.

Case Study 3

A Case of Company Survival

[2004] Alliance Textiles Ltd was the main competitor of Mosgiel Ltd (Case No 2) at the time of its collapse late in April 1980. The company was the outcome of a series of mergers and takeovers in the woollen industry, aimed at securing the benefits of rationalization and volume. In the 1979–80 year the company operated three woollen mills, two wool scouring plants, and four small garment factories. Throughout its rationalization program the company had made modest profits. Asset backing was high, but the market price of the company's 50 cents ordinary shares had ranged between 47 cents and 55 cents only during the 1979–80 year. The local (New Zealand) market for woollen goods was depressed during the year, with unused capacity across the industry, and with highly competitive pricing. The unit cost of inputs to the manufacturing processes increased by around 20% during the 1979–80 year; and this was in line with industry expectations.

Shown below are:
- consolidated revenue statement;
- consolidated balance sheet;
- selected notes to the accounts;
- a statement regarding export sales; and
- statement of accounting policies.

Let us now review the data with a view to assessing company performance in a most difficult year, and to gaining in the process some appreciation of managerial policies.

EXTRACTS FROM THE 1980 ANNUAL REPORT OF ALLIANCE TEXTILES LTD

Alliance Textiles Limited and Subsidiary Companies
Consolidated revenue statement for year ended 31 July 1980

	Note	1980 $	1979 $
Turnover			
Sales — domestic		24,072,534	21,954,670
— export		8,053,205	5,403,699
Total Group sales		32,125,739	27,358,369
Operating profit	1	1,216,429	530,941
Add: Dividends from investments		1,103	59,197
		1,217,532	590,138
Deduct: Abnormal items arising from planned restructuring	2	314,434	—
Profit before Extraordinary Items		903,098	590,138
Add: Capital profit on disposal of assets		945	2,724
Profit after Extraordinary Items (No tax payable)		904,043	592,862
Retained profits at 1 August 1979		3,353,943	2,890,801
Plus: Prior year adjustment		—	57,233
		3,353,943	2,948,034
Add: Transfers from capital reserves	3	399,526	240,047
		4,657,512	3,780,943
Less: Dividends and distributions	4	557,000	427,000
Retained Profits at 31 July 1980		4,100,512	3,353,943

Consolidated balance sheet as at 31 July 1980

	Note	1980 $	1980 $	1979 $	1979 $
Shareholders' funds					
Authorised capital					
20,000,000 Ordinary shares of 50 cents each			10,000,000		10,000,000
1,700,000 Redeemable specified preference shares of 50 cents	5		850,000		850,000
			10,850,000		10,850,000
Issued capital					
6,500,000 Ordinary shares of 50 cents each			3,250,000		3,250,000
1,700,000 Redeemable specified preference shares of 50 cents each (12%)	5		850,000		850,000
Capital reserves	6		4,100,000		4,100,000
Revenue reserves	7		1,450,578		1,850,104
			7,100,512		6,353,943
Total shareholders' funds			12,651,090		12,304,047
Liabilities					
Term liabilities	8		6,373,875		6,954,786
Current liabilities					
Bank overdraft (secured)		1,340,633		2,549,820	
Sundry creditors		2,488,138		2,260,678	
Bills payable and deposits		500,000		1,002,359	
Provision for taxation		—		4,210	
Proposed final dividend	9	260,000		130,000	
Current portion term liabilities	8	1,070,754		1,040,180	
			5,659,525		6,987,247
			24,684,490		26,246,080

	Note	1980 $	1980 $	1979 $	1979 $
Fixed assets	10				
Land and buildings		3,757,263		3,819,058	
Plant and vehicles		5,309,263		6,154,674	
			9,066,526		9,973,732
Investments (at cost)	11		402,196		407,895
Current assets					
Cash and deposits		47,038		15,459	
Debtors and prepayments		4,536,159		3,844,728	
Export incentive tax rebates and grants		699,083		584,173	
Inventories	12	9,933,488		11,420,093	
			15,215,768		15,864,453
			24,684,490		26,246,080

The Notes on pages 14 to 17 inclusive form part of this statement.

On behalf of the Board of Directors

W R Jackson, Chairman
F B McKenzie, Director

371

Notes to the Accounts
Alliance Textiles Limited and Subsidiary Companies

	1980 $	1979 $
1. *Operating profit*		
Operating profit has been shown after		
(a) Including export incentives and grants	710,937	610,099
Conversion grant export suspensory loan	—	100,000
	710,937	710,099
(b) *Providing for the following expenses and losses:*		
Audit fees	37,200	32,100
Directors' fees	20,000	20,000
Depreciation	1,028,686	1,041,003
Lease expenses	12,546	19,608
Interest — fixed loans	927,578	830,800
— others	766,770	549,348
Exchange loss on overseas loan	87,709	32,686
	2,880,489	2,525,545
2. *Abnormal items arising from planned restructuring*		
Redundancy payments to staff	161,575	
Abnormal losses incurred or provision made on stock	152,859	
	314,434	

	Consolidated $	Holding Co $
6. *Capital reserves*		
Balance from last year	1,850,104	1,632,943
Plus realized profit on sale of investments	945	945
	1,851,049	1,633,888
Less transfer of realized profits to retained earnings		
for dividend purposes	400,471	400,471
	1,450,578	1,233,417
Balances at 31/7/80 comprise:		
Realized capital profits	381,559	381,559
General capital reserves	15,728	15,728
Property revaluation reserve	418,170	—
Capital reserve on mergers	371,823	572,832
Capital replacement fund	222,035	222,035
Share premium reserve	41,263	41,263
	1,450,578	1,233,417

The following reserves are available for distribution as tax free in the hands of shareholders.

(a) Share Premium Reserve. The sum of $3,888 only has been approved by the High Court for distribution to shareholders as a tax free dividend provided revenue reserves are available to match the amount so distributed.

(b) Realized Capital Profits: $381,559.

	Consolidated		Holding Co	
	1980	1979	1980	1979
8. *Term Liabilities*	$	$	$	$
Secured loans				
Mortgages	74,826	78,826	—	—
Registered debenture stock	5,166,472	5,139,950	5,166,472	5,139,950
Second ranking registered debenture stock	316,700	316,700	288,000	288,000
Bank loans	1,210,000	1,525,000	1,150,000	1,450,000
	6,767,998	7,060,476	6,604,472	6,877,950
Unsecured loans	3,000	3,000	—	—
Obligations under capital leases	673,631	931,490	—	—
	7,444,629	7,994,966	6,604,472	6,877,950
Less Included with current liabilities repayable within one year	1,070,754	1,040,180	679,837	763,321
	6,373,875	6,954,786	5,924,635	6,114,629

1980 Term Liabilities are due for repayment as follows:

		Consolidated $	Holding Co $
New Zealand Currency:			
Year ending 31 July,	1981	862,917	472,000
	1982	638,913	521,600
	1983	710,109	664,900
	1984	414,292	231,400
	1985	467,000	463,000
After 31 July	1985	3,675,926	3,576,100
		6,769,157	5,929,000
Overseas Loans:			
Year ending 31 July,	1981	207,837	207,837
	1982	207,837	207,837
	1983	259,798	259,798
		675,472	675,472
		7,444,629	6,604,472

(a) Registered debenture stock and second ranking registered debenture stock is secured by a debenture trust deed. Mortgage advances are secured over land and buildings ranking prior to debenture stock. Bank stock ranking pari passu with the above individual categories of debenture stock has been issued to cover overdraft, term loan and other facilities. First ranking bank stock of $4,900,000 and second ranking bank stock of $1,750,000 is current.

(b) Interest rates on secured loans range from 8¼% to 16% per annum. The rates applicable to the overseas loan vary depending upon currency selected with each rollover period. At 31 July, 1980, the loan was denominated in U.S.A. dollars at an interest rate of 11.75%. This loan is covered by forward exchange contracts.

(c) Obligation under capital leases. Future payments under leases for plant including residual values, less interest costs.

373

10. Fixed Assets	At Cost $	At Valuation $	Total $	Deprec- iation $	Book Value at 31/7/80 $
Land	5,657	453,950	459,607	—	459,607
Buildings	269,015	3,257,650	3,526,665	229,009	3,297,656
Plant & vehicles	11,190,307	—	11,190,307	6,834,794	4,355,513
Plant under capital lease	1,575,000	—	1,575,000	621,250	953,750
	13,039,979	3,711,600	16,751,579	7,685,053	9,066,526
Previous year	12,979,829	3,711,600	6,691,429	6,717,697	9,973,732

The above valuation is the latest available government valuation.

12. Inventories	1980	1979
Raw materials	1,712,899	1,811,000
Work in progress	5,098,271	6,608,274
Finished goods	3,122,318	3,000,819
	9,933,488	11,420,093

Export sales: Alliance Textiles Group: $000

Year	Carpet yarns	% of export	Other products	% of export	Total exports	% of total sales	Total sales
1977/78	4,052	93	323	7	4,375	16.4	26,630
1978/79	4,169	77	1,235	23	5,404	19.75	27,358
1979/80	6,596	82	1,457	18	8,053	25	32,126

Statement of Accounting Policies

The historical cost basis of accounting has been used in the preparation of these accounts, except that land and buildings are valued at current government valuations with additions since the date of valuation at cost.

Particular policies

(a) Basis of Consolidation

The consolidated financial statements include the accounts of all subsidiary companies. All significant inter-company items, transactions, and unrealized profits are eliminated on consolidation.

Dividends only from an associate company are included, as equity accounting would have no significant effect on the group's position in the Directors' opinion.

(b) Valuation of Stock on Hand

Stocks are valued at the lower of cost or net realizable value, cost being determined principally on a first in first out basis. Cost of work in progress and finished goods includes raw materials, direct labour and factory overheads. Due allowance for obsolescence has been made in all stock valuations.

(c) Debtors

These are recorded at expected realizable value, after making provision for doubtful debts.

(d) Fixed Assets and Depreciation

For income tax purposes the Company continued to claim the maximum depreciation allowable. For accounting purposes, depreciation is calculated using straight line rates which write off the assets over the estimated economic life, ranging as follows:

Buildings	50 years
Plant	10 years
Furniture, Fittings and Motor Vehicles	5 years

(e) Capital Plant Leases

The group has some major items of plant financed under capital lease agreements. Revenue is charged with depreciation at straight line rates normally applied to the particular plant items plus interest cost calculated in the lease. Gross value of payments on these capital leases for the year was $384,686.

Other leases for motor vehicles, sundry equipment and premises are not material and are charged against revenue over the appropriate period.

(f) Taxation

The group has accumulated tax deductions from allowances for investments, export and other incentives which exceed present known tax liabilities. In assessing the accumulated tax deductions, full recognition has been given to benefits from regional and export investment allowances, export market development, and Inland Revenue Department depreciation rates. As there is no tax liability, no provision is necessary for deferred tax.

(g) Foreign Currencies

Foreign currency balances outstanding were converted to New Zealand currency at rates ruling on 31/7/80, except where forward exchange contracts are held. Realized and unrealized exchange losses are charged against profit for the year.

(h) Changes in Accounting Policies

There have been no significant changes in accounting policy during the year.

Analysis and Comments

1. Sales

	1979/80 $000	%	1978/79 $000	%	Increase $000	%
Domestic	24,073	74.9	21,955	80.3	2,118	9.6
Export	8,053	25.1	5,403	19.7	2,650	49.0
	32,126	100.0	27,358	100.0	4,768	17.4

(1) Physical volume of sales

The cost of inputs was up about 20%. If this was reflected in prices, the overall sales in physical terms would be slightly down on the previous year, and sales on the domestic market would be down about 10%. With keen competition on a depressed market, it seems more probable that some of the apparent fall in unit sales on the domestic market has been offset by lower prices.

(2) Export sales

The most notable feature is the greater emphasis on export sales, up to 49% on last year and now comprising 25% of total sales. The analysis of export sales shows that the main increase was in carpet yarns, up from $4,169,000 to $6,596,000 (58.2%).

375

2. Profit margin

	1979/80 $000	1978/79 $000	Increase $000	%
Operating profit	1,216	531	685	129.0
Add back "expenses and losses", Note 1	2,880	2,525	355	14.1
Margin	4,096	3,056	1,040	
Total sales	32,126	27,358	4,768	
% to sales	12.75	11.17		

Of the $1,040,000 increase in 1979–80:

	$000
Due to increased sales volume — 11.17% of $4,768,000	533
Due to increase in profit margin — 1.58% of $32,126,000	507
	1,040

In spite of the keen competition and price cutting on the local market, the overal profit margin is slightly higher than in 1978–79. This factor has had a significant effect on the overall results of the year.

3. Interest expense

	1979/80 $000	1978/79 $000	Increase $000
Interest — fixed loans	927	831	96
— other	767	549	218
	1,694	1,380	314
			= 22.8% up

Interest expense is 22.8% up on last year, but interest bearing liabilities are considerably lower at 31 July 1980 than a year earlier:

	1980 $000	1979 $000	Decrease $000
Term liabilities*	6,374	6,955	
Plus current portion	1,071	1,040	
	7,445	7,995	550
Bank overdraft	1,341	2,550	1,209
	8,786	10,545	1,759
			= 16.7% down

*Include obligations under capital leases (Note 8).

Interest rates range from 8¼ to 16% (Note 8). The interest cost of the year is

19.3% of debt at 31 July 1980 and 16.1% of that at 31 July 1979. It may be safe to infer:

1. That debt rose seasonally during part of the 1979–80 year.
2. That there was a sharp increase in the average interest rate on debt during the year.

4. Restructuring expense

One notes the substantial outlay ($314,434), representing a serious commitment to restructuring in order to secure the longer term future of the enterprise.

5. Rate of return

The rate of return on shareholders' funds has increased:

	1979/80 $000	1978/79 $000	Increase $000
Net profit after extraordinary items and restructuring expense	904	593	311
Shareholders' funds	12,651	12,304	(up 52.4%)
Rate of return, %	7.15	4.82	(up 48.3%)
Also the rate of return on total assets:			
Net profit as above	904	593	
Add back interest	1,694	1,380	
	2,598	1,973	625
Total assets	24,684	26,246	
Rate of return on assets, %	10.52	7.52	(up 39.9%)

6. Cash flow

	1979/80 $000	1978/79 $000	Increase $000
Net profit	904	593	
Add back depreciation	1,029	1,041	
Cash flow generated	1,933	1,634	299
Dividends	557	427	130
Cash flow retained	1,376	1,207	169

7. Dividend

The dividend on ordinary shares has been increased as shown on p 378.

This could be expected to be an indication to the market of director confidence, and to improve the market price of the share towards a more satisfactory level. At

	1980 $	1979 $
Dividends	557,000	427,000
Preference, 12%	102,000	102,000
Ordinary	455,000	325,000
= %	14	10

present share prices, an issue of ordinary shares would have been impracticable.

The comments on the capital reserves indicated that there was scope, albeit limited, to pay dividends free of tax in the shareholders' hands.

8. Control over assets

(1) Fixed assets	$000
Accumulated depreciation, 31/7/1979	6,718
Plus depreciation of the year	1,029
	7,747
Accumulated depreciation, 31/7/1980	7,685
Depreciation on assets sold or discarded during the year	62
	At Cost
Fixed assets: 31/7/1980	13,040
31/7/1979	12,980
Increase	60

There has been virtually no addition to fixed assets during the year, and the accumulated depreciation on plant sold or discarded was only $62,000. The overall investment in fixed assets, after depreciation, is down $907,000.

(2) Inventories At 31 July:	1980 $000	1979 $000	Increase/ (Decrease) $000	%
Raw materials	1,713	1,811	(98)	(5.4)
Work in progress	5,098	6,608	(1,510)	(22.8)
Finished goods	3,122	3,001	121	4.0
	9,933	11,420	(1,487)	(13.0)
Sales	32,126	27,358		
Sales to inventory	3.23	2.40		

In view of the around 20% increased cost of inputs, and the increase in dollar sales, the reduction in the inventory level suggests a strong policy of containment of investment in inventory, partly through the avoidance of build-up of work in progress (particularly) and finished goods.

(The comparison with Mosgiel Ltd in inventory breakdown is telling. Work in process was at a similar level, but raw materials and finished stocks were very much higher than those of Alliance at 31 July 1979. At 30 June 1979, Mosgiel Ltd inventory was:

	$000	Alliance $000
Raw materials	3,448	1,811
Work in progress	5,529	6,608
Finished goods	7,924	3,001
	16,901	11,420

The Mosgiel Ltd sales level was very close to that for Alliance Textiles Ltd, but the inventory was 48% higher than the Alliance inventory at the same date.)

(3) Debtors and prepayments

At 31 July	1980 $000	1979 $000	Increase $000	%
	4,536	3,845	691	18.0

The increase is close to the around 20% increase in cost inputs, which would be reflected in prices:

Sales	32,126	27,358
Sales to debtors	7.1	7.1

(The sales to debtors of Mosgiel Ltd in 1979 was 5.2.)

9. Control over liabilities

(1) *Bank overdraft*
The most significant feature of the financial position is the reduction of the bank overdraft from $2,549,820 to $1,340,633. At the same time, bills payable and deposits were reduced by $502,359 and term liabilities by $550,337.

(2) *Current ratio*
Current liabilities were reduced by $1,327,722. The current ratio improved from 2.27:1 to 2.69:1.

(3) *Debt/equity ratio*

At 31 July 1980	0.95:1
At 31 July 1979	1.13:1

There was a significant improvement, thanks mainly to the control over investment in assets during the year. The improvement was mainly in the current liabilities area, which makes it more significant.

(4) *Long-term debt*
The maturities of debt are well spread (Note 8). The interest cover is not high — at 31 July 1980 it was:

	$000
Net profit	904
Plus interest	1,694
	2,598
Interest cover	1.53 times

At these levels of profitability the company's position was not as secure as it might have been, albeit greatly improved over 1979.

10. Overall performance

The performance of the company during the year reflects a policy that was designed to meet the difficult circumstances and to help lay the foundations for secure and more profitable operations in the future. Key features were:

(1) The development of overseas markets and of products to suit those markets.

(2) Ability to earn profit from manufacturing and trading under conditions that forced the major competitor into loss and ultimate liquidation. No doubt this was related in part to the costly rationalization program undertaken by the company in this and earlier years.

(3) Strict control over investment in assets, and particularly in inventories, to achieve a stronger financial position in spite of inflationary pressure.

Case Study 4

The Importance of Analysis

[2005] The National Insurance Co Ltd carries on an insurance business mainly in Australia and New Zealand. It has its head office in New Zealand.

During the 1979–80 year, its net premium income was obtained from:

New Zealand	26%;	Fiji and Papua New Guinea	8%
Australia	54%;	Reinsurances of risks of other companies	12%

A small porportion only was in life insurance.

Among the problems of the 1979–80 year were claims arising from serious floods in Otago, New Zealand; but its most serious problem was premium cutting due to cut-throat competition for insurance business in Australia.

The chairman's review included the information that there had been substantial increases in the market value of the company's investment portfolio, due to rising share prices (particularly in Australia), and that the market value of the company's share portfolio at year's end was $10.7 million in excess of book value, compared with an excess of $6.0 million for the previous year.

The consolidated balance sheet, excluding notes, is shown on p 372.

Instructions:

A client who holds 10,000 shares in the company is concerned at the huge loss on underwriting and is considering the sale of his shareholding. He is relatively un-skilled in reading financial statements. He has asked you to analyze the accounts and to prepare a report which will give him a better understanding of the factors leading to the overal fall in profits during the 1979–80 year.

Prepare the report. It is suggested that it consist of:

(1) A concise statement comparing the total profits and overall profitability of the group in 1979–80 with those in 1978–79.

(2) An analysis and discussion of the results for 1979–80, as compared with 1978–79, for:

(a) underwriting activity (ie insurance), and

Consolidated revenue and profit and loss account
for year ended 31 August 1980

	1980 $000		1979 $000
Underwriting			
Gross premiums written	97,076		71,702
Less reinsurances	29,783		19,385
Net premiums written		67,293	52,317
Plus decrease (increase) in provision for unearned premiums		1,525	(1,268)
Earned premium income		68,818	51,049
Less			
Claims paid and outstanding	58,748		37,578
General expenses, commission and taxation	17,263		13,300
		76,011	50,878
Underwriting profit (loss)		(7,193)	171
Investment income			
Net income less taxation from:			
Government and Local Authority securities	110		89
Companies	4,457		3,644
Other investments	1,917		1,337
	6,484		5,070
Realized net gains on sale of investments	3,568		798
		10,052	5,868
Operating profit for year		2,859	6,039
Non-operating items:			
Exchange fluctuation		778	(162)
Profit on freehold properties sold		—	25
		3,637	5,902
Less minority interests in earnings of subsidiary		7	—
Consolidated profit for year		$3,630	$5,902

Consolidated Balance Sheet as at 31 August 1980

	1980 $000	1979 $000		1980 $000	1979 $000
Shareholders' funds			**Fixed assets (at book value)**		
Authorized capital — 30,000,000 Ordinary shares of 50c each	15,000	10,000	Freehold property — Land	2,803	2,722
			— Buildings	8,914	7,949
Issued capital — 16,248,738 Ordinary shares of 50c each fully paid	8,124	7,386	Office equipment and motor vehicles	1,714	1,269
				13,431	11,940
Reserves —					
Share premium reserve	1,490	1,490	**Investments (at cost)**		
Capital reserve	565	566	Government and Local Authority Securities	3,307	1,374
Exchange fluctuation reserve	—	966	Mortgages and term deposits	25,682	16,023
Retained earnings	20,739	19,782	Shares in companies	26,442	27,173
Total shareholders' funds	30,918	30,190	Company debentures and notes	33,183	26,563
Minority interests	250	—	Shares in subsidiary companies	—	—
Term liabilities				88,614	71,133
Bank term loan (secured by mortgage)	472	717			
Insurance provisions					
Unearned premiums	29,530	23,152			
Outstanding claims	66,532	38,609	**Current assets**		
	96,062	61,761	Cash at bank and on call deposit	5,877	4,102
Current liabilities			Debtors	35,561	23,696
Bank overdraft ($413,000 secured by mortgage)	2,253	928	Amounts owing by subsidiary companies	—	—
Creditors including provision for taxation	18,156	15,576		41,438	27,798
Recommended final dividend	1,868	1,699	**Intangible asset**		
Amounts owing to subsidiary companies	—	—	Goodwill on consolidation	5,937	—
	22,277	18,203	Life assurance assets	1,024	—
Life assurance fund and liabilities	465	—			
	150,444	110,871		150,444	110,871

(b) investment activity

and explaining how the non-operating item would arise.

(3) A summary showing the contributions from each area of activity for the two years and the differences that have contributed to the overall decline in profit of $2,272,000.

Suggested Answer

Report for:
Prepared by:
Date:
Subject: The National Insurance Co Ltd: Results for 1979–80 year.

1. Consolidated net profit

The consolidated net profit of the group fell from $5,902,000 in 1978–79 to $3,630,000 in 1979–80, a fall of $2,272,000 or 38.5%.

The rate of return on shareholders' funds was:

1979–80	11.74%
1978–79	19.55%

2. Underwriting results

The main cause of the fall in profit was the loss incurred in underwriting:

Business increased	1980 $000	1979 $000
Net premiums written	67,293	52,317
(an increase of $14,976,000, or 28.6%)		
After adjustment for unearned premiums, earned premiums rose:	68,818	51,049
(an increase of $17,769,000, or 34.8%)		
Claims increased significantly	58,748	37,578
(an increse of $21,170,000, or 56,3%)		
Claims as a percentage of earned premiums	85.4	73.6
General Expenses, Commission and Taxation rose	17,263	13,300
(an increase of $3,963,000, or 29.8%)		
Without a breakdown of this item, to separate out taxation, one cannot come to any conclusions.		
Overall, underwriting profit/(loss) was (a fall of $7,364,000)	(7,193)	171

Summary:

There has been considerable increase in business done. Premiums written were up 28.6%, but earned premiums were up 34.8%. This suggests some shedding of business during the year, probably because of the high claims.

The most significant factor was the increase in the incidence of claims to premium earned, up from 73.6% to 85.4%. The directors' report indicates that one cause was the losses from floods in Otago, but that the main cause was the cutting back of premiums in order to met cut-throat competition in Australia. If premiums are cut, then the percentage of claims to premiums can be expected to rise.

The overall result was an underwriting loss of $7,193,000, whereas last year more or less broke even.

3. Investment results

	1980 $000	1979 $000	Increase $000
Income less taxation from:			
Companies	4,457	3,644	813
Other investments	2,027	1,426	601
	6,484	5,070	1,414
Net gains on sale of investments	3,568	798	2,770
	10,052	5,868	4,184

The disclosed results of the year have been helped by the major gains on sale of investments — up $2,770,000 on the previous year.

It is noted that, in spite of this profit-taking, the company's share investments have a market value of $10.7 million in excess of book value, compared with $6.0 million last year, representing an additional gain of $4.7 million during the year.

4. Non-operating item: exchange fluctuation

The company holds assets in foreign currencies, and these require conversion to New Zealand dollars each year when the group's accounts are being prepared. The differences which arise through changes in the exchange rate from year to year are adjujsted through an Exchange Fluctation Account. This year the adjustment, a gain, was $778,000 compared with a loss of $162,000 last year.

Summary:

	1980 $000	1979 $000	Increase/(Decrease) $000	%
Insurance business:				
Earned premiums rose	68,818	51,049	17,769	34.8
Claims increased	58,748	37,578	21,170	56.3
% of earned premiums	85.4	73.6		16.0
Margin before expense	10,070	13,471	(3,401)	(25.2)
Less expense and taxation	17,263	13,300	3,963	29.8
Underwriting profit/(loss)	(7,193)	171	(7,364)	

Continued p 385

Investment income:

Income	6,484	5,070	1,414	27.9
Profit on sales	3,568	798	2,770	
	10,052	5,868	4,184	71.3
Operating income (net of taxation)	2,859	6,039	(3,180)	(52.6)
Non-operating etc items				
Exchange fluctuations gain/(loss)	778	(162)	940	
Other gains/(losses)	(7)	25	(32)	
Disclosed income	3,630	5,902	(2,272)	(38.5)

Unrealized gains on investments increased $4.7 million during the year.

There will be a large loss carried forward for tax purposes. The key factor in the results of the year is the serious fall in the insurance margin, the excess of earned premiums over claims. From the directors' report, it seems that this is due more to the cutting of premium rates in Australia to meet competition than to a higher incidence of claims. Future insurance results would seem to be dependent mainly on the profitability of insurance business undertaken in Australia. There is some indication from the data that steps are already in hand to reduce unprofitable business — business written was up only 28.6%, while premium income earned was up 34.8%.

Case Study 5

Historical Costs, CCA, and Purchasing Power Gains and Losses on Monetary Accounts

[2006] Following the publication by the Council of the New Zealand Society of Accountants in February 1979 of "Guidelines" regarding supplementary financial statements in terms of current costs and values, a number of large New Zealand companies included supplementary current cost accounting (CCA) statements in their 1979 annual reports. In this section we shall examine the supplementary CCA statements of one such company, the TNL Group Ltd.

One of the more serious criticisms of the CCA proposals was that they failed to take "properly" into account purchasing power gains and losses on monetary accounts. For this reason, the CCA statements of the TNL Group will be adjusted later to include a recognition of the purchasing power gains and losses on the monetary accounts of the Group.

The operations of the TNL Group involved transport and tourism mainly; the group also included subsidiaries involved in mineral extraction, wood chip production, and farming, horticulture and exporting.

In the introduction to the CCA statements, it was stated that the company had been actively engaged in promoting current cost accounting as an indication of financial performance and position. It was also stated that: "The results illustrate the harsh effect inflation has on capital intensive industries. Depreciation is a significant charge against revenue for TNL and when based on current costs needed to be increased by a further $3,024,000. A cost of sales adjustment contributed to a further loss of $566,000. "Because of restrictive pricing practices we are unable to recover costs on a current cost basis. This has inevitably contributed towards being unable to maintain the operating capability of the group to the extent of $887,000."

A summary of the consolidated CCA and reported profit and loss and balance sheet figures are shown in Figure 20.2.

Figure 20.2

Consolidated profit and loss account for the year ended 30 June 1979

	Notes re CCA figures	Current cost accounting		As reported in the unadjusted statements	
		1979 $000	1978 $000	1979 $000	1978 $000
Revenue		51,655	46,423	51,655	46,423
Operating profit before depreciation, interest and taxation		7,348	6,039	7,348	6,039
Expenses					
Difference between current cost and historical cost of sales	1	566	341	—	—
Depreciation	2	5,273	4,524	2,249	2,543
Circulating monetary assets adjustment	3	1,141	1,220	—	—
Non trading items	2	494	(7)	(154)	(451)
		7,474	6,078	2,095	2,092
Operating surplus (deficit)	4	(126)	(39)	5,253	3,947
Plus Increase in capital maintenance reserve financed from borrowings	5	1,319	1,444	—	—
		1,193	1,405	5,253	3,947
Less Interest on borrowings		1,250	945	1,250	945
Minority shareholders' share of profit		4	4	4	4
Shareholders' profit before taxation		(61)	456	3,999	2,998
Less Taxation on income	6	826	379	826	379
Shareholders' profit/(loss) available for distribution	7	(887)	77	3,173	2,619

Notes regarding the CCA figures

1 The current cost of sales was calculated by valuing opening and closing inventories at replacement cost by applying the price movement of a sample group to the total inventory for each category.

2 Depreciation and non-trading items. Depreciation was based on the current cost of assets. In the case of sale of depreciable assets, profit or loss was determined by relating the sales price to the current cost of the asset.

3 The circulating monetary asset adjustment was calculated by applying the increase in the general price index to the average of current monetary assets.

4 Operating surplus/deficit. This was the amount by which the operating capability of the company was considered to have altered during the year.

Consolidated balance sheet as at 30 June 1979

	Current cost accounting		As reported in the unadjusted statements	
	1979 $000	1978 $000	1979 $000	1978 $000
Shareholders' funds				
Issued capital	15,002	14,983	15,002	14,983
Capital maintenance reserve	24,575	20,228	—	—
Capital reserves	10,115	9,582	11,077	10,367
Retained profits	246	2,547	4,403	2,891
	49,938	47,340	30,482	28,241
Represented by:				
Fixed assets				
Land and buildings	17,634	16,652	13,151	12,285
Vehicles, plant and equipment	32,388	30,132	18,311	15,663
	50,022	46,784	31,462	27,948
Development expenditure	403	—	403	—
Investments	7,887	6,750	7,239	6,750
Current assets	13,744	14,935	13,496	14,672
Total assets	72,056	68,469	52,600	49,370
Less Deferred taxation	3,467	2,527	3,467	2,527
Term liabilities and minority interest	7,675	9,033	7,675	9,033
Current liabilities	10,976	9,569	10,976	9,569
Total liabilities	22,118	21,129	22,118	21,129
Net assets	49,938	47,340	30,482	28,241

5 Increase in capital maintenance reserve financed by borrowing (gearing adjustment). The increase in the capital maintenance reserve was represented by the writing up for the period of buildings, vehicles, plant and equipment and investments (less "backlog" depreciation), and the inventory price adjustment and circulating monetary assets adjustment. The credit to the CCA profit and loss account for the proportion of the increase in the capital maintenance reserve financed by borrowing was based on the view that to the extent that assets were financed by borrowing (rather than by equity capital), part of the increase in the capital maintenance reserve constituted a gain to equity shareholders.

6 The taxation of $826,000 was only 20.7% of the income before tax disclosed in the historical cost statements, due no doubt to various tax incentives, but according to the CCA statements, the whole of the taxation was paid from capital because there was a deficit before tax of $61,000.

7 The dividend cover was negative.

Historical cost "profit" versus CCA "loss"

	$000
The reported historical cost profit figure for the company was	3,173
The CCA statement produced a "loss" of	887
Total difference	4,060

387

There would seem to be good grounds for recognizing the deficiencies of historical cost accounting and accepting a CCA measure of profit as being closer to the reality underlying business operations in times of rising prices and inflation. Let us look closer at how the difference between the historical cost and CCA profit figures is made up:

		$000
1	The cost of the goods sold by the group increased during the year and progressively it cost more and more to replace the goods sold. The restatement of the historical cost of sales to replacement cost reflects the view that a firm cannot be deemed to have made profit unless it is able to provide from revenue for the replacement of the inventory sold. The restatement of the historical cost of sales to replacement cost required an extra:	566
2	With the rising replacement cost of vehicles, plant, etc, the depreciation charged against revenue was insufficient to cover "the maintenance of the operating capability" of the group — that is, to provide from revenue enough to replace trucks, buses, etc as they became due for replacement. The restatement of the depreciation charge in terms of replacement cost required a further:	3,024
3	The group has, as one of its important assets, the amount due to it by its customers. This and other monetary assets lost value during the year because of the inflation which took place. With inflation taken at 12.4% this loss was assessed at:	1,141
4	The group had included in its earnings profit made on the sale of vehicles, etc, of $154,000. The current cost accounts (which showed the assets at higher book values) produced a loss of $494,000 on these sales. The difference was:	648
5	All of the above meant that, instead of operating at a surplus of $5,253,000, there was an operating deficit of $126,000, an overstatement of operating surplus of:	5,379
6	The company had financed its operations in part with borrowed money. Under the CCA model used to prepare the supplementary statements of the TNL Group, the proportion of the asset revaluations (holding gains) and the loss in the value of circulating monetary assets which was financed by borrowing was recognized as part of the final income to the shareholders' interest. The amount of this gearing adjustment was:	1,319
7	Deducting this, we arrive at the overstatement of profit in the historical cost financial statements of:	4,060

CCA interpreted

What do the CCA accounts tell us? They indicate fairly clearly that this enterprise was finding it difficult to sustain itself, and eventually would have to either wind down its scale of operations or bring in more funds from shareholders and lenders just to keep going.

Monetary items: the use of loan finance

Current cost accounting (CCA) models had tended to recognize the relevance of "circulating monetary assets" such as debtors to the maintenance of the productive capability of the firm and applied a "circulating monetary assets adjustment" as a charge in arriving at current operating profit. No provision was made, however, for purchasing power losses on other monetary assets. Nevertheless, the analyst should recognize that there has been a loss of value in terms of purchasing power in respect of these assets during a period of inflation, and that the "income" derived includes part of the purchasing power of the principal advanced. A debt is principally an obligation to convey money to another person, but the significance of money lies in its purchasing power. If we look at a debt as an obligation to convey purchasing power, then in a period of inflation this obligation is reduced.

The reduction in the real principal of a debt which occurs during a period of inflation represents a gain to the borrower. Most business enterprises are net borrowers, in the sense that their liabilites exceed their total monetary assets. It is not difficult for the analyst to acquire a measure of the net gain in purchasing power accruing to a firm during a period of inflation. This gain (or loss) is independent of any changes which may have taken place in the value of the assets which have been financed by the borrowed funds.

While there is no doubt that the economic significance (purchasing power) of a liability falls during a period of inflation, it may be argued that the gain is unrealized, that there has been no direct cash inflow to the borrower to represent the gain to the borrower, nor an outflow to represent the loss to the lender. It may be argued further that if the gain to the borrower were recognized, then it may be necessary to borrow to pay the tax on this element of income and any dividend based on it. Yet it is difficult to justify differential treatment of monetary assets and liabilites. As Mr R W R White, Governor of the Reserve Bank of New Zealand at the time pointed out: "There is no difference in the characteristics of monetary assets and liabilities which warrants different treatment under inflation accounting rules. In fact, because the positive cash flow of a business can usually be directed either to the increase of a monetary asset or to the decrease of a monetary liability with equal facility, it is important that the two categories of financial contract be treated alike. If this is not done, management will have the option of directing cash flows to achieve the best tax advantage": *Reserve Bank of New Zealand Bulletin*, May 1980, p 141.

One of the more serious criticisms of certain CCA proposals was their failure to provide for a comprehensive and consistent accounting for purchasing power gains and losses on monetary accounts — both short and long term assets and liabilities. To illustrate the point, we shall modify the CCA profit and loss statement of the TNL Group Ltd so that instead of a gearing and circulating monetary assets adjustments, it incorporates purchasing power gains and losses on the net monetary accounts of the firm. The example is taken from T K Cowan, "CCA Enhanced", *Accountants' Journal*, July 1980, pp 205–11. The workings are shown in Figure 20.3. Three figures for pre- and after-tax profit (loss) are then compared: historical cost (HC) profit, as reported in the principal accounts of the group; CCA "Mark 1" profit (loss) as reported in the supplementary CCA statements of the group; and CCA "Mark 2" profit (loss) which results when the CCA figures are modified to include purchasing power gains (losses) on net monetary accounts.

Figure 20.3

	$000	$000	Profit effect $000
CCA: "Mark 1" (using gearing adjustment):			
Gearing adjustment		+	1,319
Less circulating monetary assets adjustment		−	1,141
Net adjustment re monetary items		+	178
CCA: "Mark 2" (adjusting net monetary items)			
Liabilities:			
Current		9,569	
Long term		8,953	
Deferred taxation		2,527	21,049
Assets: Monetary			
Current	14,672		
Less inventories	5,032	9,640	
Investments — as not subject to CCA adjustment		6,750	16,390
Excess of liabilities over assets			4,659
Inflation, year to 30/6/1979			12.4%
Inflation adjustment		+	578
Difference to CCA profit		+	400

Comparative results	Before tax $000	After tax $000
HC profit	3,999	3,173
CCA "Mark 1" — profit/(loss)	(61)	(887)*
CCA "Mark 2" — profit/(loss)	339	(487)*
*Based on actual tax paid.		

Review questions

20.1 (a) Discuss critically the ratios and percentages which are used to measure the profitability of an undertaking.

(b) Does a fall in the ratio of expense to turnover indicate an increase in operating efficiency?

20.2 There are two diverse companies in the AB group. A Ltd is old established, but B Ltd has been operating for only six years. For the year just ended, A Ltd showed an after-tax rate of return on funds of 12% and B Ltd 8%.

(a) What conclusions may be drawn from this data regarding the calibre of the performance of the management of A Ltd and B Ltd?

(b) If there were now $400,000 available for investment within the group, in which company should it be invested?

20.3 "The vital facts determining the future of a business are seldom to be found in the accounting statements of past years."

Examine this statement. What then is the use of analysis and interpretation of data drawn from the past?

20.4 The 19A1 profit after provision for income tax of the Albion Co Ltd was $360,000. This profit was arrived at after allowing:

	$000
For depreciation	100
For interest on: Long term loans	132
Bank overdraft	20
For rentals on long term (non-cancellable) leasehold property	28
For income tax payable	120
For deferred tax	80

The assets of the company of $8 million were financed:

	$000
From share capital in $1 shares fully paid	1,000
From asset revaluation reserve	400
From retained profits	1,600
From 8% convertible debentures of $1, convertible in 19A5, one share for one debenture stock unit	400
From provision for deferred tax	1,100
From 10% debentures	1,000
From bank overdraft	800
From trade creditors and provisions	1,700
	8,000

The rate of income tax payable by companies is 50% on the taxable balance. The Albion Co Ltd was able to take advantage in the 19A1 year of an investment allowance on plant purchased to further its production of goods for export. Sales for the year totaled $8 million.

1 From the above data, examine the profitability of the company in terms of such rates of return on sales and investment as you consider useful, indicating the significance of each, and also any limitations inherent in them.

2 Calculate the "cash flow per share", and also your measure or measures of the "earnings per share".

20.5 Consider the results of Speciality Foods Ltd for the two years ended 31 March 19A1 and 19A2 as shown on p 392. State what additional information you will need in order to reach conclusions.

20.6 Referring to Case Study 5, "Historical Costs, CCA, and Purchasing Power Gains and Losses on Monetary Accounts", specific price changes and changes in general purchasing power are realities of the business environment. Most financial statements are prepared on a basis which does not recognize either factor in the measurement of profit and position.

What is the significance of this state of affairs for the financial analyst concerned with the interpretation of financial data in such a way as to make plain the facts behind them and their significance to investors and lenders?

	19A0/1			19A1/2	
	$000	$000		$000	$000
Sales		6,000			9,000
Costs:					
Production		3,000			5,000
Administration		500			600
Marketing					
Salesmen's salaries	200			180	
Travelling expenses	160			120	
Advertising	360			600	
Sales service	60			100	
Freight outwards	240			450	
Packaging costs	300			600	
Market research costs	60			20	
Administrative salaries (marketing)	100			180	
Cash discount	120	1,600		150	2,400
		5,100			8,000
Net profit		900			1,000
Less provision for taxation		450			350*
Net profit after tax		450			650

*After allowing for export incentive reduction in tax

Case Studies for Class Assignments and Discussion

CS 20.1: Fletcher Challenge Limited 1982–1984

The figures below have been extracted from the annual financial reports of Fletcher Challenge Limited

	1984 $m	1983 $m	1982 $m
Sales	4,742	3,442	3,153
Operating earnings	189	100	173
Investment earnings	35	23	24
	224	123	197
Less funding costs — interest, lease, foreign exchange expense	132	135	96
Less Interest capitalized to assets	26	29	23
	106	106	73
Earnings before tax	118	17	124
Tax benefit (expense)	20	30	(-30)

Earnings after tax	138	47	94
Plus extraordinary items	5	5	3
	143	52	97
Less minority interest	12	7	7
Net earnings after tax	131	45	90
Shareholders' funds			
Total	962	800	760
Less minority interest	67	11	17
Equity of group share- holders	895	789	743

Included in the total figures are the following amounts relating to the operations of the Fletcher Challenge North American group:

	1984 $m	1983 $m
Sales	878	260
Earnings	24	10

The interest of Fletcher Challenge Limited in its North American Group was acquired in 1983.

The following additional information was disclosed in the 1984 financial report:
(1) The reported operating earnings for 1984 included export sales tax incentives of $29,823,000 (1983 $21,213,000). According to the Statement of Accounting Policies:

The after-tax value of government incentives convertible to cash are included in earnings and accordingly have not been deducted from taxation.

(2) *Accounting for Crown Forest Industries (of the North American Group)*: on acquisition, the Fletcher Challenge share of the net assets of Crown Forest Industries was revalued to $194 million above the purchase price. The surplus on revaluation was credited to a deferred income account and was to be amortized to the Profit and Loss Account over five years. The following statement was made about the 1984 results:

Earnings from the North American group increased to $24.2 million from $9.9 million for the three months last year. This was after the amortization of net deferred income of $55.5 million (1983 $15.2 million).

Required:

(a) Comment on the *overall* performance of Fletcher Challenge Limited for 1984 making such comparisons and using such percentages and ratios as you consider appropriate.
(b) Comment briefly on the following statement by the chairman of the Fletcher Challenge Group:

The result of $107.1 million for the New Zealand headquartered activities was outstanding. These earnings were more than three times last year's $34.7 million . . .

The New Zealand headquartered operations included all activities of the group apart from the Fletcher Challenge North American group.

CS 20.2 DIC Limited

The DIC Ltd operated departmental stores in many of New Zealand's larger cities. Its trading covered the typical range for departmental stores, including clothing, cosmetics, home appliances and television, furnishings, hardware, etc. Shown below are data from the 1978 financial statements of the company.

Trading highlights

	1978 $	1977 $	1976 $
Turnover	31,239,750	29,309,792	24,729,084
Net profit after taxation	478,488	1.003,668	1,026,590
Net profit after taxation per $ of sales (cents)	1.53	3.42	4.15
Taxes paid	—	831,496	856,675
Dividends — ordinary	12½% 396,509	14½% 459,950	14⅓% 423,703
Dividends — 12% specified preference	90,000	—	—
Revenue profit retained	(8,021)	543,718	602,887
Shareholders' funds	12,596,592	11,043,525	9,054,318
Earning rate on shareholders' funds	3.80%	9.09%	11.34%
Total remuneration paid to employees	6,188,152	5,461,649	4,396,596
Number of employees at year end	932	1,356	1,043

Excerpts from chairman's review

1 Difficult trading conditions in the current year have had a considerable influence on our profit, which can only be described as very much less than adequate.

2 In the year under review sales increased by 6.6% including 12 months trading by DIC-Beaths in Christchurch; this store had traded for only six months as part of the DIC chain in 1977. Withou the contribution of this store, sales would have been down by 0.8%.

3 In order to maintain sales at even the very modest level achieved it was necessary to accept some reduction in gross margins, the consequences of which was a lower rate of gross profit. Our expenses increased by $1,121,000 in the branches, which was mainly accounted for by wages and salaries. Head office charges increased by $467,000, the main components being interest, executive salaries, rents and superannuation. Your directors are satisfied that controllable expenses were well within budget and that management exercised every care in ensuring that cost rises were minimized.

4 The consequences of a diminished gross profit margin and increased expenses were expressed in a reduced net profit of $569,071; this was further reduced by an extraordinary item of $90,583 for redundancy pay, producing a final net profit for the year of $478,488. It was not necessary to provide for taxation in arriving at this figure and a tax loss of $270,484 is carried forward to 1979 to be offset against taxation assessed in that year.

5 An ordinary dividend of 12½ cents per share (14½%) is recommended by your directors. Together with the specified preference already paid, this will absorb the sum of $486,509. As will be apparent, dividends even at the reduced rate now recommended for ordinary shares amount to more than the net profit earned for the year. However, the cash position is reasonably liquid, stocks are in good order and prospects do not seem as forbidding as they did earlier in 1978. It will of course be the aim of your Board to restore the ordinary dividend to its former rate as soon as it is prudent to do so.

6 Following shareholders' approval, a year ago, to raise more capital by way of a specified preference share issue, non-renounceable entitlements were offered to shareholders . . . support was excellent and a total of $1.5 million dollars was raised.

7 Our original Cashel Street store and DIC-Beaths in Christchurch both traded throughout the year under review. It became apparent, however, as the year progressed, that it would be quite uneconomic to continue to operate the two stores, and a decision was reached to concentrate all our Christchurch business in the DIC-Beaths premises. To this end our original store closed in July this year . . . A redundancy agreement was negotiated with the appropriate unions and in the event . . . some $90,000 was paid out under this agreement. Trading in the combined store is so far meeting our budgeted expectations and disposal of surplus stocks has been accomplished.

8 The government's September announcement that the 5% stock valuation allowance for tax purposes would be discontinued in future was, in our view, a major disappointment and disincentive. Introduced because of liquidity problems arising from inflation, it has been discontinued because allegedly liquidity problems are less. That may be so, but unacceptable levels of inflation remain with us and seem likely to do so for yet some time. It has largely been overlooked that this measure, which has been described as crude and inequitable, nevertheless has acted as a kind of hedge against the possible introduction of inflation accounting, which will be a trader's nightmare. The stock valuation allowance as a form of relief is simple and understandable, which will be far from the case of any substitute which may have to be considered should inflation accounting come to be used as a yardstick. WE EARNESTLY HOPE THAT GOVERNMENT WILL RECONSIDER ITS STANCE [emphasis original].

Meantime, as regards our own stocks, we have taken action to ensure that these have not got out of hand, despite sales which were less than expected. In fact stocks at 31 July 1978 were $866,000 less than a year earlier and considerably reduced in terms of units.

9 *The future.* Some improvement in trading patterns has been discernable over the past few weeks and certain costs incurred in 1978 will not be repeated or will be repeated on a lesser scale in 1979 . . . there seem to be reasonable grounds for assuming that we may expect better results in 1979 than in the year recently concluded.

The following information relates to items disclosed in the financial statements:

Specified preference shares

The 1,500,000 specified shares were allotted on 6 February 1978. These shares are convertible to ordinary shares on 1 August 1984 at the rate of one ordinary share for one preference share. Dividends on these shares are deductible in arriving at the assessable income of the company, which pays income tax at the margin at 45% of assessable income.

Capital replacement fund

The company had sought the approval of the Supreme Court to pay a tax-free cash dividend out of the share premium reserve. In granting its approval the court required that an amount equivalent to the dividend paid be transferred from retained profits to a capital replacement fund.

1973 taxation deferred

This item related to arrears of tax payable by the company which had resulted from a switch to the "pay-as-you-earn" system of taxation. The arrears were payable by the company by instalments over a seven year period.

Taxation

In determining the charge for taxation, $90,000 was allowed as a deduction in respect of the dividend to the 12% specified preference shareholders and $386,556 for the trading stock allowance. These allowances together with the unearned profit on hire purchase transactions and depreciation in excess of tax rates had resulted in

The DIC Ltd
Profit and loss account for year ended 31 July 1978

	1978		1977	
	$	$	$	$
Sales		31,239,750		29,309,792
Gross profit from trading		10,472,020		10,164,468
Less expenses				
Advertising, salaries, rents, insurances, etc	8,966,515		7,611,669	
Interest on term loans	467,756		287,790	
Depreciation	504,758		499,895	
Directors' fees	18,000		18,000	
Audit fees	40,086	9,997,115	24,242	8,441,596
Trading profit		474,905		1,722,872
Add dividends from other companies	800		476	
Dividends from subsidiaries	1,500		2,500	
Interest on government stock	3,465		299	
Interest on other investments	88,401	94,166	109,017	112,292
Profit before taxation		569,071		1,835,164
Taxation		—		831,496
Profit after taxation		569,071		1,003,668
Less extraordinary item this year		90,583		
		478,488		1,003,668
Add Retained profit brought forward		2,369,524		2,378,225
Balance available for appropriation		2,848,012		3,381,893
Add bad debts reserve transfer		24,800		
		2,872,812		
Less taxation short provided prior years	4,281		—	
Bad debts provision	24,800		—	
Transfer to general reserve	600,000		600,000	
Transfer to capital replacement fund	190,324		—	
Provision for dividend as recommended	396,509		459,950	
Less transfer from Share premium reserve	190,324		—	
Capital reserve	—		47,581	
	206,185		412,369	
12% specified preference dividend paid 31/7/78	90,000	296,185 1,115,590	—	412,369 1,012,369
Retained profits		1,757,222		2,369,524

The DIC Ltd
Balance sheet as at 31 July 1978

Shareholders' funds, term and current liabilities

	1978 $	1977 $
Shareholders' funds		
Authorized capital —		
8,500,000 Ordinary shares of $1 each	8,500,000	5,000,000
1,500,000 12% Specified preference shares of $1 each	1,500,000	
	10,000,000	5,000,000
Issued capital		
3,172,070 Ordinary shares of $1 each fully paid	3,172,070	3,172,070
1,500,000 12% Specified preference shares of $1 each fully paid	1,500,000	
	4,672,070	3,172,070
Capital reserves		
Capital replacement fund	190,324	
General reserve	2,392,127	2,303,286
Share premium reserve	268,276	458,600
	2,850,727	2,761,886
Revenue reserves		
General reserve	3,316,573	2,740,045
Retained profits	1,757,222	2,369,524
	5,073,795	5,109,569
Total shareholders' funds	12,596,592	11,043,525
Deferred taxation	168,977	
Term liabilities		
Mortgages (secured)	1,998,628	2,268,963
Bank term loan (secured)	691,000	1,778,683
Other term loans	171,810	
1973 Taxation deferred	115,476	230,952
Total term liabilities	2,976,914	4,278,598
Current liabilities		
Trade creditors	2,494,447	2,636,708
Unclaimed dividends	9,443	13,010
Short term deposits	468,395	430,525
Bank overdraft and loans (secured)	1,118,691	2,279,342
Provision for taxation	396,509	282,542
Provision for dividend		459,950
Total current liabilities	4,487,485	6,102,077
	$20,229,968	$21,424,200

Fixed assets, investments and current assets

	1978 $	1977 $
Fixed assets		
Land	3,393,770	3,411,470
Buildings	3,573,698	3,319,442
Fixtures, fittings, plant and computer equipment	1,680,654	1,594,875
Total fixed assets	8,648,122	8,325,787
Investments (at cost)		
Government stock	39,000	39,000
Shares in subsidiary companies	5,100	5,100
Shares in other companies	11,681	10,134
Advances to staff	33,340	92,391
Insurance premiums paid	30,520	26,160
Mortgages and loans	484,716	468,213
Total investments	604,357	640,898
Current assets		
Trading stock	6,864,333	7,731,123
Debtors	3,611,833	3,985,702
Taxation refund due	25,750	
Cash in hand	25,573	28,311
Short term deposits	450,000	712,379
Total current assets	10,977,489	12,457,515
	$20,229,968	$21,424,200

a tax loss of $275,484 which was available to be offset against future profits. The deferred taxation account was set up by the transfer of $168,977 from the provision for taxation account and represented tax on the unearned profits on hire purchase transaction at 31 July 1977. The company's policy was to recognize the profit on hire purchase transactions at the time of sale; the profit was not taxable until realization. (This treatment by the company was adopted for the first time in 1978. According to a note on "Changes in accounting policy", the effect of this change was not material.)

Instructions:

(a) Comment on
    (i) the operating results of DIC Ltd for the year ended 31 July 1978; and
    (ii) the state of the company as at 31 July 1978.
(b) Make a forecast of the operating results of the company for the years ended 31 July 1979 and 1980.
(c) The 1980 financial statements of DIC Ltd with comparative figures are reproduced as a case study in [960].
    Check your forecasts under (b) with the figures of the case study in Chapter 9. State what additional information would have helped you to make a better forecast.
(d) Using the data in the case study in Chapter 9, make a forecast of the results and state of affairs of DIC Ltd for the 1981 and 1982 financial years.
    Having made your forecast, refer to "Note on DIC Ltd" at the end of the case studies included in the this section.

CS 20.3: The Case for Subsidizing Public Transport

The presidential address to a conference of urban public passenger transport bodies ended with this statement:

In short, it is clearly in our national economic interest, both short-term and long-term, for central government to provide real substantial assistance to both the operational costs and the capital costs of an adequate urban transport system.

Included in the evidence from which this opinion was (presumably) developed were the following statements:

1. The total number of buses operated by the group was   1,212
2. At the country's average car occupancy of 1.5, the total number of cars needed to replace them is   56,000
3. The cost of fuel for the buses to cover the annual kilometres run (45.1 million) $6.8 million
4. The cost of fuel for motorcars required to shift the same number of persons $22.0 million
5. The capital cost of the buses, at replacement cost $139.4 million
6. The capital cost of the cars needed to replace the buses is estimated at $600 million

Following the address, a submission seeking support on these grounds was sent to the Minister of Transport. You in your capacity as investigating officer for the

Department are instructed to prepare a draft report on the submission for the head of the research section of the department.

CS 20.4: A Mining Company Group

The interim report of an Australian mining group for the six months ended 31 December 1985 provided interesting information about its earnings:

	1985 $m	1984 $m
Turnover (mainly sales of nickel)	301.73	272.09
Operating costs	266.65	239.55
Income from mining	35.08	32.54
Other income (mainly interest)	14.78	7.85
Earnings before interest and taxation	49.86	40.39
Less interest	16.75	16.93
Net profit before taxation	33.11	23.46
Taxation	3.45	6.13
Net profit after taxation	29.66	17.33
Less minority interests	4.48	3.54
Net profit attributable to the shareholders of the holding company	25.18	13.79
Further information:		
Depreciation	36.91	33.64
Earnings per share (cents)	6.9	4.4

It was reported further that a factor contributing to the profit improvement was the reduction in exploration expenditure written off or provided from $19.5 million to $14.58 million, reflecting a drop from last year's abnormally high oil exploration budget.

The directors advised that they were considering the possibility of cutting production from its West Australian nickel operations if the recent renewed slump in prices continued. The price of nickel had declined from last year's high of US$2.50 to US$1.80, the main fall coming about half-way through the period ended December 31. The group earnings for that period had not been greatly affected because of the compensation of a much weaker Australian dollar. On average, the US dollar price for nickel was 5% lower, but the prices realized in Australian dollars was 10.8% higher than for the same period last year.

Some questions based on the above data

(1) Assuming that the total turnover was comprised of sales of nickel, what change has taken place in the quantity sold, compared with 1984?

(2) Assuming that all the operating costs were related to nickel mining (clearly they are not), can you compare the effectiveness of mining operations in the two periods? If not, then why not?

(3) What information can you deduce from the earnings per share about the issued share capital? Does this suggest any explanation of part of the increase in net profit before taxation?

(4) What factors might account for the low provision for taxation, in spite of increased earnings?

(5) Continuing with the assumptions in (1) and (2) above, prepare a statement explaining as far as practicable the increase in net profit before taxation of $9.65 million (41.11%).

(6) What do you see as the main factors likely to affect the earnings of the group in the next six months, in order of relative importance? Give reasons.

CS 20.5: The Adelaide Steamship Group

On 2 November 1982 the financial pages of the Melbourne *Age* provided three "perspectives" of the 1982 balance sheet of the Adelaide Steamship Group. These are shown, in abbreviated form, below:

(1) The published version

		$m
Adsteam shareholders' funds		253
Minority shareholders' funds (1)		106
Total shareholders' funds of the group		359

	$m	
Represented by:		
Assets:		
Current	171	
Investments (2)	355	
Fixed and non-current	74	599
Less liabilities:		
Current	112	
Non-current	128	240
Net assets		359

(2) Version treating redeemable preference shares as debt

		$m
Adsteam shareholders' funds		248
Minority shareholders' funds		3
Total shareholders' funds of the group		251

	$m	
Represented by:		
Assets:		
Current	171	
Investments (2)	355	
Fixed and non-current	74	599

Less liabilities:		
Current	169	
Non-current	179	348
Net assets		251

(3) Version (2), but valuing investments at market value

		$m
Adsteam shareholders' funds		115
Minority shareholders' funds		3
Total shareholders' funds of the group		118

Represented by:	$m	
Assets:		
Current	171	
Investments	222	
Fixed and non-current	73	466
Less liabilities:		
Current (3)	169	
Non-current	179	348
Net assets		118

Notes:

(1) Minority shareholders' funds are mainly redeemable preference shares issued by the subsidiary Adsteam Finance & Investment Pty Ltd instead of borrowings, for tax reasons.

(2) Investments are in the balance sheet at cost or directors' valuation. In the case of associated companies, the total investment of $310 million includes Adsteam's equity in net tangible assets above acquisition cost and at balance date had a gross market value of $176 million.

(3) Some $55.12 million of redeemable preference shares are repayable in calendar year 1983 and are treated as a current liability even though it is unclear whether the repayment is in the 1982–83 financial year.

Questions:

(1) In your opinion which version gives the "truest" and "fairest" view of the state of affairs of the company. Give reasons.

(2) Discuss the situation of the auditor of the company in respect to this balance sheet, and consider the role of accounting standards in the financial reporting process with particular reference to this case.

(3) In your opinion:
  (a) How should the investments in associated companies be valued? Give reasons.
  (b) How should the redeemable preference shares be classified? Give reasons.

CS 20.6: An Oil Refining Company

Shown below and opposite (in abbreviated form) are the profit statement and balance sheet of an oil refining company for the year ended 31 December 19A5:

Profit statement

	19A5 $000	19A5 $000	19A4 $000	19A4 $000
Income				
Processing fees (based on quantities)		12,411		12,038
Interest on short term deposits		932		719
		13,343		12,757
Expenses				
Operating costs		8,444		6,431
Overhaul expenses		738		350
Depreciation		1,025		1,127
Other expenses		38		39
		10,245		7,947
		3,098		4,810
Plus provision (made in 19A3) for loss on sale of catalyst written back		235		—
Net profit before taxation		3,333		4,810
Less taxation:				
Taxation for period	1,201		2,335	
Transfer to (from) deferred taxation provision	291	1,492	(200)	2,135
Net profit after taxation		1,841		2,675

Additional:

The following are additional facts gleaned from the company's report:

1 The plant was shut down for biennial overhaul during November/ December 19A5.

2 The 19A5 throughput was down 16% on 19A4 (in tonnes). A detailed break-down of output data is not available.

3 Imported materials and spare parts form a significant part of "processing costs".

4 The refinery complex is insured for its (depreciated) replacement value of $81,750,000. Its original cost was just over $25 million.

5 A provision was made in 19A4 for half of the estimated cost of the biennial overhaul of the refinery plant.

6 A provision was made *in 19A3* of $235,000 to cover the probable loss on disposal of a spent platinum catalyst. The balance of this catalyst was sold in 19A5 at a figure sufficient to show a minor profit over depreciated book value.

7 A plan to double the capacity of the refinery, at a cost of around $200 million, is still (after several years) under discussion with government.

8 The company pays income tax at 45% on marginal income.

Balance sheet

	19A5 $000	19A4 $000
Fixed assets		
Land, buildings, and jetties (at cost less depreciation)	3,407	3,450
Plant (at cost less depreciation)	6,270	6,182
Processing licences (at cost)	772	772
Total fixed assets	10,449	10,404
Investments	10	10
Current assets		
Stocks of materials	883	777
Platinum catalyst inventory	—	502
Debtors (*including tax overpaid $281,000)	*4,785	5,063
Cash and short term deposits	10,955	11,070
Total current assets	16,623	17,412
Total assets	27,082	27,826

	19A5 $000	19A5 $000	19A4 $000	19A4 $000
Authorized capital, in $1 ordinary shares	12,000		12,000	
General reserve	11,500		11,000	
Unappropriated profit	833		992	
Share capital and reserves		24,333		23,992
Deferred taxation liability		608		317
Long term liability		77		89
Current liabilities and provisions				
Creditors	564		1,040	
Provision for biennial overhaul			350	
Provision for taxation			538	
Provision for final dividend	1,500		1,500	
Total current liabilities		2,064		3,428
		27,082		27,826

Required:

(a) Prepare and discuss such analyses as you consider helpful to the interpretation of the "income" data (processing fees and interest) for 19A5.

(b) Working from the data disclosed in the profit statements and additional information schedule, prepare statements aimed at giving a fair view of the profits derived from the *refining operations* of the company for the 19A4 and 19A5 years. In this connection, you should make such adjustments as you consider necessary, but not adjustments for price and price level changes. Using these comparative profit figures, compare the *profitability* (ROR) of the operations side of the refinery for the two years.

(c) With a view to interpretation of the operating results of the two years, prepare an analysis of the expenses in order to explain how each factor has affected the poorer disclosed profit for 19A5; and provide comments on each of the factors that has had a material effect on the results.

(d) In the light of your analysis of income (a) and expense (c), list *in order of their importance* the *three* factors which have had the most significant effects on the results of the 19A5 year. If possible, set against each the amount of the effect of the item on profit for the year.

(e) Assuming an inflation rate of 15% for 19A5, and taking into account the information given in (3), (4) and (7) of the "additional facts" section, discuss the deficiencies of historic cost based accounts in measuring the net profit of the company in the 19A5 year. You should set out major areas of difference and where possible provide actual calculations to illustrate your views (stating any assumptions made).

NOTE ON DIC LTD

The expansion undertaken by DIC Ltd and referred to by the managing director in the 1980 financial report of the company did not prove successful and the expected substantial increase in the company's profits did not materialize. The company found itself increasingly in debt and attempts were made to restructure its operations. Its Wellington buildings were sold in 1983. By 1988, for all practical purposes the company had ceased to operate as an independent entity.

Chapter 21
Aspects of Statistical Analysis

[2101] Statistics may be defined as the science of collecting and evaluating the signficance of numerical facts. The term may also be used to describe the numerical facts themselves, for example, import/export statistics, crime statistics, health statistics, etc. Statistical analysis enables us to "digest" sets of numerical data in order to obtain a clearer understanding of what the data portray. For example, it is a simple matter to calculate an average of a set of data, but this disregards the spread of the data around that average, and that could be important. Statistical methods provide a way of measuring relationships between input factors and outputs (results) which may throw light on the causes of changes in outputs. Statistical methods may assist in the observation and study of systematic patterns of behaviour in a time series; better understanding of behavioural patterns may assist in forecasting future values of the series. Added information regarding matters such as distributions, trends and relationships constitutes the payoff from statistical analysis.

Forecasting

[2102] In the analysis and interpretation of financial statements, statistical analysis produces quantified results which may be useful in forecasting various aspects of a business enterprise's results and state of affairs. Such forecasts may then be used in decision-making by investors and other parties with interests in the operations and state of affairs of business enterprises.

[2103] The discussion which follows concentrates on forecasting for the benefit of investors. The same principles apply to other areas of forecasting.

An asset has value to the owner because of the flow of benefits which he or she expects to accrue from ownership of the asset. The flow of benefits from owning a parcel of shares is the flow of future dividends, and the market price of those shares may be taken to reflect two principal variables:

1. the forecast by the market of this flow of future dividends; and
2. the market's estimate of the level of risk that is associated with this flow of dividend income.

The capacity to declare dividends is constrained by earnings on the one hand and liquidity on the other. In theory an investor who is concerned to get value for money will make his own forecast of all these variables. Alternatively he may assume that those investors and advisers who exercise the major influence on market prices have made accurate forecasts. He may then invest at market prices with reasonable assurance, and still sleep well at night because he has invested across a range of shares in order to reduce his risk. The really desirable state for an

405

investor, however, is to be able to forecast the key variables with higher than the average precision that the market may be taken to reflect.

[2104] We may define two broad approaches to forecasting:
    (a) statistical ("objective") approach; and
    (b) subjective approach.

Statistical approach

[2105] The statistical approach to forecasting involves the manipulation of numerical data according to a predetermined model (statistical formula). The approach may be described as "objective" in the sense that, once the model has been chosen, the input of the same numerical data will produce the same result.

[2106] The statistical approach to forecasting is not strictly objective, however, in the sense that judgment would play a key role, for example, in the choice of a model — a moving average versus, say, a regression model, the number of years to use in a moving average model, whether a moving average model should involve equal weights or whether the annual figures should be differentialy weighted and the manner in which this should be done.

Subjective approach

[2107] The subjective approach to forecasting would draw on a variety of sources of information which are perceived as having a bearing on the future of the economy, specific industries and individual business enterprises in order to make what is finally a set of judgments about, say, future dividend flows and risk levels.

[2108] The statistical and subjective approaches to forecasting have a number of characteristics in common. Both are future oriented and both depend on past data. Both reflect judgment and experience. In the case of the statistical approach judgment and experience would be reflected in the model chosen, in the selection and preparation of the inputs into the model and the faith one would place in the output. Judgment and experience would play an even greater role in the subjective approach to forecasting. In both cases, the further the forecasts move from the present, the less reliable they are likely to be. In looking ahead, the future can be expected to become increasingly uncertain. Similarly, the further one goes back in an examination of past data in order to establish behaviour patterns, the less relevant the data are likely to become. Over time, the operations of business enterprises may be affected by structural changes within the enterprises, and by changes in the economic environment within which they operate, while data relating to these operations may be affected by changes in the accounting methods employed.

The Analysis and Interpretation of Time Series Data

[2109] The analysis of time series would normally involve the study and use of observed systematic patterns of behaviour to forecast future values of the series. For example, we may use the observation of a steady rise in profit averaging, say, 10% per year over a number of years to forecast similar increases in profit in the future, or we may use an observation of five-year cycles in reported profit to forecast similar profit cycles in the future.

[2110] The use of a time series in the above manner reflects the belief that the causal factors which produced the time series in the past will continue to operate and will produce similar patterns in the behaviour of the series in the future. Formal statistical models (formulas) may be developed to fit the observed data and be used in forecasting. It should be fairly evident that applying such an aproach to the anlaysis of financial statements and the forecasting of financial statement data such as earnings would be subject to severe limitations. Some of these are discussed below.

[2111] Over time changes occur which may affect the comparability of the numbers which comprise a time series and their usefulness for forecasting. These changes may be specific to the individual enterprise, particular to the industry of which it is part, or general over the whole economy. In fact, all three may apply in the one time period. Each set of data is the product of the conditions of its own time period.

[2112] For example, the New Zealand economy has experienced significant changes over the last, say, 15 years, and the effects of these changes on some industries and on some individual enterprises have been material. Economic factors affecting business have included:
• the level of inflation and changes in this;
• government economic policies; for example, prior to 1984, government support for farming and development of export markets, the removal of these following the election of a Labour government in 1984 and the changes brought about by that government in its drive to restructure the economy. We may include under this heading changes in the rate of company taxation which has varied from 45% to 48% to 28%;
• the development of closer economic relations with Australia with the objective of attaining a unified market;
• changes in the exchange value of the New Zealand dollar and their effect on exports and imports and on exporting and importing business enterprises including farming;
• evolving industrial relations over time;
• changes in New Zealand's relations with its major trading partners and material changes in the economies of those trading partners, for example, New Zealand's relations with Australia or New Zealand agricultural exports to Britain in the face of evolving common market policies regarding agricultural imports into the European Economic Community;
• the stock market crash of October 1987 which in New Zealand was the most severe in the developed world and the extended period of uncertainty which followed; etc.

[2113] At an industry wide level during a similar period we may consider:
• changes in the New Zealand meat processing industry including stormy industrial relations in the 1970s, rising industry costs to a large extent caused by substantial wage increases which could be passed on to farmers who were then receiving substantial government support, the effect on the meat processing industry of the removal of subsidies for farmers following the change in government in 1984, the

407

closure of uneconomic meat processing works, widespread redundancies among meat processing workers and the effect of these on labour relations in the industry;

• changes in the fortunes of the farming industry as a result of government support for farming in the 1970s and early 1980s, the rapid speculative increases of farm property prices during that period, the effect of the substantial 1984 devaluation of the New Zealand dollar and the removal of subsidies for farming, the floating of the New Zealand dollar and the rise in its exchange value to a level higher than that which preceded the 1984 devaluation as a result of high internal interest rates, and the effect of such high interest rates on farming, the depression that hit the farming industry as a result of the developments in the later 1980s and the dramatic falls in farm property values it helped bring about;

• changes affecting the operations of the fertilizer industry in New Zealand as a result of its close dependence on the fortunes of farming;

• the entry of the Australian airline ANSETT into the New Zealand internal air travel market and its effect on the operations of Air New Zealand and other, smaller, airline carriers;

• changes affecting the operations of the New Zealand wine industry covering periods of rapid growth, of over-production, of high taxes on wine, the effect of closer economic relations with Australia with improved opportunities for export and the prospect of increased competition from imports; etc.

[2114] At the individual firm level fundamental changes may be brought about over time because of economy or industry wide factors or changes pertaining specifically to the firm. For example, expansion through a major takeover or merger may create essentially a new enterprise with prospects and risks which are not reflected in a time series pertaining to the operations and state of affairs of the enterprise in the period prior to the takeover or merger. Diversification across industry and geographical boundaries could also affect prospects and risk. Over time there may be changes in the manner of financing of business operations such as the relative use of equity and debt finance and the acquisition of assets by means of leasing rather than purchase. Further, over time, time series may be affected by changes in the accounting methods employed by firms which in turn will impact on their comparability over time and across firms. Such changes in accounting methods and procedures may be effected in order to comply with legislative requirements, or evolving financial accounting reporting standards, or as a result of management policy.

[2115] It should be fairly obvious that, given the complexity of business operations and of the enviornment within which they take place, the mechanical application of statistical models to time series data for the purpose of forecasting would be subject to severe limitations and would produce results of dubious reliability. Past time series are the product of conditions prevailing in the past. Future time series will be the product of conditions which will prevail in the future. The model which best fits a time series of past periods is not necessarily the model which will produce the most accurate forecast of the series for future periods.

[2116] Given the above problems associated with the analysis of time series related to the operations of business enterprises, it is perhaps not surprising that investment analysts generally prefer non-statistical approaches to forecasting. Such approaches may typically involve the use of a number of economy and industry related sources of information and forecasts, as a study of firms' annual and interim financial reports, press releases, interviews with the management of firms, etc. Following a thoughtful review of the information available from all sources, conclusions will be drawn and forecasts made. While it can be expected that the accuracy of such forecast would depend on the ability and experience, and effort applied by the analyst, empirical evidence suggests that this more direct and pains-taking approach, albeit subjective, tends to out-perform forecasts produced by statistical models.

[2117] The above discussion does not imply that the subjective and statistical approaches to forecasting are mutually exclusive. As pointed out earlier, statistical models themselves are the product of choice and judgment regarding their nature, form and level of sophistication. Since the judgment applied in choosing a statistical forecasting model predetermines the nature of the forecast the model will produce, forecasts produced by statistical models are themselves essentially the product of judgment. The point being made is that given the complexity of business operations and of the dynamic environment within which they take place, statistical analysis and forecasts should be used with caution as they are not substitutes for the careful analysis and study of the economy, industry and firm related factors which have affected the operations of firms in the past, and the economy, industry and firm related factors which are likely to affect the operation of firms in the future.

The significance of detail

[2118] Key items in time series such as earnings are the net result of a set of variables which are significant in their own right. For a useful analysis, it may be essential to serparate out the significant components of the total data in the time series. Take the results of an insurance group as an example (The New Zealand South British Group Ltd, half year ended 30 September 1982).

	This Year $000	Last Year $000
Group income after taxation, as reported	19,298	20,973
A fall of 8%		
But, of this, exchange fluctuations favourable to the group produced	4,160	7,557
Income from operations was then	15,138	13,416
An increase of 12.8 percent		
This was derived from:		
General insurance	12,535	11,345
Life insurance	602	551
Trustee operations	245	195
Finance company operations	1,546	1,340
Information services, Gain/(Loss)	210	(15)
	15,138	13,416
The main contribution, from general insurance, comprised:		
Operating earnings, Gain/(Loss)	3,726	(5,230)
Realised gains on sale of investments	2,091	15,958
Realised gains on sale of land and buildings	6,718	617
	12,535	11,345

Clearly there has been a significant change in the operating results from general insurance. The factors leading to this result were:

	This Year $000	Last Year $000
Premiums earned	214,623	206,317
Less Claims incurred	147,727	158,928
Percentage of claims to premiums	68.8	77.0
Margin	66,896	47,389
Less Expenses and taxation	83,344	69,670
Deficiency from insurance	(16,448)	(22,281)
Plus Investment income net of taxation	19,565	16,146
Income from operations, Gain/(Loss)	3,117	(6,135)
Plus Share of earnings retained by associated companies (under equity accounting)	609	905
Operating earnings, Gain/(Loss)	3,726	(5,230)

To be useful in interpretation, a time series for such a group would need to include, for general insurance operations, data covering all these contributors to the end result. Changes in the difference between the book value and market value of investments should also be taken into account in a meaningful analysis. Futher, income tax expense may be affected by factors particular to each year so that it may be desirable to have before tax as well as after tax figure for income: in the above example taxation is aggregated with expenses and income from investments and share of earnings retained by associated companies are shown net of tax. The past performance may then be assessed more fairly; and projections may be made of future results in the light of past data supplemented by such information as can be obtained regarding the expectations for each contributing factor:

The significance of price changes

[2119] The significance of data incorporated in time series consists of numbers of dollars, with no regard for the fact of a changing value dollar. If one's concern is with dollar flows, then there is nothing wrong with this. For example, projections may be made in terms of dollars, using the data in a time series as part of the relevant evidence. However, if one's concern is with comparative performance, then it is necessary to express the data in common dollars, so far as this is possible. For an income series, a general price index such as the consumer price index would be applied, in order to express the data in terms of dollars of a base year. In the example in Table 21.1, taken from the annual report of a departmental store, the data are expressed in 1967 dollars. An alternative but probably more confusing treatment would have been to convert the data to 1982 dollars. An additional step towards interpretation would be to prepare an index to show each of the adjusted incomes in terms of the 1967 income, shown as 100.

If one's concern is to compare physical volumes, of sales for example, and these have not been disclosed, then an approximation may be made by developing and applying a specific price index to the series.

Table 21.1
The Effect of Inflation on Profits

	Actual Recorded Trading Profit After Tax	Adjusted to Offset Effect of Inflation (Using Consumer Price Index 1967 Base)
1967	124,800	124,800
1968	125,900	120,700
1969	124,500	113,800
1970	160,200	137,400
1971	179,000	139,100
1972	176,900	128,500
1973	311,400	209,100
1974	462,700	292,700
1975	340,500	183,000
1976	494,400	235,900
1977	547,500	219,200
1978	603,800	215,500
1979	662,800	210,300
1980	737,600	198,400
1981 (13 months)	937,000	219,200
1982	1,038,300	207,700

[2120] The adjustments in Table 21.1 are to data derived from an historical cost basis. An alternative would have been to restate the data for current cost. There are some differences of opinion regarding the usefulness of current cost and inflation adjusted data; there is reasonable consensus, however, about the inadequacies of historical cost data in times of material price and price level changes. While it may be enlightening to convert income data prepared by an historical cost system to common dollars in order to facilitate a realistic assessment of trends and cycles, it should be even more enlightening to do this with current cost data. Attempts by the accounting profession in the early 1980s to get companies to provide supplementary current cost reports met with very limited success and were abandoned.

Interim comparisons

[2121] The assembly of selected data for firms in the same industry provides a basis for making comparisons of the performance and position of the individual firm with those of firms regarded as fairly comparable. However, it is necessary to treat the analysis of data across a whole set of firms in an industry with some caution. Individual firms are likely to differ to varying extents in location, product mix, markets, ownership of assets, valuation of assets and size. Material differences reduce the fairness of the comparisons and the value that may properly be attached to the statistical analysis of the interfirm data.

The context of the industry

[2122] The fortunes of whole industries tend to fluctuate with changing conditions. One may expect the results of the individual firm to reflect to some extent the fortunes of its industry. If one can develop a set of time series data covering a whole industry, then one can compare the performance of the individual firm with that of the industry of which it is a part. One might even feel able to state that a part of a change in individual performance is due to industry influences rather than management influences. At least one can recognize that the performance of a firm is above or below the average for its industry.

The vehicles for such comparisons are industry indexes (for example, of sales and income) and industry ratios. The indexes are prepared by converting the data in the time series to an index based on a base-year expressed as 100. But there are serious problems in the gathering of industry-wide data.

There may be classification problems in defining the bounds of a particular industry. Then there are problems of composition. Over a period of years one can expect considerable changes in an industry. Some companies cease operations or are taken over, while new companies enter the scene and evolve. Here there is growth, and there decline. In an ongoing time series, one cannot select a set of firms which were operating at the start of the series and which continue to do so in each latest period. Even if one could do so, the sample would almost certainly be biased by the omissions.

[2123] The composition problem is exacerbated by the development of diversified company groups. In today's world, many enterprises carry on diverse activities, and so cannot be classified with accuracy as being part of any single industry. These segments of diversified groups may comprise major components of their respective industries. Some data regarding the segments of diversified firms may be provided in company reports, but there can be serious problems where the segments are interrelated in some of their activities. A case in point is Fletcher Chalenge Ltd, New Zealand's largest company group. The segment report ("operating Summary by Sector") included in the 1987 financial report of the Fletcher Challenge Group is reproduced and discussed as Case 1 in Chapter 15 [1534] to [1540]. The segment report breaks down the operations of the group into eight segments grouped under four broad headings: forest industry, building industry, primary industry and trading, and corporate and investment. The following figures are provided for each segment (apart from corporate and investment in respect of which turnover and tax paid earnings are disclosed): turnover, tax-paid earnings, shareholders' funds, return on shareholders' funds and exports. The following points may be noted about the segmented figures provided by Fletcher Challenge:

• Some of the segments are widely diversified themselves. For example, Primary Industry and Trading, which is shown as a single segment, includes fishing, rural servicing, meat and consumer products.

• Problems associated with arriving at the segment figures for earnings and rates of return (see [1538] to [1540]).

• Many of the individual enterprises within the Fletcher Challenge Group are among the largest of their kind in the country; few of them are fully comparable with other enterprises in their respective industries, even if separate data were available.

[2124] The problems involved in preparing data covering whole industries will be obvious. At best the data will not cover the whole population, and it may indeed exclude a significant part of the population.

An advantage of producing industry-wide data in time series is to study patterns of growth and decline, and to examine the effects of changes in the state of the economy on the industry as a whole. The existence of problems in developing reliable industry-wide data does not mean that such data have no value, but rather that they should be gathered and processed responsibly and interpreted with proper regard to their deficiencies.

The context of the economy

[2125] Some industries are more susceptible than others to changes in the state of the economy, and react in different ways to these changes. It is of some interest to investors planning investment portfolios and seeking to hedge against risk to have an appreciation of these relationships between industry and economy. Time series may be developed for companies in general, and indexes based on this data will show the economy-wide patterns of growth and decline. These indexes may then be compared with the indexes of particular industries over the same period either visually or statistically, using measures of correlation.

An economy-wide time series avoids the problem of classification into industries but inherits the other problems that relate to the preparation of industry-wide indexes. The data are drawn from companies engaged in diverse activities, so that relationships will express averages which have significance only within the context of the economy-wide series, as indicators of trends in that series.

Intercompany shareholdings cause problems in developing economy-wide data.

Firm, industry and economy

[2126] A statistician may use the appropriate techniques to relate an index series for a firm with that for its industry and that for the economy as a whole. He may conclude that a calculated percentage of the firm's index change can be associated with industry-wide influences and a calculated percentage with economy-wide influences, see P Brown and R Ball: "Some preliminary findings on the association between the earnings of a firm, its industry, and the economy", *Empirical Research in Accounting: Selected Studies*, 1967 (Supplement to *Journal of Accounting Research*, 1967, pp 55–57). It would seem to be wise to treat such statistical association as such and not as explanations. Changes in the industry and economy contexts within which a firm operates can be expected to affect its markets, its prices, its costs, its managerial decisions, and its operating results. It is going too far to actually attribute portions of those results to industry and economy influences. Without action by management and staff, there would be no operations to produce results. Business activity is not automatic. In a real sense, the results of the firm are like joint costs, strictly not divisible in this way.

The choice of ratios

[2127] There are several measures that may be used in assessing a condition such as financial leverage, or profitability.

In some cases it may be useful to use more than one measure, because each has significance in its own right. For example, profitability measures might include:
- net profit before tax plus interest, to total assets at book value;
- net profit after tax, to owners' equity.

Other measures could exclude extraordinary items from profit, or allow for assets at values other than book value. The rate of return to total assets excludes the influence of financing factors, and the rate of return on equity includes the influence of debt/equity decisions. Unless ratios supplement one another from an information viewpoint (as do these two ratios of profitability), it is desirable to concentrate on those ratios which best reflect the condition one is seeking to measure.

[2128] The application of logic, and understanding of the relative importance of the factors involved, may lead one to select the ratios used to reflect specific conditions like profitability. For example, if there have been significant changes in interest rates or taxation rates over the period of years covered in a time series, then one may conclude that the first measure of profitability shown above will be more meaningful than the second (if it became a matter of choice between them). The selection of specific ratios may make it necessary to adjust the data so that the ratios of different firms will be fairly comparable. For example it may be necessary to capitalize long term leases, as accurately as available data allow, in order to obtain comparable totals of assets and liabilities. Research may assist in the choice among alternative ratios. As we shall see in the chapter on the prediction of insolvency, it has been possible for researchers to compare the abilites of relevant ratios to predict insolvency. One may then assume that the ratios that have shown the highest capacity to predict insolvency are the best reflections of solvency. If one wishes to detemine whether it is useful to use more than one ratio to reflect a condition like profitability, some statistical aid may be called in. The extent of equivalence of say two ratios may be determined statistically if one ranks the set of data one is dealing with using each ratio and compares the rankings. The Spearman rank correlation coefficient may be calculated:

$$r_s = 1 - \frac{6 \Sigma d_i^2}{N^3 - N}$$

where r_s = the correlation coefficient;
d_i = the difference between the rankings under the two ratios;
N = the number of observations.

The higher the result, the greater the correlation. The greater the correlation, the less the need to calculate both ratios.

Averages; dispersion

[2129] Averages should be used with catuion. They do not show the components (for example, the average of 99 and 1 is 50) nor do they show the extent or direction of dispersion around the mean.

Here is an interesting illustration from the electricity supply industry:

	Cents
Revenue per unit supplied, City A	1.248
But revenue per unit — Domestic	0.936
— Non-domestic	1.832
Costs of supply per unit:	
City A	1.144
City B	1.359
City C	1.179

But these were comprised of:

	Energy cost Cents	Distribution cost Cents	Total cost Cents
City A	0.681	0.463	1.144
City B	0.932	0.427	1.359
City C	0.830	0.348	1.179

Why the 0.681 cents in City A?

	Cents
Cost per unit generated	0.478
Cost per unit purchased	0.702
Average cost	0.681

(Cities B and C purchased all their electricity)
Why the 0.702 cents?

Because purchased electricity was charged under a two-part tariff, with part dependent on maximum demand; and generation was geared to reduce maximum demand required from the seller of bulk electricity.

This is an extreme example, but the lesson is generally applicable. For example one may calculate an overall (average) rate of return on assets of an enterprise, but there may be significant variation in the profitability of segments of the enterprise.

[2130] If one is comparing the rate of return on assets of firm A with the average for its industry, the average may have been distorted by some extreme data. The standard deviation may be calculated to indicate the extent of concentration around the average, and the skewness coefficient will indicate the extent and direction of skewness of the data distribution around the average. In this way statistical tools may assist in the achievement of a fairer and more helpful comparison.

"Consensus" forecasting

[2131] It is sometimes said that the aggregation ("averaging") of individual forecasts using a variety of approaches would produce more accurate forecasts than the individual ones used in the aggregation.

The aggregation of individual forecasts will produce more accurate results provided the individual forecasts are centred around the underlying "true process", the outcomes of which the forecasts are attempting to predict. The averaging of forecasts which are "off the mark" regarding the "true process" they are trying to predict will not necessarily produce a better forecast than some of the individual forecasts used in the aggregation. While averaging may lead to the cancellation of errors in individual forecasts and, therefore, produce a more accurate consensus forecast, it may also dilute above-average forecasts included in the aggregation.

Review questions

21.1 "Statistical analysis and forecasting are not substitutes for the careful individual examination of the past and assessment of the future that are essential to rational decision-making."
Discuss in relation to the analysis and interpretation of financial statements.

21.2 "The further one goes back in an examination of past data, in order to establish behaviour patterns to be used in forecasting, the less relevant the data are likely to become."
Discuss.

21.3 "If one can develop a set of time series data covering an industry, then one can compare the performance of the individual firm with that of the industry of which it is a part."
Discuss the possible uses of such data and some of the problems associated with the development of industry performance indexes and ratios.

21.4 Discuss the proposition that in the analysis and interpretation of the operating results of a firm, it is necessary to identify and quantify three sets of influences, influences which are:
(a) economy-wide;
(b) industry-wide;
(c) peculiar to the firm.

21.5 "The model which best fits a time series of past periods is not necessarily the model which will produce the most accurate forecast of the series in the future."
Discuss.

21.6 Discuss the view that the aggregation (averaging) of individual forecasts using a variety of approaches will produce a more accurate forecast than the individual ones used in the aggregation.

21.7 "Each set of data is the product of the conditions of its own time period."
Discuss in relation to the use of past data to make forecasts about the future results and state of affairs of business enterprises.

Chapter 22

The Prediction of Insolvency; Trade Credit

Insolvency

[2201] Insolvency is the inability to pay one's debts as they fall due. It is a financial condition that may but does not necessarily lead on to bankruptcy or liquidation of an enterprise. From time to time business enterprises may find great difficulty in meeting their financial commitments, but may avoid collapse by taking appropriate and timely action to remedy the situation.

There are many losers from the financial collapse of a business enterprise. These may include: employees; managers; owners/shareholders; providers of trade credit; providers of loan finance; local communities.

Where the indications are that the enterprise is headed towards insolvency, all of these parties have a need to know of this situation so that they can protect their interests as far as possible. Hopefully, timely action will result in either the avoidance of collapse or the avoidance of loss by interested parties.

The question discussed in this chapter is the extent to which the analysis and interpretation of the financial statements of business enterprises assist in the prediction of insolvency.

Sources of information for predicting insolvency

[2202] The financial statements of past periods are not an adequate basis for predicting insolvency (or any other future condition for that matter). The analysis of these historical statements may indicate more or less financially comfortable conditions and more or less satisfactory trends in key ratios; but our concern in prediction is with the uncertain future.

Some help in the prediction of insolvency may be obtained from the study of relevant financial ratios and of trends in those ratios over the last, say, five years; but in the end prediction of outcomes in the business sector has to be based on informed judgment regarding what the future holds for each individual enterprise rather than on the analysis of data from the past and its statistical projection, or on the application of ratio cut-off criteria and multi-ratio formulas developed for general aplication. If there were a reliable formula for the prediction of insolvency, and everyone applied it, it would continually prove its own infallibility. But there is no such formula.

[2203] That is not to decry the value of ratio analysis. Ratio analysis provides a fuller understanding of performance and position, and of trends in these. But, in the context of the prediction of insolvency, its main purpose is to indicate cases requiring detailed study and as a background to the exercise of judgment. Some useful research has been carried out in this area which can assist in the selection of ratios for use in the assesment of insolvency.

[2204] Any analysis of the solvency position of firms should be carried out in the context of relevant economy, industry and firm related factors. The ultimate concern should be how these factors will impact on the solvency position of specific firms.

[2205] At the economy-wide level concern should be with existing and expected levels of inflation, with interest rates, with government fiscal policies and their effect on the economy in general and impact on particular industries. Government policies regarding support for exports and protection of local industries from imports and changes in these policies could have major effect on the viability of some industries and firms within industries.

[2206] At the industry level concern would be with the general performance and prospects of the industry, with existing and prospective competition (for example from imports), with the ability of the industry to pass on cost increases, etc.

[2207] At the level of the individual firm the concern will be with the prospects of the firm in the context of the economy and industry environment within which the firm operates, with the cost structure of the firm in absolute terms and in relation to the industry to which the firm belongs, with existing and prospective competition, with the ability of the firm to pass on cost increases, with the quality of the firm's productive assets in relation to those of its major competitors, with the ability of the firm to raise additional funds by way of debt or equity capital, with the quality of the firm's management and changes in this quality.

[2208] The analysis of debt and the timing of its maturity may provide key information regarding the financial health of the firm. For example, major debt maturing in the near future may be of crucial importance to the solvency of the firm if difficulties are expected in its repayment by refinancing.

[2209] The share market can also provide useful information for evaluating the solvency position of a firm. For example, a share price at or below par is an indication not only of lack of enthusiasm from the market but also of lack of ability of a company to issue additional equity capital in order to reduce its dependence on debt finance.

[2110] Credit ratings provided by credit agencies may be used as indicators of enterprise solvency. The issue of judgment summonses is likely to indicate serious financial stress.

[2211] Finally, since the solvency of a firm depends on its ability to pay its debts as they fall due, the study of solvency should be carried out with emphasis on expected cash flows.

The importance of cash flow analysis

[2212] One of the best approaches for predicting solvency is to carry out a financial budgeting exercise, beginning with immediate past data and using such relevant quantitative and non-quantitative information as is available, to project likely future operating results and state of affairs. In Chapter 20 we saw that this could have been done fairly readily in the case of Mosgiel Ltd (Case Study 2, "A Company Failure in Hindsight").

[2213] In the case of Mosgiel Ltd we projected the financial needs of the company for the year following its last published financial report, 1 July 1979 to 30 June 1980, the year which saw the company's demise. We assumed that in that year the company would have been faced, on the average, with 20% cost/price increases, not an unrealistic expectation under the then prevailing economic conditions. We saw that in order to maintain its 1979 level of operations, the company would have needed something like $4 million in additional funds to finance the expected increase in the monetary amounts of its inventories and debtors (ie 20% of inventories of $16.9 million and debtors of $5.5 million at 30 June 1979). We saw little possibility of the company obtaining that amount of additional funds from debt since the company was already operating at, if not beyond, its safety debt level. It was equally unlikely that the company could have raised this amount by the issue of equity capital given its low reported profitability and lack of enthusiasm for its shares which at the time were selling at about or below par. An alternative would have been for the company to sell selected sections of the enterprise and to cut back on the level of its operations. This would not have been easy given the depressed state of the industry at the time. For example, Mosgiel's main competitor, Alliance Textiles Ltd, reported a similar position to that of Mosgiel (some reported figures and ratios of Mosgiel and Alliance Textiles are compared later in this chapter; see also Case Study 3, "A Case of Company Survival", in Chapter 20).

The difference between the two enterprises, one failing and the other not only surviving but also operating profitably the following year, lay in the medium term policies and short term responses of management to a very difficult situation. Alliance accepted and operated within the unavoidable constraints by raising operational efficiency, rigidly controlling the investment in inventories and trade debtors, linking production closely to sales, and further developing a growing export market for which it had planned earlier. The management of Mosgiel failed to do these things, with company failure as a result. These interesting cases indicate clearly that ratios from the past are not reliable signals of impending failure, that assessment of the effects of expected factors influencing cash flows in the ensuing period (and longer term) is essential to informed judgment regarding solvency, and that the assessment of the calibre of management and the soundness of its longer-term policies may be the most important element in the prediction of outcomes. There is no substitute finally for detailed study and judgment at the level of the individual enterprise. What prediction models may do for us is to indicate a set of enterprises whose position is such that individual detailed study is warranted.

Research into the Prediction of Financial Distress

[2214] The ability to predict insolvency or get early warning signals of impending insolvency has undisputed advantages to investors, creditors and auditors, to name three groups with vested interests in the financial state of business firms. It is an area which has attracted considerable interest and research.

419

A large part of the research into the prediction of financial distress has concentrated on business failure as evidenced by the liquidation of the distressed firm rather than on insolvency which is a condition which may be rectified by actions of management, including arrangements with the firm's creditors, or by restructuring the firm's operations which may involve its merger with or takeover by another enterprise. It is within the broader context that insolvency is considered in this chapter.

[2215] The research aimed at helping the prediction of financial distress has primarily centred on determining which variables expressed as financial ratios, are the best indicators of approaching failure. The results have been expressed in univariate models (incorporating a single variable) or multivariate models (incorporating more than one variable).

[2216] A pioneer study of 79 failed and 79 non-failed companies was carried out by Beaver: W H Beaver, "Financial Ratios as Predictors of Failure", *Empirical Research in Accounting: Selected Studies 1966*, supplement to Vol 4 *Journal of Accounting Research*, pp 71–127. Thirty ratios were calculated for each company each year. The mean of each ratio each year for the set of failed companies was compared with that for the set of non-failed companies. The trends in these means for failed and non-failed companies were plotted over the five years up to failure. The extent of the difference, and the movement in the ratio over the five years, were regarded as indicators of the capacity of the ratio to predict failure. It is interesting that the ratio of cash flow to total debt was seen as having the highest rating as a predictor.

The criticisms that have been made of the research methods applied in this study include:

1. The selection of matching non-failed companies was a subjective exercise.

2. The comparison of failed companies with an equal number of non-failed companies was out of line with the relative populations of failed and non-failed companies.

3. The study was limited to failed companies with financial data over five years, so excluding from the study the more failure prone recently established enterprises.

4. The selection of non-failed companies of similar size to the failed companies meant that the important factor of size was excluded from the study. It was common knowledge that the incidence of failure is greater among small enterprises than among larger ones.

5. The fairness of comparing the means of the ratios for each set of companies where one is dealing with a range of companies in different industries and in different degrees of financial stress is open to question. For example, how relevant is it to apply to an individual enterprise in a particular industry a ratio-based measure derived from a set of enterprises in a range of industries each with its own set of assets and appropriate sources of finance?

[2217] It is more realistic to see ratios in terms of sets rather than separately. For example, one may improve the current ratio by raising more long term finance and so worsening the debt/equity ratio. The calculation of a range of ratios relating to the operating results and financial structure would outline an operating and financial profile of an enterprise the study of which will provide a more informed basis for assessing the prospects of the enterprise in terms of

- profit and profitability and trends in these;
- relative reliance on debt and trends in this as measured for example by a gearing ratio;
- the ability of the firm to meet recurring charges arising from the cost structure of the firm and its financing policies; etc.

The use of ratios to outline operating and financial profiles of firms is the general approach to the analysis and interpretation of financial statements adopted in this book.

[2218] As we saw in the Mosgiel case which was discussed in Chapter 20 and was referred to earlier in this chapter, a reference to the share market's assessment of a firm's prospects as reflected in the market value of its shares will give an indication of the ability of the firm to overcome an apparent financial distress by going to the market for additional equity finance.

Multivariate Discriminant Analysis (MDA)

[2219] It is reasonable to think that some of the ratios in a set are more relevant to the prediction of failure than others. It may be practicable through research and statistical analysis to select and to give weight to ratios which reflect their relevance to the prediction of failure. Multivariate discriminant analysis is a statistical technique which incorporates a number of variables in a distress prediction model to produce a single statistic, "Z score", which is then used to classify firms into failed and non-failed.

A multivariate discriminant function will take the form of:

$$Z = a_1X_1 + a_2X_2 + \ldots + a_nX_n$$

where

$X_1, X_2, \ldots X_n$ are the variables (eg financial ratios) incorporated in the model;

$a_1, a_2, \ldots a_n$ are the discriminant coefficients (weights) assigned to the variables; and

Z is the "Z score" used in the classification of firms into failed and non-failed.

[2220] A pioneering work in the field of multivariate discriminant analysis is that of Altman (E I Altman, "Financial Ratios, Discriminant Analysis and the Prediction of Corporate Bankruptcy", *Journal of Finance*, September 1986, pp 589–609).

[2221] Key issues in developing multivariate discriminant functions are the selection of variables (eg financial ratios), the determination of discriminant coefficients (weights) to assign to the variables, and the choice of a "cut-off" point for the Z score such that would minimize misclassification (for example of non-failed firms as failed and of failed firms as non-failed). An approach, not without problems is to derive a discriminant function and cut-off point from a sample of failed and non-failed companies and a combination of ratios which best discriminate between the two groups of companies. The model may then be tested for its ability to classify correctly the firms included in the sample from which the model was derived, and, much more importantly, for its ability to classify correctly firms other than those included in the samples. The ultimate test of a predictive model is its continuing ability to recognize firms headed for financial distress before rather than after financial distress becomes a condition beyond dispute.

[2222] An initial attempt to develop a multivariate discriminant model for New Zealand conditions was made by Tabb and Wong (J B Tabb and J Wong, "Predicting Company Failure", *The Accountants' Journal*, May 1983, pp 176–8). In this study, 20 public companies which had failed in the preceding 10 years were chosen and ratios were calculated using the last financial statements of the companies prior to the appointment of a liquidator. An attempt was made to pair each failed company with a non-failed company matching it in size, type of industry, and period. Problems were encountered in finding a sufficient number of public companies to obtain matches in all respects. Seven variables were used to derive a discriminant function. The function was standardized so that the line between potential failure and potential non-failure was set at 0 with centroids ("centre of gravity") of –1.1 and +1.1 (ie a Z score equal to or less than –1.1 indicated a high probability of failure within the next 12 months, while a Z score equal to or greater than +1.1 indicated a high probability of not failing over the next 12 months). The authors claimed an 80% success rate for the model in predicting failure one year prior to the event for the sample companies. They expressed the belief that they could, in time, improve the success rate by modifying the model and enlarging the sample.

[2223] An MDA model, based on New Zealand conditions, with a claim to a considerably higher rate of success was developed by Ferner and Hamilton (D G Ferner and R T Hamilton, "A Note on the Predictability of Financial Distress in New Zealand Listed Companies", *Accounting and Finance*, May 1987, pp 55–63).

Ferner and Hamilton distinguished between the ability of a model to correctly *classify* into failed and non-failed the companies included in the sample from which the model was derived and to correctly *predict* failure when applied to companies other than those included in the original sample. They believed a model's predictive power to be less than its classification power.

Ferner and Hamilton defined "financial distress" to have been present in those companies which were delisted from the New Zealand Stock Exchange between 1964 and 1983 which failed to continue trading as independent entities. This definition produced 16 distressed companies comprising 8 liquidations, 4 receiverships and 4 acquisitions involving financial restructuring. Each of the distressed companies was then matched with a non-distressed listed company selected as far as possible from the same industry at that point of time. Difficulties were encountered in obtaining such matching companies. A set of 11 financial ratios was used to produce a three-variable discriminant model estimated on the financial ratios for the year preceding the financial distress and then used to calculate Z scores for earlier years.

In considering the results of the study, Ferner and Hamilton noted a marked deterioration in the mean Z score of the distressed companies in the three years leading to their ceasing to trade independently. The model was found to be 95% correct for *classifications* made on the last annual report of the companies prior to failure and to retain the same degree of correctness for two further years preceding the year of failure. The model was tested for *predictive* ability on 23 arbitrarily selected listed companies not included in the original sample. It was found that in relation to "Type 2" errors (the classification as distressed of companies which were not in fact distressed) the model misclassified two companies, an error rate of 9%. In relation to "Type 1" errors (the classification of non-distressed companies which were in fact distressed), the model predicted distress in six of seven cases, an error rate of 14%, when data for the year preceding failure was used and in three out of six cases, an error rate of 50% when data of three years preceding failure was used.

[2224] The preceding discussion illustrates some of the major problems involved in the development of "formal" models for predicting financial distress:

(a) the definition of financial distress;

(b) the selection of "appropriate" samples of failed and non-failed firms to develop the model and then to test it;

(c) the selection of relevant variables to include in the model and the determination of weights to assign to the variables;

(d) the determination of the cut-off point for the Z score of the MDA model (or for a ratio in the case of a univariate model) such that will minimize misclassification;

(e) the bias which may enter into the model and its testing as a result of the selection of failed and non-failed firms;

(f) determining the validity of the model across firms and over time;

(g) in the New Zealand context, the very small numbers of firms included in the statistical analysis have to be recognized in considering the relative importance to be attached to its conclusions.

[2225] There are a number of factors which add to the above problems.

[2226] Given the very low rate of failure among listed companies, it would be practically impossible to base the formulation and testing of models on samples of listed companies which are representative of the total population, at least in a country the size of New Zealand. If, under "normal" circumstances, on the average, fewer than one in a hundred listed companies fail per year, then a distress prediction model which states that no company will fail will have a statistical rate of success of at least 99%, a high rate of success by any count; the model will be costless to apply and will be useless for any of the purposes for which distress analysis and prediction may be required. Any model that attempts to make a prediction other than that no firm will fail is likely to be statistically less successful as it would be prone to make "Type 2" errors (to classify as distressed a company which is not) instead of only "Type 1" errors (to classify as non-distressed a company which is distressed).

[2227] A key issue in the evaluation of a distress prediction model is the model's performance at the margin — in the grey area around the discriminatory cut-off point. The shortcomings of applying statistical formulas to marginal cases of financial distress will be illustrated later in this chapter by some comparisons between a failed company, Mosgiel Ltd, and its non-failed main competitor Alliance Textiles Ltd, both discussed in Chapter 20 and referred to earlier in this chapter.

[2228] Further complications in forecasting financial distress are introduced by the diversification of business operations across industries and geographical boundaries. Overall risk may be affected by the financial arrangements which may exist among the members of company groups.

A pragmatic approach

[2229] The model builder may use his experience and the results of research in selecting a set of ratios for use in measuring a condition, in this case solvency. Again using his jugdment, he will attach a weight to each ratio in the set, according to its relative importance (as he sees it). He will then determine norms for each ratio that are seen as appropriate to the particular industry (possibly an average for a fair sample of companies). The next step is to relate the ratio to the norm, and to calculate its value as part of the set. For example, if the current ratio were given a relative weight of 0.30 in a set aimed at measuring credit rating (or solvency), the current ratio were 1.5:1, and the norm for the industry were 2:1, then the measure of this component of the set might be calculated:

$$0.30 \left[1 + (1 - \frac{1.5}{2}) \right] = 0.30 \, (1.25) = 0.375$$

A similar calculation would be made for each of the other components of the set. The results may then be added so as to provide an index which expresses the set of ratios as a single number. In this model, a number in excess of unity is an adverse departure from the industry norm. Detailed study and monitoring would be required if the number exceeded a set figure.

An alternative procedure used in credit rating is to allocate numbers, as weights, to each ratio. For example, the current ratio may be allocated 30 points. Upper and lower limits are then set for each ratio, and a range of scores is set between these limits. Total scores are then obtained for each enterprise, as indicators of the condition being measured (say credit-worthiness). A cut-off point may be set for total scores, not as a basis for final decisions but rather as an indicator of the margin around which close examination of individual cases should precede any decision. This examination would have regard to both financial and non-financial factors.

Some variables used in prediction models

[2230] It would be useful at this point to list the variables used in the studies discussed in the preceding paragraphs as examples of financial relationships which have been considered as relevant for the prediction of financial distress.

I H Beaver

Thirty ratios for failed and non-failed companies were calculated and compared. The ratio with the highest rating as a predictor was
  cash flow to total debt.

E I Altman

Five variables were used to develop an MDA model:
  • working capital to total assets;
  • retained earnings to total assets;
  • earnings before interest and tax to total assets;
  • market value of equity to total debt;
  • sales to total assets.

J B Tabb and J Wong

Five variables were used to develop an MDA model:
- (current assets less current liabilities)/total assets;
- retained earnings/total assets;
- cash flow/total assets (cash flow being net profit plus depreciation);
- log (total assets/1,000,000)^{10} (as a means of relating financial risk to size);
- earnings before tax/shareholders' funds;
- log (total liabilities/total assets)^{10} (as a measure of gearing);
- (current assets less current liabilities/total liabilities (as a measure of a firm's ability to service its liabilities).

D G Ferner and R T Hamilton

Eleven variables were studied to derive a model based on three variables:
- earnings before interest and tax to total assets;
- current liabilities to total assets;
- no credit interval (net current asssets to annual cash expenditure, ie operating expenditure less depreciation).

The eleven variables considered in the study were:
- from Altman, the five variables listed above;
- from Taffler and Tisshaw (R Taffler and H Tisshaw, "Going Going, Gone — Four Factors Which Predict", *Accountancy*, 1977, pp 50–4):
  – profit before tax to current liabilities;
  – current assets to total liabilities;
  – current liabilities to total assets;
  – no credit interval (net current assets to annual cash expenditure);
- from Beaver:
  cash flow to total debt;
- added by Ferner and Hamilton:
  cash flow to interest paid.

Warning signals

[2231] It is evident from the above discussion that the prediction of financial distress is a complex exercise and that the use of statistical models would not necessarily simplify the matter. This is not to say that prediction models, statistical or otherwise, should not be used. Even when the approach is subjective, the perception of the factors which indicate impending financial distress, even when not specifically stated, would represent a distress prediction model.

[2232] The availability of information on computer files, coupled with the capacity of computers to process data in accordance with set programs quickly and economically, has opened up the posibility of systems calculated to produce warning signals of the need for closer study of particular companies. It is in this area that statistical distress prediction models can make a significant contribution. It should be noted, however, that the usefulness of such prediction models would depend on their ability to identify potentially distressed firms. As we pointed out earlier, given the low rate of company failure, a mode which predicts that no firm will fail will have a very high rate of statistical success and be useless for the purpose of distress prediction.

Decomposition analysis

[2233] Decomposition analysis is another statistical tool which may be applied conveniently through the use of computer programs.

The objective of decomposition analysis is to provide a single figure measure of the extent of the change that has taken place in the composition of a total between two points of time. In financial analysis, the model may be used to measure the extent of overall change in the asset mix, in the sources of finance, in the sources of revenue, in the elements of cost, and in the various categories of expense. For example, it may be applied broadly, to the major classes of assets; less broadly in, say, the allocation of the total investent in current assets among inventories, accounts receivable, short term investments, and cash; and in finer detail to the allocation of the investment in inventories among raw materials, work in process and finished goods. If company financial data are converted to computer input as it becomes available, and a decomposition analysis applied, the output will indicate those companies whose results may warrant more detailed and individual study by the analyst: For a more detailed discussion of the decomposition method see B Lev, *Financial Statement Analysis: A New Aproach*, Prentice-Hall Inc, 1974.

[2234] The following information has been drawn from the 1979 report of Mosgiel Ltd, which was the subject of Case Study 2, in Chapter 20.

Mosgiel Ltd
Investment in assets 1978 and 1979

Assets By class	Value ($000)		Relative Shares	
	1978	1979	1978	1979
Fixed assets	10,656	10,547	.341	.317
Current assets	20,286	22,416	.648	.675
Other	354	271	.011	.008
	31,296	33,234	1.000	1.000
Current Assets				
Cash	19	14	.001	.001
Debtors and prepayments	5,521	5,481	.272	.244
Inventories	14,746	16,921	.727	.755
	20,286	22,416	1.000	1.000
Inventories				
Raw materials	3,819	3,468	.259	.205
Work in process	5,068	5,529	.344	.327
Finished goods	5,859	7,924	.397	.468
	14,746	16,921	1.000	1.000

A decomposition measure may be developed by multiplying the 1979 relative share of each component by a fraction, being the 1979 relative share over the 1978 relative share, and then adding the products. To illustrate, the decomposition measure for assets by class (that is, fixed, current and other) is based on the calculation:

$$0.317 \left(\frac{0.317}{0.341}\right) + 0.675 \left(\frac{0.675}{0.648}\right) + 0.008 \left(\frac{0.008}{0.011}\right)$$
$$= 0.2947 + 0.7031 + 0.0058$$
$$= 1.0036$$

For current assets, the decomposition measure is based on the calculation:

$$0.001 \left(\frac{0.001}{0.001}\right) + 0.244 \left(\frac{0.244}{0.272}\right) + 0.755 \left(\frac{0.755}{0.727}\right)$$
$$= 0.0010 + 0.2189 + 0.7841$$
$$= 1.0040$$

For inventories, the decomposition measure is based on the calculation:

$$0.205 \left(\frac{0.205}{0.259}\right) + 0.327 \left(\frac{0.327}{0.344}\right) + 0.468 \left(\frac{0.468}{0.397}\right)$$
$$= 0.1623 + 0.3108 + 0.5517$$
$$= 1.0248$$

Unless the relative shares are identical, the calculation will yield a total greater than one. The excess over one is then expressed in terms of 10^{-4}; that is, multiplied by 10,000. In the case of Mosgiel Ltd, the decomposition measures, 1979 over 1978, are:

For assets by asset class	36
For current assets	40
For inventories	248

[2235] It will be apparent that the decomposition measure for inventories was significant, indicating that this item in the report of Mosgiel Ltd might warrant detailed study, as indeed it did. The company had been maintaining production in spite of a decline in the market, and a receiver was appointed some 10 months later.

The technique may be applied to a time series for an individual firm. By relating the decomposition measures of a firm with an industry average, one may obtain some appreciation of the extent to which the differences are due to internal factors. The most significant contribution of decomposition techniques is the economical provision of signals to the researcher that detailed investigation may provide useful information. It should be recognized that change in the elements comprising a total may be found to be desirable, and reflect deliberate management policy. On the other hand, it may be found to reflect a departure from plan, as was certainly the case with Mosgiel Ltd's investment in inventories.

Distress prediction at the margin

[2236] We pointed out earlier that distress prediction at the margin is of crucial importance and that such a prediction cannot normally be handled by a statistical prediction model. We will illustrate the problem by comparing some of the reported figures of Mosgiel Ltd from the company's last published financial statements (year ended 30 June 1979) and ratios and percentages derived from them with corresponding figures, ratios and percentages for its main competitor, Alliance Textiles Ltd, derived from the latter company's financial statements for the year ended 31 July 1980 (Figure 22.1). The comparison is of Mosgiel figures for 1978 and 1979 with Alliance Textiles figures for 1979. The financial statements of the two companies are reproduced as Case Studies 2 and 3 in Chapter 20.

In relation to the question of forecasting financial distress, the comparison of the figures of these two companies is particularly appropriate because both companies were of approximately the same size, both companies were in approximately the same geographical location and both operated under the same economy-wide and industry conditions.

Figure 22.1

Mosgiel Ltd and Alliance Textiles Ltd
Comparison of Published Figures – 1979

	Mosgiel		Alliance
	1979 $000	1978 $000	1979 $000
Sales	28,540	26,116	27,358
Net profit before tax (operating profit for Alliance)	1,166	1,362	531
Less tax	250	189	—
Net profit after tax	916	1,173	531
Net profit after tax to sales	3.21%	4.48%	1.9%
Net profit before tax	1,166	1,362	590
Add back financing costs:			
interest paid	1,509	1,075	1,380
leasing costs	207	139	20
total financing costs	1,716	1,214	1,400
Net profit before tax and financing costs	2,882	2,576	1,990
Add back depreciation	568	578	1,041
Net profit before tax, financing costs and depreciation	3,450	3,154	3,031
Financing costs to			
(a) profit before tax and financing costs	59.5%	47.1%	70.4%
(b) profit before tax, financing costs and depreciation	49.4%	38.5%	46.2%
Return on shareholders' funds	5.95%	7.73%	4.8%
Return on total assets (net profit before tax, interest and extraordinary items to total assets)	8.4%	7.5%	7.5%
Working capital and current ratio:			
current assets	22,416	20,286	15,864
current liabilities	10,248	9,820	6,987
working capital	12,168	10,466	8,877
Working capital to sales	42.3%	40.0%	32.4%
Current ratio	2.19:1	2.07:1	2.27:1
Proprietary ratio (shareholders' funds to total assets)	46.4%	48.5%	46.9%

A superficial examination of the amounts, ratios and percentages in Figure 22.1 could well lead one to conclude that it was Alliance Textiles which was heading for failure. It may be interesting to note that at the time the share market did not differentiate between the two companies. The shares of both companies were trading at about or just below par value.

Summary:

[2237] It should be evident from the preceding discussion that the prediction of financial distress and insolvency is a complicated matter which cannot be readily delegated to statistical models. While the use of such models may facilitate the procedure, in the final count, one cannot avoid the necessity to use judgment applied intelligently to both financial and non-financial data perceived to be relevant to each case. Research into the use of data bases and models should aim to reduce the burden of analysis and prediction by effectively reducing the number of cases which should be singled out for individual attention.

Review questions

22.1 " ... since the solvency of a firm depends on the firm's ability to pay its debts as they fall due, the study of solvency should be carried out with emphasis on expected cash flows."
Discuss.

22.2 "The ultimate test of a predictive model is its continuing ability to recognize firms headed for financial distress before rather than after financial distress becomes a condition beyond dispute."
Discuss.

22.3 "A key issue in the evaluation of a distress prediction model is the model's performance at the margin — in the grey area around the discriminatory cut-off point."
Discuss.

22.4 What are some of the problems encountered by researchers in attempts to develop financial distress prediction models?

22.5 (a) Name some groups with vested interests in the early prediction of impending financial distress of business enterprises and explain the nature of their interests.

(b) Given early warning of impending financial distress, what steps may be taken by interested groups to avoid financial collapse or to minimize its effects?

22.6 Four models for the prediction of financial distress in listed companies have shown the following statistical success rates:

Model	Success rate
	%
A	85
B	90
C	95
D	98

Which method, in your opinion, would be most useful for the prediction of financial distress?

22.7   "Research into the use of data bases and models should aim to reduce ... the number of cases which should be singled out for individual attention." Discuss.

Chapter 23
Analysis and Interpretation for Investors

[2301] In this concluding chapter we shall consider financial statements and their analysis and interpretation as sources of information for investment decisions.

[2302] In Chapter 3 we considered the information content and objectives of financial statements and saw that, according to FASB Statement of Financial Accounting Concepts No 1, "Objectives of Financial Reporting by Business Enterprises" (November 1978), the function of financial reporting is to provide information which is useful for making economic decisions about business and about investment in or loans to business enterprises (para 15). According to the Statement, financial reporting is primarily concerned with the needs of users who, because of limited authority to obtain the information they want from an enterprise, must use the financial statement information provided by management (para 28).

[2303] On the other hand we noted that supporters of the efficient market hypothesis (EMH) have questioned the usefulness of financial statements for decision-making. According to the EMH (for example at the semi-strong level of market efficiency) the market impounds in share prices, promptly and without bias, all publicly available information including financial statement data. That being so, share prices are the best available estimates of value, and analysis based on financial statement data will not lead to abnormal returns being earned on security investments even by the sophisticated, well-informed investor. In an efficient market, market return will compensate investors only for risk which cannot be diversified away. The services of an expert may be utilized for the purpose of planning an investment portfolio given the risk preferences of the investor, and where an expert may be expected to obtain information prior to its being made public. Once an investor has established a portfolio at a given level of largely undiversifiable risk, he or she should pursue a buy-and-hold policy, since switching from one group of securities to another at the same level of risk would not hold advantages but will result in transaction costs.

[2304] Notwithstanding the efficient market hypothesis, evidence provided by surveys shows that shareholders/investors, even those with a high level of experience and sophistication, do use financial statements as an important primary source of information, indicating, by implication at least, a belief that the study of financial statements can improve investment decisions and investment returns.

[2305] It seems reasonable to assume that financial (and other relevant) information may have different implications for different investors. It follows that

431

investors' diverse expectations may be expected to produce a dispersion around the resulting average market response. In this context, some expectations could be superior due to superior analytical and predictive ability of some investors which will allow them to earn abnormal returns.

[2306] In Chapter 3 we saw that some strong doubts exist about the efficiency of the share market. In particular the EMH ignores market cycles and the need at times to move in and out of the market, for example moving out when the market is high. It has been argued that contrary to the assumption of the EMH that speculation moves the market towards equilibrium, a good deal of speculation is in fact destabilizing; for example, a rising trend in share prices may attract interest which leads to further rises, a process which may be self-sustaining for a period. Further, investors' perception of financial data and their reaction to it may be influenced by the mood of the market. Events on the New Zealand stock market preceding and following the stock market crash of October 1987 are a case in point.

The stock market crash, October 1987

[2307] In the two years or so which preceded the stock market crash there was a growing feeling in New Zealand that company shares were overvalued in relation to company earnings. Interest rates were high, at times exceeding 20%. Caught in a frenzy of speculation, many people borrowed at high interest rates to invest in company shares, whereas events were to show that, in fact, it was time to get out of the share market. Yet people continued to invest in shares. For example, prior to the crash, the market value of some company shares was more than four times the reported net asset backing of the shares. The market price of the shares of a property investment company with reported net asset backing of about 77 cents exceeded $3.

Could one say that the expectations of the investors who paid these prices in the hope of making substantial market gains were in any way rational or realistic? The expectations must have been for subsantial market gains given the opportunity cost of high interest rates. When the stock market crash came in October 1987, the price falls on the New Zealand stock market were more severe than in any other country in the developed world. Further, the shock and loss of confidence caused by the crash resulted in a stock market recovery much slower than in other countries.

[2308] A thoughtful study of the financial statements of companies should have warned investors of an impending major readjustment of market prices and, if adequately heeded, it could have lessened the severity of the crash when it came. Even in periods of relative market stability the analysis and study of financial statements should give signals of overpricing of shares and of market cycles nearing a peak or low point.

[2309] Notwithstanding their limitations which have been extensively discussed in some of the preceding chapters, financial statements do contain important information regarding the operating results and state of affairs of companies. This information, considered in the broader context of industry and economy, and in the light of the continuing flow of new relevant information, provides an essential framework for making an informed forecast of future outcomes for the individual enterprise.

[2310] In spite of their limitations and associated problems of analysis and interpretation, financial statements are the best framework within which information about the operations and state of affairs of companies may be formally presented and subjected to audit and compliance with legal and professional standards regarding form, content and disclosure.

Risk and uncertainty

[2311] Investment decisions are concerned with the future. Rational investment decisions are based on expectations which range from the certain, such as interest on securities issued by or on behalf of central government, to the very uncertain, such as the rate of inflation over the next 10 or 20 years. As we saw in earlier chapters, much of accounting measurement itself is based on expectations about the future and is therefore permeated by uncertainty.

[2312] The evaluation of investment opportunities should be concerned with the underlying level of risk and the required rate of return given the level of risk.

[2313] The level of risk which an analyst will attach to an investment opportunity could be the result of subjective evaluation after taking into account what are considered to be relevant factors or it could be the result of hunch based on personal knowledge and experience.

[2314] Regardless of the approach adopted for dealing with risk, uncertainty can never be entirely removed in the evaluation of investment opportunities. Consider for example the case of two New Zealand based companies which in the early 1980s embarked on substantial expansion. The expansion of the first company was designed to give its operations nationwide coverage. Shop premises were purchased in most of the country's main centres and the managing director's report to the financial statements spoke confidentially of expectations of major increases in profit as a result. The second company undertook expansion overseas by acquiring a major subsidiary at what was described as a very advantageous price in a depressed market. The New Zealand sharemarket adopted a "wait and see" attitude in both cases and there were no significant changes in the share prices of either company. Subsequent events did not confirm the expectations of the first company. The expected increases in profit failed to materialize, the company which had borrowed heavily found itself in increasing difficulties and, after several attempts at restructuring it virtually ceased to exist. In the case of the second company, subsequent events proved that the overseas acquisition was in fact a very successful one and in a matter of several years the overseas subsidiary became a major contributor to the total profit of the group.

[2315] A market oriented approach of assessing the risk associated with a particular investment is to consider the extent and pattern of the fluctuations in the return obtained from the investment over time. The greater the fluctuation in returns around the mean, the greater the risk is assumed to be. From the viewpoint of an investor, the return on an investment in shares is normally taken to include both dividends received and changes in the market value of the shares; a measure of this return may be obtained by dividing the sum of the dividend per share paid during the period and the ending market price of the share by the market price of the share at the start of the period (that is, the end of the preceding period).

[2316] To the extent that it is possible to place limits on the range of possible outcomes, and to fairly assess probabilities within the range, one can develop an expected outcome (the mean), and also a standard deviation, a dispersion of possible outcomes around the mean, which provides a measure of risk. Let us consider alternative investment in shares A and B as illustrated in Example 23.1.

Example 23.1

Shown below are the ranges of expected returns, corresponding probabilities and expected average rates of returns on the shares of companies A and B from the viewpoint of a prospective investor:

Co A			Co B		
Expected rates of return (1)	Probability (2)	Expected average return (1) x (2)	Expected rates of return (1)	Probability (2)	Expected average return (1) x (2)
%			%		
4	0.10	0.40	4	0.15	0.60
7	0.25	1.75	10	0.20	2.00
10	0.30	3.00	14	0.30	4.20
13	0.25	3.25	18	0.20	3.60
16	0.10	1.60	24	0.15	3.60
	1.00	10.00%		1.00	14.00%

In Example 23.1 the expected average rates of returns are:
Shares in A = 10%, Shares in B = 14%.

The respective standard deviations of the expected rates of return (σ_A and σ_B) are:
$$\sigma_A = 3.42\% \text{ and } \sigma_B = 6.03\%.$$

The standard deviation of the expected future returns is a measure of the risk associated with a given investment — the smaller the standard deviation (that is, the tighter the probability distribution) the lower the risk associated with the investment.

In Example 23.1, from the viewpoint of our investor, investment in shares in Company B will be more risky than investment in shares in Company A as the expected return from Company B share has a higher standard deviation than the expected return from investment in company A.

On the other hand, the expected return on Company B shares is higher than the expected return on company A shares. This is a normal state of affairs as usually a relatively higher return is expected from an investment considered to be more risky than a given alternative.

[2317] The calculation of expected rates of return and relative risk in Example 23.1 would be made on the basis of the market prices of the shares and the investors' own assessment of relative returns and probability distributions. Whether the investor would choose to invest in company A or company B shares would depend on his own attitude to risk. The current market prices of company A and company B shares reflect the market's "average" expectation regarding expected returns and assessment of relative risk arrived at by the interaction of buyers and sellers of shares. If the expected return differential between company A and company B shares (10% v 14%) is more than enough to compensate our investor for the higher risk involved in company B shares, he will buy company B shares at the going price or may be prepared to bid the price up. By doing this he will enter the interaction of buyers and sellers which ultimately determines the market price of shares.

Systematic and unsystematic risk

[2318] As pointed out in the preceding section, fluctuations in the rate of return represent a measure of the risk associated with an investment in company shares. A distinction is made in the finance literature between systematic and unsystematic risk.

Fluctuations in the rate of return can be due to general market movements because of changes in the general economic climate. In addition, changes in rates of return will be affected by conditions, events and expectations peculiar to individual companies and the industries within which they operate. As a result, the returns on investments in individual companies will move, to some degree, independently from movements in the market as a whole.

Systematic risk relates to fluctuations in the rate of the return which reflect changes in market conditions in general. *Unsystematic risk* relates to fluctuations in the rate of return peculiar to a particular company and independent of the general trend of the market. The total risk associated with an investment in company shares therefore consists of systematic plus unsystematic risk.

[2319] The relationship between systematic and unsystematic risk is illustrated in Example 23.2.

Example 23.2

Shown below are relative returns on shares in Company Z and the average return on the share market:

Period	Return on shares in Z %	Average market return %
1	8	6
2	9	7
3	4	3
4	6	4
5	8	5

The returns on shares in Z and the corresponding average returns on the share market may be plotted on a graph as shown in Figure 23.1. A line may then be drawn on the graph showing the "characteristic" relationships between average market rates of return and the return on Z shares. This line may be drawn "by sight" or, more accurately, by the use of simple linear regression, that is a least squares fit.

The equation which will give a least squares fit of the data in Example 23.2 is:

$$Y = 1 + 1.2X$$

The above least squares equation, which has been used to fit the "characteristic" line in Figure 23.1 can be interpreted as follows: to the extent that there is correlation between the return on Z shares (Y) and the average market return (X), the return on Z shares is equivalent to a fixed factor 1 plus 1.2 times the average market return.

For example, if the average market return is 10%, the return on Z shares can be expected to be

$$Y_Z = 1 + 1.2(10\%) = 13\%$$

The "beta" coefficient

[2320] The slope of the "characteristic" line (1.2 in our example), is called the beta coefficient of a share and is used to measure the volatility of the return on the share in relation to the return on the market as a whole.

The beta of a share is used to measure the *systematic risk* associated with an investment in the share. The greater the beta, the higher the systematic risk. For example, to the extent that the return on a particular share is regarded to be positively correlated with the average return on the market, the return on a share with a beta of 2 is likely to be twice as volatile as the average market return which is assumed to have a beta of 1; similarly, the return on a share with a beta of 0.5 will be half as volatile as the average market return. In Example 23.2 the beta of 1.2 indicates a volatility of return of 1.2 times that of the market.

Unsystematic risk and total risk

[2321] The difference between the return indicated by the "fitted" or "characteristic" line and the actual returns on a share as observed in the data used to establish the correlation between individual and market returns is taken as a measure of *unsystematic* risk.

In the above analysis, the relationship between the return on any share j and the average return on the stock market is assumed to be linear in the form of the following equation:

$$R_j = \alpha + \beta_j R_m + e_j$$

where R_j = the return on any particular share j;

β_j = the beta of share j;

R_m = the average market return; and

e_j = movements in the return of share j independent of average movements on the market.

In Example 23.2 the return on Z shares of 8% observed in Period 5 can be analyzed as follows:

$$R_Z = 8\% = 1\% + 1.2(5\%) + 1\%$$

Figure 23.1

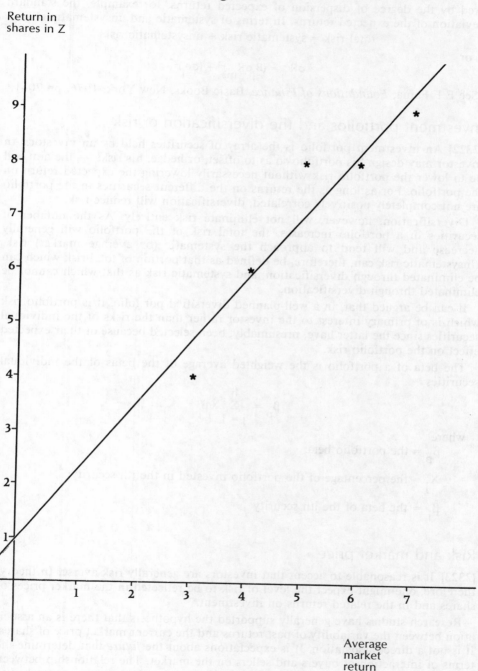

Return in
shares in Z

9 -

8 -

7 -

6 -

5 -

4 -

3 -

2 -

1 -

1   2   3   4   5   6   7

Average
market
return

As stated earlier, the risk associated with an investment in shares may be measured by the degree of dispersion of expected returns, for example, the standard deviation of the expected returns. In terms of systematic and unsystematic risk

$$\text{total risk} = \text{systematic risk} + \text{unsystematic risk}$$

or

$$\sigma R^2_j = (B_j \sigma R_m)^2 + (\sigma e_j)^{2*}$$

*See E F Fama, *Foundations of Finance*, Basic Books, New York, 1976, pp 70–1.

Investment portfolios and the diversification of risk

[2322] An investment portfolio is the array of securities held by an investor. An investor may design his portfolio so as to offset, or hedge, his risks — the aim will be to lower the portfolio risk without necessarily lowering the expected return on the portfolio. For as long as the returns on the different securities in the portfolio are not completely positively correlated, diversification will reduce risk.

Diversification, however, will not eliminate risk entirely. As the number of securities in a portfolio increases, the total risk of the portfolio will generally decrease and will tend to approach the systematic (or average market) risk. Unsystematic risk can, therefore, be defined as that portion of total risk which can be eliminated through diversification, and systematic risk as that which cannot be eliminated through diversification.

It can be argued that, in a well-planned diversified portfolio, it is portfolio risk which is of primary interest to the investor rather than the risks of the individual securities since the latter have, presumably, been selected because of their expected effect on the portfolio risk.

The beta of a portfolio is the weighted average of the betas of the individual securities:

$$\beta_p = \sum_{j=1}^{h} X_j \beta_j$$

where

β_p = the portfolio beta;

X_j = the percentage of the portfolio invested in the jth security;

β_j = the beta of the jth security

Risk and market price

[2323] It is reasonable to accept that investors are generally risk averse. In theory, therefore, one might expect the level of risk to be reflected in the market prices of shares and in the related returns on investment.

Research studies have generally supported the hypothesis that there is an association between the variability of past returns and the current market price of shares. It is not a direct association. It is expectations about the *future* that determine the terms of interaction of buyers and sellers on the market. The relationship between price and risk is complicated by the ability of investors to hedge the risk attached to individual share investments. One can expect there to be some reflection in share prices of the extent to which this risk can be eliminated through the diversification process.

Interpretation of Statistical Measures of Risk

[2324] Statistical measure of risk, like most statistical measures, should be interpreted with caution — they are derived from past events whereas the interest of investors is in the future. Enterprises change in structure over time and so does the perception of investors of the risks associated with their operations and prospects.

Changes in investor's perceptions of the risk associated with investment in particular companies may reflect changes in the nature of the firm's operations, its financial and cost structures, its managerial and personnel policies and the economic environment within which the firms operate. In the final count, at least some degree of judgment is unavoidable no matter what statistical analyses are made in support of investment decisions.

Relevance to the analysis and interpretation of financial statements

[2325] One may ask what has the preceding discussion in this chapter got to do with the subject of this text — the analysis and interpretation of financial statements?

The connection is at least two-fold:

(a) To the extent that analysis and interpretation is carried out on behalf of investors, an understanding of the share market and of the factors which affect investor decisions becomes important.

(b) To the extent that financial statements contain useful information, an effective analysis of financial statements becomes an important part of the process leading up to informed investment decisions.

The importance of the latter, and indeed of the analysis and interpretation of financial statements generally, has been underlined by the events of October 1987. These events made very clear the dangers involved in neglecting the message of financial statements as to the future prospects of business enterprises.

Index